Praise for *Christianity and Transforming States*

While it cannot be gainsaid that Christians are frequently targeted for oppression in a variety of global contexts, the opposite is also sadly true: Christians can also become the oppressors of persons and peoples they regard as deviant or repugnant, even those whose only fault is being Christian differently. David Emmanuel Singh's essay collection evinces a badly needed balance between this double-sided truth. Euro-inclusive without being Euro-exclusive, the book documents some of the lesser-known struggles of Global South and Global North Christians—Catholic and Orthodox, Protestant and Pentecostal—against one ideological juggernaut or another (Hindu[tva]ization or Islamicization, Sinicization, or Secularization, to mention but a few of the many discussed). A serious book for perilous times, argued with rigor and vigor. I recommend it highly.

—Richard Fox Young, Timby Chair Emeritus,
History of Religions, Princeton Theological Seminary

This book unveils that there are as many Christianities as there are nation-states since each of the latter features both evolving histories of Christians in relationship to the state and shifting majority-to/from-minority positionalities of Christians across national demographic spectrums. Scholars of World Christianity, religion and politics, and political/public theologies, among those working in related fields, will benefit from these interdisciplinarily researched and presented case studies.

—Amos Yong, former dean of the School of Mission and
Theology, Fuller Theological Seminary

Diving into the intricate tapestry of state-religion dynamics and the varied ties between states and minorities, this illuminating volume presents a series of captivating case studies. Unveiling the multilayered nature of these relationships with nuanced precision, this work stands unparalleled in capturing the contemporary global landscape of minority construction and the practice of 'minoritization.' With its cutting-edge approach and incisive analyses, this book is a valuable resource for the interested public and scholars of religion, theology, politics, sociology, anthropology, and beyond. Prepare to be enthralled by the remarkable depth and breathtaking geographical scope this exceptional volume uncovers.

—Felix Wilfred, editor in chief, *International Journal of Asian Christianity*, and emeritus head of the Department of Christianity, State University of Madras

This book brings into focus the diversity of Christian experience and its intra-religious dynamics. It highlights the reality of Christianity as both victim in one setting and victimizer in another. As more than two-thirds of Christians globally live in religiously pluralistic environments, the book challenges today's believers to take to heart teachings of Christ in those socioreligious contexts, but also not to ignore the reality of intra-Christian contact, conflict, and exchange as illustrated in the book.

—Wonsuk Ma, executive director, Center for Spirit-Empowered Research, Oral Roberts University

Each essay in this fascinating volume gives us a remarkably enlightened, well-informed, and penetrating grasp of grassroots experiences of a different Christian community striving to survive within an often hostile political environment. With deft sophistication, all focus on struggles and tensions between 'minority rights' (and/or survival) and 'majority rule' that all too often, under the cloak of 'majoritarian democracy,' can become oppressive and tyrannical, if not totalitarian.

—Robert Eric Frykenberg, professor emeritus, University of Wisconsin–Madison

Any simplistic tendency to see the Christian's relationship to other religionists in today's multi-polar world merely in terms of victims or victimizers is promptly debunked by the abundant evidence gathered here. This volume provides much insight for Christians to be 'wise as serpents and innocent as doves' in their engagement with the non-Christians amongst whom they live. I commend it heartily.

—Hwa Yung, bishop emeritus, Methodist Church in Malaysia

This book brings to light the complex contexts in which Christianity exists as a minority and majority faith and offers profound insights into the nature of their varied experience and response.

—Esther Mombo, professor, School of Theology,
St. Paul's University, Kenya

CHRISTIANITY AND TRANSFORMING STATES

CHRISTIANITY AND TRANSFORMING STATES

Mapping Varied Christian Experiences and Responses

Edited by
David Emmanuel Singh

FORTRESS PRESS
MINNEAPOLIS

CHRISTIANITY AND TRANSFORMING STATES
Mapping Varied Christian Experiences and Responses

Copyright © 2024 by Fortress Press, an imprint of 1517 Media. All rights reserved. Except for brief quotations in critical articles or reviews, no part of this book may be reproduced in any manner without prior written permission from the publisher. Email copyright@1517.media or write to Permissions, Fortress Press, PO Box 1209, Minneapolis, MN 55440-1209.

29 28 27 26 25 24   1 2 3 4 5 6 7 8 9

Library of Congress Control Number: 2024938171

Cover design: Brittany Becker
Cover image: Sameba Cathedral in Abstract Watercolors, Tbilisi, Georgia - stock photo by kampee patisena/Getty Images

Print ISBN: 978-1-5064-9335-0
eBook ISBN: 978-1-5064-9336-7

In honour of my parents who first introduced me to 'World Christianity' and my colleagues-friends, Wonsuk & Julie Ma, Damon Wai-Kwan So and Thomas Allan Harvey, with whom I have shared years of service in understanding World Christianity in its diverse expressions and settings.

CONTENTS

Introduction   1
David Emmanuel Singh

Part I
Transforming States and Christian Experience

1. Sabotage, Violence, and Distraction since the Adoption of the Citizenship Amendment Act in India   15
   David Emmanuel Singh

2. Chinese Christians and Post-Maoist Polities   35
   Michel Chambon

3. Christians as a Religious Minority in Modern Islamising Pakistan   53
   Farhana A. Nazir

4. Christians in Indonesia, Malaysia, and the Philippines: The Minority–Majority Experience   73
   Peter G. Riddell and Amos Sukamto

5. The Impact of *Velayat-e Faqih* on Iranian Christians in Post-Revolution Iran   97
   Michael Nazir-Ali and Amir S. Bazmjou

Part II
Christian Minority Responses

6. From Retreat to Social Engagement: The Dynamics of Marginalisation among Pentecostal-Catholic Relationships in Rural El Salvador   117
   Ronald T. Bueno and James G. Huff Jr.

7   What Then Shall We Say?: Responses of
    Tibetan Christians to Victimisation in a
    Time of Heightening Sinicisation   139
       Gangri "Philip" Gobu

8   As in Heaven, so on Earth?: A Response to a
    Dominant Religious Ideology from a Mizo
    Christian Tribal Perspective   159
       Marina Ngursangzeli Behera

9   Fear and Inwardness: An Examination of the
    Responses of Church of Pakistan and Full
    Gospel Assemblies Churches in Modern Pakistan   177
       Gloria Calib

10 Christian-Muslim Dialogue as Socio-Political
    Action in Egypt   199
       Toby Kan and Henrik Lindberg Hansen

11 Living as Followers of Jesus in Disfavoured
    Communities: Perspectives from the Northern
    Nigerian Context   219
       Uchenna D. Anyanwu

Part III
States and Christian Majority

12 Persecution in a Land of Religious Freedom:
    The Jehovah's Witnesses' Experience in
    Malawi 1964–1993   243
       Klaus Fiedler and Kenneth R. Ross

13 Rehashing the Alliances of Throne and Altar:
    On the Instrumentalisation of Religion in
    Contemporary Central and Eastern Europe
    and Building Resilience   263
       Pavol Bargár

14 The Romanian Orthodox Church and the
    Evangelicals: Conflicts and Collaborations   283
    Cristian-Sebastian Sonea and Teofil Stanciu

15 Christianity in Kenya: When Would-Be
    Liberators Are Marginalised in a Country
    Where They Are a Majority   303
    Oliver Kisaka Simiyu

16 Orthodox Christianity in Ethiopia: The Shifting
    Influence of a Religious Majority   323
    Ralph Lee

17 Between Politics and Religion in Eastern Europe:
    Eastern Orthodoxy, State, and Religions in
    Contemporary Bulgaria   339
    Valentin Kozhuharov

About the Authors   357
Subject Index   367
Country/Region/Place Index   369
Names Index   371

INTRODUCTION

David Emmanuel Singh

My readings of the nineteenth-century sources,[1] particularly those of Robert Durie Osborn (1835-1889), led me to guest-edit an issue of the *International Journal of Asian Christianity* (*IJAC*) in 2002. This contained both historically and empirically informed papers by several authors. These papers served as a critique of what I have suggested is an oversimplified binary of 'faith as meekness and polity'.[2] Christianity's founding principle, Osborn had argued, was the opposite of Islam's, and this was rooted in its founders' teaching and example. Christ appeared meek and feeble in comparison to Muhammad, and the cross was the final evidence of his frailty. 'The church of Christianity', Osborn would argue, illustrated it in its emphasis on Christ-like meekness, self-sacrifice, love, and undeserved forgiveness.[3] Qur'anic Surah 19.93, for Osborn, exemplified the nature of Islam or 'the Muhammadan theology:' 'there is no one in the heavens and earth who will not come as a slave to the Merciful'. This, Osborn argued, was a useful tool for Muslims who claimed the authority of God and required people to submit with 'meekness and resignation'.[4] Simply stated, Christianity demonstrated meekness and servanthood, whereas Islam exemplified power and submission and, hence, a political faith.

I noted in my *IJAC* editorial that while there is truth in Osborn's view of Christianity and Islam, it is not fully borne out by the actual historical expressions of both faiths. Medieval Christendom was an embodiment of faith as polity. Christendom's polity was expressed also in the 'doctrine of

---

1   David E. Singh, *Christian-Muslim Relations: A Bibliographical History 1800-1914*. Vol. 17 (Brill: 2021), 220-223 and 259-264.
2   David E. Singh, 'Christianity and Islam: Meekness-Servanthood and Faith as Polity Majesty,' *International Journal of Asian Christianity*, 5(2), 2022, 163-179.
3   Singh, 'R. D. Osborn,' *Christian-Muslim Relations*, 2021.
4   Robert D. Osborn, *Islam under the Khalifs of Baghdad* (London: Seeley, Jackson & Halliday, 1878/1880), 281.

the two swords'. It interpreted Luke 22:38 in a particular way to justify the authority of the priesthood and royal power.[5] The suffering and sacrificial Christ was re-imagined in terms of the temporal king or priest representing the majesty of Christ; his followers were re-imagined as his soldiers and not as those who were expected to 'take up their crosses' like Christ did for his non-physical kingdom.[6] Today, we see examples not only of majority Muslim states but also Hindu and Buddhist faiths as polities, as is evident in India and Myanmar with increasing evidence of the persecution of minorities.

Just before COVID brought the world to a halt, I travelled to India for a visit. I was drawn, however, into a countrywide dissent movement led by Muslims but supported by a wide range of minority faiths, including Indian Christians. This followed the controversial Citizenship Amendment Act (CAA) and the discourse on the National Register of Citizens (NRC). The protestors argued the act was manifestly anti-secular (as per the constitution) in defining citizenship, for the first time since independence, along religious lines. This was, however, in line with the manifesto of the Hindu nationalists who had played no role in India's independence as a secular democracy or the development of its high-minded constitution. Richard F. Young was editing a volume for Fortress Press with a focus on world Christianity and interfaith relations, and I offered to contribute to this. The volume highlighted that 'religion is in fact deeply integrated into the lives of those in the Global South, even though "secularism"—a political philosophy that requires the state to treat all religions equally—predominates in many of the regions'.[7] My paper on the grassroots collaboration between the minorities showed that Christians are not the only ones in focus of coercive polity. In my case, the victims of a Hinduizing state were primarily Muslims, but the other minorities, including Christians, collaborated in a sustained opposition of the act. I showed evidence of minority religions' collaboration in expressing peaceful dissent instead of meek submission.[8] This to

---

5   See P. S. Healy, 'The Doctrine of the Two Swords' in *The Oxford Dictionary of Middle Ages* (OUP, 2010).

6   Singh, 'Christianity and Islam,' 2022, 163–179.

7   Richard F. Young (ed.) *World Christianity and Interfaith Relations*. United States. (Fortress Press 2022).

8   David E, Singh, 'Emerging Cooperation among Minorities in Defense of Indian Secularism since the Adoption of the Citizenship Amendment Act

my mind helped in further nuancing the meekness-polity binary referred to above.

Following the publication of Young's volume, I chanced upon the University of Notre Dame report on the 'Contexts of Persecution'.[9] It offered both 'a geographic band' of Christian persecution and the types of responses (*survival, association,* and *confrontation*), which directed me to begin a search of my own. My initial approach was simple, though the expectation was that the evidence would colour the discourse. I decided on seeking the help of regional experts as potential contributors to assist me in interrogating both the diverse Christian contexts and Christian experience/response. Upon closer view, I saw that the 'Contexts of Persecution' had excluded Europe or the West altogether. A wider view of world Christianity was needed, I reasoned, with a qualitative flavour to it and, hence, this edited volume.

I began with a simple 'two-sided approach'—one that examined Christians in contexts where they would be a disfavoured minority as well as where they would be a dominant or favoured faith with other minority Christian denominations around them. The idea was that while it is true that many Christians suffer because of Muslim, Hindu, Buddhist, and secular polities, if one reviewed their experience and response as a whole, could Christians be both victims and victimisers? This, I suggested to the contributors to this volume, was where the uniqueness of our approach would be. However, the evidence we see in this volume shows a far more layered and complex reality of Christianity in Asia, Africa, and Europe than we had imagined. We have attempted to present this nuanced evidence under three main sections: Transforming States and Christian Experience, Christian Minority Responses, and States and Christian Majority.

The contexts represented here include both the 'geographic band' highlighted as 'Contexts of Persecution' and those that are normally not included in such a 'band', namely, Europe / the West. In terms of the countries represented here, we have China, the Philippines, Indonesia, Malaysia,

---

(CAA) under the BJP' in Series on World Christianity and Public Religion Vol. 4, Young (ed.), *World Christianity,* 2022.

9   See 'Under Caesar's Sword' 2023 at https://ucs.nd.edu/report/the-contexts-of-persecution/.

India, Pakistan, and Iran in Asia; Czech Republic, Romania, and Bulgaria in Europe; Malawi, Kenya, Nigeria, and Egypt in Africa; and El Salvador in South America. We wanted a contribution from North America but could not include it mainly because of the lack of space in the volume.

The chapters in this volume highlight aspects of the changing political landscapes, but they also bring to light, as already indicated, a far more varied a picture of Christian experiences and responses than we had initially anticipated. Allow me to expound this a bit below.

The Citizenship Amendment Act (CAA) and the proposed National Register of Citizens (NRC) offer us a window into the changing idea of India; an idea that is particularly inclement for minorities, including Christians. This India is divorcing itself from a unique permutation of secularism that Charles Taylor admired. With the Bharatiya Janata Party (BJP) winning federal elections, one witnesses a new kind of politics in the erstwhile context of an 'open' and 'responsible secularism'. Here one has a glimpse into, in the words of Charles Taylor, 'the mobilisation of popular piety in a very sinister fashion'.[10] The 'Indian secularism' was a negotiated construct combining the Gandhian and Nehruvian positions. This allowed equal respect to all religions within a secular state. The constitution reflected this and the Indian National Congress largely safeguarded it. Under the BJP, arguably, the state employs disruption, violence, and diversion as part of statecraft. Informed by an ideological version of Hinduism, this state tends to be particularly intolerant toward non-Indic religious minorities as it seeks homogeneity and suppresses dissent.

While the BJP-run federal state does not openly target Christians, in most states of India they are often easy targets of violence because they are fewer in number and they seek converts. The Northeast of India presents a contrasting scenario. Christianity is a majority in three of the seven states here. The BJP's last election manifesto was exceptional in sparing these states from the mandatory CAA more because of their tribal identity than their Christian affiliation. Of these, Nagaland, with over 90 percent

---

10   Sonali Campion interview with Charles Taylor at LSE. January 20, 2016 at: https://blogs.lse.ac.uk/southasia/2016/01/20/a-lot-of-the-thinking-about-secularism-that-ive-done-has-grown-out-of-intensive-discussions-about-the-indian-situation-charles-taylor/.

Christian population, has chosen an alliance with the BJP. The case we present in this volume is that of Mizoram, a Christian majority state that chose a different trajectory than did Nagaland. It could just be a matter of time before they follow suit partly under pressure for survival as a state dependent on federal funding. This paper offers a glimpse into the thinking of many still seeking to negotiate their 'identity as citizens of heaven' and collaboration or partnership with the BJP. This is presented creatively as a tension between two types of citizenships: heavenly and earthly. This view sees Mizo Christianity as being essentially compatible with being Indian as enshrined by the high-minded constitution of the makers of India but incompatible with Hindu nationalism. If this vision prevails, unlike Nagaland, Mizoram could continue to stand firm in solidarity with the rest of Indian Christians and resist the powerful influence of the BJP.

In Southeast Asia, one encounters three different cases of countries possibly on a similar trajectory as India but with Islam and Christianity as the majority contexts. Indonesia and Malaysia are Muslim majority, the Philippines is majority Christian. They each present a mixed history of domination of minorities and conflicts. In Malaysia, state-supported Islamisation has been part of the wider global Islamic revival. From the state's point of view, Islamisation assisted with the construction of alliances around a state-subscribed ideology. Islamising identity is not far off a fully acknowledged theocracy in Pakistan. The blasphemy law arises out of an intent to safeguard the sacred; however, it is widely misused against the minorities. The state, perhaps in response to the international pressure, makes the right noises about minority protection; however, the application of the law continues to have serious consequences for Christians. Christians experience what it means to be second-class citizens, vulnerable to the whims and fancy of their accusers and the use of a law whose application is less about real evidence and more about punishing the guilty even if unproven, usually to death. Unsurprisingly, fear and inwardness characterizes the Christians here, as illustrated by the cases of the Church of Pakistan and Full Gospel Assemblies.

Unlike Pakistan, Iran, in West Asia, is a declared theocracy. It is a prominent example of a rapid anti-secular/anti-west Islamization. Iran capitulated to the Islamic revolution beginning in 1978. Iran's long and varied pre-revolution history included openness toward religious diversity.

Khomeini's overthrow led to the establishment of Shi'a theocracy and Muslim clerics took control of the state as rulers and lawyers representing God's rule on earth. A new constitution temporally legitimized narrow sectarian rule in a land known for its internal diversity. Its religiously diverse population includes, even today, Sunnis, ancient Zoroastrians, and 'the recognized Christians', namely, the Armenians and Assyrians. The recognized Christians have conditional protection of the state, which is denied to the newer Christians (converts to Christianity). Both recognized and unrecognized Christians experience marginalisation in their own ways. The recognized Christians are considered second-class (protected as *dhimmi*); their experience is relatively better than that of other Christians, who are often treated as anti-Muslim pro-west infidels.

China is another interesting case, which adds greater depth to our volume. The state is known for various forms of pressures and religious coercions toward minorities, which include Muslims and Christians on the mainland, and Tibetan Buddhists and Christians in Tibet. The Peoples' Republic of China annexed Tibet in 1950s. The Dalai Lama and many Tibetans fled because they were prevented from running their own state. Tibetan tradition, culture, political system, economy, and religious beliefs have since been in the process of being 'sinicised'. Sinicisation is widely recognised, but the sinicisation of Tibet and the strategic responses of Tibetan Christians are relatively less known. Some examples of their agency in the face of aggressive sinicisation are notable: (1) safeguarding *sola scriptura* in challenging the project of 'Bible-rewriting', (2) contact-exchange with churches abroad, and (3) expressing identity both in cultural and religious senses (being Tibetan and Christian). These strategies give them a sense of being part of a much bigger story of faith and a base for launching a subtle resistance to the Chinese project of socialization.

The Chinese Christian agency in mainland China adds another level of complexity in the face of sinicisation. The phrases 'vitality of responses' and 'Christian networks' underline the diversity in responses and networks. This is important because the discourse on Christian minorities often not only totalizes them as a homogenous mass, it also abstracts them purely as objects of suffering and persecution with little agency of their own. Thus, while one must acknowledge the well-known reality of a split between registered and unregistered Christians (comparable to the

Iranian case of recognised and unrecognised Christians) in China and the reality of Christian suffering, we know that scholars and observers have dwelt on this reality before. What is new here is the recognition of a range of responses by Chinese Christians; these responses are 'neither binary, static, nor homogenous across the country'. It is true that Chinese Christianity is a minority, but this minority has internal differentiation of 'ecclesial traditions, business networks, and clan-based identities'. These are not static, but in flux on account of their in-house concerns and on account of their aims related to the internal Chinese or external international dynamics. The changes in the political leadership of China also determine their responses. There are therefore constant alignments and realignments in Chinese Christian responses.

The Egyptian case also highlights the point about diversity and agency. Here, one sees the mainstream churches' accommodation with the state, described as 'clientelism', but also sees the opening of other avenues for concrete action or engagement. Clientelism is arguably a way of relating with the state and vice versa; it is a mechanism for minimising the gap between the rulers and socio-religious groups. It affords religious groups space to express themselves within rules set by the state and for the state to keep an eye on them or 'control' them for what is seen as the greater good of the nation and order in society. The 2011 Revolution saw a weakening of this system as the space opened for new discussions on interfaith dialogue with arguments drawn from human rights and humanism. In this alternative space, many Christian groups relatively free from clientelist obligations are able to engage collaboratively in society. Informed by humanism, they are able to start from a more fundamental premise than one presented by religion. Seeing the religious others primarily as human beings offers them an opportunity for conversations on equality, citizenship, discrimination, and so on. Its future is yet to unfold but this is an additional avenue outside of the state-circumscribed patron-client relations for Christians to collaborate with different traditions within Egyptian Christianity as well as with Muslims.

The examples of coercive states so far have been either Muslim or Hindu. Are states with Christian majority any different?

Our first case here comes from a seemingly peaceful and 'strongly Christian' country of Malawi. This shows evidence of 'persecution in a land of religious freedom'. Jehovah's Witnesses (JW) are a millenarian sect of Christianity. Malawi is considered Christian because its 'public morality was shaped by biblical teaching and a large majority of its population' are professing Christians. Why then did a Christian country persecute Malawi's JW from 1964 and 1993? This happened seemingly inexplicably to 'law-abiding, tax-paying citizens' and their victimisation was permitted under the watch of, or even led by, a one-party regime simply because JW, as part of their expression of faith, refrained from involvement in Malawian politics. The public and the mainline churches showed their collusion with the government through their silence. This level of collusion between a majority community and the state against a minority among them has parallels in the state of Gujarat in India, where the state seemingly supported the mob violence against Muslim minorities and the Hindu religious bodies condoned these actions.[11]

One sees the dynamics of the church and state perhaps more clearly in Central-Eastern Europe; this includes the states that are rapidly secularizing (e.g., the Czech Republic). Here, the evidence points toward a 'misuse of religion" or its use involving a religious rhetoric in support of a particular vision of nationalism—one that is inward-looking, exclusive, and critical of the liberal democratic values of the European Union or Western Europe. The religion that is often visible here is Christianity or its dominant expression in the country concerned. The rhetoric employs the language of 'Christian values', by which is normally meant either Orthodox or Roman Catholic values. Internally, such a rhetoric enables the state in alliance with the church to both control and exclude those considered 'the other'. This other includes religions or minority Christian denominations and more broadly other ethnicities, genders, cultures, sexualities, and political views. Here one sees the dominant tradition of Christianity in alliance with the state; the minority traditions of Christianity here often appear as victims.

The Romanian case highlights this, but in addition to the reality of the Orthodox Church's dominance in the religious and public spheres, one also sees the emerging evidence of collaboration between

---

11 See more in David E. Singh, 'Hindu-Muslim Violence in Gujrat and a Profile of Christian Mission' in *Transformation* 20 no. 4 (2003): 206–216.

the Orthodox (dominant tradition) and evangelicals (minority traditions). This is a particularly interesting detail easily missed in the context of a discourse on Christianity and state in Central-Eastern Europe. Protestant Christianity in Romania is relatively recent when compared with Orthodoxy. The Evangelicals among them have been growing rapidly, especially the Charismatics/Pentecostals. Their stories acknowledge 'oppression' meted out by the Orthodox tradition. Their Orthodox counterparts have their own allegations against the Evangelicals, which are offered as reasons for their marginalisation. After the Communist takeover, as a way of better controlling the disparate non-Orthodox traditions, the regime set up a Federation of Evangelical Denominations, which included among the Pentecostals and the Adventists some relatively older traditions of the Baptists and the Brethren. In the post-Communist and secularizing state of Romania, there seems to be increasing collaboration between them and the Orthodox tradition. What is bringing them closer is the shared pressure of the issues of abortion, same-sex marriage, and a new definition of the family. They still differ on the finer details involving these issues and the specific arguments used by them to counter the liberal position, but there is some cooperation. There remains, however, an absolute parting of ways among them on matters involving theology and the specifics of their respective traditions. Their joint actions are all around ethical issues, which is promising. Similarly, in Bulgaria, Orthodox Christians understandably engage in safeguarding their historic faith and practice in the face of what they perceive to be challenges from outside their tradition. However, especially in light of increasing secularisation, they recognise the importance of not going alone in their dissent. For this reason, they are more willing, as in the Romanian case, to collaborate with the minority Christian traditions they had previously opposed.

Our case from Kenya is unique in that it does not fit in any category explored so far. Kenya is multi-ethnic and majority Christian (approximately 85.5 percent), of whom a little over 60 percent are Protestant, about 20 percent Catholic, and the rest others. There is a fair degree of collaboration between Christian denominations in much of Kenya, but Christians experience marginalisation in counties with a majority Muslim population. This makes the case interestingly different from the rest. A narrative emerging from Muslim sources has been that Christians, being the majority, collaborate with the state against Muslims. There may be some truth in this, but the counterevidence from the counties where Muslims are in majority shows that Christians experience increasing marginalisation despite being in majority nationally and despite their inter-denominational unity in the public sphere. Perhaps this experience of Christians in the Muslim majority counties is akin to another case of Christians from northern Nigeria. Christians arguably account for nearly 50 percent of Nigeria's population, even though they have been a demographic minority in the North. In the North, they have experienced marginalisation and much worse: kidnapping, violence, and death. Despite such experiences, the Christian majority in the rest of Nigeria has never treated Muslim minorities in ways that match their experience in the North. While their experience of suffering may have contributed to intra-Christian cohesion in the North, their experience has certainly led them to engage in deeper theologizing. In this sense, they are ahead of their counterparts in the Kenyan counties with Muslim majority. This theological engagement is unsurprisingly centred on the cross of Jesus, which for his followers in Nigeria is a source of hope in the middle of violence and death. This hope is about triumphing like Christ their master, who died on the cross but rose again. This is a source of assurance for Nigerian Christians in the North. Evil and violence others perpetrate will not triumph over those who adopt the way of Christ.

That there are conflicts and tensions between the Orthodox and Evangelical churches is not surprising. The Orthodox regard all Protestants 'as imposters' and agents of secularization and globalization. The Orthodox belief and practices are considered by the non-orthodox as being heretical. Despite being a minority, Pentecostalism's impact in the public sphere has been unmistakable. The fall of Communism highlighted difference in choices among Orthodox churches, Evangelicals, and especially the Pentecostals. The minority churches showed greater resolve for engagement in political and social spheres in order to challenge the rising secularism and play a role in Ethiopia's economic development. Pentecostalism has also been responsible for charismatic renewal of Christianity in Ethiopia. The schism within the Orthodoxy took place because some within it favoured charismatic 'renewal'. Despite schism, the Orthodox Church remains a powerful institution with links with the state. However, its position as a historic church and its continued power and presence in society still does not ensure its self-assured engagement with plurality in Ethiopia. Catholics in particular, even as a small minority, are still regarded by the Orthodox with suspicion owing to their encounters with Jesuit missionaries. It is in these interstices of conflict and change within the Orthodox Church that one sees some promise of a desire for a better mutual understanding and partnerships in the days to come.

Another case involving the minority Pentecostal church's role in socio-political-economic makeover in rural El Salvador could add to the evidence on how even minority traditions of Christianity can make a large-scale impact on nations with a Catholic or Orthodox tradition. This is despite a history of marginalisation of Pentecostal Christians across Central America but especially in the case presented in this book invoicing El Salvador. The case shows how the experience of marginalisation and the sense of being a minority changes over time. This contributes to change also in the way Pentecostals and Catholics are moving beyond historic exclusion toward practical partnerships. The broader socio-economic consequences of these partnerships are creating openings for the Pentecostals to relate meaningfully with the Catholics. This change occurs not through theological or religious dialogue but through evolving shared visualizations of the transformation of their communities on the ground. Our hope is that readers will receive with appreciation this multilayered narrative and add to this picture of World Christianity from their own research and scholarship.

PART I

TRANSFORMING STATES AND CHRISTIAN EXPERIENCE

1

SABOTAGE, VIOLENCE, AND DISTRACTION SINCE THE ADOPTION OF THE CITIZENSHIP AMENDMENT ACT IN INDIA

David Emmanuel Singh

In another writing, I have highlighted the 'emerging cooperation among minorities in defence of Indian secularism'.[1] Here the focus is on the state and not on minorities' agency under it. In this chapter, I highlight the evidence of a changing India around the discourse on the Citizenship Amendment Act (CAA) and the proposed National Register of Citizens (NRC). Inspired by Acts 4–6, I also offer my reflections around the themes of disruption, violence, and diversion.

With the highest representation in Parliament, the Bharatiya Janata Party (BJP) is the largest political party in India today. In terms of its ideology, it is often linked to V. D. Savarkar (1883–1966; Hindu Mahasabha) and K. B. Hedgewar (1889–1940; Rashtriya Swyamsevak Sangh [RSS]). As a political organisation, the BJP has roots in an older right-wing party, the Jan Sangh (1951–1977). The State of Emergency under the Indira Gandhi

---

[1] See David E. Singh, 'Emerging Cooperation among Minorities in Defense of Indian Secularism since the Adoption of the Citizenship Amendment Act under the BJP', in *World Christianity and Interfaith Relations*, vol. 4, ed. Richard F. Young (Minneapolis, MN: Fortress Press, 2022).

Congress led to its demise, but it spawned a grand alliance against the Congress in the form of the Janata Party (JP). A split in the JP in 1980 led to the creation of the BJP with a right-wing agenda endorsed by the RSS. The BJP struggled to gain traction in the wake of Indira Gandhi's (1917–1984) assassination and Rajeev Gandhi (1944–1991), her son, winning a landslide victory. The tide turned through the revival of the Ram Temple Movement under the leadership of L. K. Advani (b. 1927). The BJP-led alliance won the national elections in 1998 and, despite a hiccup in 1999, regained its position until the end of the term in 2004. Although the BJP remained out of power for the next ten years, since 2014 it has focussed on realising its vision of Hindu nationalism or Hindutva. The BJP's aim has increasingly become manifest since its second round of electoral victory in 2019; it now appears less about development and more about Hindu nationalism. The CAA and NRC have been part of this direction.

INDIAN CITIZENSHIP

The clearest evidence of the Hindutva agenda surfaced after the BJP's re-election in 2019: to a lesser extent in the abrogation of Article 370 in Jammu and Kashmir but principally in the passing of a new bill on Indian citizenship into the CAA.[2]

The act in itself is unexceptional. Similar acts had been passed before under both the Congress and the BJP. For example, the acts in 1987 and 2003 stated that those born in India on or after 26 January 1950 but before 1 July 1987, and on or after 1 July 1987 but before 2003, will be deemed citizens of India by birth.[3] The years 1950, 1987, and 2003 are significant because (1) the Indian constitution came into force as of January 1950, and (2) in July 1987 and in 2003 the Citizenship Amendments Acts (as well as a third one in 2019) were passed. Significantly, one of these Acts was passed under the Congress (1987) and two under the BJP rule (2003 and 2019).

Fundamentally, India follows a system whereby an individual acquires citizenship by the nationality or ethnicity of either or both their

---

2   Scrapping Kashmir's special status and autonomy.
3   Citizenship Act 1955 (CA), clau.3a&b at https://indiacode.nic.in/bitstream/123456789/4210/1/Citizenship_Act_1955.pdf.

parents (based on the 1987 Act). The 2003 Act under the BJP made a finer distinction. This act stated that one acquires citizenship not simply by birth in India but by proving that either or both of one's parents are citizens, or one parent is a citizen and the other is 'not an illegal immigrant' at the time of the birth.[4] The specific condition relating to the legality of one parent's immigration status was introduced as part of the BJP's policy that has echoes in both the 2019 amendment and the discourse on the NRC. The definitions of citizenship by birth and citizenship by descent have had minor revisions both under the Congress (in 1992) and under the BJP (2003).[5]

Other routes to acquiring Indian citizenship bring the current discourse into sharper focus: (1) Citizenship by Registration and (2) Citizenship by Naturalization (CN).[6] CN is especially significant today because it allows an individual (excluding an illegal immigrant) to acquire Indian citizenship.[7] This route to Indian citizenship, however, became slightly more complicated with the insertion of 'special provisions' by the Act of 1985 under the Congress. These special provisions were added to align with the Assam Accord following the agitation led by the Assam movement against mostly Bangladeshi immigrants.[8]

It is one thing to pass an act, but the reality on the ground is often quite messy. It would be impractical to simply repatriate all those deemed illegal immigrants under the 1985 Act; many of them might have lived in India for years and might have had children. In such cases, children's citizenship would be decided by recourse to the principles outlined under citizenship by birth above, where at least one parent had to be a citizen and the other (after the amendment of 2003 under the BJP), if not a citizen, would have to prove they were not an illegal immigrant. This left room for a determined state to enforce laws that would consequently break up families and transfer those deemed illegal (including children) to detention centres. We know the first such centres emerged around 2008 on the

---

4   CA clau.3c.i/&ii.
5   CA clau.4.
6   Citizenship by Registration in CA clau.5; Citizenship by Naturalisation in CA clau.6.
7   CA clau.6.1.
8   CA clau. 6A.

orders of the High Court of Assam.[9] The intention was to house 'illegal immigrants' temporarily until their status was clarified, but this could and has often resulted in a hopeless route for many.

So, in this background, what is different about the CAA of 2019 under the BJP?

MANIFESTO AND CAA

The CAA of 2019 needs to be seen through the lens of the BJP's *Sankalp Patra* (BJP's election manifesto).[10] That it is nationalistic is evident from the start given that the very first item on the agenda is about keeping the 'Nation First'.[11] The top ten promises in it include Article 370 and the CAA, it adopts a zero tolerance policy toward terrorism, and it places 'national security' and 'combatting infiltration' high on the agenda.[12] The specific incorporation of both Article 370 and the implementation of the new Citizenship Amendment Bill (CAB)/CAA manifests an India that demonstrates leadership and strength domestically and internationally. Clause 12 of the *Sankalp Patra* clearly states:

> We are committed to the enactment of the Citizenship Amendment Bill for the protection of individuals of religious minority communities from neighbouring countries escaping persecution. We will make all efforts to clarify the issues to the sections of population from the Northeastern states who have expressed apprehensions regarding the legislation. We reiterate our commitment to protect the linguistic, cultural and social identity of the people of Northeast. Hindus, Jains, Buddhists and Sikhs escaping persecution from India's neighbouring countries will be given citizenship in India.[13]

---

9   Prakash K. Dutta, 'NRC and Story of How Assam Got Detention Centres for Foreigners', *India Today*, 27 December 2019.
10   *Sankalp Patra: Sankalpit bharat—sashakt bharat* (Determined and strong India) (New Delhi: BJP, 2019).
11   *Sankalp Patra*, 2019, 13–14.
12   'BJP Manifesto 2019: Top 10 Promises for Next 5 Years', *India Today*, 8 April 2019.
13   *Sankalp Patra*, 2019, 4–12.

SABOTAGE, VIOLENCE, AND DISTRACTION: THE CAA IN INDIA 19

Following a massive mandate of 351 seats for the alliance compared to 336 in 2014 and an increased vote share of 45 percent in 2019 compared to 38 percent in 2018,[14] the BJP lost little time in implementing some of the top ten promises. The CAB sought to amend the Citizenship Act of 1955. Its passage was understandably smooth in both houses and was signed by the BJP-nominated president on 12 December 2019. It came into force as per clause 1.2 with its notification in the official gazette of the central government of India.[15]

On the surface, the Citizenship Amendment Act exceeds the *Sankalp Patra* at least by adding two religious minorities not named before: Parsees and Christians. It is unclear why they were missed in the manifesto or why it was thought necessary to include them in the act. It appears that despite the projection of strength, the BJP does care about Western attention. It does not want to be seen as anti-Christian. In terms of its manifesto,[16] the BJP wanted the international community to see that its decision to include or exclude minorities was fair-minded and 'informed' by an accompanying narrative about terrorism. It could also be a strategy to divide the minority faith communities up in such a way that they would not have any serious reason to form a united dissent. Following Modi's 'grand welcome' in Texas in 2019, as the protests against the CAA in India continued, expensive preparations led to the hearty welcome of the president of the United States (POTUS) to India in February 2020. There were no substantive gains for India except the optics of power by association. POTUS, on his part, appeared eager 'for more business and looking to find a counterweight to the rise of China',[17] and/or he saw in Modi a fellow nationalist fighting a battle against terrorism and immigration.

The *Sankalp Patra* also lacked specificity in that it did not detail from which 'neighbouring countries' the named 'persecuted minorities' would be welcomed. The act addresses this gap, specifies the countries,

---

14   Raj Chengappa, 'Mandate 2019: The Republic of Narendra Modi', *India Today*, 5 May 2019.
15   'The Citizenship Amendment Act', *Bharat ka Rajpatr (The Gazette of India)* 47, 12 December 2019.
16   *Sankalp Patra*, 2019, 13–14.
17   Jeffrey Gettleman and Vindu Goel, 'Modi Prepares to Welcome Trump to India', *New York Times*, 28 January 2020.

and strategically limits them to three that are majority Muslim: Afghanistan, Bangladesh, and Pakistan.[18] It excludes Nepal, Bhutan, Myanmar, Sri Lanka, and the Maldives; it remains silent on Muslim minorities like the Rohingya, the Ahmadiyya, and the Shia. The act's silence on Muslim minorities highlights its bias but is consistent with the BJP's narrative on terrorism and security; it thereby appears to construct its nationalistic discourse (for now) purely in relation to Islam and the selected neighbouring Muslim nations. It shows that religious minorities (non-Muslims) who might have illegally entered India to escape persecution (impossible to prove apart from qualitative autobiographies) on or before 31 December 2014 (when BJP came into power) qualify for naturalisation.[19]

REASONS FOR PROTESTS

The discussion above states that CAAs were common across party lines (the Congress and BJP). The CAA of 2019 was different in that its intent appeared altruistic (accommodating in India the persecuted religious minorities from neighbouring countries). However, if the CAA of 2019 was altruistic as claimed, why were there spontaneous public protests? In answering this question, one needs to look at (1) the CAA in relation to what it is popularly believed to prepare the ground for, namely the NRC; (2) the exceptional results of the NRC in the state of Assam; and (3) the reasons for the focus on three neighbouring countries and the exclusion of Muslims from the 2019 CAA. This exclusion has implications for Muslims and Christians should a nationwide NRC be executed.

CAA-NRC Linkage

BJP sources mostly deny a link between the CAA and NRC. Harsh Mander, a highly respected commentator-activist, calls any link a 'lie'.[20] The BJP's Home Minister has outlined the strategy in the recorded sessions of Parliament. There have been denials of the linkage in the backdrop of the

---

18   *Bharat ka Rajpatr*, 2019, 2.
19   *Bharat ka Rajpatr*, 2019, 3.
20   Akhil Kadidad, 'BJP Claim over NRC-CAA Linkage Is a Lie', *Deccan Herald*, 23 December 2019.

protests against the CAA throughout India. A BJP minister, Ravi Shankar Prasad, speaking at *Agenda AjTak*, said, 'NRC hasn't been finalised yet. There is no question of joining CAA with NRC as the draft is yet to be completed'; he said too that the country belonged equally to Muslims and Hindus.[21] BJP's Information Technology Cell has been flooding the space with this new narrative. A counternarrative, which takes Home Minister Shah's statements at face value, says: 'Now don't be so innocent that's [sic] at present it's [sic] only CAA. Chronology is already defined...'.[22]

It is apparent to most people that the CAA is not as altruistic as it appears; its intent is to introduce religious criteria to India's citizenship laws, which makes the linkage to the NRC evident. The act allows only non-Muslims from the three Muslim countries a route to citizenship; Muslim minorities are excluded. The intent of the NRC is to headcount all those living in the country in order to separate citizens from non-citizens. Home Minister Shah's official X profile (formerly Twitter) has: 'First we will pass the Citizenship Amendment bill and ensure that all the refugees from the neighbouring nations get the Indian citizenship. After that NRC will be made and we will detect and deport every infiltrator from our motherland'.[23] In a video uplinked by the BJP, Shah clearly says: 'First the CAB will come. All refugees will get citizenship. The NRC will come. This is why refugees should not worry, but infiltrators should. Understand the chronology'.[24] In another speech in 2019, Shah again said: 'We will ensure implementation of NRC in the entire country. We will remove every single infiltrator from the country, except Buddhists, Hindus and Sikhs'.[25] This statement is obviously incorrect because it leaves out Christians and Parsee originally included in the CAA 2019. However, in another statement Shah corrected this: 'All the Hindus, Sikhs, Buddhists, Christians, they will get citizenship, so where is the question of NRC? We

---

21 'No Question of Linking CAA to NRC', *India Today*, 17 December 2019.
22 Twitter page at https://twitter.com/search?q=%22don%27t%20link%22%20NRC&src=typed_query&f=live 2019.
23 Amit Shah (@AmitShah). Twitter, 1 May 2019.
24 *BJPlive*, Amit Shah speech at https://www.youtube.com/watch?v=Z__6E5hP-bHg&feature=youtu.be it Shah, @syedrafi, 11 April 2019.
25 *BJPlive*, 2019.

want to walk up to them and give them citizenship. They wouldn't be asked for any documents'.[26]

The CAA and NRC are linked also because, as Jayal says, 'While one carves out a path to statelessness for the disfavoured groups, the other creates paths to citizenship for preferred groups'.[27] The link between the two can be seen in that these are BJP's instruments for changing the very meaning of citizenship in India's secular constitution.

Exclusion of Muslims

As noted, Clause 12 of BJP's manifesto excludes Muslims. It also does not name the countries: '[those from] India's neighbouring countries will be given citizenship in India'.[28] The 2019 CAA, however, specifies three countries, which are all Muslim. The fundamental assumptions are that (1) only Muslim countries in India's neighbourhood persecute minorities and (2) Muslims as minorities are not persecuted either in these three countries or in other countries in India's neighbourhood. This needs to be seen also in the broader context of BJP policies relating to Muslim minorities within India. Muslims are viewed with suspicion and are often encompassed in the broader security narrative with Pakistan. The revocation of Article 370 in Kashmir, the criminalisation of triple *talaq*, incidents of reconversions or *ghar vapasi*, the Ram Mandir discourse, and vigilantism and lynching all revolve around Muslims.

The attempt at singling out Muslims reminds observers of the Partition; it also indicates the state's intent to move toward 'majoritarianism' (a sort of 'Hindu Pakistan'). Unsurprisingly, the chants of *azadi* (freedom) are rising.[29] The BJP, on its part, has also made a convenient political use of popular chants as an election slogan against the Congress: a 'Congress *mukt bharat*' (India free from Congress), which is a shortcut for freedom from the idea of secular India. In the contexts of the protest, *azadi*

---

26   Amit Shah, Shivam Vij@DilliDurAst, 18 December 2019.
27   Niraja Gopal Jayal, 'The CAA and NRC Together Will Reopen Wounds of Partition and Turn India into a Majoritarian State', *The India Forum*, 29 December 2019 at Scroll.in/947458.
28   *Sankalp Patra*, 2019, 4–12.
29   Sukant Deepak, 'Kamala Bhasin on Why *azadi* Was Never Kashmir's Alone', *DailyO.in*, 5 March 2016.

arguably refers to the attempt at another historic division of Indians along Muslim-Hindu lines and the replacement of a secular with a Hindu India.

The attempts made in both the BJP manifesto and the resulting CAA stand somewhat at odds with Clauses 6 and 7 of the Constitution of India (COI) concerning the rights of citizenship. Clause 6 outlines the right to citizenship for anyone who migrates from Pakistan into India if 'either of his parents or any of his grandparents was born in India'. Even if this clause is argued to be historical in nature, clause 7 could be argued to offer more explicit support against Muslims even where it is proved they had migrated to Pakistan but choose then to return to India:

> Notwithstanding anything in articles 5 and 6, a person who has after the first day of March, 1947, migrated from the territory of India to the territory now included in Pakistan shall not be deemed to be a citizen of India: Provided that nothing in this article shall apply to a person who, after having so migrated to the territory now included in Pakistan, has returned to the territory of India under a permit for resettlement or permanent return issued by or under the authority of any law and every such person shall for the purposes of clause (b) of article 6 be deemed to have migrated to the territory of India after the nineteenth day of July, 1948.[30]

Unconstitutionality of CAA

Stanford- and Harvard-educated lawyer Abhinav Chandrachud works at the Bombay High Court. In a talk widely circulated on YouTube, he revisits the debate surrounding the CAA. That the CAA is unconstitutional seems evident, but Chandrachud offers a more nuanced perspective on it and, hence, his viewpoint is worth visiting.[31] As noted above, the CAA of 2019 does not stand on its own. It has a history—some of which I have

---

30 COI.II.7 at https://www.india.gov.in/sites/upload_files/npi/files/coi_contents. pdfCongress@ 2019INCIndia, 22 December 2019.
31 Abhinav Chandrachud, 'History of CAA Lies in the History of 1948' posted by Satyen K. Bordoloi at YouTube, https://www.youtube.com/watch?v=gife GicNLfl. 2020.

outlined but that goes back to 1947–1948, that is, before the constitution was adopted. Following Partition, there were two waves of migration from West Pakistan into India: the first was that of Hindus and Sikhs. The second took place in 1948 and involved Indian Muslims who had migrated to West Pakistan after Partition but had returned or were returning into independent India. A distinction was made early on in describing Hindu and Sikh refugees (known as displaced persons) and the Muslim returnees (known as evacuees). The Muslims who had migrated to Pakistan left behind properties known as evacuee properties.[32] Giving these properties to the refugees helped Hindu and Sikh refugees from Pakistan to resettle in India. The retuning Muslims presented Indian politicians and administrators with a problem; it meant displacing Hindu or Sikh refugees a second time to make way for the returning Muslims. This, they felt, could easily fuel the communal passion of Hindu fringe elements and hence had to be carefully managed.

So, in this context of a complex post-Partition influx, in July 1948 the permit system was invented.[33] This system sought to stem the flow of Muslim evacuees into India. Although those returning were not identified by their religion in documents, in practice, a distinction between Muslims and Hindus/Sikhs was made. After leaving India, many Muslims chose to return, whereas the Hindus and Sikhs travelled only one way. Therefore, the returnees were easily identifiable as Muslims and, under the permit system, were easily denied resettlement rights in their own properties. Their right to permanent resettlement was possible only if they were not displacing those displaced. One can see this system embedded in clauses 5, 6, and 7 of the constitution.[34] The language of these clauses is indeed secular and non-discriminatory, but these clauses contain two hidden premises: (1) those who came before the permit system was adopted on 19 July 1948 were largely understood to be Hindu/Sikh, and in these cases, the granting of the citizenship was automatic; (2) those who came after 19 July 1948, and

---

32 See more in Joya Chatterji and David Washbrook, *Routledge Handbook of the South Asian Diaspora* (Abingdon, UK: Routledge, 2014), 187.

33 Vazira F-Y. Zamindar, *The Long Partition and the Making of Modern South Asia: Refugees, Boundaries, Histories* (New York: Columbia University Press, 2010).

34 COI.II, 5–7.

having first evacuated at the Partition (Muslims), now needed a permit for permanent resettlement. It is clear this strategy worked: By March 1948 (before the adoption of the permit system), twenty-two thousand Muslims had returned to India, but after the permit, only about two thousand were admitted.

I have no evidence of the actual number of those who were denied resettlement. This was, however, not as simple as Chandrachud makes it out to be. It was not possible to enforce the system of permits uniformly because, as today, most people had few or no documents; in many cases, permits were fabricated; and many returnees claimed never to have left India in the first place.[35] Therefore, the notion of an appreciable reduction in the number of returnees because of the permit system needs a separate interrogation. The fact is that the government of India simply could not enforce the system in order to prevent evacuees from returning.

What is clear is that the permit system succeeded in keeping Muslims out. It can therefore be seen that the bias against Muslims goes back to a time before and around the establishment of the constitution of India. This bias is also evident when the West Pakistan case is compared with that of the East. The permit system was applied to the West but not to East Pakistan. This is, as Chandrachud argues, because whereas in the West there were only about 700,000–800,000 Hindus/Sikhs around the time the permit system was adopted, there were over 16 million Hindus in the East. It was not applied to East Pakistan so as not to obstruct the movement of displaced Hindus into India.

Clearly, this narrative tarnishes the secular origins of India's constitution, but this is not to say the constitution was and is not secular. In fact, the CAA (and not just the planned NRC) of today is plainly unconstitutional in light of article 14 of the constitution: 'The State shall not deny to any person equality before the law or the equal protection of the laws within the territory of India'.[36] It is this equality provision, Chandrachud argues, that the current CAA violates in more than one way, not the least of which is that it excludes many other minority groups apart from Muslims, such as the Jews, Bahai, Atheist, agnostics, and others. Thus, it is true that

---

35   Chatterji & Washbrook, *Routledge Handbook*, 2014, 188.
36   COI.III, 14.

the CAA under the BJP is unconstitutional, but one needs to understand that this is part of a long history of bias against minorities that predates the BJP.

STATE'S RESPONSE TO PROTESTS

While Muslims appear to be the obvious target of exclusion, other minorities, including Christians (excluding the Northeastern Christian states) understand that non-Indic religious minorities are not safe. This explains the widespread and mixed dissent movements. As an Indian Christian, I find it impossible not to take a side. Stott's review of Acts 4–6 highlights for me something evident in that good stories often get blighted by evil; the Pentecost leading to a closely knit community was followed by moral subversion, physical violence, and distractions.[37] This to me is a helpful way of limiting the scope of my review of the state's response to minority dissent in India, which included Christian participation as I have outlined in my work 'Emerging Cooperation'.[38]

Subversion

Subversion can be a way of counteracting imbalance where a community comes into being 'to control the violence that would otherwise prevail'.[39] This would have been the case when Gandhi chose to encourage non-cooperation/civil disobedience against an empire that sanctioned Jaliawala Bagh (13 April 1919). Popular dissent in India today could be characterised as subversion in this sense. Turiel's work, however, suggests that subversion is not exclusive to those with 'little power' but also is practised by those in power. In the case of those in power, subversion can also entail deceptive actions.[40] One example of this would be when some in the BJP go openly after certain religious minorities (as when churches are destroyed, pastors beaten up or imprisoned, etc.) while others higher up the 'food

---

37   John Stott, *The Message of Acts* (Leicester: IVP, 1990).
38   Singh, 'Emerging Cooperation', 2022.
39   Orlando Fals-Borda, *Subversion and Social Change in Columbia,* (New York: Columbia University Press, 1969).
40   Elliot Turiel, 'Resistance and Subversion in Everyday Life', *Journal of Moral Education* 32 no. 2 (2003): 115–130.

chain' resort to outright lying, deception, or plausible deniability. This is evident in the BJP's outreach into the 'Christian' Northeast where Christians in majority are treated with respect but Christians in minority in the mainland are persecuted.

Hazra calls BJP's politics 'sanctioned communalism'.[41] This is especially evident during election campaigns. An accused (Pragya Thakur) waiting to stand trial for her role in the 2008 Malegaon blast was fielded by the BJP in the 2019 elections. Having now been embraced by the BJP, she is known to have made a number of incendiary comments; for example, she has talked about 'climbing atop the Babri Masjid . . . to help demolish it'—all this to clear the path for the temple promised in the manifesto. Amit Shah is said to have talked about purging 'infiltrators except Buddhists, Hindus and Sikhs', clearly a veiled reference to non-Indian religious minorities. The chief minister of a populous state, Uttar Pradesh, is said to have referred to Muslims as 'the Green virus' or 'termites'. A BJP leader threatened to 'bring machines from China to shave 10–12 thousand Muslims and later force them to adopt Hindu religion' as part of what has been known since the nineteenth century as *gharvapasi* (reconversion) of Indian Christians and Muslims.[42]

According to a report, most political leaders lie or deceive and the real question is 'Why do leaders lie?'[43] Outside the context of the campaign trail, the top leadership of the BJP has generally been more discreet. A *Business Standard* article reports that India has 'never seen any leader lie and deceive like Modi before'.[44] While this might be an exaggeration, we know that the CAA protests have elicited some uncoordinated responses and even lies from the leaders. Perhaps the best place to start is Modi's speech at the Ramlila Maidan in Delhi on 22 December 2019. I heard the speech in India, and it is available in full on several media platforms, such as *India Today*, *NDTV*,

---

[41] Indrajit Hazra, 'By Nominating Pragya Singh Thakur, BJP Has Crossed over into the Domain of Sanctioned Communalism', *TOI*, 19 April 2019.

[42] Nikhil Inamdar, 'Five Instances That Bear Out the BJP's Anti-Muslim Stance on the Campaign Trail', *Quartz India*, 23 April 2019.

[43] John Mearsheimer, *Why Leaders Lie: Truth about Lying in International Politics* (Oxford University Press, 2013).

[44] 'Never Seen Any Leader Lie and Deceive Like Modi Before: Siddaramaiah', *Business Standard*, 4 May 2019.

ABP, and *YouTube*, along with commentaries and articles about the speech. An analysis of the main points covered shows its relevance for the issues of subversion and distraction. Just a few examples should suffice.

One of Modi's assertions was: 'Since my government first came to power in 2014, I want to tell my 1.3 billion countrymen, there has never been a discussion on NRC.' This was as brazen a lie as can be. We know that Modi's deputy, Amit Shah, said in Parliament, 'First we will pass the Citizenship Amendment bill and ensure that all the [non-Muslims] refugees from the neighboring nations get the Indian citizenship. After that NRC will be made and we will detect and deport every infiltrator from our motherland.'

Another statement speaks of the absence of detention centres: 'There have been multiple rumours about NRC too. NRC was implemented in Assam on the Supreme Court's orders. No rules have been framed for bringing it to the whole country; it has not been introduced in Parliament. There is no detention centre in India.' Many of his listeners may have overlooked this at the Ramlila Maidan, but this was clearly a lie. India not only already has such camps; others are being built. One of India's largest camps is nearly done in Goalpara Assam.[45] Since the NRC in Assam, 1.9 million people who have been found to be 'not citizens of India' need to be housed until their cases are cleared. Some, if not all, Muslims among them could remain there until the end of their lives if Bangladesh refuses to accept them. This could become a lot messier if NRC is implemented nationwide.

According to a newspaper, Prime Minister Modi said, 'The Citizenship Act NRC has nothing to do with Indian Muslims'.[46] I have already cited the words of Minister Ravi Shankar Prasad and Home Minister Amit Shah's testimonies that suggest the opposite view.[47] What makes Modi's lies deadlier than most is that he has the backing of his party (BJP), of the largest right-wing volunteer force in the world (RSS), and of the state institutions all eager to execute his plans.

---

45 Tawqeer Hussain, '"How Is It Human?": India's Largest Detention Centre Almost Ready', *Al Jazeera*, 2 January 2020.
46 'Never Seen Any Leader Lie', 2019.
47 'No Question of Linking CAA to NRC: Union Minister Ravi Shankar Prasad', *India Today*, 17 December 2019; see also Rohan Venkataramakrishnan, 'Who Is Linking Citizenship Act to NRC? Here Are Five Times Amit Shah Did So', *Scroll.in*, 20 December 2019.

Violence

Following the BJP-led 'pro-CAA protest' in the RSS bastion, one popular slogan used was *desh ke gaddaron ko, goli mari salon ko* ('shoot the traitors of India').[48] In Delhi, responding to the nationwide protests, a Union minister, Anurag Thakur, chanted the same slogan.[49] This was directed especially to the never-ending protests led by women (and children) at Shaheen Bagh (SB). The slogan reflects the BJP narrative that non-Indic minority religions have extraterritorial loyalties and hence are *gaddars* (traitors) worthy of elimination. This discourse is not against infiltrators from Pakistan or Bangladesh but against India's own citizens. Seeing this as a licence to kill, lone gunmen have attacked protestors at SB. One of them was heard shouting '*sirf hinduon ki chalegi*' ('only what Hindus say will go');[50] another nationalist fired on students protesting against the CAA. In pictures, he can be seen waving his gun near a large police force and inviting students: 'Come, I will give you freedom' (*azadi*).[51] This has also encouraged widespread right-wing vigilantism against Christians and Muslims all across India.

The Gujrat Riots of 2002 saw an estimated death toll of about two thousand people[52] under Modi as the Chief Minister (CM) of the state.[53] In 2012, a special committee of the Supreme Court cleared Modi of involvement. The state police and government officials played a role in pointing the Hindu rioters to properties to destroy while citizens were murdered and raped.[54] Following the CAA, a BBC report called a state in India as being the

---

48 'No question of linking CAA to NRC.'
49 'MoS Finance Anurag Thakur Leads *goli maaro saalon ko* Chant at BJP Rally in Delhi', *Outlook*, 27 January 2020.
50 'Shaheen Bagh Firing: Shooter Shouts *sirf Hinduon kin chalegi*, Detained', *Ojha*, 1 February 2020.
51 'Gunman Injures Indian Student in Attack on Citizenship Protest', *Guardian*, 30 January 2020.
52 Christophe Jaffrelot, 'Communal Riots in Gujarat: The State at Risk', (2003). DOI:10.11588/heidok.00004127.
53 'India: The Modi Question', episodes 1 and 2, series producer Richard Cookson, executive producer Mike Radford, aired January 17, 2023 on BBC, https://www.bbc.co.uk/programmes/p0dkb144.
54 Richard Jackson, Eamon Murphy, and Scott Poynting (Eds.), *Contemporary State Terrorism: Theory and Practice* (Abingdon, UK: Routledge, 2011).

'worst affected in the ongoing protests'. Many people lost their lives; many were shot by the police. One of the survivors asked, 'Did we die because we are Muslims? Are we not citizens of this country?' The CM talked of *badla* (revenge) for the destruction of public property: 'their property will be confiscated to make up for the loss of public assets'. The protestors said they were only exercising their democratic rights but the inordinate state response led to chaos and angry reactions from the protestors. Reportedly, police detained thousands for days; they were intimidated by the police; police also took part in vandalizing properties of those suspected of dissent.[55] More recently, it was reported 'over 10 Jamia students were admitted after a scuffle with police;' the students alleged they were hit in their 'private parts'—many of them had to be taken to hospital because their injuries were 'serious in nature' according to doctors.[56]

The BJP leaders have repeatedly highlighted protests as minority-led versus Hindu/India struggle; for example, in his speech, Modi said, 'People who are setting fire can be seen on TV . . . they can be identified by the clothes they are wearing'.[57] People who are from different walks of life, like a deported German student, have made comparisons between Modi and Hitler; the Hollywood actor, John Cusack, and the actor turned politician, Prakash Raj, have also made such allusions and have even shared a picture of Modi dressed like Hitler.[58] We know Rahul Gandhi has alluded to this as well: 'the brutal attack on JNU students & teachers by masked thugs, that has left many seriously injured, is shocking. The fascists in control of our nation are afraid of the choices of our brave students. Today's violence in JNU is a reflection of that fear'.[59]

While a large number of the senior leadership was in Gujarat with Modi to welcome POTUS on his last visit to India, parts of Muslim areas

---

55 Tanushri Pandey, 'Cops Hit Us in Our Private Parts: Over 10 Jamia Students Admitted after Scuffle', *India Today*, 11 February 2020.
56 Pandey, 'Cops Hit Us', 2020.
57 '"Can Be Identified by Their Clothes": PM Modi on CAA Protesters', *The Quint*, 15 December 2019.
58 'Hollywood Actor John Cusack, Prakash Raj Share Image Comparing Modi with Hitler', *The Week*, 7 January 2019.
59 'Kerala Leads the Way in Anti-CAA Protests on Republic Day', *The Week*, 26 January 2020. http://tinyurl.com/yr4xfbfs

burned. Likely encouraged by the perceived American/Trump support, BJP supporters (again with tacit support from the state authorities, including the police) launched an offensive leading to many deaths, looting, and burning of homes and places of worship by 'Hindu mobs'. A large number of people affected in these also had 'gunshot wounds, acid burns, stabbings and wounds from beatings and stone pelting'.[60] The Asrar Ahmed interview with some Hindus shows their view was that some BJP politicians actually played a role in inciting violence against Muslims who had been protesting peacefully. The main accused named was a member of the BJP. Another bold Hindu woman reporter pointed out that the Hindu mob was shouting slogans of '*jai shri rama*' and encouraging the mob members to 'remove the trousers of the protester to separate Muslims from the rest' (circumcision being a way of identifying Muslims). This, she reported, was happening in Delhi following the model of the Gujarat riots; she also bravely named two BJP leaders in this context: Kapil Mishra and Amit Shah. We know there is some truth to it because we have clips of Mishra standing with a police officer and giving the police an ultimatum 'to clear the roads of anti-CAA protesters or else [he said] they would have to hit the streets'.[61] Via Tweets, Misra defiantly denies the charge he is a 'terrorist'.[62]

Misdirection

Stolberg writes about politicians lying and argues that 'Trump has elevated the art of fabrication'. 'The Art of Political Distraction' describes it as a way of capturing 'the public imagination by tapping into some larger fear or existing perception'. It is 'a proxy for a bigger concern'.[63] Jamieson's work shows there is a link between distraction and deception.[64] Modi and Trump seem to admire each other. Arguably, Modi is far behind in the art of

---

60 Hannah Ellis-Petersen, 'Delhi Protests: Death Toll Climbs amid Worst Religious Violence for Decades', *Guardian*, 26 February 2020.
61 'They Are Calling Me Terrorist: Defiant, BJP's Kapil Mishra Tweets Again', *NDTV*, 26 February 2020. http://tinyurl.com/3dc539ha
62 'They Are Calling Me Terrorist', 2020.
63 Sheryl Gay Stolberg, 'The Art of Political Distraction', *New York Times*, 21 March 2009.
64 Kathleen Hall Jamieson, *Dirty Politics: Deception, Distraction and Democracy* (New York: Oxford University Press, 1993).

distraction and deception. Chaudhari and Sinha offer evidence of what they describe as 'a combination of falsehood and half-truths' in Modi's speech at Ramlila on 22 December 2019.[65] Just a few examples should suffice: His speech claimed that the 'NRC word has not been discussed anywhere' and that it 'had to be implemented in Assam only under the Supreme Court's direction'. The reality is that, as noted before, NRC was part of the BJP's manifesto for the 2019 elections, it has been raised in Parliament, and Modi's own home minister promised in the Upper House that NRC would be executed throughout India. In his speech, Modi also claimed that the CAB was passed by Parliament 'for the future of Dalits, the oppressed and the exploited'. In the same speech he contradicted himself by saying that CAA 'is not for any citizen—Hindu or Muslim . . . This law has nothing to do with the 130 *crore* [1.3 billion] people who stay in this country'.

Because the CAA is linked with NRC, we know from the exercise in Assam that it did affect many Indians and potentially will affect many more if it is implemented nationwide. Modi blamed the Congress and 'urban naxals' for spreading the rumor that 'all Muslims will be sent to detention camps'.[66] The Congress did not make this sort of overgeneralisation. All they said was factually accurate: 'An Indian citizen without the requisite document will be forced to suffer the ordeal of several court cases and may eventually end up in a detention camp'.[67] If CAA-NRC really have nothing to do with '130 *crores* Indian' (which includes Indian Muslims), why did the chief minister of the largest and politically most important state of Uttar Pradesh say, 'Muslims should be fed with bullets'?[68]

More solid evidence of distraction in the face of the protests is the new discourse about the National Population Register (NPR). It was updated in 2015, a year after the BJP came to power in 2014. It is a 'register of usual residents of the country'. A 'usual resident' is 'a person who has resided

---

65   Pooja Chaudhary and Pratik Sinha, 'PM Modi's Speech on CAA/NRC: A Combination of Falsehood and Half-Truths', *Alt News,* 24 December 2019.
66   Congress@INCIndia, 22 December 2019, https://twitter.com/INCIndia/status/1208692404099919873.
67   Congress@INCIndia, 22 December 2019, https://twitter.com/INCIndia/status/1208692404099919873.
68   'Chief Minister of Indian State Says "Muslims Should Be Fed with Bullets",' *PressTV,* 6 February 2020.

in a local area for the past 6 months or more or a person who intends to reside in that area for the next 6 months'. The aim of NPR is 'to create a comprehensive identity database of every usual resident in the country' and its intention therefore is not to determine the resident's nationality.[69] In his commentary titled 'The Five-Step Game', one of India bravest political analysts, Yogendra Yadav, explains the sense in which NPR serves as a proxy for CAA-NRC. He also argues how NPR could lead to the detention of many Indian citizens and naturalisation of 'foreigners' if they are from a minority religion (except Islam) and hail from the three designated countries. Yadav's analysis shows that the exercise to begin in due course is not meant to create a register of 'the usual residents of India'; rather, it is the first step toward determining Indian citizenship. The five steps of this exercise will be NPR (possibly imminent), Doubtful Citizens List (largely a job of government administrators), NRC (a massive and costly nationwide exercise), Foreigners' Tribunal (for those on the doubtful list and those who fail NRC criteria), and finally Detention.[70]

---

69   'Introduction to NPR-2010 Section A', *Census of India* (2011) at http://censusindia.gov.in/2011-Common/IntroductionToNpr.html.
70   Yogendra Yadav, *The Five-Step Game of NPR+NCR+CAA*, 10 February 2020 at https://www.youtube.com/watch?v=Zy5guWl4Amg.

2

CHINESE CHRISTIANS AND POST-MAOIST POLITIES

Michel Chambon

This chapter explores the ways Chinese Christians, Catholics, and Protestants have responded to coercive polities deployed in post-Maoist China. While international attention has widely focused on the split between Chinese Christians who accept supervision by the state and those who refuse (Patriotic and underground Catholics, Three-Self and House Church Protestants), this chapter argues that the range of Christian anti-coercion responses is neither binary, static, nor homogenous across the country. Chinese Christians are not a single minority but a diversified body of ecclesial traditions, business networks, and clan-based identities. Furthermore, the nature and intensity of coercive polities have evolved over time and space. While the post-Maoist state had gradually loosened its control over religious groups, church-state relations tightened again under Xi Jinping's leadership. However, depending on the local religious landscape and the ways local officials implemented state policies, Chinese Protestants and Catholics, who make a little less than 10 percent of the total population, have deployed various strategies to respond to oppressive administrative measures. Yet, competition among Christian networks and with other religious movements, which are unequally active across the country, have also impacted their way of collaborating with local officials and accepting state supervision. Therefore, Chinese coercive polities and anti-coercion responses are complex and changing, calling for constant re-investigation.

BACKGROUND CONTEXT

To explore this spectrum of Chinese Christian responses, this chapter is divided into four sections. Each covers one decade of the past forty years. During each period, specific religious dynamics emerged and forms of continuity existed. Religious, political, and economic events also reframed the ways the state had defined and implemented coercive polities. Similarly, Christian communities and networks adjusted their social, religious, and political positioning. Thus, I argue that the past four decades each had their own specificities. Distinguishing them helps a better understanding of the variety of Christian responses and the diversity of factors behind these specificities.

Data presented in this chapter are based on two primary sources. First, I elaborate on personal observations collected during the past twenty years. From September 2003 to June 2006, I worked as a seminarian and pastoral worker for the Catholic diocese of Hong Kong, where I learned Cantonese and collaborated with the French Paris Foreign Missions. As my Chinese improved, I regularly visited various parts of China, especially Guangdong and Guangxi provinces. While I have continued to visit China almost every year since then, I lived in Taiwan from September 2009 to February 2011, where I learned Mandarin and researched local Christianity. Then, with the help of Dennis Balcombe, an influential Pentecostal missionary based in Hong Kong, and as part of my PhD program in anthropology, I lived in a Three-Self Protestant Church in Nanping, Fujian Province from January 2015 to June 2016.[1] I conducted systematic ethnographic fieldwork among the six local Christian networks.[2] This in-depth engagement with Chinese registered and non-registered Christian networks was an opportunity to pay recurrent visits to Christian communities along the Fujian and Zhejiang coasts, as well as to the cities of Guangzhou, Shanghai, and Beijing. My second source of information and insights is the ever-growing scholarship produced by sociologists, anthropologists, and political scientists researching Chinese Christianity and religion in

---

1   Michel Chambon, *Making Christ Present in China, Actor-Network Theory and the Anthropology of Christianity* (Cham: Palgrave Macmillan, 2020).
2   Michel Chambon, 'How Do Chinese Christians Draw Boundaries among Themselves? Reassessing the Question of Chinese Christianities', *Religions* 13 (2022): 258.

China. Although I do not pretend to summarise their increasingly nuanced work, I am deeply indebted to Elizabeth Allès, Cao Nanlai, Jean Charbonnier, Antony E. Clark, Vincent Goossaert, Huang Jianbou, Ji Zhe, Eugenio Menegon, Pan Juliang, Chloé Staar, Nicolas Standaert, Benoit Vermander, Robert Weller, Yang Fenggang, and many more.

Before discussing what happened in the 1980s, one must briefly summarise the political background from which Chinese Christians of that time emerged. After decades of war against Japan as well as civil war, the Communist Party seized power over all of China, Manchuria, the Tarim Basin, and Tibet. On 1 October 1949, Mao Zedong proclaimed the People's Republic of China. Chinese Christian networks and communities knew that things would become more complicated for them. Within a few years, all foreign members were expelled and heavy bureaucratic control was imposed upon religious activities. In line with the Communist agenda, all private and often Christian schools, dispensaries, and hospitals were nationalised. During the Cultural Revolution (1966–1976), all religious activities and publications were strictly prohibited. By the late 1960s, Christianity had disappeared from the public space of the People's Republic of China.

Nonetheless, Chinese Christians had developed various ways to adjust their religious commitment to this new socio-political situation. Catholics, who have had a few centuries of experience on how to survive under large-scale state persecutions, let their faith withdraw within the privacy of their families. Where Catholicism had a long historical presence, family clans became the guardians of the faith. At night, relatives gathered discreetly, recited traditional prayers like the rosary, and waited for better days. Consecrated women (*beatas*), who have been less targeted by the state than priests and bishops, went back to their families and helped to supervise religious education, devotional practices, baptism, and funerals.[3] The lived realities of Catholicism became a family-based religion hidden from the public sphere and under the strict protection of the kinship group. This response to communist persecution helped to transmit a certain form of Catholicism to the next generation but not to other social circles and happened without clerical participation.

---

3   Michel Chambon 'Chinese Catholic Nuns and the Organization of Religious Life in Contemporary China', *Religions* 10 (2019): 447.

On the Protestant sides, things were different. While pastors and leaders were often targeted by the state, Protestantism had more difficulties in withdrawing within family circles. Chinese Protestantism was a more recent Chinese religion. It gave more importance to individual choice and education, and it was deeply associated with countless schools and hospitals. In most regions, kinship groups with their codified mechanisms of mutual support were less a Protestant resource. Yet, many individual Christians, often women, maintained their faith privately.[4] They continued to chant Christian hymns, usually alone at home, and kept a life of prayer. During the worst years of the Great Leap Forward (1958–1962) and of the Cultural Revolution (1966–1976), they were also more lenient to share their faith with acquaintances in distress. They believed that their God could help with physical health and national salvation. Furthermore, in regions where Protestantism had stronger roots, families were more likely to identify with Christianity and to become the collective shelter of the Christian faith. In poorer regions of the country, Protestant families were more inclined to support each other and, therefore, to attract neighbours.[5]

While it seems that the number of Chinese Catholics stagnated—or even declined—during the Maoist period, Protestantism had indeed begun to attract converts in some regions of the country. The two Christian traditions have lost their political influence, their clerical apparatus, and most of their social footprint, but Maoism has also transformed the way they differ from each other. It is from this unique socio-religious context that Chinese Christians emerged at the end of the 1970s.

THE REBIRTH: 1978–1989

With the death of Mao Zedong in 1976 and the politico-economic reforms instigated by Deng Xiaoping in 1977, the whole country began to look for new modes of production without questioning its political order. Rural

---

[4] Kao Chenyang, 'Reassembling Christianity: Fuzhou Protestantism under China's Cultural Revolution from the Perspective of Life-History Research', *Sino-Christian Studies* 31 (2021): 7–44.

[5] Nanlai Cao, *Constructing China's Jerusalem: Christians, Power, and Place in Contemporary Wenzhou* (Stanford: Stanford University Press, 2011).

populations, where Catholics were better established, were the first ones to benefit from this partial opening. They began to cultivate their own crops, to sell their products, and to have cash-based income. This was a revolution at that time. With the entrepreneurial mindset encouraged by the state, they invested in the production of basic manufactured products and began to build small merchant networks.

While the Chinese economic landscape was rapidly changing, the state also reduced its pressure against religion. After decades of unsuccessful ideological eradication, the government opted for administrative control and legal containment. The goal was not anymore to eradicate all religions but to control them until the time when prosperity and modernity would make them irrelevant. Old sites of worship were gradually returned to religious communities as long as they had a properly registered religious leader. The state started to pull Christian priests, bishops, and pastors out of labour camps to put them in charge of specific churches. Despite a certain return of Christianity, the state was still eager to monitor Christian networks and communities in order to prevent any political activity.

In a rapidly changing society, however, where the social support and safety provided by socialist organisations and work-units were collapsing, Chinese citizens looked for alternative resources that could provide moral values, mutual support, and a sense of purpose. Soon, numerous people began to return to temples, and religious practices reappeared at an unexpected scale.[6] In this context, rural Catholics began to practise their faith more publicly. Their new income, the support of their whole clan, and the broader religious fever affecting Chinese society encouraged them to make their religiosity more public. During the following two decades, their priority was to give visibility to their family God and to erect churches.

Yet, most Catholics distrusted the religious policy of the state and did not value legal recognition. In line with anti-communist Catholic movements of the 1950s, they usually remained underground while becoming more publicly visible and socially confident. In larger cities, however, the social footprint of Catholicism was weaker and city governments more determined to maintain full control. Through the careful reopening of

---

6 Vincent Goossaert and David A. Palmer, *The Religious Question in Modern China* (Chicago: University of Chicago Press, 2011).

specific churches, the administration imposed its regulation upon urban Catholicism and forced Catholics to choose between Rome and Beijing. In order to reassign a cathedral or a church to Catholic worship, associated priests and bishops were forced to join the patriotic association controlled by the Chinese administration. Soon, the split between patriotic and underground Catholics re-emerged.

For Protestants, the 1980s marked a period of rapid numerical expansion. In line with China's religious fever, Chinese Protestants were eager to share their own spiritual resources with friends and acquaintances. Many citizens were curious about the teaching of Christ associated with the wealthy and healthy West. Christians and non-Christians would gather at home to hear stories and tales about Christianity, pray, and sing while building informal fellowships. Without yet generating very distinct structures and churches, Protestantism spread across interpersonal relations and touched numerous people. Remaining informal, Protestant Christianities circumvented anti-religious policies.

Chinese socio-economic transformations also generated new forms of social inequalities. The work-units of large cities were losing their competitiveness. Soon, urban and more educated populations felt that they were disadvantaged compared to rural populations. By May 1989, public protests broke out in several cities of the country and called for further reforms. After weeks of hesitation, the state decided to send the army and to reassert its firm political control, opening a new page in Chinese history.[7]

FINDING LANDMARKS: 1989–1999

After the events of Tiananmen on 4 June 1989, the Chinese Communist Party reaffirmed its monopoly over the society while encouraging the economy to continue its expansion. With an impressive growth rate, the entire country became a gigantic factory, with millions of people migrating to new industrial zones and Maoist socio-economic structures collapsing. Meanwhile, Chinese families and traditional kinship networks lost their capacity to stand as a site of collective identity and support. In this

---

7   Joseph Fewsmith, *China since Tiananmen: The Politics of Transition* (New York: Cambridge University Press, 2001).

economic boom combined with brutal social changes and strict political control, Chinese citizens were left alone in their competition for economic survival.

Not surprisingly, the Chinese religious fever became even stronger. New religious movements and syncretic cults that had appeared during the preceding decades gained wider influence and pushed the state to readjust its religious policies.[8] Monitoring the slow disappearance of religion was an outdated approach, a remnant of Maoism that needed urgent updates. For Chinese officials, it was time to counter 'evil cults' that could challenge the leadership of the party. Since eradicating religion had proved to be impossible, discriminating between religious traditions that could be socially useful and those that could be politically dangerous became essential. With the help of their growing revenues, local administrations began to work at re-establishing formal religious institutions that could monitor and channel religious aspirations of the population. New registration systems were systematised, and Christian leaders were encouraged to have more formal and explicit leadership of their fellow Christians.

On the Catholic side, priests and bishops were no longer in charge of a specific religious venue, but territorialised parishes and dioceses were revived, updated, and systematised. In the eyes of the administration, it was time for religious leaders to cover clearly defined territories. Even though suspicion against the Vatican and foreign influences remained high, the Chinese administration wanted a clear and systematic cartography of the Chinese Catholic Church. Administrative control that was stronger in urban centres became more generalised across the country, especially in Catholic rural strongholds. The imposition of administrative regulations renewed tensions between the state and underground Catholics. On several occasions, the state forced a priest to become a bishop without papal approval, a breach of Catholic canon law unacceptable for most Catholics. The split between patriotic and underground Catholics became even deeper. In places where new and illicit bishops were notoriously immoral, Catholics would refuse to join their religious ceremonies or make donations. Rejected by local churchgoers and the Vatican, these

---

8   David A. Palmer, *Qigong Fever: Body, Science, and Utopia in China* (New York: Columbia University Press, 2007).

Catholic leaders as well as state officials behind them found themselves in a difficult situation.

At the same time, significant numbers of younger rural Catholics were migrating toward large industrial hubs. Away from their hometown, working endless hours, and exposed to a new lifestyle, their religious practice shifted. Some maintained some forms of regular piety, but most waited for their annual Chinese New Year vacation to receive the sacraments at their hometown. However, to overcome the moral ambiguities of their new socio-religious lifestyle, they also sent donations to their home church to help with the renovation or construction of impressive buildings. With this new influx of money, rural Catholic communities gained confidence and resisted even more the intrusion of the state.[9] Through family ties and financial incentives, they worked at convincing at least one local administration (the police, the united front, or the office for religious affairs) that Catholics were not dangerous or subversive citizens. With new allies within the administration, Chinese Catholics organised their activities more publicly and expanded their churches. In the 1990s, although urban Catholicism was fairly weak and unable to resist state control, Chinese rural Catholicism was at the peak of its socio-religious influence.

On the Protestant side, Christian networks began to take a more formal shape. In front of the theological challenges raised by syncretic cults claiming a Christian identity while worshipping, for instance, the female reincarnation of Jesus Christ, a new generation of better-trained leaders emerged. These younger pastors believed that Chinese Protestantism needed a more defined theology rooted in the Bible and systematic study. Often, they were willing to work with state officials as long as their administration was willing to give recognition to Christian communities. This gave even more visibility and stability to a rich network of Protestant churches across China.

Yet, in growing industrial zones where large proportions of the population were made of young migrant workers without a local residency permit, many Protestant leaders did not see the need for an ambiguous administrative support. Aware of the atheist agenda of the communist

---

9   Richard Madsen, *China's Catholics: Tragedy and Hope in an Emerging Civil Society* (Berkeley: University of California Press, 1998).

state, many Christian communities preferred to remain unregistered. Their priority was to believe in Jesus, nourish their faith, and help each other. Spending hours at banquets with state officials and engaging in bribes appeared as a waste of time and as a betrayal of their moral aspirations.[10] Although the 1990s urban and rural Protestantism was expanding rapidly, internal distinctions and competition between registered and unregistered communities became sharper.

The more the state wanted to localise Christian communities and to rule them through the administrative unit they geographically belonged to, the more Protestant evangelists looked for trans-local connections. As a way to resist the state, but also as a participation in the entrepreneurial and risk-taking mentality promoted by the state during the Reform era, numerous Protestants were eager to circulate across prefectures and provinces to learn from various churches and share Christian materials. Zealous and confident, these new Christian leaders built far-reaching networks and social capital. Through various organisational patterns, Chinese Protestantism expanded in all directions, and anti-religious policies had less impact on it than on Catholicism, which remained more localised.

THE GOLDEN AGE: 1999–2008

After two decades of rapid economic growth and socio-religious changes that came on the heels of the tormented Maoist era and war against Japan, Chinese leaders and society began to look for more stability. For years, the whole country was a gigantic construction site. The search for endless profits, the massive air pollution of the late 1990s, and the widespread presence of corruption and prostitution affected all sectors of society. The side effects of the one-child policy were also becoming palpable and social cohesion was under threat. In some sense, in the midst of rapid economic growth, the country was facing a moral and identity crisis.

Voices began to advocate for a return to the socio-cultural roots of Chinese society. During the first years of the new millennium, Confucianism, a politico-religious ideology that modern China has fought hard,

---

10 Mayfair Mei-hui Yang, *Gifts, Favors, and Banquets: The Art of Social Relationships in China* (Ithaca: Cornell University Press, 1994).

made its great return. The teaching of the old master Kong and its interpretations by his disciples appeared as a valuable resource to stabilise the country, encourage morality, and rejuvenate the nation.

This ideological experimentation was also a potential resource to channel religious forces. Under a Confucian reinterpretation, Catholicism and Protestantism could appear as respectable traditions contributing to the moral edification of the universalist and inclusive Chinese civilisation. Furthermore, Confucianism allowed a variety of Chinese scholars to express their interest in the teaching of Christ while cultivating an intellectual approach to its subsequent traditions. These academic figures did not ask for baptism and did not formally convert to Christianity. Rather, they claimed to be 'Cultural Christians', a new kind of Chinese Christian able to resolve tensions between Chineseness and foreignness, denominational Christianity, and church and state relations.

Chinese Protestantism had to address other issues as well. The large number of converts, the challenging proselytism of Korean missionaries, and the multiplication of syncretic movements pushed mainstream denominations to strengthen their institutionalisation and theology.[11] Even though the anti-religious sentiment of the state remained real and its intrusive policies constant, Protestant leaders were more frequently willing to collaborate with officials. They wanted to secure construction permits for much-needed larger churches or to be able to report aggressive preachers of millenarian movements proselytizing at the footstep of their worship venues.

In line with the Confucian revival, Protestant communities were also willing to establish homes for the elderly. Because of massive migrations toward cities and growing individualism, elderly people were often left alone in the countryside. The state was looking for ways to outsource the cost of this social problem and Christian churches appeared to be an accommodating partner. During the entire decade, the number of Christian homes for the elderly multiplied. Church leaders allocated a growing proportion of their income and human resources to this social issue. This provided not only social and political merits but also helped numerous

---

[11]   Jie Kang, 'The Rise of Calvinist Christianity in Urbanising China', *Religions* 10 (2019): 481.

non-Christian families to approach the Christian faith. Homes for the elderly implicitly helped to address administrative pressures and traded social services for religious visibility.

Non-registered Protestant communities were also evolving. With more believers interested in their collective support and fellowship, house churches saw their financial resources and social footprint increase. They began to rent larger venues, such as multifunctional rooms in commercial buildings or reception halls in hotels. These venues were convenient for Sunday services with numerous worshippers.[12] It also made Protestant house churches look even more modern and appealing. Unlike gatherings in private apartments, this kind of Sunday gathering attracted less attention from local authorities. House churches would rotate between a few venues where landlords turned blind eyes to the religious but lucrative nature of these meetings.

To cope with state surveillance, house churches were also easily willing to split into smaller entities. Instead of becoming mega-churches that would attract the concern of state officials, they preferred to establish small, independent, and flexible networks of Christian fellowships. This organisational pattern allowed them to remain under the political radar. Young neo-urban settlers who were seeking strong social bonding and friendship were also more attracted to this kind of organisation. These small networks allowed more Christian leaders to stand up and take responsibility.[13]

It was also during the first decade of the twenty-first century that Wenzhou churches became a national phenomenon. These Protestant communities were rooted in the religious and economic history of Wenzhou, a coastal city of Zhejiang province, which was poor during the Maoist period. Wenzhou churches have a specific way to combine Christian values, ecclesial structures, and entrepreneurial goals. In these Protestant networks, churchgoers were also co-workers and economic salvation was a collective issue.

---

12   Fenggang Yang, 'Lost in the Market, Saved at McDonald's: Conversion to Christianity in Urban China', *Journal for the Scientific Study of Religion* 44 no. 4 (2005): 423–441.

13   Li Ma, *Religious Entrepreneurism in China's Urban House Churches: The Rise and Fall of Early Rain Reformed Presbyterian Church* (London: Routledge, 2020).

Therefore, Wenzhou churches operated as a corporation of co-workers moderated by a team of elected members. For their Sunday services, they hired a visiting preacher and avoided having a stable and unique pastor.[14] Although these churches and business networks appeared in the 1980s, they became extremely strong and wealthy in the early 2000s. Able to demonstrate their economic success to local officials, they built massive and numerous churches across the region of Wenzhou and beyond. Those buildings were often the headquarters of their combined economic activities and oversaw trading networks across all of China and beyond. In a period giving priority to economic success, but marked by identity and moral crisis, Wenzhou churches had powerful leverage to subjugate state officials.

Meanwhile, Catholic communities were also benefitting from the rapid socio-economic changes of Chinese society and the relative relaxation of religious control that characterised the early 2000s. During this period, even though state suspicion against the papal religion remained high, urban communities became the driving force of Chinese Catholicism.[15] In the countryside, despite the newly rebuilt churches, young churchgoers were migrating toward large cities with no desire to come back. In these new urban centres, migrant Catholics began to have stronger revenues and social connections. Gradually, they decided to keep their children with them in order to give them better education opportunities. This new family dynamic, combined with the Chinese identity crisis of that time, encouraged neo-urban Catholics to reclaim their religious heritage and to translate it into their new urban realities. To create places of worship where they could immerse their children into the ritualist and devotional apparatus of twentieth-century Chinese Catholicism, factory owners converted a room of their workplace into a private chapel. There, urban Catholics could gather for daily rosary and prayers. Similarly, some private apartments became venues for daily and weekly collective devotions. Those places remained extremely discreet and centred on the recitation of prayers. However, they allowed migrant Catholics to reclaim their religious heritage and to modernise it.

---

14 Cao, *Constructing China's Jerusalem*, 2011.
15 Michel Chambon and Antonio Spadaro, 'Urban Catholicism in China', *La Civiltà Cattolica*, English Edition 3 (2019): 26–38.

Both patriotic and underground communities also networked more actively with visitors coming from Hong Kong, Taiwan, and elsewhere. After two decades of efforts to implement the ecclesiological and liturgical norms of Vatican II, the priority started to shift toward new ways to educate children into the Catholic faith; visitors from outside of China were a precious source of inspiration. Despite the suspicion of the state and police controls, Catholic communities generalised the organisation of summer youth camps during which young Catholics were exposed to alternative ways to envision and experience the faith. Initially, camps were mostly organised in the countryside where things were economically and politically easier to handle. Urban and young Catholics would return to their hometown to attend these camps. This illustrates how, in the early 2000s, urban and rural Catholicism were still deeply intertwined, collaborating, and interdependent. To circumvent state control as well as practical difficulties, churchgoers, religious practices, and financial donations circulated back and forth between urban and rural Catholicism.

In the 2000s, nonetheless, modernizing cities started to become the beating heart of Chinese Catholicism. Although the anti-Catholic sentiments of some state officials and the ups and down of the Sino-Vatican relations continued to impact and sometimes harm relations between underground and official communities, Chinese Catholics found ways to move forward and to not focus exclusively on the coercive polities of the state. In rural and urban China, priority was given to training a new generation of Catholics and clergy members.

In sum, the early 2000s was the period during which the coercive polities of the state were the least intense. Even though some Catholic priests were ordained bishops by force and some Protestant leaders were put under arrest, Christian communities grew and evolved quickly. In many ways, Protestant networks were the most successful at escaping state control, building strong networks across the country, and attracting new converts.[16] Tensions between registered and

---

16   Francis Khek Gee Lim, *Christianity in Contemporary China Socio-Cultural Perspectives* (New York: Routledge, 2013). Carsten T. Vala, 'Negotiations and Diversifications of China's Christianities', *Review of Religion and Chinese Society* 1 (2019): 1–4.

unregistered communities decreased and various forms of collaboration appeared discreetly to foster the numerical growth and religious maturity of Chinese Christianity. However, this decade of Christian growth and institutionalisation soon had to face a new political climate triggered by economic changes and political rivalry at the global scale. This is what the next and final section discusses.

THE RETURN OF THE CLOUDS: 2008–2019

By the end of 2007, with the collapse of major hedge funds in the USA and economic signals suggesting a major financial crisis on the horizon, China faced a serious challenge. For decades, its political stability had been built upon the ability of the Chinese Communist Party to deliver economic growth and channel social change. Despite intense tensions at home and abroad, the party did boost the Chinese economy, maintain national unity, and tackle inequalities. To address the Great Recession of 2008, which revealed the unsustainability of the Chinese economic model and its political risks, the Chinese leadership decided to reset its political agenda and economic strategy. In late 2008, it introduced the largest stimulus package in the world to encourage domestic consumption, develop infrastructure, and upgrade China's industrial and high-tech capacities. Similarly, facing growing security issues at home (protests in Tibet and Xinjiang) and abroad (Arab Spring, colour revolutions, Snowden revelations), the party decided to tighten its socio-political control. Over the next few years, a new political leadership emerged to coordinate and embody this drastic shift, which has allowed China to not only continue its tremendous economic growth but also to reinforce its national security, strengthen its political resilience, and challenge the global order.

Under the renewed leadership of Xi Jinping, Confucianism was not selected as the driving force to secure national cohesion and socio-economic progress. Instead, it was nationalism combined with centralisation of power, reaffirmation of socialism with Chinese characteristics, anti-corruption policies, and a global projection of China. For an entire decade, China implemented the Chinese dream of President Xi. In this new socio-economic and political environment, religious groups were also forced to comply with state priorities. During this period, the intensity and systematic nature of coercive polities imposed upon Christian groups increased constantly.

Still, the state did not return to the anti-Christian persecutions and anti-religious ideologies of the Maoist regime. Rather, the Xi Jinping administration imposed growing regulations upon all sectors of society, including the Christian ones. Like major companies being partially nationalised and co-opted by the party, all religious groups saw the growing presence of the state invading and constraining their daily functioning. From the late 2000s through early 2010s, national and international attention was caught by the highly publicised destruction of some Wenzhou churches that officially did not have the proper construction permits. This campaign was symbolised by the systematic removal of the extremely large red crosses found at the top of most Wenzhou churches. This campaign mostly aimed at decoupling the religious and financial facets of these networks in order to limit the scope of Christian churches.

Under this renewed political pressure, which forced Chinese congregations to clarify the nature of their activities, the majority of Christian networks did gradually accommodate and looked for ways to show their love of the nation.[17] Once it became clear that the Chinese Communist Party was not going to reduce its control over Christian churches, Wenzhou churches began to hire properly trained and ordained pastors. Under the threat of destruction, they also found ways to differentiate between economic activities and religious fellowship. Large Three-Self Protestant Churches, which had invested funds in private sectors, reoriented them toward charitable purposes like Christian homes for the elderly. Some house churches that had built a formal church registered their organisation under the relevant administration.

Still, many house churches found ways to escape what they perceived as an increasing intrusion of the state. In addition to the various anti-coercive strategies already mentioned in this chapter, house churches amplified their use of digital media and the internet. Following the rapid digitalisation of Chinese society, they learned to use social media and websites to spread religious material. They also established small chat groups

---

17 Carsten T. Vala, *The Politics of Protestant Churches and the Party-State in China: God Above Party?* (New York: Routledge, 2018).

to allow their members to virtually gather and pray on a regular basis. For instance, numerous micro-groups would meet every morning for 30 to 45 minutes while members were commuting to work. Sitting or standing anonymously on the subway, they put their headphones in their ears, read sections of the Bible together, and listened to Christian hymns and sermons while sending emojis to each other.[18] Without much visibility, Christianity became virtually present everywhere.

For Catholics, the situation was more paradoxical. A key factor to explain this was the new leadership of Pope Francis and his persistent efforts to reset dialogue with Chinese leaders. Instead of letting numerous clerical voices and prelates share their views about how the Vatican should approach Beijing and whether anti-communist resistance should be encouraged, Pope Francis reduced the number of people directly involved in diplomatic dialogue with the Chinese administration as well as the number of questions to negotiate. In the eyes of the new bishop of Rome, it was necessary to work with the Chinese administration and build mutual trust. For this purpose, he asked clergy members to refrain from interfering with these negotiations. On 22 September 2018, the Holy See and Beijing announced that they had reached a provisional agreement on the appointment of Chinese bishops. Several excommunicated Chinese bishops were included within the communion of the Catholic Church and the territories of some Chinese dioceses were formally recognised by the Vatican. In the eyes of the Holy See, and despite remaining difficulties, China had only one Catholic Church and all its bishops were in communion with the pope. Under these circumstances, all Chinese Catholics were called to honestly collaborate with local authorities—yet, without giving up what they considered morally right. The Vatican made clear that no one was expected to join the problematic patriotic association imposed by the Chinese Communist Party.

Nonetheless, as the good faith of the Chinese administration became increasingly unclear, various Chinese and non-Chinese Catholics began to openly disagree with the new policy of the Vatican. To challenge the imposed and coercive nature of Pope Francis's approach, opponents like

---

18   Jinrui Xi, 'Christian New Media in China', *Asian Survey* 59 (2019): 1001–1021.

Cardinal Joseph Zen of Hong Kong gave numerous interviews to the international press.¹⁹ The Holy See was accused of being played by Beijing while Chinese Catholics faced increased control and discrimination. Pope Francis was rarely directly attacked. The blame was usually oriented toward his administration, but complaints and critical views became more public and recurrent during the late 2010s.

CONCLUDING REMARKS

After more than a decade of growing coercive measures and administrative control upon Christian circles, China and the rest of the world met a new challenge, the COVID-19 pandemic. In January 2020, medical reports about an unknown disease began to circulate on the web. Soon after, most of China went into lockdown, followed by three years of zero-COVID policy. Travel to China became almost impossible and information coming out of Chinese churches became difficult to verify; it is still impossible to analyze the exact impact of the pandemic upon Chinese Christians and their coercive environment.

However, as I write the final version of this chapter, numerous protests against the zero-COVID policy imposed by Xi Jinping have broken out and the Chinese administration has suddenly lifted all travel and medical restrictions. Once again, and despite alarmist claims in global media, the Chinese socio-political situation seems neither entirely fixed nor under control. Thus, one must emphasise the capacity for change and resilience of the two main actors studied in this paper, the Chinese communist regime and Chinese Christian networks.

Over the past forty years, the Chinese administration has continuously adjusted its approach to Christian networks. Although coercive measures have always been present, the religious policy of the state has been constantly evolving and often accommodating. Similarly, the social scope

---

19   Joseph Zen Ze-Kiun and Pierre G. Rossi, *For Love of My People I Will Not Remain Silent: A Series of Eight Lectures in Defense and Clarification of the 2007 Letter of Pope Benedict XVI to the Church in the People's Republic of China* (San Francisco: Ignatius Press, 2017).

and religious nature of Chinese churches have unceasingly changed—and so has the entire Chinese religious landscape. Consequently, the Chinese Christian minority has deployed a variety of responses to the coercive polities of the state. These Christian responses were neither simply antagonistic nor homogenous across the country. They have and will continue to evolve.

3

CHRISTIANS AS A RELIGIOUS MINORITY IN MODERN ISLAMISING PAKISTAN

Farhana A. Nazir

Historically in Pakistan religious parties were never able to establish a government, yet the country remains deeply religious. Pakistan was formed using Islamic symbolism, Muslim identity, and 'yet disclaiming any ideas of a theocracy'.[1] The application of the law of blasphemy has been particularly grim for minorities. Christians have been prosecuted under this law for years. The misuse of the law of blasphemy has been widely recognised by the judiciary, government, and even Muslims of Pakistan but nothing significant has been achieved to reduce the violence. The roots of this problem lie in the past, but my aim here is to discusses how the protection of the citizens of Pakistan, especially from religiously motivated violence, has become a crucial issue today and how it splits those who want reform of the law (especially laws passed between 1980 and 1986) and those who oppose all reforms.

CHRISTIANS AND PROTESTS

On 9 March 2013, over 175 houses, a church including religious books, and all the belongings of the Christian community were torched by a mob over a blasphemy accusation. The matter went to the Supreme Court and the

---

1 Iftikhar H. Malik, 'The State and Civil Society in Pakistan: From Crisis to Crisis', *Asian Survey* 36 no. 7 (1996): 676.

accusations of blasphemy were dismissed. This is just one example of many where Christians have been prosecuted under the blasphemy law. Bishop Azaraiah, noting a different verdict, said, 'the blasphemy sentence has shocked the Christian community', and Bishop John Malik said, 'the sense of insecurity would increase following the convictions'.[2] Jilani said, 'The blasphemy law now has become a tool in the hands of criminal minded persons. They have now started using them to embroil their opponents in highly questionable litigations, which get so controversial and dichotomous during the course of trial that it becomes almost unfeasible to decipher the truth.'[3]

While there have been many individual protests against the blasphemy law, the death of Manzoor Masih (in 1994) sparked agitation across the country as Christians demanded repeal of this law and security for their lives. The sentencing of 12-year-old Salamat Masih was accompanied by mob violence against Christians and their places of worship in 1997.[4] Many affected people have expressed how the blasphemy issue has affected the social life and relationship of Christians and Muslims. One of the victims said,

> We [Christians] and Muslims have been living here for generations. Both communities were on good terms, but, due to this incident, we have disconnected forever. In the past, we were friends. Now we are enemies. This incident has left long lasting effects. It is not possible for us to forget what Muslims have done to us. A personal dispute was turned in to a communal dispute and as a result, unending enmity and abhorrence has emerged in the heart of both communities.[5]

---

2   'Bishop Azraiah and Malik in Churches Observe Day of Fasting in Amritsari', *The Blasphemy Law*, 12 February 1995.
3   Anees Jilani, 'Blasphemy Law and the Minorities', *The News*, 14 May 1998.
4   About eight hundred of the nine hundred houses, churches, schools, and shops of Christians were burned without confirmation of blasphemy. Sookhdeo, Patrick. *A People Betrayed: The Impact of Islamization on the Christian Community in Pakistan* (Fearn, Ross-shire, Scotland: Christian Focus Publishing, 2002), 8.
5   Samuel Masih expressed his thoughts in the interview with Jinnah Institute team after the attack in Bahmni Wali, Kasur, and Punjab on 23 January 2009.

A Roman Catholic bishop, John Joseph, chair of the Christian-Muslim relation commission and the National Commission for Justice and Peace Pakistan, said, 'Since the Government failed to fulfil its commitments, we have no alternative but to launch a countrywide agitation and to adopt other tactics for the abolition of blasphemy law...such "verdicts" are not only detrimental to national unity, they created hatred among the minority community... we are united for our rights and are prepared to sacrifice even our lives'.[6]

Four years after witnessing the death of Manzoor Masih, Joseph shot himself outside the Sahiwal Court in Punjab province. This followed Ayub Masih's sentencing to death for blasphemy on 5 May 1998, although Ayub Masih was later released by the Supreme Court for lack of evidence of blasphemy.[7] To Bishop Joseph, it had become clear that 'lives destroyed by false allegations meant nothing to the authority'.[8] Bishop Joseph, in his letter faxed to the press just before his death on 5 May 1998, stated,

> Section 295-C is the greatest block in the good and harmonious relations between Muslims and the religious minorities in Pakistan. In order to achieve national harmony, let us give a push to this immense boulder, before it crushes all of us. Once the obstacle is away, each Pakistani will be able to live and work in peace and our beloved motherland, Pakistan will prosper.[9]

Bishop Joseph hoped his suicide would galvanise authorities and communities of Pakistan for the repeal of the blasphemy law in order to

---

6   John Joseph, 'Reaction to death verdict, Christians to start nation-wide protest', in Amritsari, *The Blasphemy Law*, 25.

7   Following are some cases: *Salamat Masih v. The State, 1995* and *Ayub Masih v. The State P. L. D. 2002.*

8   John Joseph, 'Reaction to death verdict', in Amritsari, *The Blasphemy Law*, xv.

9   John Joseph's letter *The Final Step Against 295-C.* can be found in Amritsari, *The Blasphemy Law:* xiii. Bishop wrote various letters to the authorities as well as church authorities about discrimination and the misuse of the law throughout 1990s. See details of writing in Khalid Ashi Rashid, *A Peaceful Struggle: A Collection of Bishop John Joseph's Writings against Black Laws and Discrimination* (Faisalabad: National Commission of Justice and Peace, 1999).

create peaceful co-existence. On the one hand, the Christian community discussed whether he was a martyr and great leader and protested against the misuse of the blasphemy law.[10] However, on the other hand, religious and political organisations condemned the act of suicide by claiming that the bishop wanted to embarrass Pakistan in the eyes of the world. Some condemned misusing the law and argued that the law of blasphemy has added to the corpus of discriminatory legislations against minorities and led to distortion.[11] Whatever he may become for future generations of Pakistan, today his death is a symbol for a powerless minority, which lives through continuing struggle under the threat of blasphemy laws.

Many Muslims condemned the death of Bishop Joseph, while sympathising with his family. For example, in 1998, the Prime Minister Nawaz Sharif expressed deep sorrow over the suicide of Bishop John and, in a condolence message to the bereaved family and the Christian community, insisted that the constitution of Pakistan guaranteed full freedom and fundamental rights to the minorities.[12] Opposition leader Benazir Bhutto also expressed shock and grief over the tragic death of Bishop John. In a message, she said that it was a traumatic event that focused the deep sense of frustration felt by the members of the minority communities at the misuse of the blasphemy law by extremist and bigoted elements.[13]

The Federal Minister of Religious and Minorities Affairs Raja Zafer ul-Haq, while insisting that the law is not against particular religions, urged the government to re-examine the law.[14] However, most of those sympathetic to Islamic parties who wanted the law to remain feared that the government might act toward reforming the law. They criticized Christians' protests over the law and argued that section 295-C is not discriminatory

---

10 Christians critically protested against blasphemy as observed in Karachi (*The Frontier Post*, 11 May 1998) and across Punjab: in Faisalabad (*The Nation*, 12 May 1998) (*Dawn*, Lahore, 12 May 1998), in Multan (*Dawn*, 13 May 1998), in Lahore (*Dawn*, Lahore, 16 May 1998).
11 Shamsul Islam Naz, "Bishop Joseph to Be Buried," *Dawn*, 9 May 1998.
12 *The Nations*, 9 May 1998, in Amritsari, *The Blasphemy Law*, 24.
13 See "Pope, WCC Pray that Bishop John Joseph's Struggle Will Bear Fruit" *Union of Catholic News*, 10 May 1998.
14 See more in Zahid Husain Khan, "Pakistan Senators Seek to Reform Blasphemy Law," *Union of Catholic News*, 31 January 2017.

because it is the same for anybody found to have committed blasphemy.[15] All communities are indeed equally vulnerable to accusation, but the critical question of who actually suffers remains unanswered. There are clear attempts to silence people. For example, the Minister for Religious Affairs Ijazul Haqq stated that 'the people of Pakistan would come out on the streets if attempts were made to change the blasphemy law'.[16] He also stated vehemently that even if one hundred thousand Christians lost their lives under the blasphemy law, it would not be repealed.[17]

The refusal to review the blasphemy law in terms of protecting minorities and the insistence on keeping the law even if minorities continue to suffer suggests an uncertain future for the minorities as well as others who support the repeal of the law. However, it will be helpful to examine how blasphemy accusations are dealt with by the apparently independent judicial system, assuming the law stays.

MISUSE OF THE LAW

The judicial system of Pakistan claims to follow the rules, providing justice to all, a point insisted upon by Jinnah in his informal talk to civil officers at Peshawar in April 1948, when he said, 'You should try to create an atmosphere and work in such a spirit that everybody gets a fair deal and justice is done to everybody. And not merely should justice be done but people should feel that justice has been done to them.'[18] However, the justice system has become controversial, and some have suggested even notorious, in terms of dealing with blasphemy accusations. The judicial system for dealing with blasphemy cases has been affected by the pressure and threats of the masses. Justice Munir, who headed an investigation into anti-Ahmadi

---

15   See more in Farhana Nazir, *The Evolution of Legislation on Religious Offences: A Study of British India and the Implications for Contemporary Pakistan* (Carlisle: Langham Monographs, 2019).

16   *The Times,* 11 May 1998, in Gabriel, *Christian Citizens in an Islamic State: The Pakistan Experience* (England: Ashgate, 2007), 64.

17   *BosNews Life,* 27 June 2006, in Gabriel, *Christian Citizens in an Islamic State,* 65.

18   Jinnah in Syed Sharifuddin Pirzada, *Fundamental Rights and Constitutional Remedies in Pakistan* (Lahore: All Pakistan Legal Decisions, 1966), 86.

agitation in 1953 and reviewed how the legislation on 'Offences Relating to Religion' was misused, commented, 'Pakistan is being taken [over] by the common man—though it is not—as an Islamic state. This belief has been encouraged by the ceaseless clamour of Islam and an Islamic state that is being heard from all quarters since the establishment of Pakistan.'[19]

It has been observed that not only those accused of blasphemy but also the judiciary and courts are exposed to mob pressure. The issue of repealing the law and the threats to the lives of minorities have also split the judiciary. Various lawyers and judges support the inevitably arbitrary imposition of the death sentence under blasphemy accusation, but others regard the death sentence as discriminatory and find it unacceptable for non-Muslims to face criticism and threats from Muslims. For example, it was noted that the lower courts, in cases such as Salamat Masih's in 1994, passed the death sentence against the accused despite inadequate evidence. Although Salamat was released later by the High Court, the judge who ordered his release was threatened and later murdered. On 4 September 1999, Lahore High Court Justice Nazir Akhter reportedly said that those accused of blasphemy 'must be punished or killed on the spot without any trial and there is no need of the law'.[20] Judgements mentioned above clearly show how the judicial system or individuals in it can fall under suspicion of failing to provide justice in some blasphemy cases. According to Asma Jahangir, former Chairperson of the Human Rights Commission of Pakistan and current UN Special Rapporteur on Extrajudicial, Summary or Arbitrary Executions, 'The anti-blasphemy law has tended to be abused. Because of the public sentiment the allegation arouses, the law has also been liable to a miscarriage of justice. Clearly, the incidence of blasphemy was no greater than before the law came in than it is after it. There are certainly more allegations of it now. The experience points to the need for serious rethinking of the law.'[21]

---

19   Muhammad Munir, 'Christians in Pakistan Bear the Cross of its Blasphemy Laws', *Navhind Times*, May 1998 in Amritsari, *The Blasphemy Law*, 186.

20   *International Religious Freedom: Report to Congress by the Department* edited by Barbara Larkin (Washington, US Governing Printing Office, 2000), 519.

21   'State of Human Rights in 1998 Report', (Human Rights Commission of Pakistan, February 1999), 164.

Though the judicial system as a whole came under suspicion of not providing full justice to victims, the High Court has generally struggled to provide justice on the basis of requiring firm evidence to prove the case, provided the accused survives to reach the High Court stage.[22] It has been expressed by the judiciary that it 'must seriously consider the ways it [blasphemy accusation] can badly affect the innocent people'.[23] Ismail Qureshi, though regarding the death sentence as the final verdict and seeing section 295-C as an important piece of legislation to prevent defiling the name of the Prophet, nevertheless emphasises that Muslims should not take the law into their hands 'when there is recourse to a court of law against the contemnor'.[24] However, the contemporary practice of the law in the hands of local communities presents just this situation, and due process of law has been critically affected by violence motivated by blasphemy accusations. The most critical examples of this disregard for proper practice can be seen when a local community does not care about the judgement of the courts concerning the innocence of an accused, preferring to kill the accused.

Judges have made some judicial suggestions regarding both the law and its possible amendment. The case of *Riaz Ahmad v. State* in June 1994 is worth highlighting—particularly the question of whether the language used by the accused (even though it was said to be in accord with the teaching of Ghulam Ahmad), is derogatory to the Prophet Muhammad and whether this constituted an offence (section 295-C).[25] This case was tried on the behalf of Ahmadi and Christian parties. During the trial, the counsel representing Christian parties discussed and argued that section 295-C should be extended in order to prohibit contumacious reproaches against Jesus Christ so that those who indulge in defiling the name of Christ are also punished with death. The trial Judge Mian Nazir Akhtar expressed his hope that 'the provision be made more comprehensive to as to make blasphemy qua other prophets including the Holy Christ, punishable with

---

22 *Ayub Masih v. The State* PLD 2002 Supreme Court 1048.
23 Faizan Usmani, 'Blasphemy Law: To Repeal or not to Repeal'? Posted on 2 December 2010. Available on www.pkarticleshub.com.
24 Muhammed Ismail Qureshi, *Muhammad: The Messenger of God and the Law of Blasphemy in Islam and the West* (Lahore: Nuqoosh, 2008), 69.
25 *Riaz Ahmad v. State* PLD (1994) Lahore 504.

the same sentence'.[26] The first problem here is that under such a suggestion Christians could be alleged to commit blasphemy against Muslim beliefs when they declare their belief that Jesus is the Son of God unless such a statement is allowed as it would have been under the 1860 law allowing mutual and courteous discussion of faith. Secondly, religious leaders and founders, such as the Prophet Muhammad and Jesus Christ, are already included in section 295-A, which can defend any religious community from outrage against their religious personages and faith through malicious speech and writing. However, this clause was rarely used in Pakistan, and after 295-C was enacted, it was annulled. Therefore, suggestions such as those of Akhtar do not seem particularly useful.

Given the continuing protest and violence concerning whether the law should be repealed or not, governing authorities did introduce a few changes in the legal procedure concerning the procedure for accusation. Abdulfateh Amor, the Special Reporter of UN Commission on Human Rights on the Elimination of All Forms of Religious Intolerance, concludes that 'the blasphemy law should not be discriminatory and should not give rise to abuse ... If offences against belief are made punishable ... then procedural guarantees must be introduced and a balanced attitude must be maintained'.[27]

EFFORTS TOWARD CHANGING THE LEGAL PROCEDURE

In 1988, Benazir Bhutto (1953–2007) became prime minister and began arguing that the religious offences law should not be misused. During her regime, political authorities delivered various statements regarding the protection of minorities for religiously motivated violence under the blasphemy law, but her political power collapsed in 1991. In 1992, the Federal Minister of Religious Affairs Mawlana Abadu Sitar Niazi issued 'a *fatwa* against her declaring her to be a *kafir* (infidel) liable to the death penalty'.[28]

---

26 *Riaz Ahmad v. State* PLD (1994) Lahore 504.
27 Recorded in the report to the 52nd Session Commission on Human Rights, E/CN.4/1996/95/Add.3.
28 Patrick Sookhdeo, *Freedom to Believe: Challenging Islam's Apostasy Law* (McLean, VA: Isaac, 2009), 66–67.

A year later, 'a case was brought against her in the Lahore High Court under section 295-C . . . accusing her of criticising the blasphemy law'.[29] Though she was not convicted of blasphemy, this is an early example that shows how the law started to be used against the governing officials to weaken their power.

In early 1994, after being re-elected prime minister, Benazir Bhutto again intended to introduce two procedural changes to lessen the possibility of abuse of Section 295-C. The first was to require formal authorisation by a judicial magistrate before a complaint of blasphemy could be registered and arrests made. Second, a false allegation of blasphemy would itself be made a criminal offence to be punished with up to seven years' imprisonment.[30] In February 1994, the Chief Justice of Pakistan, the chairman of the Council of Islamic Ideology, and chief justices of the four provincial high courts sent an Amendment Bill to the Council of Islamic Ideology for further revision of the misuse of the law. Mawlana Kausur Niazi, Chairman of the Council of Islamic Ideology, commented that 'the law needs modification to ensure that it is not abused. . . . The procedure for police registration of a case, the judicial level at which it should be considered and the suitable criteria for admission of witnesses have to be looked at thoroughly'.[31]

The judiciary has frequently agreed that the blasphemy law has been misused to accuse anyone of false allegations. One example is the case in Shantinagar of Salamat Masih and the mob violence that was incited by unproven allegations of blasphemy. Similar incidents occurred in other places. Making knowingly unfounded allegations a punishable crime may have constrained malicious accusations and protected the innocent to a certain extent, but this proposal did not become law. On 28 May 1995, Bhutto, after facing critical widespread strikes and protests across Pakistan against any changes to the blasphemy law, declared that her government had only envisaged procedural changes and 'will not amend the law'.[32]

---

29   Sookhdeo, *Freedom to Believe*, 66–67.
30   Amnesty International Report on Pakistan, September 1996 (ASA 33/10/96).
31   Moulana Kausur Niazi quoted in Amnesty International Report on Pakistan, September 1996.
32   Benazir dealing with section 295-C in Amnesty International Report on Pakistan, September 1996.

In the 1990s, Nawaz Sharif, elected twice as prime minister, also faced pressure and demands to apply *Shari'a* because it was part of his political manifesto.[33] His government removed the optional sentence of life imprisonment for defiling the name of the Prophet, and imposed the mandatory death sentence in section 295-C of PPC in 1992.[34] Although he was also one of those political leaders who condemned the misuse of the law, he remained convinced that the law should not be repealed. Given this apparent impasse, the question of what should be done to stop the misuse of the law to protect the citizens of Pakistan became increasingly important.

In October 1999, Pakistan's political and constitutional evolution was interrupted when General Pervez Musharraf, a military chief army officer, came to power as president of Pakistan till 2008. During his presidency, he said publicly on several occasions that there needed to be procedural changes in the existing law to check its frequent misuse.[35] In 1999, Musharraf's agenda appeared to maintain a moderate Pakistan in which 'minorities enjoy full rights and protection as equal citizens and in the letter and spirit of Islam'.[36] In 2000, he promised to amend the blasphemy law to allow only senior district officials to register blasphemy cases, but soon withdrew the proposed change under pressure from the religious lobby. In 2004, under critical pressure, he too was forced to back down and stopped reforming the law,[37] although, in 2005, Parliament passed a law requiring that a senior police official investigate a blasphemy accusation before a complaint was filed in the courts.[38] Later, in May 2007, a bill

---

33   Malik, "The State and Civil Society in Pakistan", 19.
34   Mariam Faruqi (Ed.), *A Question of Faith: A Report on the Religious Status of Minorities of Pakistan* (Karachi: Jinnah Institution, 2011), 39.
35   Emanuel Yousaf Mani, *Human Rights Monitor 2008: A Report on the Religious Minorities in Pakistan* (Lahore: National Commission of Justice and Peace, 2008), 44.
36   "Pakistan: Open Letter to General Parbez Musharaf" in Amnesty International, 19 October 1999, ASA 33/028/ (www.amnesty.org.uk); Shaun Gregory, 'Under the Shadow of Islam: The Plight of the Christian Minority in Pakistan', *Contemporary South Asia* 20 no. 2 (2012): 203.
37   Gregory, 'Under the Shadow of Islam', 203.
38   Amnesty International reported 44 registered blasphemy cases in 2006. 'Country Report: Pakistan', *Amnesty International*, 2007.

by a ruling party parliamentarian calling for changes that would make the blasphemy law less discriminatory was rejected. The parliamentary affairs minister was quoted as saying, 'Islam is our religion and such bills hurt our feelings. This is not a secular state but [the] Islamic Republic of Pakistan.'[39] Musharaf resigned and went into exile in 2008.

Thus, from 1988 till 2007, the political and governing power represented by Benazir Bhutto, Nawaz Sharif, and Pervez Musharraf all tried making some changes either to uphold the death sentence or make some procedural changes in blasphemy accusation. When non-Muslims were accused of blasphemy during this period, even mere suspicion brought critical damage to lives and all religious objects of communities. In many cases, before any prosecution and legal trial, churches and bibles, Hindu temples and religious deities, Christian schools, and hostels, residences, or neighbourhoods of an accused or their community are damaged or burned with consequent loss of property or lives of innocent people, as occurred in Gojra, Korian, Shantinagar, Sanglahill, Sialkot, and Lahore in Punjab.

Even the dead among the Muslim minorities have been attacked, in violation of section 297, such as when in July 2010 the Liaqatabad police station was approached with the demand to remove the Islamic inscriptions such as *kalima tayaba* (there is no god but God and Muhammad is His Prophet) from the tombstones of Ahmadis' graves.[40] Punishing the dead went further when about fifteen to twenty unknown persons deliberately entered the Ahmadi graveyard in Model Town, Lahore, and desecrated and damaged 120 Ahmadis' graves in December 2012. In Pakistan today 'violence is inflicted on the living as a matter of course, [but] the visceral hatred ... on Ahmadis' graveyard [dead people] is chilling'[41] and such accusations do not allow them 'to rest in peace even after [they] are dead'.[42]

It is equally bad for Christians. An accused is never safe, not even under the protection of the state. For example, Robert Fanish, (19 years

---

39   Sohail Khan, 'Government Rejects Bill to Amend Blasphemy Law', *The News*, 9 May 2007; Amnesty International, *Pakistan: Blasphemy Acquittal Welcome but Law Must be Amended* (ASA 33/026/2002).
40   'Police Removed Quranic Verses from Ahmadi Graves to Avert Clashes', *The Tribune Express,* 18 August 2010.
41   'Chilling Act', *Dawn,* 5 December 2012.
42   Gulmina Bilal Ahmad, *Daily Times,* Pakistan, 7 December 2012.

old), a Christian from Jatheki, Sialkot, known to be having an affair with a Muslim woman, was accused under section 295-B for throwing down a copy of the Quran in September 2009.[43] Before his arrest, the local church, including all religious books and bibles, was set on fire. Fanish was later arrested and, before any trial and inquiry, was found dead inside his jail cell. All those who spoke at the news conference said that the death of Fanish raised suspicion of the involvement of jail officials in his murder.[44] Suspected of murdering Fanish, Assistant Superintendent Sibtain Raza, Head Warden Mohammad Yusuf, and Warden Javed Iqbal Awan were suspended and Salim Shahid Beg of Lahore said that the suspended officials would face an inquiry under the Punjab Employees Efficiency, Discipline and Accountability Act.[45] Clearly, the state cannot guarantee the safety of the accused and the fear of trial for the perpetrators has not led to a significant reduction in blasphemy charges.[46]

Amnesty International notes that continuing complex religious issues are a result of long negligence of successive governments demonstrating an overruling concern for power and rule rather than principle.[47] Government of Pakistan ensured that:

> While the law remains on the statute book, everyone charged under the blasphemy law receives a fair trial and is not subjected to any form of ill-treatment; to declare a moratorium on carrying out the death penalty under this law and to take steps to abolish the death penalty for this offence; to take adequate steps to ensure the safety of members

---

[43] Emmauel Zafar, 'The Minorities View', *Hamsookhan* 7 no. 9 (September 2009): 19.

[44] On the death of Fanish, Asma Jahangir (a lawyer and chairperson of the Human Rights Commission), Secretary-General I. A. Rehman, Muhammad Tehseen, Nadeem Anthony, Shahtaj Qazilbash, Joseph Francis, and Farooq Tariq concluded that minorities should be protected either in their homes or in jails. Newsletter of National Commission for Peace and Justice, *The Mirror* 13, no. 1 (January–March 2010): 4–6.

[45] News Letter of National Commission for Peace and Justice, 4–6.

[46] Amnesty International reported 44 registered blasphemy cases in 2006. 'Country Report: Pakistan', *Amnesty International*, 2007.

[47] Amnesty International, *Pakistan: Use and Abuse of the Blasphemy Laws*, AI Index: 33/08/94.

of the religious minorities in general and anyone at present charged with blasphemy in particular; and to implement international standards for the protection of the rights of religious minorities.[48]

One of the most important further steps has been the tabling of the Amendment of Blasphemy Bill, which is the basis of the following discussion.

PROPOSED AMENDMENT OF BLASPHEMY BILL

In February 2008, Asif Ali Zardari became president of Pakistan.[49] His government was not free from religious agitation; killings after accusations of blasphemy continued. The problem is well illustrated by the case of Aasia Bibi, a Christian sentenced to death for allegedly insulting the Prophet Muhammad in 2010. Two members of Parliament, Sulman Taseer and Shahbaz Bhatti, were killed in early 2011 for supporting legal and social reforms.

Aasia was accused of committing blasphemy when she was fetching water. It was argued that non-Muslims should not drink from the same because as the water was impure, *haram*. Aasia was asked to convert to Islam, which she declined.[50] Aasia's sentence was internationally condemned. Amnesty International, a Human Rights organisation, demanded her death sentence be commuted and argued for the law of blasphemy to be reformed. The Supreme Court in Islamabad, Pakistan, finally acquitted her of the charges after which she took asylum in Canada, where she now lives.[51] Likewise, Pope Benedict XVI appealed that Pakistani Christians 'are often victims of violence and discrimination' and urged that their 'dignity and fundamental rights be fully respected'.[52]

---

48 It was declared during the rule of Musharaf. Amnesty International, *Pakistan: Use and Abuse of the Blasphemy Laws*, AI Index: 33/08/94, 2.
49 Gregory, 'Under the Shadow of Islam', 204.
50 For the whole story on Aasia Bibi, see Anne Isabelle, *Blasphemy: The True Heart Breaking Story of the Woman Sentenced to Death Over a Cup of Water* (London: Hachette Digital, 2011).
51 Amnesty International, *Urgent Action: Pakistani Woman Sentenced to Death*, Index: ASA 33/011/2010.
52 'Pope Pleads for Life of Condemned Pakistani Woman', *BBC News*, 17 November 2010, http://bbc.co.uk/news/world-south-asia-11777482.

Aasia Bibi's case also provoked a storm nationally. Mariam Faruqi notes that President Zardari ordered a ministerial review, which concluded that 'the verdict was legally unsound and sought a presidential pardon for her'.[53] The government gave in to a long-standing demand of its coalition partner, the *Jamiat-e-Ulema-e-Islam* led by Maulana Fazlur Rehman, and appointed a hardline cleric from the party to head the Council of Islamic Ideology to decide whether the country's laws are in conformity with Islam. On 29 November 2010, the Lahore High Court barred the president from issuing a pardon despite this privilege being granted to him by the constitution.[54] On 30 November, Sherry Rehman, Member of National Assembly (MNA) of Pakistan People's Party, submitted a bill to the National Assembly Secretariat seeking an end to the death penalty under the existing blasphemy laws in order to reduce misuse of the law.[55] On 30 December, the government publicly reneged on a commitment to review the blasphemy laws, announcing that it had 'no intention' to repeal or amend the law. Sensing the government's lack of resolve and supported by sections of the media, extremists offered head money to anyone who killed Assia Bibi and issued death threats to opponents and critics of the blasphemy law.[56] Assia's case received serious attention when Salman Taseer, a Muslim governor, visited her in jail for justice.[57] In December 2010, Taseer stated that 'the sentence against Assia is inhumane.... I have handed over the appeal for a presidential pardon, which I will take to the president and soon Assia

---

53   Faruqi, *A Question of Faith*, 4.
54   Faruqi, *A Question of Faith*, 4.
55   See Amir Waseem, 'Sherry Submits Bill for Amending Blasphemy Law', *Dawn* 30 November 2010; Sherry Rehman, 'Amendments to the Blasphemy Laws Act 2010', submitted on 30 November 2010, published by Jinnah Institute, available on www.jinnah-institute.org.
56   In December 2010, a leading Urdu daily published an editorial in support of a Peshawar cleric's call for head money on Aasia Bibi. It praised the cleric's move, stating, "What the government couldn't do after a court decision, the nation will." See Faruqi, *A Question of Faith*, 4, 43. Assia Bibi was in the jail in Shekhupura, Punjab, from where she lodged an appeal at the High Court.
57   United States Department of State Bureau of Democracy, Human Rights and Labor, *International Religious Freedom Report for 2011*, available at http://www.state.gov/documents/organization/193145.pdf; M. A. Niazi, 'Blasphemy Case Shakes the Nation', 3 December 2010, www.pkarticleshub.com.

will be pardoned'.[58] His bodyguard, Malik Mumtaz Hussein Qadri, on 4 January 2011, assassinated him.

The *Jammat-e-Ahl-e-Sunnat*, Pakistan warned that those who expressed grief over the assassination could suffer like Taseer, insisting 'no Muslim should attend the funeral or even try to pray for Salman Taseer or even express any kind of regret or sympathy over the incident'.[59] Moreover, Qadri's appearance at the court attracted large crowds, including lawyers who showered rose petals to welcome him and support him for killing Taseer. Qadri admitted killing the governor and argued in the court that 'I did not kill anyone unlawfully. I have taught a lesson to apostate Salman Taseer in the light of the teachings of the Quran and the Tradition of the Prophet.'[60] This was another in the line of cases showing how one who murders the blasphemer becomes a hero, as did Qadri, following the legacy and example of Illam Din, still known as 'the martyr', who killed Rajpal for publishing the offensive pamphlet insulting the Prophet Muhammad in 1927 in Lahore, in British Pakistan.[61] Taseer's daughter, Sarah, said, 'This is a message to every liberal to shut up or to be shot'.[62]

Shahbaz Bhatti, a Christian Federal Minister of Minorities, and one of the supporters of the government making efforts to ameliorate the problems of all religious minorities, faced threats to his life for his stand against Pakistan's blasphemy law. He commented during a trip to Canada, 'I have been told by pro-Taliban religious extremists that if I will continue to speak against the blasphemy, I will be beheaded. . . . As a Christian, I believe Jesus

---

58   Salman Taseer, 'Violence Brings Pakistan's Women Advocates to Aid Religious Minorities', 19 August 2011, http://womennewsnetwork.net.
59   'Salman Taseer: Thousands Mourn Pakistan Governor', *BBC News*, 5 January 2011.
60   'Mumtaz Qadri Charged with Salman Taseer Murder', *BBC News*, 14 February 2011, http://www.bbc.co.uk/news/world-south-asia.
61   This case study has been discussed in detail in 'The Question of Religious Communities and Their Religious Rights' in Nazir, the Evolution of Legislation on Religious Offences: A Study of British India and the Implications for Contemporary Pakistan (Carlisle: Langham, 2019), Chapter 6.
62   *New York Times*, 4 January 2011 in Paul Marshal and Nin Shea, *Silenced: How Apostasy and Blasphemy Codes Are Choking Freedom Worldwide* (Oxford: Oxford University Press, 2011), 99.

is my strength. He has given me power and wisdom and motivation to serve suffering humanity. I follow the principles of my conscience, and I am ready to die and sacrifice my life for the principles I believe'.[63]

On 4 March 2011, Bhatti was murdered in Islamabad and his assassins left leaflets proclaiming that they killed him because he committed blasphemy and warned others to be aware of meeting the same fate if they criticised the law of blasphemy.[64] Maulana MA Chinioti, a leader of a right-wing Islamic party, said, 'They should know that true Muslims will spill their last drop of blood to protect the sanctity of holy personalities and the book'.[65] After the assassination of Minister Bhatti, President Asif Ali Zardari stated in a local newspaper, 'This is a concerted campaign to slaughter every liberal, progressive and humanist voice in Pakistan. The time has come for the federal government and provincial governments to speak out and to take a strong stand against these murderers to save the very essence of Pakistan.'[66]

The government was keen to investigate both murder cases but largely kept silence over the future implications of the blasphemy law. Yet, despite the clear problems attached to change, a bill to amend the law was tabled.

AMENDMENTS TO THE BLASPHEMY LAWS ACT 2010

Sherry Rehman, former minister for information and Pakistan People Party (PPP) legislator, proposed a Bill to the National Assembly on 30 November 2010. For Rehman, repealing the law would be the ideal situation because 'its formulation and mechanisms of implementation have serious implications for social, constitutional and natural justice in Pakistan'.[67] To her, such change and amendment are needed for the sake of minorities and

---

63   Bhati's statement is recorded from one of his videos. See Ashish Kumar Sen, 'Pakistani Government Official Murdered for Criticism of Islamic Blasphemy Law', *Daily News*, 4 March 2011, http://www.studentnewsdaily.com.
64   Gregory, "Under the Shadow of Islam," 204.
65   Muddassir Rizvi, 'Pakistan: Abuse of Blasphemy Law', *The Manila Times*, 20 November 2003.
66   International Religious Freedom Report for 2011, 9.
67   Sherry Rehman, "Gojra and Pakistan's Identity', *Dawn*, Lahore, 9 August 2009.

this 'can be obtained if made politically palatable'.[68] She declared that PPP 'is the government that can review the blasphemy laws. It is a moment in history that must be seized. Pakistan's identity may be ambiguous, but it is precisely [its] space that can be used as an opportunity to steer our fragile nation-hood in another direction'.[69] Some of the major objectives of the proposed amendment bill were to:

> Avoid miscarriages of justice in the name of Blasphemy. . . and reduce the penalties to each offence so that punishments are proportionate and any incentive to use these laws to settle scores removed. Include the concept of premeditation or intent, which is key to criminal procedure. The terminology of the legislation has been clarified to include in the concept of '*mens rea*' or intent behind the criminal act. Ensure that anyone making false or frivolous accusation under the legislation is penalised as befitting the section under which original claim was made.[70]

The first change Rehman proposed was to change punishments given under sections 295-A, 295-B, and 295-C. It was proposed to amend the punishment given under section 295-A for outraging religious feelings through malicious writing and speech from ten years to imprisonment of either description up to 'two years'. Notably, Rehman intended to revive the originally prescribed punishment of two years and fine for outraging the feelings of any class under section 295-A, a clause applied by the British in 1927 and amended in 1992 in Pakistan. She also proposed to add the same 'malicious and outrageous intention' contained in section 295-A to the new sections 295-C, 298-B, and 298-C. Currently, section 295-A, which had been successfully applied to deal with offensive writings in the pre-1980 period, is rarely if ever used.[71] According to the new Amendment Bill, the death penalty inserted in section 295-C for defiling the name of

---

68 Sherry Rehman, "Blasphemy Law Needs Rectification", *The News*, 17 December 2010.
69 Rehman, "Gojra and Pakistan's Identity".
70 Sherry Rehman, Amendments to the Blasphemy Laws Act 2010.
71 The successful prosecution and judgement given under section 295-A are discussed in detail in F. A. Nazir, *The Evolution of Legislation on Religious Offences*, Chapter 4, 164–183.

the Prophet should be removed and any words, either spoken or written, 'should be punished with imprisonment of either description for a term which may extend to "ten years" or with a fine or with both'. Likewise, the punishment of life imprisonment for defiling the copy of the Quran given under section 295-B should be replaced with 'either description for a term which may extend to "five years" or with fine or with both'.[72]

The second major change according to the Amendment Bill is related to 'intention,' which is the most important ingredient of the law and has been recognised as an error, especially in section 295-C and section 298-A. Notably, these sections do not distinguish between intentional, deliberate acts and unintentional acts, which is an important ingredient necessary to convict anyone in criminal law. Sections 295 and 295-A, the previous clauses applied by the British, specify the 'deliberate and malicious intention' (to punish offensive writing and speech under section 295-A) and deliberate acts (to punish who defiles and damages the place of worship under section 295). The new additions (section 295-C and section 298-B), though containing most of the description of the old law, omit the crucial point of intention in defining the crime. Rehman regards this error as one of the major reasons for the misuse of the law that leaves accusations open to widespread abuse, placing the burden of proving innocence on the accused in the face of prosecution witnesses who tailor their evidence through prejudice or malice.[73] To deal with this issue, Rehman proposed adding intention with words like 'malicious and deliberate intention' to secure blasphemy convictions. These terms were originally added in section 295-A in 1927 by the British to convict those who insulted the Prophet Muhammad through offensive publications done with deliberate and malicious intention.[74]

According to Sherry Rehman, the government must reconsider the introduction of the provision that 'would make it easier to award punishment to those who file fake cases'. To tackle this issue, it was proposed to add a new section, 203, to the Pakistan Penal Code, which could punish 'anyone making a false or frivolous accusation under any of the sections

---

72   Rehman, Amendments to the Blasphemy Act 2010, 1.
73   Rehman, 'Blasphemy Law Needs Rectification'.
74   Section 295-A is discussed in detail in Nazir, *The Evolution of Legislation on Religious Offences*, Chapter 2, 90–96.

of 295A, 295B and 295C . . . shall be punished in accordance with similar punishments prescribed in the section in which the false or frivolous accusation was made'.[75] Furthermore, anyone making false or frivolous accusations under sections 295A, 295B, and 295C may be arrested without a warrant and such a person can be tried in Sessions Court.[76] To Rehman, by enforcing this change, the complainants or accusers take full responsibility whether the case is false or true. By reviewing various cases in the Amendment Bill, Rehman argued that the lack of a clear government response gave freedom to accusers to incite acts of violence and intimidation against religious minorities.[77] Rehman hoped that these changes 'would take away the impunity afforded to malicious accusers and inciters to hate, whose victims may find acquittal but also find that their lives, reputations, security and mobility destroyed by such charges'.[78] To reduce the risk of mob violence, Rehman proposed adding a new section 298-E in Chapter XV of the Religious Offences law. This law prescribes punishments for seven years with a fine for 'any advocacy of religious hatred that constitutes incitement to discrimination or violence'.[79] According to Rehman, initial reports of blasphemy accusations, pre-trial, and trial procedures to convict the accused are frequently incorrectly done at the level of the lower courts. Rehman proposes to amend the Court of Criminal Procedure by adding section 190 (3) to insist that 'all offences falling within sections of 295A, 295B and 295C of Pakistan Penal Code shall exclusively be taken cognizance of by the Court Sessions and Tried by the High Court'.[80] The change was proposed to prevent injustice in lower courts, because the higher courts afford judges better protection against extremists, as well as place the trial under greater public scrutiny.[81] It was also an investment in the future: 'it's going to be a long haul but I don't think it's impossible. It just looks that way sometimes. If we are to live in

---

75 Rehman, Amendments to the Blasphemy Act 2010, 1.
76 Rehman, 'Gojra and Pakistan's Identity'.
77 Rehman, 'Gojra and Pakistan's Identity'.
78 Rehman, 'Blasphemy Law Needs Rectification'.
79 Rehman, 'Blasphemy Law Needs Rectification'.
80 Rehman, Amendments to the Blasphemy Act 2010, 1.
81 Rehman, 'Blasphemy Law Needs Rectification'.

Pakistan, to invest in Pakistan's future, then we do have to think about how to find this glass half full'.[82]

The Bill was likely to get cross-party support from liberal legislators but the religious parties opposed it. The government halted the bill's progress after violent protests demanded the bill be withdrawn and disbanded the committee set up under the Minister for Minorities, Shahbaz Bhatti. Both Rehman and Bhatti were declared 'liable for murder' by the rallies.[83] Sherry Rehman withdrew her commitment to repealing the law. Though Rehman is still alive, 'the blasphemy issue is still haunting [her]'.[84] Rehman, according to the petitioner, committed blasphemy on *Dunya* Television program *Dunya Meray Aagay* ('The World in Front of Me') on 30 November 2010 while talking about the misuse of the law of blasphemy.[85]

CONCLUSION

Religion and religious offences were and still are areas of significant legislation and a sensitive matter in South Asia, especially in the Punjab. The blasphemy law and its interpretations remain as complicated today as before. The authorities continue to claim their commitment to protect all communities from religiously motivated violence by applying and practising Chapter XV on 'Offences Relating to Religion'. Today, the law has gained a quasi-sacred nature. Internationally, the implications of the 1980s laws have been condemned, and suggestions have been made to protect religious communities and their rights—protections that already exist in the law of Chapter XV of PPC. One expects the situation to become more difficult for Christians, however, in the days to come, especially when Western governments criticise Pakistan or impose sanctions. It highlights the charge that Pakistani Christianity is a Western religion. This further alienates indigenous Christians from their Muslim neighbours.

---

82 Rehman, quoted by Issam Ahmed, 'Could There Be a Liberal Resurgence in Pakistan?' www.pakteahouse.net.
83 Faruqi, *A Question of Faith*, 42.
84 Azam Khan, 'Blasphemy Petition against Sherry Rehman Accepted,' *The Express Tribune*, 18 January 2013.
85 Khan, 'Blasphemy Petition against Sherry Rehman Accepted'.

4

CHRISTIANS IN INDONESIA, MALAYSIA, AND THE PHILIPPINES
The Minority–Majority Experience

Peter G. Riddell and Amos Sukamto

Christian-Muslim encounters in Southeast Asia are most in evidence in Indonesia, Malaysia, and the Philippines. In the former two countries, Muslims constitute a majority, whereas the Philippines hosts a massive Christian majority of almost 90 percent. Such a demographic situation has produced a mixed history of tension, conflict, and some reconciliation. This chapter will consider how oppositions have been entrenched in all three countries and how efforts at building harmony across religious lines are establishing firm foundations in the early twenty-first century.

INDONESIA

Indonesia has the largest Muslim population of any country in the world.[1] In 2022, Muslim numbers were estimated at 231,000,000 people, or 86.7 percent of the total population of Indonesia,[2] making Islam the majority

---

1 "Muslim Population by Country 2022," accessed December 3, 2022, https://worldpopulationreview.com/country-rankings/muslim-population-by-country.
2 Komaruddin Hidayat and Dadi Darmadi, 'Indonesia and Two Great Narratives on Islamic Studies', 26 no. 1 (2019): 201–205; 'Muslim Population by Country 2022'.

religion in the country. Besides Islam, there are various minority religious groups, such as Protestants and Catholics (9.90 percent), Hindus (1.69 percent), Buddhists (0.72 percent), and Confucianists (0.05 percent).[3] Local primal religions do not increase their numbers to any significant degree. Each religious group has various sects, ranging from moderate to radical approaches to faith. Such diversity often creates conflict, both between adherents of one religion and another and between adherents of various streams within that religion. Religious conflicts intersect with ideological conflicts, such as occurred between Muslims and Communists (mostly *abangan* groups) from independence to 1965.

After the 1965 coup, known as the *Gerakan 30 September* (G30S-30 September Movement), there was a massive rate of conversion to Christianity.[4] This triggered great anxiety among the Islamic elites, who accused Christians of fishing in murky waters, taking advantage of adversity.[5] After the G30S, the Islamic elites felt they were facing a new threat from Christianity. Since then, inter-religious conflict in Indonesia has been dominated by Muslim-Christian tensions. In 1967, there were incidents of church destruction in Meulaboh, Aceh, and in Makassar, South Sulawesi. To defuse the heated situation, the government held deliberations among religious leaders for the first time, in 1967. However, these deliberations did not succeed in reducing the Muslim-Christian tension because each group was preoccupied by defending the interests of its religion. The Islamic elite did not wish its community to be accessible to missionary activity. On the other hand, the Christian elite did not agree with any limitations in spreading the gospel.[6] One of the Christian representatives at the deliberations, Albert Mangaratua Tambunan, stated,

---

3   Robert W. Hefner, 'Islam and Institutional Religious Freedom in Indonesia', *Religions* 12 no. 6 (2021), https://doi.org/10.3390/rel12060415.

4   Amos Sukamto, 'Dampak Peristiwa G30S Tahun 1965 Terhadap Kekristenan Di Jawa, Sumatera Utara Dan Timor', *Journal Amanat Agung* 11 no. 1 (2015): 85-130, https://ojs.sttaa.ac.id/index.php/JAA/article/view/199.

5   Hyung Jun Kim, "The Changing Interpretation of Religious Freedom in Indonesia," *Journal of Southeast Asian Studies* 29 no. 2 (1998): 357-373, https://doi.org/10.1017/S0022463400007499.

6   Weinata Sairin, ed., *Departemen Agama Dan Hubungan Agama-Agama Di Indonesia* (Bandung: PT Danamartha Sejahtera Utama, 2000), 100-101.

as Christians we are bound by divine commandments which, among other things, are formulated as follows: 'and you will be my witnesses in Jerusalem and in all Judea and Samaria, and to the end of the earth'. (Acts 1:8). In another verse it says: 'Go into all the world and proclaim the gospel to the whole creation'. (Mark 16:15)[7]

This government-sponsored deliberation did not result in an agreement. Responding to this, Natsir, the representative of Islam, stated that 'since then what has been called "free fight for all", with "survival of the fittest" in the field of religion, applies'.[8] At the grassroots level, another church was destroyed in 1968 in Jatibarang (West Java).[9] In early 1969, a Protestant church in Slipi, Jakarta, was damaged.[10]

The policies of the New Order government under President Suharto (1966–1998) under the influence of the military tended to regard Islam as a challenge to the official national philosophy of Pancasila,[11] which enshrined equality among the different faiths, so many government policies increasingly marginalised Islam on the Indonesian political stage. In the 1970s and 1980s, Islamic groups were increasingly active at the grassroots level and radical Islamic groups went underground. Several Islamic figures suspected that Christian groups played a role in marginalising Islamic interests during the New Order era.[12]

The 1970s have been called the wonderful period of tolerance in Indonesia. The Indonesian government developed a three-day harmony program, focusing on harmony between and among religious adherents and between religious adherents and the government. Viewed from the outside,

---

7 Weinata Sairin (Ed.), *Tatkala Pesan-Pesan Merambah Zaman: Himpunan Naskah Pesan Di Lingkungan PGI Dilengkapi Berbagai Dokumen Penting* (Jakarta: Persekutuan Gereja-gereja di Indonesia, 2000), 118.
8 M. Natsir, *Islam Dan Kristen Di Indonesia* (Bandung: Peladjar dan Bulan Sabit, 1969), 248.
9 Sahibi Naim, *Kerukunan Antar Umat Beragama* (Gunung Agung, 1983), 73.
10 Natsir, *Islam Dan Kristen Di Indonesia*, 1969, 238.
11 Pancasila comprises five principles: (1) belief in one Almighty God; (2) just and civilised humanity; (3) the unity of Indonesia; (4) democracy under the wise guidance of representative consultations; and (5) social justice for all the peoples of Indonesia.
12 Douglas E Ramage, *Percaturan Politik Di Indonesia: Demokrasi, Islam, Dan Ideologi Toleransi* (Jogjakarta: MataBangsa, 2002), 168–169.

this program appeared quite successful. No significant inter-religious conflicts occurred during this period. Viewed more closely, the relationship between Islam and Christianity was like simmering embers of a fire. Tensions could be seen in various publications, such as *Panji Islam* magazine and *Media Dakwah* (magazine of the Indonesian Islamic Da'wah Council), which highlighted cases of Christianisation in Indonesian regions.[13] Fulfilling the demands of Muslims regarding Christianisation, the Minister of Religion on 1 August 1978 issued Decree No. 70 of 1978 concerning Guidelines for Religious Propagation. The main content of the decision was that it was not permissible for religious preaching to be aimed at people who had embraced another religion.[14] In the same month, the Minister of Religion issued decree No. 77 of 1978 regarding foreign assistance to religious institutions in Indonesia. It stated that foreign aid must go through the Minister of Religion.[15]

The polemic about the domination of Christians in government institutions also received attention from several Islamic figures in Indonesia.[16] Some Muslim groups felt threatened by Christianity.[17] When the New Order government began to decline, the feeling of threat and prejudice by Muslims against Christianity in Indonesia turned into violent actions in the form of closing, destroying, and burning churches as of the mid-1990s.

ENTRENCHING OPPOSITIONS SINCE THE MID-1990S

As it declined, the New Order government drew closer to Islam in the early 1990s and introduced various Islam-friendly policies, such as the

---

13 M. Natsir, *Islam Dan Kristen Di Indonesia* (Jakarta: Media Dakwah, 1983).
14 Amos Sukamto et al., 'Impacts of the Religious Policies Enacted from 1965 to 1980 on Christianity in Indonesia', *Mission Studies* 36 no. 2 (July 10, 2019): 204, https://doi.org/10.1163/15733831-12341649.
15 Sukamto et al., 'Impacts of the Religious Policies Enacted from 1965 to 1980 on Christianity in Indonesia', 204.
16 Ramage, *Percaturan Politik Di Indonesia: Demokrasi, Islam, Dan Ideologi Toleransi*, 178.
17 Mujiburrahman, *Feeling Threatened: Muslim-Christian Relations in Indonesia's New Order*, vol. 3 (Leiden University Press, 2006).

establishment of the Association of Indonesian Muslim Intellectuals (ICMI), allowing headscarves for female students in state schools, abolishing Social Funding Assistance with Prizes, and accommodating Islamic interests in the state legislature and executive.

In the mid-1990s, the pressures on Christianity increased. Several church closures and cases of burning began to emerge, especially in Java.[18] In early 1996, closing and destruction of churches occurred in various places, such as in Cikampek on 12–13 April 1996 and Bogor on 14 April 1996.[19] These incidents spread to East Java in Sidotopo, Surabaya, on 9 June 1996. Ten churches in this area were destroyed. On 10 October 1996, there was a riot in Situbondo, East Java, that resulted in the death of a pastor's family and the burning of dozens of church buildings.[20] On 26 December 1996, the Tasikmalaya Riot, West Java (*Peristiwa Kerusuhan Tasikmalaya* abbreviated as PKT), occurred.[21] On 30 January 1997, in Rengasdengklok, several churches were burned by a mob.[22] On 22–23 November 1998, churches were destroyed in Ketapang, and in Petojo, Central Jakarta. These riots culminated in widespread violence and attacks in the Maluku islands in eastern Indonesia, first occurring from January to early April 1999, with a recurrence from late July to October 1999, a further series of incidents from November to December 1999, and a further recurrence from April 2000 to 2001.[23]

---

18 In areas where Christians are the majority, mosques had been vandalised and burned by the mob, for example, in Kupang, East Nusa Tenggara, on 30 November 1998 and in Tolikara Regency, Papua, on 17 July 2015.

19 Amos Sukamto and Rudy Pramono, 'The Roots of Conflicts between Muslims and Christians in Indonesia in 1995-1997', *Transformation: An International Journal of Holistic Mission Studies*, July 11, 2020, 214, https://doi.org/10.1177/0265378820937722.

20 Sukamto and Pramono, 'The Roots of Conflicts between Muslims and Christians', 214.

21 Sukamto and Pramono, 'The Roots of Conflicts between Muslims and Christians', 215.

22 Sukamto and Pramono, 'The Roots of Conflicts between Muslims and Christians', 215.

23 Cerita secara lengkap mengenai peristiwa konflik ini bisa dibaca dalam Lambang Trijono, *Keluar Dari Kemelut Maluku: Refleksi Pengalaman Praktis Bekerja Untuk Perdamaian Maluku,* (Yogyakarta: Pustaka Pelajar, 2001).

EFFORTS TO BUILD HARMONY SINCE THE MID-1990S

Facing these various social challenges and pressures, the responses of Christians in Indonesia varied greatly. The theological construction developed by Christian sects in Indonesia largely determined the form of their response. These challenges also stimulated interest in cooperation among various Christian denominations in Indonesia. Christian responses in Indonesia included collaborating to lobby for government policies, developing a theology of brotherhood and the praxis of living together, strengthening interfaith dialogue, forming the Indonesian Christian Communication Forum, and forming the Prosperous Peace Party. A more detailed discussion of these responses follows.

Collaborate to Lobby for Government Policies

The above-mentioned decrees of the Minister of Religion No. 70 and 77 of 1978 had limited the space for the development of Christianity in Indonesia. The Communion of Churches in Indonesia (at that time known as the Council of Churches in Indonesia, DGI) as the largest organisation of Protestant churches in Indonesia, in collaboration with the Catholic Supreme Council of Indonesian Bishops (MAWI), filed an objection to the Indonesian government over these two decrees.[24] This objection did not receive a positive response from the government. Indeed, the Minister of Religion together with the Minister of Home Affairs issued joint decree No. 1 of 1979 concerning Procedures for the Implementation of Religious Propagation and Foreign Assistance to Religious Institutions in Indonesia.

As a result of restrictions on foreign aid (including mission personnel), many mission personnel working in Indonesia had to return to their countries of origin. Facing the threat of a Catholic human resource crisis in the 1970s, a program called 'Program to Accelerate Indonesianization of Catholic Church Workers in Indonesia' was implemented. The program proved successful. In 1970, of the total 1,462 priests, 27 percent (400) were Indonesians and 73 percent (1,062) were foreign nationals, but by 1990 the

---

24 *Tinjauan Mengenai Keputusan Menteri Agama No. 70 Dan 77 Tahun 1978* (Jakarta: Sekretariat Umum Dewan Gereja-gereja di Indonesia dan Sekretariat Majelis Agung Waligereja Indonesia, 1978).

situation had reversed. Of the total 1905 priests, 81 percent (1,535) were Indonesian and only 19 percent (370) were not Indonesian.[25]

Developing a Theology of Brotherhood and the Praxis of Living Together

The social pressures that arose in the mid-1990s made several Christian leaders in Indonesia realise the need to re-evaluate both their theological positions toward other religions and their practice of living in society. The process of building a theology of dialogue with other religions had been initiated among Indonesian theologians in 1960 by Walter Bonar Sidjabat after he completed his doctoral studies at Princeton Seminary that year with a dissertation entitled 'Religious Tolerance and The Christian Faith'.[26] This kind of theological effort was continued by Victor I. Tanja, who completed his doctoral studies at the Hartford Seminary Foundation in 1979. According to Tanja, in the context of the diversity of Indonesia, dialogue among religious communities is needed, involving dialogue with open principles and a willingness to listen to the teachings and beliefs of others.[27] Missions must be carried out through conversation, not one-sided action. The theological basis for this view is that Jesus also conversed with the crowds.[28] Tanja further stated that 'in the view of the Bible all human beings, even though they have different religions, nations, races, and ethnicities, are God's family'.[29] S. Wismoady Wahono, a theologian from the Jawi Wetan Christian Church (GKJW), discussed the theology of living together (pro-existence), which means that religion exists not only for itself but for living together.[30]

---

25 Huub J. W. M. Boelaars, *Indonesianisasi, Dari Gereja Katolik Di Indonesia Menjadi Gereja Katolik Indonesia* (Yogyakarta: Kanisius, 2005), 236; Sukamto et al., 'Impacts of the Religious Policies Enacted from 1965 to 1980 on Christianity in Indonesia', 211–212.

26 Walter Bonar Sidjabat, *Religious Tolerance and the Christian Faith* (Jakarta: BPK Gunung Mulia, 1982).

27 Victor I. Tanja, *Tiada Hidup Tanpa Agama: Bunga Rampai Tentang Peranan Agama Dalam Berbagai Dinamika Kehidupan* (Jakarta: BPK Gunung Mulia, 1988), 49.

28 Tanja, *Tiada Hidup Tanpa Agama*.

29 Tanja, *Tiada Hidup Tanpa Agama*.

30 S. Wismoady Wahono, *Pro-Eksistensi: Kumpulan Tulisan Untuk Mengacu Kehidupan Bersama* (Jakarta: BPK Gunung Mulia, 2001), 6.

National awareness of the need for this kind of dialogue was achieved at the PGI General Assembly in Tomohon in 1980 when it was decided to hold a structured Seminar on Religions (SAA), which presented speakers from various religious groups addressing the theme of the relationship between religion and society. One outcome of the SAA was the published proceedings under the title *Meretas Jalan Teologi Agama-agama di Indonesia: Theologia Religionum* (Opening the Way of the Theology of Religions in Indonesia: Theologia Religionum).

The Bandung Diocese gave an excellent reflection in responding to the 1996 Tasikmalaya Riot (PKT). The experience of the PKT that had impacted the life of the Catholic Church needed to be used as material for correcting their ecclesiological model. This experience was reviewed and reflected on, drawing clear lessons leading to a more mature pilgrimage for Catholics.[31] The PKT made them aware that, in social life among Tasikmalaya residents, they were still considered foreigners (*orang asing*). For this reason, it was necessary to develop a call to cultivate brotherhood by building a moral movement and building true brotherhood.[32] This could be achieved by changing four paradigms: (1) from strangers to friends, (2) from being less caring to caring, (3) from personal piety to community piety, and (4) from a hobby to enjoy to a willingness to sacrifice.[33] It was hoped that this paradigm shift would produce a new form of ecclesiology, namely that 'the church must walk together with all humans in solidarity between humans'.[34]

Strengthening Interfaith Dialogue

To strengthen inter-religious dialogue, Sumartana, after discussions with Romo Mangunwijaya, Adnan Buyung Nasution, Parakitri, and Abdul Rahman Wahid, formed the Institute for Inter-Faith Dialogue in Indonesia (Interfidei) on 20 December 1991. The Interfidei board members came from various religious groups: Daniel Dakhidae (Catholic), Djohan

---

31 Keuskupan Bandung, *Refleksi Peristiwa Tasikmalaya*, (Bandung: Keuskupan Bandung, 1997), 1.
32 Bandung, *Refleksi Peristiwa Tasikmalaya*.
33 Bandung, *Refleksi Peristiwa Tasikmalaya*.
34 Bandung, *Refleksi Peristiwa Tasikmalaya*.

Effendi (Muslim), Haksu Thjie Tjai Ing (Kong Hu Cu), Zulkifli Lubis (Muslim), Bikkhu Sri Pannavaro Mahathera (Buddhist), Mrs. Gedong Bagoes Oka (Hindu), Pastor Eka Darma Putra (Protestant), and Th. Sumartana (Protestant).[35]

Interfidei was established by considering the context of pluralism in Indonesia. The reality of pluralism, apart from requiring a creative interpretation of the national motto 'Bhinneka Tunggal Ika' (Unity in Diversity), also requires cooperation and dialogue among religions. Three areas covered by Interfidei to produce productive dialogue are a dialogue between adherents of the same religion, dialogue between religions, and dialogue between religions and society.[36]

Forming the Indonesian Christian Communication Forum (FKKI)

After the destruction of ten churches in Sidotopo, Surabaya, on 15 June 1996, law enforcement officers took no action. Some unscrupulous officials even dismissed Christian complaints, saying, 'You guys just go home because you are a minority, just give in, there's no need for a lot of protests'.[37] On the other hand, a church that had received such treatment could not do much except remain silent. Several Christian mass organisation leaders agreed to form an advocacy organisation called the Surabaya Christian Communication Forum (FKKS). FKKS was formed on 13 June 1996 in Surabaya.[38] One of the movers of FKKS was a legal expert from Airlangga University (UNAIR) Surabaya, namely Professor J. E. Sahetapy. The FKKS work program involved consolidation, information, and communication

---

35   Johannes B. Banawiratma and Bagir Zainal Abidin, *Dialog Antarumat Beragama: Gagasan Dan Praktik Di Indonesia* (Bandung: Mizan Publika dan Program Studi Agama dan Lintas Budaya, 2010), 51.

36   Eka Darmaputera, 'Institut DIAN/Interfidei: Sebuah Sumbangan Dialog', in *Dialog: Kritik & Identitas Agama*, eds. Elga Sarapung, Noegroho Agoeng, and Alfred B. Jogoena (Yogyakarta: Institut DIAN?Interfidei, 2004), 325–329.

37   Paul Tahalele, 'Apa Dan Mengapa Forum Komunikasi Kristiani Surabaya—Indonesia', in *Beginikah Kemerdekaan?* (Surabaya: Forum Komunikasi Kristiani Indonesia, 1997), 1.

38   Tahalele, 'Apa Dan Mengapa Forum Komunikasi Kristiani Surabaya—Indonesia', 1.

about the condition of churches in Surabaya. FKKS recorded the churches that were damaged, closed, and burned in the previous five years, providing legal and rehabilitation services. FKKS also conducts dialogues and consultations with formal leaders such as the Mayor, Commander of the Military Resort, Commander of the Regional Military Command, Governor, and Regional People's Representative Assembly (DPRD) of East Java.[39]

After the destruction of the church in Situbondo, East Java, on 10 October 1996, the FKKS, on 15 October 1996, was upgraded to the East Java Christian Communication Forum (FKK East Java).[40] East Java FKK sent a Statement of Concern to the President of the Republic of Indonesia regarding the Situbondo incident. On 17 October 1996, FKKS together with the Nahdlatul Ulama (NU) organisation and the Ansor Youth Movement made a joint statement of concern.[41] Responding to the destruction of churches, which became more widespread in almost the entire island of Java, on 26 January 1997 the East Java FKK was upgraded to the Indonesian Christian Communication Forum (FKKl).[42] One of FKKl's important contributions was to collect data and publish books in both Indonesian and English on details of various church closures, vandalism, and burning in Indonesia.

Prosperous Peace Party (Partai Damai Sejahtera, PDS)

Before the 2004 election, a group of Pentecostal and Charismatic leaders agreed to form a political party called the Prosperous Peace Party (Partai Damai Sejahtera abbreviated as PDS), chaired by Ruyandi Hutasoit. The PDS was formed because (1) there had been no political party that accommodated the aspirations of Christians when the burning and destruction of churches occurred starting in 1996, and (2) it was difficult to obtain permits to build houses of worship.[43] The church was very weak in the face of

---

39　Tahalele, 'Apa Dan Mengapa Forum Komunikasi Kristiani Surabaya—Indonesia'.
40　Tahalele, 'Apa Dan Mengapa Forum Komunikasi Kristiani Surabaya—Indonesia'.
41　Paul Santoso Tahalele and Thomas Santoso Tahalele, *Beginikah Kemerdekaan Kita?* (Surabaya: FKKS-FKKl, 1997), 184.
42　Tahalele, 'Apa Dan Mengapa Forum Komunikasi Kristiani Surabaya—Indonesia'.
43　'Mengapa PDS?', *Majalah Damai Sejahtera*, 2004, 9.

such challenges. One way to strengthen the bargaining power of Christians in government circles was to have Christian representatives sitting in both the executive and legislative bodies. Therefore, PDS developed the Yusuf 04 program, with the goal of placing Yusuf (a figure who was used as a model from the Old Testament Bible) in the executive branch of the state and placing Daniel, Shadrach, and Meshach in the legislature.[44] Yusuf, Daniel, Shadrach, and Meshach were minority figures who succeeded in becoming influential people in the political decisions of a nation.

The PDS program soon bore fruit. Based on the results of the 2004 election, PDS managed to have thirteen representatives in The People's Representative Council of the Republic of Indonesia (DPR RI), fifty-two in The Regional People's Representative Council (DPRD I), and 329 in the Regency People's Representative Council (DPRD II).[45] However, from 2006, the PDS was affected by internal divisions and, consequently, in the 2009 elections, they did not gain any seats in the DPR RI.

MALAYSIA

Malaysia's population, an ethnic and religious kaleidoscope where Muslims constitute a modest majority (63.5 percent) of the population,[46] provides an opportunity to test whether Islam, when empowered, can reflect the democratic, pluralist values espoused by much of the world in the twenty-first century. Tunku Abdul Rahman, the first Prime Minister of Malaysia and father of the nation, declared in Parliament at the time of Malaya's independence in 1957, 'I would like to make it clear that this country is not an Islamic State as it is generally understood; we merely provide that Islam shall be the official religion of the State.'[47] Thus, although Islam was defined as the official religion of Malaya (1957) and Malaysia (1963), its primary

---

44 'Program PDS', *Majalah Damai Sejahtera*, 2004, 7.
45 M. Imaduddin Nasution, *Partisipasi Politik Umat Kristen Indonesia: Studi Kasus Partai Damai Sejahtera* (Jakarta: Verbum Publishing, 2012), 57.
46 Statista Research Department, 'Share of Population in Malaysia 2020, by Religion', 5 October 2022, https://www.statista.com/statistics/594657/religious-affiliation-in-malaysia/.
47 Mohammad Hashim Kamali, *Islamic Law in Malaysia. Issues and Developments* (Kuala Lumpur: Ilmiah Publishers, 2000), 30.

functions at the national level in the early years were ceremonial and ethnic, serving to define the identity of the majority ethnic group, the Malays.

Entrenching Oppositions: The Mahathir Legacy

In Malaysia, former Prime Minister Mahathir Mohamad (b. 1925) has made a regular appearance in the annual publication that identifies the world's most influential Muslims, *TheMuslim500*.[48] However, a range of legislative initiatives before and during his first tenure as prime minister had a marked negative impact on interreligious harmony. From his position as education minister (1974–1978) and then as prime minister (1981–2003), Mahathir was a key driving force in building an Islamic bureaucracy, with a raft of Islamisation legislation that privileged Islam through diverse mechanisms. These included state funding of Islamic programs on the media, establishment of an Islamic university, creation of a Department of Islam within the Prime Minister's Department, establishment of an Islamic bank, founding of the Institute of Islamic Understanding, and diverse other initiatives. Such developments have been a source of great anxiety to minority faiths since the early 1980s. Mahathir and his various ruling administrations amplified Islamic consciousness to the point where many Malaysian Muslims came to see non-Islam in threatening terms. This easily translated to a fear of imagined advances in Malaysia by other faiths, especially Christianity.

Faced with growing Islamisation and perceived discrimination from the Malaysian administrations under Mahathir, religious minorities formed the Malaysian Consultative Council of Buddhism, Christianity, Hinduism, Sikhism, and Taoism in 1983. Since its formation, the Majlis, as it is popularly known, has lobbied government about religious rights of non-Muslims, for example, burial grounds, obstacles to construction of places of worship, banning of Christian symbols, banning of teaching of non-Muslim faiths in schools, exclusion of non-Muslim programming from public media, restriction over distribution of Bibles in hotels, and other issues.

Following the formation of the Majlis in 1983, Christians, who constitute 9 percent of Malaysia's population, came together three years later to

---

48 Abdallah Schleifer (Ed.), *The Muslim 500: The World's 500 Most Influential Muslims, 2019: With Cumulative Rankings over Ten Years* (Amman, Jordan: The Royal Islamic Strategic Studies Centre, 2018), 109.

form the Christian Federation of Malaysia (CFM) as the government-driven Islamisation program picked up steam. The CFM represented over 90 percent of the Christian population of Malaysia: Catholic, Council of Churches of Malaysia, National Evangelical Christian Fellowship, and Pentecostal groups. At one point, school textbooks, following standard Islamic teaching, stated that Jesus was not crucified. Lobbying by the CFM succeeded in having such texts revised.

In May 1986, during Mahathir's second term as prime minister, the Malaysian Ministry of Home Affairs issued a letter to the Christian community identifying a number of words deemed sensitive to persons professing the religion of Islam, and a Non-Islamic Religions Enactment followed in 1988 banning non-Muslim use of the word 'Allah'.[49] A multi-decade-long tussle ensued between the Malaysian government and the Malaysian churches, with a challenge to the government ban led by the *Herald*, a Malaysian Catholic newspaper. On 31 December 2009, Malaysian High Court Justice Datuk Lau Bee Lan issued a ruling allowing Catholics to use 'Allah' to describe the Christian God in the national language. Faced with a public backlash from Muslim conservative groups, newly installed Prime Minister Datuk Seri Najib Razak declared that the Home Ministry would appeal against the ruling. Fire-bombings of several churches were accompanied by an attack on a convent school. Meanwhile, police stepped up security at Christian houses of worship around the country.

In Malaysia, a particularly contentious obstacle to Christian-Muslim harmony was a document published in 2014 by the Selangor Council of Islamic Scholars (MAIS). Entitled *Pendedahan Agenda Kristian* (An Exploration of the Christian Agenda), the 120-page booklet, carrying only sporadic source referencing and lacking a bibliography, portrays Christians as agenda-driven, devious, purveyors of evil, and Machiavellian: 'the agenda and evil intentions of evangelical groups and Christian preachers need to be exposed. Muslims must know and act on this. Their agenda really

---

49　Deemed as exclusive to Muslims under a gazette (Warta P.U (A) 15/82) and circular (Pekeliling KKDN. S.59/3/6/A) dated 5 December 1986, http://malaysia-update.blogspot.com/2010/01/jakim-says-allah-ban-must-include-sabah.html.

threatens the welfare and sanctity of Islam'.[50] By contrast, the document quotes Q3:110, which states that Muslims are 'the best of people born to mankind'.[51] The document mistranslates the name of The Voice of the Martyrs, a non-violent group dedicated to advocating on behalf of persecuted Christian minorities, as "Pejuang Jihad Kristian" (Christian Jihad Fighters).[52] The booklet's potted history of colonialism is brief and superficial, suggesting in conspiratorial terms that the Portuguese, Spanish, and British colonial powers collaborated in an overall goal of Christianising the world.[53] Finally, the document implies that the formation of the Malaysian Consultative Council of Buddhism, Christianity, Hinduism, Sikhism, and Taoism[54] in 1983 was a Christian-driven attempt to Christianise.[55] In fact, the Majlis was a multi-faith gathering formed to discuss concerns of minority faiths with the Islamisation policies of the Mahathir government of that time. The document expresses disappointment 'because the representatives of Islam did not participate in the Council'. Muslim representatives had been invited to participate but declined.[56]

Returning to the ongoing dispute about legislation against Christian use of the term 'Allah' to refer to God, on 10 March 2021 the Malaysian High Court ruled that the use of the word 'Allah' by non-Muslims all over Malaysia was allowed. This re-ignited the debate and tension between Malaysia's ruling Muslim-dominated government and the Christian churches. On 15 March 2021, the federal government filed its appeal (at the appellate court) against the previous week's High Court ruling.[57] The ongoing awkwardness

---

50 MAIS, *Pendedahan Agenda Kristian (An Exploration of the Christian Agenda* (Shah Alam, Malaysia: Majlis Agama Islam Selangor, 2014), 55.
51 MAIS, *Pendedahan*, 56.
52 MAIS, *Pendedahan*, 58.
53 MAIS, *Pendedahan*, 61–108.
54 The Malay title is *Majlis Perundingan Malaysia Agama Buddha, Kristian, Hindu, Sikh dan Tao*, known in abbreviated form as the Majlis.
55 MAIS, *Pendedahan*, 63.
56 Peter G. Riddell, 'Islamisation, Civil Society and Religious Minorities in Malaysia', in *Islam in Southeast Asia: Political, Social and Strategic Challenges for the 21st Century*, eds. K.S. Nathan and Mohammad Hashim Kamali (Singapore: Institute of Southeast Asian Studies, 2005), 170–171.
57 FMT Reporters, 'Putrajaya Files Appeal in Use of "Allah" Case,' *Free Malaysia Today*, 15 March 2021, https://www.freemalaysiatoday.com/category/nation/2021/03/15/putrajaya-files-appeal-in-use-of-allah-case/.

of the Christian-Muslim relationship in Malaysia poses challenges as the country moves further into the twenty-first century.

Building Harmony and Dialogue Initiatives

Countering the statements by mainstream religious scholars and organisations as discussed above, some Muslim scholars in Malaysia have contributed in positive ways to Christian–Muslim harmony. This has been seen especially regarding the government ban on Christians using 'Allah' as the term for God in their worship and literature. Ustaz Maszlee Malik and Musa Mohd Nordin, writing in the online periodical *Malaysiakini*, stated the following:

> Muslim secularists from within political parties are now usurping the role as custodians of Islam . . . and juxtaposed with religious zealots from within 'religious' parties as well as Muslim NGOs; they form a lethal concoction of religious intolerance in their 'jihad' to *'mempertahankan kalimah Allah'* (uphold the name of the Lord). . . This is quite obviously another reflection of the 'siege mentality' of the 'Malay Muslim governance' which has since independence played on the fears of the Malay Muslim populace easily riled by such non-issues due to their 'hypersensitive and touchy Malay gene'.[58]

A long-term challenge facing inter-religious relations in Malaysia has been limited contact between the different faith communities. A survey of churches in 2001 conducted by the National Evangelical Christian Fellowship revealed that around 48 percent of Christians surveyed rarely interacted with Muslims, while 36 percent of churches did not organise any activities that involved interaction with non-Christians in their neighbourhoods.[59] The Roman Catholic St Francis Xavier Parish in Kuala Lumpur launched a 'Movement for Interfaith Enhancement' in 1999,

---

58 Maszlee Malik and Musa Mohd Nordin, 'Non-Issue from Angle of Islamic Law but. . .', *Malaysiakini*, 6 January 2010, http://www.malaysiakini.com/letters/121300.

59 Edmund Ng, 'A Post-Survey Analysis: Towards Greater Community Involvement', *Berita NECF* March/April 2002, 11.

focusing on meetings with other faiths, with the church becoming a catalyst to involve other Catholic parishes in dialogue. Similarly, the Protestant Council of Churches of Malaysia issued a statement around the same time calling for increased dialogue with other faiths.[60] Such initiatives in Christian–Muslim dialogue have met with mixed success. Civil society groups, both Muslim and Christian, have pursued some of the most effective activities.

The IMAN Research group, coming out of Muslim roots, is a think tank seeking to enhance community harmony, peacebuilding, and sustainable development. IMAN is active in publication, issuing many research reports, such as 'Malaysia, Identity Politics and the Future of Our Democracy'.[61] Of particular interest is a research project entitled "The Sentiments of Inter-Faith Relations', which was designed to research 'the sentiments behind inter-faith relations in Malaysia and the Philippines, specifically the narratives that drive communal tensions between Muslims and Christians and which may be employed and exploited by violent extremist groups'.[62]

Another civil society group to implement activities designed to enhance inter-religious harmony is the Christian group UID Sejahtera, established in 2018 by the Gabungan Bertindak Malaysia, a coalition of twenty-seven civil society organisations in Malaysia. UID-Sejahtera collaborated with the Malaysian Alliance of Civil Society Organisations (MACSA) and the Muslim group Yayasan Dakwah Malaysia (YADIM) to organise a seminar on 20 January 2021, entitled 'Religious Perspectives in Strengthening Family Values'.

---

60 'Prime Minister's Assurance to Religious Groups', Press Statement, Council of Churches of Malaysia, https://web.archive.org/web/20021224140619/http://www.ccmalaysia.org/netscape/events/past1.htm accessed May 20, 2002.
61 Nadia Lukman. "Malaysia, Identity Politics and the Future of our Democracy", IMAN Research Society Brief, April 2022, https://www.imanresearch.com/wp-content/uploads/2022/04/brief-2022-04-April.pdf, accessed January 21, 2024.
62 IMAN Research, 'The Sentiments of Inter-Faith Relations: Narratives behind Muslim-Christian Tensions in Malaysia and the Philippines', Concept Paper, Kuala Lumpur, 2018.

THE PHILIPPINES

Unlike Muslim-majority neighbours of Malaysia and Indonesia, the Philippines comprises a vast population (over 100 million) that is around 90 percent Christian. Muslims are 6 percent of the population. This has created an inter-religious situation that has often resulted in tension and conflict through the centuries.

Entrenching Oppositions: Internal Population Movements

After the USA took control of the Philippines from the Spanish in 1898, there was a provincial restructuring that created the Moro Province, covering the former regions of Zamboanga, Lanao, Cotabato, Davao, and Jolo. The military governor of Moro Province, General George W. Davis, wrote a report on 25 August 1902 that encapsulated negative attitudes to Muslim Filipinos:

> With a people who have no conception of government that is not arbitrary and absolute; who hold human life as no more sacred than the life of an animal; who have become accustomed to acts of violence; who are constrained by fear from continuing the practice of piracy; who still carry on slave trade; who habitually raid the homes of mountain natives and enslave them; ... —it is useless to discuss a plan of government that is not based on physical force, might, and power.[63]

In subsequent decades, increasing numbers of Christian Filipinos from the north were resettled in Muslim-majority Mindanao, increasing rapidly after independence in 1946.[64] The population of Mindanao increased gradually from 1913 to 1939 by barely 100,000 to pass 1,000,000 overall in the latter year. In 1948, two years after independence, the population of Mindanao had grown to 1,216,348, but by 1960, it had exploded to 5,090,433,[65]

---

63 Dean Conant Worcester, *The Philippines Past and Present, Volume 2* (New York: Macmillan, 1914), 681–682.
64 Reynaldo M. Aquino, *Land Ownership and Migration Impact on the Muslim Secessionist Conflict in the Southern Philippines* (Monterey, California: Naval Postgraduate School Master of Science Thesis, 2009), 41.
65 George Farwell, *Mask of Asia: The Philippines* (Melbourne: F.W. Cheshire, 1966), 108.

with settlement from the Christian northern Philippines largely accounting for this growth.

Prior to independence, legislation on land ownership in Mindanao discriminated heavily in favour of Christians. According to the Public Land Act No. 2874 of 1919, a Muslim Filipino was allowed a maximum of ten hectares in homestead lots in Mindanao, while non-Muslim Filipinos could own twenty-four-hectare lots.[66] Commonwealth Act No. 141 of 1936 declared all Muslim ancestral land holdings to be public lands. This trend continued after independence, with other land settlement programs continuing into the 1960s.[67] Over time, the Muslim communities on Mindanao became a minority in their own homeland; Bacani reports that 'the proportion of Muslim inhabitants to the population of Mindanao declined from 98% to 40% by 1976, and to around 20% in 1995'.[68] By 1982, Muslims on Mindanao owned only around 18 percent of the land.[69]

A series of Muslim rebellions were the result of these demographic changes; the Tausug Maas Kamlon rebellion in the 1940s and 1950s derived essentially from conflict over land ownership in Sulu.[70] In 1968, Nur Misuari founded the Moro National Liberation Front (MNLF) with the aspiration of establishing Mindanao as an independent republic. Ten years later, a breakaway movement from the MNLF led by Hashim Salamat led to the formation of the Moro Islamic Liberation Front (MILF), which set more religious goals by aiming for an Islamic state in the Southern Philippines. The peace agreement of 1996 ended the MNLF armed rebellion, with Misuari becoming the elected governor of the new Autonomous Region in Muslim Mindanao (ARMM).[71]

---

66   Aquino, *Land Ownership*, 42.
67   Aquino, *Land Ownership*, 45–46.
68   Benedicto R. Bacani, *The Mindanao Peace Talks: Another Opportunity to Resolve the Moro Conflict in the Philippines* (Washington, DC: United States Institute of Peace, 2005), 4.
69   Aquino, *Land Ownership*, 47.
70   Ruben D. Torres, 'Never-Ending Quest for Peace', *The Manila Times*, June 25, 2021, https://www.manilatimes.net/2021/06/25/opinion/columns/never-ending-quest-for-peace/1804559.
71   Torres, 'Never-Ending Quest'.

The conflict between the Philippines government and the MILF concluded when the Comprehensive Agreement on the Bangsamoro was signed on 27 March 2014. The Bangsamoro Organic Law of 26 July 2018 established the Bangsamoro Autonomous Region in Muslim Mindanao (BARRM), which replaced the ARMM and was controlled by the MILF, led by its chairman and Governor Murad. The history of fragmentation of resistance movements in the south continues, with the Bangsamoro Islamic Freedom Fighters (BIFF), a splinter group from the MILF, maintaining armed resistance to government control.[72]

It is difficult to find theological statements by mainstream Christian organisations or individuals in the post-colonial Philippines that negatively typecast Muslims as seen with the negative stereotyping of Christians in the case of Malaysia above. One reason is that an opposite process of secularisation was taking place among Christian communities in the Philippines, resulting in different language being used by the different communities to explain relational problems. Peter Gowing, writing in 1977 about the Philippines, offers interesting perspectives:

> In contrast to the growing secularism of Philippine Christian Society, Philippine Muslim Society has for the past thirty years or so seen a vigorous resurgence of Islam... Christian Filipinos... tend to see their relationships with Muslims in political terms. They are puzzled as to why the Muslims present obstacles to the unity of the nation and threaten secession or press for autonomy. Christians argue that the war on Mindanao has nothing to do with religion.... Muslims tend to see their relationships with Christians in religious terms. The Muslims cannot understand or accept the religiously indifferent secularism or the enlightened humanitarianism of the modern Philippines. Having been subjected for so many centuries to efforts at forcing them to abandon their religion and culture, the Muslims suspect that the Christian population and their government are still motivated by those objectives.[73]

---

72   Torres, 'Never-Ending Quest'.
73   Peter G. Gowing, 'Of Different Minds: Muslim and Christian Perceptions of the Mindanao Problem', *Philippine Quarterly of Culture and Society* 5, no. 4 (December 1977): 244.

Building Harmony and Dialogue Initiatives

In the Philippines, faced by Christian–Muslim problems in the south of the country, there have been various Presidential Decrees and calls for dialogue since independence in 1946. Ferdinand Marcos, president from 1965–1986, issued Presidential Decree 1803 (The Code of Muslim Personal Law) on 4 February 1977 whereby Islamic personal laws based on Qur'anic principles were recognised as part of the legal system of the Philippine Republic.[74] The Second Philippine National Christian–Muslim Dialogue, which met in Marawi City in January 1976, endorsed this Muslim claim as a right, with similar declarations subsequently issued by the National Council of Churches and the Catholic Bishops' Conference.

President Gloria Arroyo (in office 2001–2010) was committed to greater Christian–Muslim harmony. Speaking in 2010, she declared that 'interreligious dialogue is the only solution for peace and stability in Mindanao', after much conflict between Islamic rebels of the Moro Islamic Liberation Front (MILF) and the Philippines government.[75] Christian–Muslim dialogues began in the 1960s in Mindanao as tensions continued between the communities. According to Nieva Manzano,

> One of the major reasons for the frequent conflicts between Muslims and Christians is the prejudice that Christians have against Muslims or vice-versa. Muslims presented Christians as land grabbers and oppressors who took away their lands from them.... On the other hand, Christians considered the Muslims as murderers, thieves and dirty.[76]

---

74 Gowing, 'Of Different Minds', 247.
75 Anon., 'President Arroyo: Interfaith dialogue only solution for peace in Mindanao'. *AsiaNews.it*, 19 March 2010, http://www.asianews.it/news-en/President-Arroyo:-Interfaith-dialogue-only-solution-for-peace-in-Mindanao-17935.html.
76 Sr. Nieva Manzano, 'The Christian-Muslim Relations in the Philippines and the Daughters of Charity Apostolate with Muslims'. *Vincentiana* 43 no. 4–5 (1999): 1.

Various Christian–Muslim initiatives were launched, especially in Mindanao, in a search for interreligious harmony. These included the Silsilah Dialogue Movement; the creation of the SALAM Foundation, with a social and literary program for Muslims; AZ (Peace Advocates Zamboanga); Interfaith Dialogue centres established in many dioceses and parishes in Mindanao; and Education for Peace Centres created in practically all Catholic schools in Mindanao with the primary objective of having peace education in the curriculum or integrating it in all subject disciplines. Arguably, the most important of these initiatives is the Silsilah Dialogue Movement (SDM), founded in Zamboanga City on 9 May 1984. The key inspirational founding figure was Father Sebastiano D'Ambra, together with Muslim friends. D'Ambra is a prolific author and addresses the goals and advantages of dialogue in his books, affirming the goals and activities of the international Christian–Muslim dialogue entitled *A Common Word between Us and You*, writing:

> Often we find Christians or Muslims who do not know their religion. A little knowledge of religion is often the beginning of misunderstanding, religious apathy or religious 'radicalism'. The basic elements of our religions have the foundation in the love of God and love of neighbor.[77]

The successes of the Silsilah Dialogue Movement since its foundation in 1984 are witnessed to in the testimonies of participants, both Christian and Muslim. Nor Asiah Madale Adilao, a young Muslim woman who in time became Muslim Coordinator of the Silsilah Forum Davao, attended a SDM event for the first time in summer 2000 and wrote:

> Everything for me is first time. First time to sleep together inside the room with a Christian nun from the Oblates of Notre Dame (OND sisters) from Jolo, first time to eat together during meal time, first time to pray together inside the four corners of the session hall. Finally, it was my first time to stay overnight with a Christian

---

77   Sebastiano D'Ambra, *A Path to Peace. Culture of Dialogue: Path to Peace* (Zamboanga City: Silsilah Publications, 2014), 26.

family on a weekend. . . . It was through Silsilah that I found an inner silence within myself; and it gave birth to dialogue. I started to reflect and pray for peace not only for my Muslim brothers and sisters, but also for the Christians. I found a place where I could perform my prayers. Eventually, I felt comfortable with other people who are different from me in culture and religion.[78]

Elsewhere in the Philippines, diverse groups pursue other dialogue activities. The Daughters of Charity and their Apostolate with the Muslims are working in schools in various parts of Mindanao. Their activities focus on the integration of Christian and Islamic teachings in Values Education classes; separate classes for the two religions; shared co-curricular activities; supporting the Parents' Councils Organization; and regular visits to the families of students.[79] Dialogue groups do not only address matters related to theology and belief but also issues usually considered as part of secular dialogue. For example, the National Interfaith Dialogue on Climate Change Philippines, first convened in 2010, is a recurring event, promoting action on environmental protection and sustainability based on religious teachings.[80]

More broadly, at the micro level in society, it is common for a Catholic priest, a Protestant pastor, and a Muslim imam to recite prayers in turn for wide-ranging activities and on special days. For example, both Muslims and Christians in the Philippines observe the feast of Eid al-Fitr, which marks the end of the Muslim fasting month, as a holiday.[81]

CONCLUSIONS

This survey of Christian–Muslim relations in Indonesia, Malaysia, and the Philippines might have expected the greatest problems to occur in the most

---

78   Nor Asiah Madale Adilao, 'Silsilah: A Chain of Dialogue and Beyond', *Silsilah Bulletin* 27 no. 1 (January-December 2016): 13.
79   Manzano, 'The Christian-Muslim Relations'.
80   Anon., *National Interfaith Dialogue on Climate Change Philippines*, n.d., https://www.facebook.com/InterfaithDialogueonClimateChangePhilippines.
81   Elizabeth T. Urgel, "Christian-Moslem Relations in Southeast Asia: Towards Peace and Harmony," *Changing Religious Movements in a Changing World Conference* (Falun, Sweden: Dalarna University, 21–24 June 2013).

geographically and ethnically diverse countries of Indonesia and the Philippines. Indeed, significant Christian–Muslim relational challenges have occurred in those countries since they gained their independence in the late 1940s. However, while ongoing, such challenges in Indonesia and the Philippines have been more characterised by periodic flashpoints rather than chronic crises, with concerted efforts by governments to address and resolve these tensions.

The Southeast Asian country where the magnitude of Christian–Muslim problems has been most in evidence, and most chronic, is Malaysia. This is due especially to a set of Islamisation policies introduced by governments from the 1980s onwards in order to shore up the ruling coalition in the context of worldwide Islamic resurgence that impacted Malaysia's Muslim community, just as it affected every other Muslim community across the globe. The creation of a powerful Islamic bureaucracy and a raft of Islamisation legislation and institution-building measures over a forty-year period has triggered great anxiety among all religious minorities in Malaysia, which constitute over 35 percent of the national population. Christian–Muslim tension has been at the heart of the interreligious instability that is chronic in Malaysia.

Nevertheless, our examination of Christian–Muslim relations in Southeast Asia in the post-colonial period, while identifying challenges, ends up being weighted toward more positive trends and outcomes in the early twenty-first century. The intervention of political, social, and religious leaders in all countries has been key in producing a balance sheet that is positive overall. That process will need to continue in coming decades for Southeast Asian Christians and Muslims to live in harmony and friendship.

5

THE IMPACT OF *VELAYAT-E FAQIH* ON IRANIAN CHRISTIANS IN POST-REVOLUTION IRAN

Michael Nazir-Ali and Amir S. Bazmjou

Christians in Iran have faced opposition and persecution from before the advent of Islam. After its arrival, they continued to experience serious restrictions under the Islamic *dhimma* as Iran Islamised, as indeed, Christians and Jews did elsewhere. Christianity continued to grow, however, and the Church of Iran has even been involved in missions to Central Asia, India, and China. In the twentieth century, the churches began to acquire relative freedom of worship, service, and witness. However, since the revolution in 1979, it is often asked to what extent *Velayat-e Faqih* has impacted Iranian Christians. Various attempts have been made, in the form of articles and resources, to respond to such a question. Although it is difficult to find many concrete responses to such a question, we attempt to address it in its diverse aspects. We have both been immersed in Iranian culture and life; one of us was born three years before the revolution and converted to Christianity at a young age, became a senior church leader, and belongs to the post-revolution generation, which has experienced the full impact of *Velayat-e Faqih*. The other is a student of Iranian language, culture, and religion and has been in Iran many times since the Islamic Revolution.

PRE-REVOLUTION CHRISTIANITY

Most New Testament scholars agree that the Magi, in the Gospel of Matthew, were from the Parthian Empire (ruled by one of the Iranian dynasties), which was centred in present-day Iran and Iraq.[1]

Biblically 'Parthians, Medes and Elamites, three tribes from Iran, were in Jerusalem on the day of Pentecost, and could have brought back Peter's message to their homeland'.[2] Historically, Christianity seems to have arrived in Iran from near the eastern borders of the Roman Empire, possibly during the second century CE. The ancient Liturgy of Addai and Mari bears witness to an early presence in and around Iran of the church that came to be called the Church of the East (sometimes erroneously called 'Nestorian').[3] Since the emergence of Christianity in Persia, converts have faced various kinds of opposition. However, there was no systemic persecution of Christians in the early period, although there was harassment. From the middle of the third century, the Sassanids gained ascendancy. They were heavily influenced by a Magian form of Zoroastrianism and wanted to emphasise their 'Persian-ness'. At first, there seems not to have been any extraordinary persecution of Christians, but this changed after the conversion of Constantine. In the very year that Christianity became the official religion of the Roman Empire, Constantine sent a letter to the Shahinshah Shapur II in which he asked for protection for Christians in the Persian Empire. This did not matter much while there was peace between the two superpowers, but when war broke out between them in 337 CE, Christians were accused of being sympathisers of the Romans and systematic persecution erupted.

At first, punitive taxation was levied on Christians. When they could not pay, their properties were expropriated, and they were imprisoned. When even this did not lead them to renounce their faith, churches were

---

[1] Dwight Longenecker, 'We Three Kings' Who Were the Magi? (2014) at https://www.catholiceducation.org/en/controversy/common-misconceptions/we-three-kings-who-were-the-magi.html (accessed 9 January 2022).

[2] Mark Bradley, *Iran and Christianity: Historical Identity and Present Relevance* (London, New York, Continuum International Publishing Group, 2008), 138.

[3] L. E. Browne, *The Eclipse of Christianity in Asia,* (Cambridge, CUP, 1933); Atiya Aziz, *A History of Eastern Christianity* (London, Methuen, 1968).

demolished, their sacred objects were confiscated, and bishops, priests, and deacons were imprisoned, tortured, and executed. The suffering of the Christians under Shapur was such that it is remembered in the region to this day. This continued until the accession of the Emperor Yazdigard, who concluded a peace treaty with the Romans and, in 410 CE, issued an Edict of Toleration for the Christians in his Empire. The edict gave Christians some freedom to worship and to regulate the internal life of their communities; it also gave the state a role in the church's affairs.[4] The edict did not mean the end of all persecution. The Law of Apostasy, forbidding a Zoroastrian to change his religion, was often a cause of persecution. The Magians were alarmed at the rapid growth of the church and sometimes incited persecution for this reason. If, moreover, there was conflict between the two empires, Christians were immediately viewed with suspicion and encountered hostility.[5] Despite all the socio-political challenges, Christianity survived and developed in the next centuries.

Islam arrived in Persia around 636 BCE when the Sassanids were defeated by the Arabs. As a result, most Iranians were gradually converted either forcibly, to escape the *dhimma*, or through assimilation mainly to Sunni Islam over a period of three centuries. Shi'ism begun to arise following the development of the Shi'a Twelver ideology,[6] and Shi'ism and the Shi'a population became the majority within society during the Safavid dynasty (1501–1736). They established Twelver Shi'ism throughout the dynasty as the state religion of Iran, and it 'was a major factor in the emergence of a unified national consciousness among the various ethnic and religious elements of the country'.[7] Shah Ismail Safavid (1501) was the pioneer who formed the first Shi'a state, and he later brought about the importation of Shi'i religious scholars from abroad. They came

---

4   William Young, *Patriarch, Shah and Caliph* (Rawalpindi, Christian Study Centre, 1974), 8.
5   Young, *Patriarch, Shah and Caliph*, 60.
6   Richard Bulliet, 'Islamic Iran, through the Eighteenth Century', Centre for Global Education, ASIA Society (2022), https://asiasociety.org/education/islamic-iran (accessed 3 September 2022).
7   *Encyclopaedia Iranica*, 'Constitutional Revolution', iii. The constitution, (2022) https://www.iranicaonline.org/articles/constitutional-revolution-iii (accessed 25 August 2022).

predominantly from the great scholarly school in Lebanon, which the Safavids used to legitimise their rulership, although Sunni Muslims initially were the native Muslims in Iran.[8]

Although Christian mission was increasingly circumscribed under Islam in Persia, the Church of the East continued, sometimes with renewed vigour, its missionary work in Central Asia, China, and India.[9] Assyrians[10] (Nestorians) and Armenians were the major ethnic Christian groups who were residents of Persia during Islamic rule as a minority among a Muslim majority under the socio-political arrangement of the *dhimma*.[11] Under the Ottomans, the ancient millet system of the Persians was adapted to the Islamic *dhimma* and served as a basis for the social and political organisation of the non-Muslim religious communities of the Empire until the reforms of the *tanzimat* in the nineteenth century. It has defined the thinking of many of these communities since, posing a challenge to national integration and unitary forms of government.[12] Some of the Georgian Christians and Armenians,[13] for instance, were enslaved and converted to Islam under the reforming but also cruel Shah 'Abbas I. Those who insisted on retaining their faith were forcibly moved from one place to another. The Armenians

---

8 Ori Goldberg, *Shi'a Theology in Iran, The Challenge of Religious Expectance* (Abington & New York: Routledge, 2012), 6–7.

9 See Igor De Rachewiltz, *Papal Envoys at the Court of the Great Khans* (Stanford: Stanford University Press, 1971); Henry Hill (Ed.), *Light from the East: A Symposium on the Oriental Orthodox and Assyrian Churches*, (Toronto: Anglican Book Centre, 1988).

10 Until modern times, the Assyrians—Syriac-speaking Middle Easterners—belonged throughout the medieval period to either of two branches of Eastern Christianity (Jacobite and Nestorian) The Assyrian community examined here was concentrated in Iranian Azerbaijan, mainly around the town of Urumiyah (Rizaiyah).

11 The Arabic term of *dhimma* or *dhimmi* refers to the status of Christians and Jews who are named as *ahl al-dhimma* 'protected peoples' (People of the Book) in and by Islamic states and countries, but this condition was not, at first, applied to other religious groups, although Zoroastrians were later included.

12 Michael Nazir-Ali, *Conviction and Conflict: Islam, Christianity and World Order* (London and New York: Continuum, 2006), 85.

13 Armenians have lived in Iran for around four centuries.

were given, however, some trade concessions; their newly established centre of New Julfa, near Isfahan, became and remains an important Christian site. Shah 'Abbas also allowed some Western religious orders to establish monastic houses in his territories. Later on, in the nineteenth century, many Armenians migrated to Russia but those who remained were used by the Qajar dynasty to open up Iran to the outside world.[14] Armenians along with Assyrians remained as major ethnic Christian minority groups in Iran.

In the nineteenth century, mission agencies from various Christian denominations began to work widely in Iran. For example, Henry Martyn, the great Anglican missionary and linguist, completed his translation of the New Testament into Farsi in 1812. Martyn's translation was soon complemented by William Glen's translation of the Old Testament.[15] Regarding the mission activities of various Western-origin denominations, Assyrians and Armenians as ethnic Persian Christians were at times not welcoming of the missions, but the most attractive aspect of the these missionaries was that they built schools and hospitals, and Muslim children were often the majority of those attending these schools.[16] Although the original aim of many of the missions had been to revitalise the ancient churches of Iran so they could engage in mission to the Muslim, Jewish, and Zoroastrian communities there, in fact, the result was often that members of the ancient churches broke away and formed Protestant churches of different kinds.[17] Alongside traditional/ancient churches, other evangelical churches and denominations emerged, such as Presbyterian and Pentecostal churches (Assemblies

---

14   P. M. Holt, Ann K. S. Lambton, and Bernard Lewis (Eds.), 'The Central Islamic Lands from Pre-Islamic Times to the First World War,' *The Cambridge History of Islam*, Vol IA, (Cambridge, CUP, 1970); Paul Hunt, *Inside Iran*, (Tring, Hertfordshire: Lion, 1981), 419; Hill, *Light from the East*, 14; Aziz, *A History of Eastern Christianity*.

15   David Bebbington, *Evangelicalism in Modern Britain: A History from the 1730s to the 1980s* (London, Unwin Hyman, 1989), 86; Jocelyn Murray, *Proclaim the Good News: A Short History of the Church Missionary Society* (London: Hodder and Stoughton, 1985), 137; Kelsey M. Finnie, *Beyond the Minarets: A Biography of Henry Martyn* (Chatham: CLC Publications, 1999); John Rooney, *The Hesitant Dawn* (Rawalpindi: Christian Study Centre, 1984), 77.

16   Eliz Sanasarian, *Religious Minorities in Iran* (Cambridge: CUP, 2000), 43–44.

17   Hill, *Light from the East*, 113; Murray, *Proclaim the Good News*, 136 and 290.

of God Church). Conversions to Christianity happened for Shi'a Muslims because of the work of missionaries, as well as evangelism by and the work of Armenians and Assyrians as ethnic Christians who were sometimes church leaders among believers of a Muslim background. The Church of Iran, with the mobilising and working of missional activities by foreign missions and ethnic Christians, continued to grow in various aspects. However, almost all foreign mission work ended abruptly with the revolution in 1979.

SOVEREIGNTY OF *VELAYAT-E FAQIH*

Iran had a long royalist history before revolution began in 1978. Iranian political identity has deep roots in the ancient Persian kings—Cyrus, Cambyses, Darius, Bahram, Ardeshir, Shahpur, Khosrow, and Nader Shah. Pride in being an Iranian goes back to this royalist history. The majority of Iranians do not acknowledge the tyrannical aspects of their kings; the focus is on their code of justice and charismatic rule under divine force or favour (*farr-i īzadī & Far-i Kayani*).[18] Despite the royalist political identity, however, the revolution in 1979 (later named the Islamic revolution) terminated the long history of the monarchist era and ushered in the Islamic Republic of Iran, an authoritarian theocratic regime formed by Shi'a clergy.[19] Ayatollah Ruhollah Khomeini as a Shi'a *Faqih* and a grand ayatollah overthrew the Pahlavi dynasty,[20] declaring the Islamic republic of Iran.[21] The Islamic revolution of 1979 in Iran can be compared with the French revolution of 1789 and the Russian revolution of 1917. This revolutionary event provided essential change when Ayatollah Ruhollah Khomeini succeeded in raising the banner of Islamic Shi'a theocracy in the royalist land of the kings.[22]

---

18 Mark Bradley, *Iran and Christianity: Historical Identity and Present Relevance*, 45.
19 Alexandros Simoglou, *Iran: A Brief Study of the Theocratic Regime* [Electronic], (2005), 5–8, https://www.files.ethz.ch/isn/26514/PN05.07.pdf, (accessed 10 August 2018).
20 The word 'ayatollah' means 'exemplar of Allah' or 'miraculous sign of God'.
21 BBC History, *Ayatollah Khomeini*, (2014), http://www.bbc.co.uk/history/historic_figures/khomeini_ayatollah.shtml, (accessed 07 July 2021).
22 Said Amir Arjomand, *The Turban for the Crown: The Islamic Revolution in Iran (Studies in Middle Eastern History)* (Oxford: Oxford University Press, 1988), 3.

Moreover, 'the Islamic Revolution was in effect the redefining of clerical aspirations no longer congruent with the temporal power of the state but in competition with the state and eventually taking control of the state.'[23] Khomeini was considered the founder of this new state with himself as the supreme leader.

Khomeini established the 'Twelvers' or *Ithna 'ashariyya*[24] domination with the Imams as the divinely appointed successors of Muhammad. Khomeini insisted that in the beginning God created human beings and that God has never left humanity without a leader. Subsequently, from Adam to Muhammad, prophets were appointed by God to guide the people to show them the righteous path and to forbid deviation. After the death of Muhammad, his twelve successors were to be the guiding Imams in the world.[25] Similarly, Shi'a clergy claim that Sharia law was given by God to Muslims that it might be implemented correctly and that no one knows Islam and its divine law better than the clergy. Khomeini himself insisted, 'it was natural that clergy (*Velayat-e Faqih*) should rule as guardians of the state until the return of the 12th divinely ordained Shi'a Imam al-Mahdi'.[26]

Khomeini had the power to engage in *ijtihad*,[27] and, following him, the jurisprudents (*fuqaha*) govern the state in the absence of the Twelve Imams. They are the appointed by God to rule and guard the Shi'a state.[28] 'The Shi'a classic law generally holds the position that in the absence of the Imam of the Age, any form of government, presumably even a government led by the jurists, is fundamentally "unjust" and therefore

---

23 Abbas Amanat, *Apocalyptic Islam and Iranian Shi'ism* (New York: I.B. Tauris & Co. Ltd., 2009), 11.

24 The mainstream Shi'ia Islam which believes in the 12 Shi'ia Imams; hence the name which means 'Twelvers'.

25 Imam Ruhollah Khomeini, *Islamic Government*, (Tehran: Entesharate Daftare Tablighate Islami, 1998), 24–25.

26 Kasra Aarabi, *What Is Velayat-e Faqih?* (2019), https://institute.global/policy/what-velayat-e-faqih (accessed 10 September 2021).

27 *Ijtihad* refers to independent reasoning and is contrasted with *taqlid* (conformity to legal precedent).

28 Tamara C. Mackenthun, 'Continuity in Iranian Leadership Legitimization: Farr-I Izadi, Shi'ism, and Velayat-e Faqih', (master's thesis, Boise State University, 2009), 82.

theoretically illegitimate'.[29] There is therefore no Shi'a classic traditional model that acknowledges the direct role of the *fuqaha* in governing the state. Yet, Khomeini arrogated for himself (and the clergy) the role of deputy in the absence of Imam al-Mahdi (a capable *Faqih*—*Velayat-e Faqih* is *Niyabat-i Imam*).

The new constitution was written in the light of Shi'a Twelver belief and Khomeini's theocratic concept. It was sanctioned by divine legitimisation of political authority.[30] After the revolution, the non-Shi'a Twelver minorities, including Christians, were deeply impacted socio-politically by the manifestation of *Velayat-e Faqih*. 'For Khomeini, Iran should not just be an Islamic republic but a clerical republic'.[31] He saw Iran as a pure Shi'a Muslim country, regardless of its ethnic and religious diversity. Subsequently, Article 12 of the 1979 Shi'a constitution recognised Iran as a Twelvers state despite the opposition of the Sunnis.[32]

Historically, over the centuries, the population of Iran has remained ethnically, linguistically, and religiously diverse. Religion has been an important constituent of the Iranian identity for millennia, and Iran is home to many diverse and ancient religions.[33] Before the revolution of 1979, every citizen, including the religious minority groups, were described as 'Irani', but after the Islamic revolution, 'Irani' was replaced by *aqaliyat* (minority) for Christians, Jews, and Sunnis. Likewise, 'Muslim sisters and brothers' replaced the term *hamvatan* (compatriot). There were objections to the use of the term of *aqaliyat* in Article 13 of the Islamic constitution for minorities at the Assembly of Experts,[34] because they rather preferred

---

29 Amanat Abbas, *Iran: A Modern History*, (New Haven & London: Yale University Press, 2017), 907. See also Tamara C. Mackenthun, 'Continuity in Iranian Leadership Legitimization', 82.
30 Ervand Abrahamian., *A History of Modern Iran*, (Cambridge and New York: Cambridge University Press, 2008), 163.
31 Khomeini, *Islamic Government*.
32 Sanasarian, *Religious Minorities in Iran*, 154.
33 United States Commission on International Religious Freedom (2016), https://www.uscirf.gov/sites/default/files/USCIRF_AR_2016_Tier1_Iran.pdf (accessed 4 July 2020).
34 The Assembly of Experts (*Majlis-e Khobregan*) for the Leadership is an 88-member body of Islamic jurists elected by direct popular vote every eight

the term *jawami* (communities), but later they agreed upon the use of *aqaliyat* to refer to the religious minority groups.³⁵ Khomeini's theocracy thus produced an authoritarian government and socio-political system with a dogmatic Shi'a ideology that does not tolerate differences in views or practice.

CONSTITUTIONAL RECOGNITION

The Shi'a constitution after the revolution recognised religious minorities, as did the 1906–1909 constitution (the Qajar and Pahlavi).³⁶ This is rooted, as noted, under the *dhimma* rule and the influences of Khomeini's view on *kafir dhimma*.³⁷ Here even the *ahl al kitab* are classified as infidels!

Article 13 recognised merely three minority religious groups: Armenian and Assyrian as Christian, Zoroastrians, and Jews. Article 14 of the Iranian constitution ensures the rights and protection of these religious minority groups. Article 64 allows the religious minorities to elect their own representatives to Parliament. The Majles (Parliament) has 270–290 representatives, including separate seats allocated to five non-Muslim members (five MPs) who are legitimately recognised by the constitution.³⁸ Article 26 provides permission to recognise religious groups as being able to establish socio-political and religious gatherings/societies, but they must not do anything that violates the principles of Iran's theocracy. Essentially, their purposes and activities within such gatherings/societies must not be against the Shi'a system created by *Velayat-e Faqih*. Finally, Article 19

---

years. According to the Constitution, the Assembly's mandate is to appoint, monitor, and dismiss the supreme leader.

35   Sanasarian, *Religious Minorities in Iran*, 154.
36   Edalatnejad Saeid, *Shiite Tradition, Rationalism and Modernity: The Codification of the Rights of Religious Minorities in Iranian Law (1906–2004)* (PhD thesis, The Department of History and Cultural Studies Institute for Islamic Studies, Free University Berlin, 2009), 165.
37   *Kafir dhimma* has been used by Khomeini and other Shi'a *Fuqaha* in Iran and is the same term and meaning as the Arabic word *dhimmi*, referring to followers of monotheistic religions, known as "People of the Book". The word *Kafir* means infidel.
38   Abrahamian, *A History of Modern Iran*, 166.

defines the equality of all people (citizens), groups, and ethnicities, regardless of the tribe or ethnic group to which they belong, and there is no specific indication of religion in that article. Constitutionally, all these five articles recognise and define the socio-political rights of three minority groups, and their positions are classified within the Shi'a system.

Nonetheless, there are other Iranian religious groups, such as the Buddhists, Hindus, Gnostics, Bahais, and, in particular, Christian converts from Islam. These are all unrecognised by the Shi'a constitution, for they are not part of the *dhimma*. In other words, there is no social-legal definition of Christian converts from Islam, because they are not part of the two ethnic Christian groups (Armenian and Assyrian). In post-revolution Iran, the legal terms of 'Recognised' and 'Unrecognised' have been used to distinguish religious minority groups legally and constitutionally, particularly in distinguishing Armenians/Assyrians and converts to Christianity. Thus, the undefined rights of such minorities have had unpleasant socio-political implications.

IMPLICATIONS AND RESPONSES

The application of Khomeini's ideology created a complex totalitarian system. It privileged the Shi'a. Although Articles 14, 19, and specifically Article 23 in the constitution promised freedom of belief,[39] nevertheless, gradually the ideal of these articles changed with socio-political pressure. This led to the persecution of religious minorities and, particularly, Iranian Christians.[40]

Recognised Christians (Armenian/Assyrian) as Iranian citizens, based on Article 19, are entitled to all the rights of equality in the country. Yet these rights are limited under the 'Islamic law and some of those limitations have been outlined in the Iran Penal Code of Practice'. State legislation sets and defines the socio-economic and religious boundaries/limitations for their governmental and social relationships, as well their

---

39   Article 23: The investigation of individuals' beliefs is forbidden, and no one may be molested or taken to task simply for holding a certain belief.
40   Mark Bradley, *Iran and Christianity: Historical Identity and Present Relevance*, 3 and 164.

political and economic engagement.[41] Despite recognition of their legal rights by the Constitution, they are liable to face socio-political challenges because they do not technically belong to the pure Shi'a society and the state.

Armenian and Assyrian Christians do have representatives in the *Majles*, but all such positions are vetted by the *fuqaha*.[42] Islamic Shi'a tradition forms and spreads a social mentality against Christians, stating that they are *najess'*(unclean) and *kafir* (infidel). Christian religious practices have been tolerated by the state, and they are allowed to hold their religious services, events, ceremonies, and holidays, though the authorities must be notified in advance regarding each religious event and the exact dates of these observances. All notes of speeches and talks delivered must be submitted for authorisation to the *Vezarat-e Farhang va Ershad-e Islami* (the Ministry of Culture and Islamic Guidance). Additionally, restrictions are applied for religious publications; particularly, it is forbidden to import and print the Bible in Iran. Christians are to avoid proselytising and not allowed to invite any outsider to their religious ceremonies. All church leaders are forced to 'sign a form confirming that Muslims would not be allowed into their religious centres and gatherings'.[43] This has pushed non-Muslims to become segregated within their communities. Archbishop Sebouh Sarkissian, the prelate of the Armenian Church in Iran, responded to the socio-political pressures on Armenians in order to protect the religious and national identity of the group:

> Keeping the language and keeping the Christian faith as our identity is the way to protect our existence. Either you are Armenian and part of the church community or you are not. If you are part of the church community, then you are in and you will be under the protection of the Armenian community in the country.

---

41   Sara Afshari, 'Marginalization and Negotiation of Boundaries: The Case of the Armenian Church in Iran', *Mission Studies* no. 38 (2021): 283. https://doi.org/10.1163/15733831-12341794.

42   Christian A. Van Gorder, *Christianity in Persia and the Status of Non-Muslims in Iran*, (Lanham, Boulder, New York & Plymouth, UK: Lexington Books, 2010), 176.

43   Sanasarian, *Religious Minorities in Iran*, 74, 77.

> Otherwise, in a global society, you will get lost.... We have many restrictions, and some of these restrictions have been created by ourselves over time to protect our existence in this country. For example, we don't allow mixed marriages. You have to understand our situation. Our main aim is to protect our religious identity, national identity, and language identity. Secondly, within the political situation of Iran, one needs to be more careful even in choosing friends.[44]

Inwardness is an inevitable response to ongoing discrimination and restrictions on all Christians. The power of the Shi'a state has been absolute: 'If you do not obey, you will be annihilated.'[45] Since Khomeini, the state's tolerance has been further reduced. Even recognised Christians face discrimination and restrictions; in order to survive, many of them emigrate to the West.

One of the significant impacts of Khomeini's *Velayat-e Faqih* on Shi'a Muslims in Iran has been conversion to Christianity. Based on the latest official reports, post-revolution, Iran has shown an increase of Muslim Shi'a converting to Christianity as an 'unrecognised religious minority'. For example, referring to the latest statistics, 'researchers have credited the underground evangelical house church in Iran as the fastest growing Christian church in the world, and it has unique characteristics that defy comparison with churches in America and Europe'.[46] The majority of those in the underground house churches are not from the ethnic minority Christianity (Armenians, Assyrians); rather, they are from Iranian Shi'a background. The number of conversions has also significantly increased. These groups are largely Protestant and evangelical, actively share their

---

44 Sara Afshari, 'Marginalization and Negotiation of Boundaries: The Case of the Armenian Church in Iran', *Mission Studies* 38 no. 2 (2021): 290. doi: https://doi.org/10.1163/15733831-12341794

45 James A. Haught, *Holy Horrors: An Illustrated History of Religious Murder and Madness* (Buffalo, New York: Prometheus Books, 1990), 200.

46 Mark Ellis, 'Fastest Growing Church Has No Buildings, No Central Leadership, and Is Mostly Led by Women', God Reports (2019), http://godreports.com/2019/09/fastest-growing-church-has-no-buildings-no-central-leadership-and-is-mostly-led-by-women/ (accessed 6 July 2020).

religious beliefs, and, according to the International Federation for Human Rights, have been subject to persecution.⁴⁷

Many factors have led to such conversions. These include personal evangelism by evangelical house church groups despite persecutions and 24/7 Christian satellite channels used for preaching and teaching the Bible in Farsi. However, one of the main reasons seems to be the increasing disillusionment and scepticism among ordinary and intellectual people toward the totalitarian system and its consequences over the past forty years. Being a spiritual people, most Iranians are unable to ignore Christianity as an alternative.

Traditionally, Islam does not allow conversion. Those who violate this rule are commonly considered apostates and legally the penalty could be death.⁴⁸ However, the level of punishment for apostasy is left to the judges; the term is *Ta'zir*;⁴⁹ consequently, converts could face a variety of sentences short of death. One of the key roots of opposition and mistreatment goes back to Khomeini himself. In his addresses, he encouraged anger against religious minorities, including Christians, as well as marginalising them.⁵⁰ Khomeini in his speeches (post-revolution) referred to religious minorities, including Christians of all denominations, as conspirators and economic plunderers who were enemies of the truth of Islam and of all Muslim intellectuals.⁵¹ In the era of his successor, Khomeini's legacy remains. 'The regime's revolutionary ideology has had all the necessary elements for nurturing prejudicial tendencies: anti-Israeli and

---

47   Federation for Human Rights (FIDH), (2019), 21, https://www.fidh.org/IMG/pdf/IrandiscrimLDDH1545a.pdf (accessed 6 July 2020).

48   Bijan DaBell, 'The Iran Primer, Iran Minorities', (2013), https://iranprimer.usip.org/blog/2013/sep/03/iran-minorities-1-diverse-religions (accessed 7 September 2019), 1.

49   *Ta'zir* literally means to prohibit, to assist, and to punish. In the jurisprudential terminology, it refers to punishments that inhibit the commitment of sins. It is a sort of punishment that is not explicitly specified in shari'a and the specification of its type and amount is left to the shari'a ruler or the judge.

50   A. Christian Van Gorder, *Christianity in Persia and the Status of Non-Muslims in Modern Iran*, (Lexington Books, 2010), 182.

51   Kathryn Spellman, *Religion and Nation: Iranian Local and Transnational Networks in Britain* (New York: Berghahn Books, 2004), 165.

anti-Zionist feelings, anti-imperialism, anti-Westernism, and xenophobia. Consequently, espionage, conspiracy, sabotage, serving as agents of some perceived enemy became convenient accusations to be used against anyone for any reason.'[52]

The Shi'a state justifies persecution of Christians in the name of national security. This is why all foreign Christian missionaries were forced to leave the country. The state issued no further missionary or humanitarian visas for foreign workers. Clearly, there was high suspicion of foreigners who could serve as spies. In February 1979, actual persecution began, when some Anglican institutions were closed down, properties were confiscated, and some Anglican Church members were arrested and held without trials. Eight days after the revolution began, on 19 February 1979, Rev. Arastoo Sayyah, an Anglican priest, who had converted from Islam, was brutally murdered in the offices of his Anglican church in Shiraz. 'The Anglican hospital in Isfahan was closed by the government, and the Anglican Church and its offices were raided and looted by known members of the Islamic Propagation Society who declared that the hospital was a first-class spy base of the West.'[53] Later, an attempt was made to assassinate the Anglican Bishop Hasan Dehqani-Tafti (a convert from Islam) and his wife in their bedroom with gunshots, but both survived.[54] Their 24-year-old son, Bahram Dehqani, was murdered 'when his car was forced off the road and then commandeered by a gunman who took him to a remote spot in northwest Teheran before executing him'.[55] There are other Anglican Church leaders who have been imprisoned or exiled, but all denominational churches in Iran suffered greatly from the beginning of the *Velyat-e Faqih*.

The Protestant churches suffered even more severe persecutions than the Anglican Church and Catholic Church, partly 'due to their tendency to proselytise, and because many of their adherents were converts. In 1988 three protestant churches closed down and later, a few more in the 1990s, including the Bible Society, the Garden of Evangelism, a

---

52 Sanasarian, *Religious Minorities in Iran*, 128.
53 Van Gorder, *Christianity in Persia*, 178–180.
54 Sanasarian, *Religious Minorities in Iran*, 123.
55 Van Gorder, *Christianity in Persia*, 181–182.

camp and training centre.[56,57] Several Protestant-Evangelical Christian church leaders have been executed extrajudicially since the early days of the revolution.[58] The manner of their disappearances and the consistency of the design of their deaths have made most observers suspect the Iranian governmental authorities themselves.[59] For example, Rev. Hossain Soodmand, who converted before the 1979 revolution and was the pastor of a house church in Mashhad, was arrested and tortured before being hanged after a ruling by an Islamic clerical court convicted him of apostasy, without his family's knowledge. He was the first and the last convert who was executed officially by the Shi'a state, then buried in the place titled as the 'cursed ground' in the city of Mashhad.[60] Afterwards, a number of other Protestant leaders were pursued and mysteriously killed, such as Bishop Haik Hovsapain-Mehr, Rev. Mehdi Dibaj, Rev. Tateos Michaelian, Pastor Mohammad-Bagher Yusefi, and Pastor Ghorban Tourani.

In recent years, most church buildings, including Armenian and Assyrian churches, which held Farsi language services, have been shut down. The converts are forced to go underground and meet for worship in homes instead of church buildings; from this have emerged the house church groups throughout Iran. The *Telegraph* newspaper reported in 2018:

---

56 Sanasarian, *Religious Minorities in Iran*, 123, 125.
57 Examples include closing church bookstores in four cities; closing churches in Sari and Mashhad; limiting the activities of the Ahvaz church to Sundays only; threats against and beating of church members for obtaining information; etc.
58 This includes Christian converts from Muslim backgrounds and Armenian and Assyrian Christians who were involved in serving Muslim-background converts.
59 Eliz Sanasarian and Avi Davidi, *Domestic Tribulations and International Repercussions: The State and the Transformation of Non-Muslims in Iran* (Business Source Premier, 2007), 2.
60 Leah MarieAnn Klett, 'Iran Bulldozes Over Grave of Pastor Executed for Converting to Christianity after Seeing Jesus in Dream', *The Christian Post* (2020), https://www.christianpost.com/news/iran-bulldozes-over-grave-of-pastor-executed-for-converting-to-christianity-after-seeing-jesus-in-dream.html (accessed 25 October 2022).

> There are no official records, but there are estimated to be some 350,000 (Christians) remaining in Iran—some one per cent of Iran's population, with a rising trend toward converting to Christianity. . . . While worship is permitted under the Islamic Republic's constitution, conversion to Christianity can be a crime meriting a sentence of more than 10 years imprisonment. Iran's powerful mullahs are committed to expanding the influence of Shia Islam and blame "foreign influence" for the conversions. There are many reports that this has contributed to the government's ever-increasing dependence on hard-line Islamic ayatollahs, who naturally see Christianity as a threat to their power. For this reason, it's not surprising that we're seeing an increase in Christian persecution. It has become increasingly common for authorities to arrest worshippers, raid house churches, and confiscate Bibles.[61]

Human Rights organisations have organised the long list of intensified persecution of Anglican and Protestant converts. Consequences of conversion include closing several churches, banning the use of Persian language in sermons and services, restricting the publication of Bibles, and strictly prohibiting Muslims from attending services. Existing converts from Islam are put under particular surveillance, suffering denial of freedom of assembly and association; denial of freedom of expression; state systematic discrimination, harassment, and monitoring; arbitrary arrest and detention; employment discrimination; denial of education (higher education); and discrimination in marriage and family life. There is deprivation of access to justice, lack of due process in court proceedings, and finally the state prosecution of converts as national security threats. All of these lead to many Christians fleeing the country.[62] Frequently, Articles 499 and 500 of the penal code in Iran have been used 'in the prosecution of converts and have

---

61   Josie Ensor, 'Iran Arrests More Than 100 Christians in Growing Crackdown on Minority', *The Telegraph*, 10 December 2018, https://www.telegraph.co.uk/news/2018/12/10/iran-arrests-100-christians-growing-crackdown-minority/ (accessed 9 September 2019).
62   International Campaign for Human Rights in Iran, *The Cost of Faith: Persecution of Christian Protestants and Converts in Iran*, (New York Headquarters: 2013), 8–12.

been amended to widen the scope for prosecuting Christians, especially converts from Islam to Christianity, whom the regime defines as members of "sects" and "cults"'.[63]

CONCLUSION

We conclude with the following observations.

The first is a socio-political observation: the Shi'a Twelver ideology of *Velayat-e Faqih* is a form of rulership that is religiously justified and is totalitarian in system. It recognises some and excludes others, especially minorities, in varying degrees. Shi'a Muslims also feel the effect of this in that they are not free to be nominal Muslims and are not permitted to exercise agency through conversion to Christianity or any other faith. The so-called recognised Christians, Armenian or Assyrian, have the *dhimmi* status but they also experience being second-class citizens. Christian converts are seen as *kafirs* and apostate, members of sects and cults, pro-west, pro-Zionist (Christian Zionist), and anti-Islamic; they have, therefore, been treated as a national security threat. The manner of the state's understanding of conversion causes real problems as a result of the absence of legal recognition, civil-social rights, protection and safety by the country's law, and a place to worship or have fellowship. All this leads to their marginalisation and suffering as described above; in many cases, this also leads to some finding ways to leave the country.

The second observation is a spiritual one: Iran and Persia have had a special place in the Bible. In the midst of the darkness of Shi'a totalitarianism and *Velayat-e Faqih,* God has begun a new chapter for Christianity in Iran since the 1979 revolution. This is evidenced by the Christian faith spreading widely among Shi'a Muslims compared to the pre-revolution period. Since the revolution, a common expression among worldwide Christians is 'Ayatollah Khomeini was an influential evangelist for Iranians!' To some extent, this is true because the sense of disillusionment

---

63   Pat Ashworth, "Christians in Iran under Pressure, COI Report Says', Church Times (2022), https://www.churchtimes.co.uk/articles/2022/14-october/news/world/christians-in-iran-under-pressure-coi-report-says (accessed 25 October 2022).

among the Shi'a people and their scepticism about their Shi'a context/faith has grown. The house churches in Iran (and among Iranians abroad) have consequently seen rapid growth, new forms of worship, and godly leaders. One needs to see the impact of *Velayat-e Faqih,* therefore, also in terms of church growth. We have directly experienced how Jesus Christ changes and transforms people's lives and uses them to witness to the Kingdom of God in the nation of Iran and beyond. It is our prayer and hope that this work will continue in the years ahead.

PART II

CHRISTIAN MINORITY RESPONSES

6

FROM RETREAT TO SOCIAL ENGAGEMENT
The Dynamics of Marginalisation among Pentecostal-Catholic Relationships in Rural El Salvador

Ronald T. Bueno and James G. Huff Jr.

The rapid growth of Pentecostal churches in El Salvador over the past five decades offers a rich opportunity to explore how relationships between Salvadorans who affiliate with different Christian faith traditions have evolved over time. For most of its history, the Republic of El Salvador (which means The Saviour) was a place where the institutional Catholic Church exercised considerable influence over the economic, political, and socio-cultural dynamics of everyday life. Until recently, the overwhelming majority of Salvadorans identified as Catholics and maintained strong attachments to the church. The emergence of the first Pentecostal congregations in rural communities among peasant (*campesino*) households at the beginning of the twentieth century marked an inconspicuous start to a movement that eventually transformed the religious landscape of El Salvador. One hundred years later, nearly 40 percent (roughly 2.7 million) of Salvadorans identify themselves as Protestant *evangelico* Christians, and the overwhelming majority of these adherents attend churches that are part of various Pentecostal movements.[1]

---

[1] IUDOP, *Encuesta sobre la religión para las y los salvadoreños,* Serie de Informes 122 (San Salvador: Universidad Centroamericana 'José Simeón Cañas', 2009);

Since the early 2000s, our scholarly and practitioner work has focused on documenting and understanding the dynamics of religious and social change generated by the growth of the Pentecostal movement in contemporary El Salvador. Our research has detailed how Pentecostals in rural communities engage in projects of social change and has explained how such work shapes their self-understandings, practical theologies, ritual practices, and internal organisation as local congregations.[2] Notably, our studies have examined how relationships between diverse religious and social actors have changed over time as leaders and members of Pentecostal churches have steadily increased their involvement in the political, economic, and social dimensions of rural community life. The question proposed here—what it means to be a Pentecostal Christian in communities where the dominant Christian tradition has been Roman Catholicism—offers an opportunity to reconsider our own research findings in a novel way.

The chapter traces three historical periods to describe how relationships between Catholic and Pentecostal Christians in El Salvador have evolved since the beginning of the twentieth century. In each period, we consider the dynamic interplay of culture and power in the reproduction of social relationships between Catholic and Pentecostals in rural

---

Timothy Wadkins, 'Getting Saved in El Salvador: The Preferential Option for the Poor', *International Review of Missions* 97 (2008): 31–49.

2   Ronald Bueno, 'Translating Pentecost into Transformed Communities in El Salvador: Social Engagement as a New and Contested Ritual', in *Pentecostals and Charismatics in Latin America and Latino Communities*, eds. Nestor Medina and Sammy Alfaro (New York: Palgrave Macmillan, 2015), 67–79; Ronald Bueno, 'Community Engagement as a New and Contested Ritual: An Ethnographic Study of Five Pentecostal Congregations in El Salvador', (PhD thesis, Middlesex University London, 2019); James G. Huff, 'Pentecostalized Development and Novel Social Imaginaries in Rural El Salvador', *Journal of Latin American and Caribbean Anthropology* 19 no. 1 (2014): 22–40; James G. Huff, 'Pentecostal Socialities and Transforming Rural El Salvador', in *Global Renewal Christianity: Spirit-Empowered Movements Past, Present and Future, Volume 2: Latin America*, eds. Vinson Synan, Amos Yong, and Migual Alvarez (Lake Mary: Charisma House, 2016), 55–76; James G. Huff, 'Of Specters and Spirit: Neoliberal Entanglements of Faith-Based Development in El Salvador', *Urban Anthropology* 46 no, 3,4 (2017): 173–220.

communities. To delineate these dynamics, we use Sidney Mintz's concepts of inside and outside meaning.³ In his studies of food and power, Mintz employs the concept of inside meaning to highlight how humans create meaning within their shared, ordinary routines of food production and consumption. We use inside meaning, or the 'interior embedding of significance in the activity of daily life, with its specific associations (including affective associations) for the actors' involved,⁴ to explore the significance of being a Pentecostal Christian in communities where Catholicism was the default lived religion for most of the twentieth century. Mintz clarifies that the production of inside meaning always occurs within 'larger, more encompassing social, economic, political, and institutional systems and environs,' which he identifies as 'outside meaning'.⁵ Outside meaning refers to the 'background conditions against which inside meaning takes its characteristic shape'.⁶ In each of the historical periods we consider, we describe the conditions that shaped how Pentecostals made sense of their experience and how they interacted with their Catholic neighbours.

A primary claim of our discussion is that Pentecostal social engagement shifted in form and meaning as the historical and cultural conditions changed in El Salvador throughout the twentieth century.⁷ The Pentecostal movement began toward the end of the 1800s during a turbulent re-ordering of social and economic relationships. The earliest Pentecostal

---

3   Sidney Mintz, *Sweetness and Power: The Place of Sugar in Modern History* (New York: Penguin Books, 1986); Sidney Mintz, *Tasting Food, Tasting Freedom: Excursions into Eating, Culture and the Past* (Boston: Beacon Press, 1995); Sidney Mintz, 'Food and Its Relationship to Concepts of Power', in *Food and Agrarian Orders in the World-Economy*, ed. Philip McMichael (Westport: Praeger Publisher, 1995), 3–13.
4   Mintz, 'Food and Its Relationship to Concepts of Power', 6.
5   Mintz, 'Food and Its Relationship to Concepts of Power', 5.
6   Mintz, 'Food and Its Relationship to Concepts of Power', 6–7.
7   The chapter includes data generated from a five-year ethnographic study of five Pentecostal churches within their social fields of development in El Salvador. The field research included extensive participant observation in church services, community meetings and events, and project worksites. The research also included forty-five semi-structured interviews of pastors, volunteer church leaders, and members and thirty-one semi-structured interviews of community leaders from five different communities.

adherents were displaced and marginalised peasants who sought safe relationships outside of the primarily Catholic-controlled socio-economic order. They restricted their public activities to evangelism. As broader political-economic and institutional changes occurred, such as the eroding of the Catholic canopy, the entrenchment of neoliberal development capitalism, and shifts in the social locations of some of its adherents, different Pentecostal groups became more socially engaged.

CATHOLIC RETRENCHMENT AND LIBERAL REFORMS

The origins of the first Pentecostal groups in El Salvador occur against the backdrop of larger religious and political-economic changes unfolding at the dawn of the twentieth century. The power of the Catholic Church, which had maintained considerable influence over most aspects of social, political, and economic life in El Salvador for nearly four centuries, was greatly diminished by the end of the nineteenth century. Although Catholicism was recognised by the Salvadoran government as the official religion in 1862, church and state relations became increasingly strained as liberal politicians gained power and legislated reforms that aimed to 'secularize and laicize El Salvador'.[8] In the ensuing decades, consecutive liberal governments further diminished the power of the Catholic Church by introducing constitutional provisions that granted freedom of religion to citizens, authorised public education, and greatly restricted the church's landholdings.[9]

Although the influence of the institutional Catholic church was greatly reduced by liberal reforms, Catholicism remained the default lived religion for the majority of Salvadorans at the beginning of the twentieth century. Local institutions and public gathering spaces that were built or sponsored by the Catholic Church (e.g., schools and community halls) still shaped community life, and Catholic leaders continued to wield influence

---

8   Edward Mikus, 'The Catholic Church and the Formation of Human Rights Doctrine in El Salvador', (master's thesis, CUNY Hunter College, 2017), 28.
9   Mikus, 'The Catholic Church and the Formation of Human Rights Doctrine in El Salvador', 28.

over local social hierarchies. Catholic pastoral workers, for example, generally 'directed their attention to parishes and schools serving the wealthier class' and 'church officials sided with the ruling classes on most social issues'.[10]

The transformation in church-state relations in El Salvador in the late nineteenth century was initiated in part by the actions of landed elites, who sought to move El Salvador toward an export-led, cash-crop economy. To this end, the government conscripted and privatised common lands held by indigenous groups to increase agricultural production of cash crops such as coffee, sugarcane, and indigo. The landed elite established large plantations called *haciendas* that created two new classes in the Salvadoran population: peasant labourers, who had inadequate land to support their families and worked on the hacienda during and beyond the harvest season, and the *colonos,* or resident labourers whom landlords provided with land in return for labour services.[11] With limited access to credit and legal recourse, many peasants lost their common lands to a group of wealthy families, which by the twentieth century owned 80 percent of the arable land in the country.[12]

Peasant populations were displaced from fertile common land, which they had cultivated for subsistence and economic growth, and were forced into exploitative labour on the *haciendas*.[13] Many peasant households were forced to move to remote, less arable locations to live, obligating them to migrate during the harvest season and work for three months on large plantations as day or seasonal labourers. Other peasant

---

10 Philip J. Williams and Anna Peterson, 'Evangelicals and Catholics in El Salvador: Evolving Religious Responses to Social Change', *Journal of Church and State* 38 no. 4 (1996): 875.

11 Jeffrey Gould and Aldo Lauria-Santiago, *To Rise in Darkness: Revolution, Repression, and Memory in El Salvador, 1920–1932* (Durham: Duke University Press, 2008).

12 Alastair White, *El Salvador*, 6th ed. vol. 12, *Colección Estructuras y Procesos* (San Salvador: UCA Editores, 2001), 66.

13 Aldo Lauria-Santiago, 'Land, Community, and Revolt in Late Nineteenth-Century Indian Izalco', in *Landscapes of Struggle: Politics, Society, and Community in El Salvador*, eds. Aldo Laurie-Santiago and Leigh Binford (Pittsburg: University of Pittsburgh Press, 2004).

households stayed close to the large plantations to find work and lived as squatters with limited access to land to cultivate for their subsistence; yet others became *colonos* on the haciendas. Such economic dynamics made it very difficult for most peasant families to sustain their livelihoods. Most peasant households had little to no influence over political life at the communal, municipal, or national levels. Many of these same marginalised and displaced peasants were among the first congregants in Pentecostal gatherings in El Salvador.[14] The steady increase of Protestant missionaries in Latin America in the early twentieth century was viewed by Catholic officials as another concerning development that threatened to further undermine the church's influence. The expansion of Protestant mission 'coincided with the advent of US imperialism' in Latin America, and even though most 'Protestant missionaries did not actively promote [US] intervention . . . or the institutionalization of the agro-export economy . . . Protestantism was nevertheless linked to the festering issue of US domination' in the region.[15] Not surprisingly, the Catholic hierarchy considered the 'influx of Protestant missionaries as a way for liberal governments to further neutralize the role of the Church'.[16] Some officials went as far as endorsing aggressive tactics to dissuade Protestant missionaries from working in Latin America, 'such as locking evangelical halls, slashing tires on missionary vehicles, and even organizing Bible burnings'.[17] Such tactics suggest, at the very least, that conversion to Protestant Christianity could come with considerable social costs.

---

14   Everett Wilson, 'Sanguine Saints: Pentecostalism in El Salvador', *Church History* 52 (1983), 186–198; Philip J. Williams, 'The Sound of Tambourines: The Politics of Pentecostal Growth in El Salvador', in *Power, Politics, and Pentecostal in Latin America*, eds. Edward L. Cleary and Hannah W. Stewart-Gambino (Boulder: Westview Press, 1997), 179–200.

15   Michael Dodson, 'Tradition and Change in the Latin American Catholic Church: A Comparison of El Salvador and Nicaragua', *Renaissance and Modern Studies* 36 no. 1 (1993): 127.

16   Mikus, 'The Catholic Church and the Formation of Human Rights Doctrine in El Salvador', 43.

17   Mikus, 'The Catholic Church and the Formation of Human Rights Doctrine in El Salvador', 43.

We turn here to consider how the first groups of Pentecostal adherents managed their religious and social lives in contexts where their faith was viewed by some as a threat to dominant forms of Christianity. Scholars have noted that the first Protestant churches in El Salvador generally belonged to one of two groups: the historical or mainline Protestant churches (e.g., Lutherans, Methodists, etc.) and the 'evangelical' churches, which are primarily affiliated with Pentecostal movements.[18] The origins of Pentecostalism in El Salvador occurred around the same time as the revival at the Azusa Street Mission (1906) in the United States. Robeck notes that the first report of Pentecostalism in El Salvador was in 1905 by Central American missionary Robert Bender.[19] Although Bender did not identify as Pentecostal, one of his missionary communiques to his constituents in the United States observed:

> On the last day of our meetings there we taught them the condition for the reception of the Holy Ghost with power. Some thirty remained to an aftermeeting [sic.]. We together waited upon God for the infilling of the spirit and all of a sudden, the power came upon us, and we were all filled with the Holy Ghost to which all testified. God has most graciously visited us with salvation.[20]

Wilson has offered a similar description of the meeting of a small congregation in western El Salvador among coffee plantation workers:[21]

> Worship in the rustic church on the Volcano of Santa Ana was simple and spontaneous. Meetings often were extended prayer sessions, developing occasionally into boisterous displays of emotion, tongues, and ecstasy. Members perceived these episodes of visions, weeping, and healings, accompanied by a sense of prophetic power, as self-authenticating evidence of divine presence.[22]

---

18   Williams and Peterson, 'Evangelicals and Catholics in El Salvador,' 876.
19   John Mark Robeck, *Towards a Pentecostal Theology of Praxis: A Case Study* (Lanham: Rowman & Littlefield), 73–76.
20   Robeck, *Towards a Pentecostal Theology of Praxis*, 73.
21   Wilson, 'Sanguine Saints', 186–198.
22   Wilson, 'Sanguine Saints', 189.

Notably, the congregants of these churches tended to withdraw from the social life of the communities they inhabited, a pattern that has been documented in other Latin American countries.[23] US missionaries affiliated with the 'holiness traditions' of Protestant Christianity encouraged the first converts to separate themselves from the 'corrupting' world.[24] This meant breaking from previous relationships and cultural practices, which were rooted in catholicised traditions and were viewed as impediments to converts' new spiritual trajectories. Church leaders also insisted that new members be grafted into a new community—the local Pentecostal congregation. The more embedded converts became in their congregations, the more they abandoned their affiliations with the local Catholic Church and became disconnected from their Catholic family and friends.

The imposed segregation and voluntary retreat from previous relationships further drove converted Pentecostal members away from social and political events and activities at the community level. Many retreated from formal political activities because they believed that the activities were corrupt or corrupting to their primary goal of 'personal transformation'.[25] Others felt that participating in such activities was unsafe and 'ineffective'.[26] Yet, even as they opted to retreat into their congregations to focus on projects of self and family transformation, Pentecostals shared certain eschatological beliefs (e.g., that Christ's return was imminent) that promoted evangelism as the primary purpose of interacting with non-Pentecostal (e.g., Catholic) neighbours and family members.[27] Accordingly, the one-on-one conversations they had with 'non-believers' and the

---

23   David Martin, *Tongues of Fire: The Explosion of Protestantism in Latin America* (Oxford: Basil Blackwell, 1990).

24   Allan Anderson, *An Introduction to Pentecostalism* (Cambridge: Cambridge University Press, 2004); Frans Kamsteeg, *Prophetic Pentecostalism in Chile: A Case Study on Religion and Development Policy* (Lanham: The Scarecrow Press, 1998).

25   Steve Offutt, *New Centers of Global Evangelicalism in Latin America and Africa* (New York: Cambridge University Press, 2015); Timothy Wadkins, *The Rise of Pentecostalism in Modern El Salvador: From the Blood of the Martyrs to the Baptism of the Spirit* (Waco: Baylor University Press, 2017).

26   Offutt, *New Centers of Global Evangelicalism*, 6.

27   Offutt, *New Centers of Global Evangelicalism*, 131.

small public meetings they organised on street corners and plazas aimed primarily to convert their Catholic neighbours.

We note a few patterns in this first phase of Catholic and Pentecostal social relations. First, the political-economic changes generated by liberal reforms significantly impacted the influence of the Catholic Church. Such structural changes are fundamental to understanding the dynamic evolution of Catholic and Pentecostal relationships at the community level for the remainder of the twentieth century. Second, Catholic officials viewed newly forming Pentecostal groups as another threat to power just as the Catholic influence over social and political life was diminishing. The actual numbers of Pentecostal converts at the time was small, and these new adherents remained a minority Christian group in El Salvador for most of the twentieth century. Third, everyday life for this small group of Pentecostal converts was challenging, given that most were from economically marginalised and politically disenfranchised households located in rural communities. Although they coped with similar socio-economic conditions as their Catholic neighbours, their conversion to Pentecostalism engendered new forms of differentiation in local social and religious networks. Their retreat to their new congregation was likely prompted as much by internal dynamics (e.g., spiritualties that stressed separation from a corrupt world) as by external ones (e.g., experiences of exclusion in the wider community).

POLITICAL VIOLENCE, CATHOLIC SCHISM, AND CRISIS

Liberal reforms created political and economic foundations that shaped state-society relations for the rest of the twentieth century. The establishment of the coffee economy and the 'expropriation of indigenous lands' corresponded with the 'creation of a repressive security apparatus' that regularly used lethal violence to eliminate popular resistance to the status quo.[28] Various 'crises of hegemony' for the 'original liberal state model'[29] shaped the dynamics of Catholic and Pentecostal relationships.

---

28 Joaquin M. Chavez, 'An Anatomy of Violence in El Salvador', *NACLA Report on the Americas* 37 no. 6 (2016): 32.
29 Chavez, 'An Anatomy of Violence', 32.

The first crisis was the 'indigenous uprising' and the subsequent ethnocide, known as *La Matanza* (The Massacre), which occurred in 1932.[30] Rapidly decreasing coffee prices in the 1930s resulted in massive unemployment and civil unrest in the countryside. Peasant groups, composed mostly of indigenous people, mobilised protests to demand better wages and working conditions on coffee plantations. The state responded with lethal violence, and soldiers killed an estimated thirty thousand peasants in approximately one week. *La Matanza* marked the beginning of decades of authoritarian rule by military dictatorships that regularly exercised 'state terror and terrorism' to 'mediate class and ethnic conflicts'.[31] The military, bolstered by the oligarchy, ruled the country until the late 1980s.

Several important changes in outside meaning developed in the years following *La Matanza*. The first concerned structural changes in the economy, which remained organised around the cultivation and export of agricultural commodities (e.g., coffee, sugar, and cotton), but became increasingly industrialised over time. By the mid-twentieth century, military leaders implemented import substitution industrialisation to stimulate domestic manufacturing,[32] and the steady growth of local industry in turn 'attracted migrants to the cities and converted urban poor into workers'.[33] As we note below, some Pentecostal groups in these newly forming urban communities began to experiment with novel forms of social engagement during this period.

A second dynamic concerns the living conditions of Salvadorans who remained in rural communities. Many *campesinos* were 'landless or nearly so' and during the harvest seasons migrated to large farms and 'coffee

---

30 Chavez, 'An Anatomy of Violence'.
31 Chavez, 'An Anatomy of Violence', 32-33.
32 Import substitution industrialisation refers to a set of national economic development policies adopted by various Latin American governments in the 1950s and 1960s to spur the growth of domestic markets and the production of manufactured goods.
33 Kati Giffith and Leslie Gates, 'Colonels and Industrial Workers in El Salvador 1944-1972: Seeking Societal Support through Gendered Labor Reforms', in *Landscapes of Struggle: Politics, Society, and Community in El Salvador*, eds. Aldo Laurie-Santiago and Leigh Binford (Pittsburg: University of Pittsburgh Press, 2004), 72.

estates' where they earned meagre wages.³⁴ The overwhelming majority of rural households 'labored for little pay with little access to education or medical services, enduring extraordinary poverty and social exclusion, even among Latin American standards'.³⁵ The conditions of material poverty, insecure employment, landlessness, and political marginalisation would eventually compel *campesinos* in certain parts of the countryside to participate in collective action to demand economic reform and political inclusion.³⁶

The Catholic Church in El Salvador experienced significant change during this same period. Some of the changes were facilitated by Archbishop Luis Chavez y Gonzalez, who, beginning in the 1940s, guided the archdiocese of San Salvador to promote more progressive social causes. His work as Archbishop 'laid the groundwork for [the clashes] between a Church for the poor and a State for the elite'³⁷ that occurred in the 1960s and 1970s. In response to Vatican II (1962–1964), a growing number of Salvadoran priests, nuns, and catechists, along with missionaries from North America and Europe, began working in rural communities and marginalised urban neighbourhoods to lead bible studies and provide pastoral care as an exercise of the 'preferential option for the poor'.³⁸

This new pastoral ethic and practice was not endorsed by all in the Salvadoran Catholic Church. In urban areas, many church leaders remained connected to the elite and other conservative, 'apolitical' movements, like Opus Dei.³⁹ The oligarchy sought to destabilise the authority of the leadership of the Catholic Church by dividing it into political and apolitical church movements.⁴⁰ Such divisions impacted Catholics in rural communities differently, with some relying primarily on itinerant priests who travelled from one church to officiate the sacraments and offer

---

34 Elisabeth Jean Wood, *Insurgent Collective Action and Civil War in El Salvador* (Cambridge: Cambridge University Press, 2003), 58.
35 Wood, *Insurgent Collective Action*, 58.
36 Wood, *Insurgent Collective Action*, 11.
37 Mikus, 'The Catholic Church and the Formation of Human Rights Doctrine in El Salvador', 53.
38 Wood, *Insurgent Collective Action*, 90–91.
39 Wadkins, *The Rise of Pentecostalism in Modern El Salvador*.
40 Wadkins, *The Rise of Pentecostalism in Modern El Salvador*.

social assistance to needy parishioners. In communities where priests and congregants began to organise to challenge the status quo, local elites, state agents, and security forces collaborated to threaten and repress local Catholic Church groups.

In the 1970s, Salvadorans experienced increased levels of violence as peasant groups and urban workers increasingly 'challenged state terror and terrorism'.[41] A second crisis of hegemony erupted in 1979, when El Salvador was plunged into civil war, which lasted until 1992. During the conflict, more than seventy-five thousand Salvadorans lost their lives (an estimated one in fifty-six Salvadorans), and the entire landscape of the country was transformed.[42] During this period of civil war, Pentecostal adherents grew steadily while many of their Catholic counterparts experienced internal division and intense repression by state agents.

The growth of Pentecostal churches came primarily from individuals and families who left Catholicism to join congregations affiliated to traditional denominations (e.g., Assemblies of God) in the central and western regions of the country. Several urban congregations, which were founded in the capital city of San Salvador by US missionaries and Salvadoran pastors in the 1960s, also experienced significant growth during the war as cities swelled with people displaced by the conflict occurring in rural areas. From 1978 to 1982, the average annual growth rate for evangelical church membership was 22 percent and was 15.7 percent from 1982 to 1984; estimates for evangelicals as a percentage of the total population during the late 1980s range from 12 to 23 percent.[43]

Pentecostals generally avoided civic and political engagement during the civil war, and most did not offer public support for either the *Frente Farabundo Marti de Liberación Nacional* (FMLN) or the Salvadoran government. There is evidence that a few Pentecostal leaders and US missionaries supported the repressive actions of the state in the 1970s and 1980s, and some US missionaries convinced local pastors that the Marxist-Leninist ideologies held by the guerrilla groups that formed the insurgency would

---

41 Chavez, 'An Anatomy of Violence', 32.
42 Wood, *Insurgent Collective Action*, 8.
43 Williams, 'The Sound of Tambourines'.

eliminate freedom of religion.[44] Deep misgivings about (and opposition to) leftist groups and political parties among Pentecostals persisted for the better part of the twentieth century and are still echoed among some adherents today.

Existing divisions and relational strains between Pentecostals and Catholics in rural communities were exacerbated during the civil war. Pentecostals further differentiated themselves socially from Catholic neighbours who joined peasant organisations in support of the FMLN. The Pentecostal church building was a safe space from the threat of conflict and the dangers of Catholic priests and neighbours who promoted revolution. For many Catholic leaders, the possibility that congregants might convert to Pentecostalism became increasingly real as their evangelisation efforts increased during the war. Pentecostals expanded their own 'grassroots efforts' by 'members of local churches [who] invited family members, friends, and co-workers to attend services, and [who] organized prayer meetings in their homes'.[45] For some Catholic leaders, the perception that 'Pentecostal groups rarely faced persecution by the [state] regime'[46] was further proof that Pentecostals were complicit in state repression.

During the civil war, Pentecostals continued a similar pattern of social engagement, which was steady recruitment of neighbours through evangelisation and invitation to church meetings or to home prayer groups. The message of personal transformation was appealing to many Salvadorans impacted by the civil war. Conversion to Pentecostalism did not mean that they had 'to risk their lives by joining a political movement or a trade union ... instead they had to first put their own lives in order ... [which appealed to] many poor Salvadorans, who had grown skeptical of corrupt politicians and the dangers of political activism encouraged by progressive Catholic leaders'.[47]

---

44   Leigh Binford, 'Peasants, Catechists, Revolutionaries: Organic Intellectuals in the Salvadoran Revolution, 1980–1992', in *Landscapes of Struggle: Politics, Society, and Community in El Salvador*, eds. Aldo Laurie-Santiago and Leigh Binford (Pittsburg: University of Pittsburgh Press, 2004), 93.
45   Williams and Peterson, 'Evangelicals and Catholics in El Salvador', 880.
46   Williams and Peterson, 'Evangelicals and Catholics in El Salvador', 880.
47   Williams and Peterson, 'Evangelicals and Catholics in El Salvador', 881.

Several developments created opportunities for Pentecostal groups to experiment with new forms of social engagement during the 1970s and 1980s. First, the steady urbanisation of the Salvadoran population corresponded with the emergence and growth of numerous Pentecostal congregations within urban, working poor communities, especially in San Salvador. These congregations were often larger than their rural counterparts and had access to infrastructure (e.g., building space) that enabled the development of programs to address the needs of their congregants. In 1962, for example, John Bueno and the *Centro Evangelistico* church began a private Christian school to address poverty in San Salvador. By the late 1980s, the school had grown from one campus to a national network of thirty-five campuses serving over fifteen thousand students per year. Second, some Pentecostal congregations gained access to external resources from international faith-based organisations, like World Vision, which began operations in El Salvador in 1975 and increased its aid and relief work during the war. A third dynamic was the tacit support that Pentecostal groups received from Salvadoran government officials during this period. Whereas some Catholic groups sought to mobilise communities to oppose the government, Pentecostal churches carried out ministries that focused narrowly on meeting the economic and material needs of poor congregants and neighbours. Such 'apolitical' forms of social engagement did not challenge the status quo and reinforced Pentecostal aims to reach the lost through charitable acts.

DIVERSE RELIGIOUS MARKETPLACES AND NEOLIBERAL CAPITALISM

Before signing the peace accords to end the civil war, the government had already started to implement structural changes that would shape the social and economic life of El Salvador. By the late 1980s, import-substitution was failing, and the state was unable to repay its national debt. President Cristiani began implementing economic stabilisation and structural adjustments upon becoming president in 1989. By 1991, the government had signed its first of multiple Structural Adjustment Loans (SALs) with the World Bank, which required the government to promote an export-led economy, deregulate currency, and invest in public infrastructure.[48] SALs also required the state to reduce public spending in education, health, and other public services.

A direct consequence of neoliberal reforms was a shift in public investment strategy from national to local development. In 1994, the government launched a new strategy to re-allocate development investment from federal funds to mayoral offices.[49] The state provided block grants to implement local development initiatives through certified community development associations (*ADESCO*). Nevertheless, mayors often complained that they did not have sufficient resources to train *ADESCO* members in community development. The lack of public funding in both training and projects created new incentives for local mayors and community leaders to seek out and partner with NGOs and other civic actors, such as churches.

The neoliberal turn in El Salvador ultimately decentred and reorganised the role of the state, transforming it from implementer to regulator in all areas of social and economic life. Under neoliberalism, the 'market is the organizing and regulative principle underlying the state'.[50] Comaroff states that, under neoliberalism, the state exists to 'enhance profitability and promote entrepreneurial citizens'.[51] She argues that in a decentred state, where individual subjectivities and entrepreneurs are encouraged and formed, the space for religious movements that prioritise personal or individual transformation—such as Pentecostalism and some Catholic Charismatic movements—can compete effectively in an open marketplace to recruit new adherents.

Since the 1990s, Pentecostalism has continued to grow in rural and urban settings as well as among different socio-economic sectors of

---

48 World Bank, 'Project Completion Report: Republic of El Salvador' Report No. 145131, (1995).
49 Red Para el Desarrollo Local, 'El Salvador, Desarrollo Local y Descentralización del Estado: Situación Actual y Desafíos' *Informe:* enero 2003-diciembre 2005 (2006).
50 Jean Comaroff, 'Pentecostalism, Populism and the New Politics of Affect', in *Pentecostalism and Development: Churches, NGOs and Social Change in Africa*, ed. Dena Freeman (Basingstoke: Palgrave Macmillan, 2012), 55.
51 Comaroff, 'Pentecostalism, Populism and the New Politics of Affect', 55.

society. El Salvador has become a 'modern, pluralized, religious marketplace where voluntary choice and competition for souls is as frenetic as it is in the newly emerging capitalist economy'.[52] Wadkins adds, 'hierarchical and corporately organised social structure in El Salvador, which was dominated by the aristocracy, military and the Catholic Church, has given way to a more democratic social order, a market economy, and the opening of free social spaces for greater levels of civic participation'.[53] The increase in number and influence of Pentecostal congregations also shaped the liturgical rites and organisational cultures of the Charismatic Catholic movement. Much like Pentecostalism, the movement encourages lay preaching, lively worship, dancing and singing in the Spirit, speaking in tongues, and an emphasis on healing.[54] According to the 2014 Pew survey on Latin American religion, some 50 percent of all Salvadoran Catholics claim to be Charismatic.[55]

The pluralisation of religious marketplaces has encouraged a shift in relationships between Catholics and Pentecostals in rural communities from marginalisation to coexistence and, in some cases, collaboration. For the most part, Catholic and Pentecostal congregations coexist within a religious marketplace that is defined by competition, at differing levels of intensity, for new converts. Nevertheless, the decentring of the state and the erosion of the Catholic canopy left community leaders to fend for themselves in addressing the needs of their families and communities. The increased pressure and responsibility to identify and mobilise local resources to address community needs created opportunities for some Catholic leaders to be openly befriend and work with Pentecostal neighbours. In short, the decreased funding from public entities created new spaces for Catholic and Pentecostal leaders to work together to develop projects to address community needs.

Although the majority of Pentecostals primarily provide services independently or through a faith-based organisation's program to individual families, there is evidence that some Pentecostal congregations are starting to

---

52   Wadkins, *The Rise of Pentecostalism in Modern El Salvador*, 15–16.
53   Wadkins, *The Rise of Pentecostalism in Modern El Salvador*, 39.
54   Wadkins, *The Rise of Pentecostalism in Modern El Salvador*, 24.
55   Wadkins, *The Rise of Pentecostalism in Modern El Salvador*, 25.

work with public and civic organisations to address community-wide issues.[56] Active participation in novel forms of social engagement has created new opportunities for some Pentecostals that blur the social boundaries of their previously prescribed and formal relationships with Catholic members.[57] Some Pentecostal leaders talk about engaging their Catholic neighbours in meaningful conversations regarding personal and community problems.[58] Several pastors and church leaders described the new relationships as *casi hermanas/os*—almost like Pentecostal sisters/brothers. They stated that they lent each other money, vehicles, and equipment. They also visited each other's houses and shared important moments, such as birthdays and anniversaries, as if they were *hermanas/os*.

For example, Marcos,[59] a Pentecostal pastor, described his new relationship with a Catholic leader named Cesar. Pastor Marcos said that they had become friends while working together on several community projects and serving on the *ADESCO* board. They lent each other their vehicles for projects and shared food and supplies between their families. Cesar even sold the *La Paz* Church a piece of land at a lower price than what was offered by a private developer. He also asked Pastor Marcos for advice on marital and other family problems.

Pastor Marcos, likewise, shared personal and church problems with Cesar. He officiated the burial service of Cesar's mother, who was an active member of the local Catholic Church. He also cared for Cesar through his fight with cancer and officiated his funeral. Pastor Marcos stated that Cesar had asked him for prayer many times and had even 'confessed his sins' to him, but never had done so publicly or joined the Pentecostal church to avoid offending his Catholic family. Pastor Marcos mourned deeply Cesar's death. He said, 'I will miss him dearly. He was my closest friend.'[60]

---

56 James G. Huff, 'Pentecostalized Development and Novel Social Imaginaries in Rural El Salvador', *Journal of Latin American and Caribbean Anthropology* 19 no. 1 (2014): 22–40; James G. Huff, 'Of Specters and Spirit: Neoliberal Entanglements of Faith-Based Development in El Salvador', *Urban Anthropology* 46 no. 3,), (2017): 173–220.

57 Bueno, *Community Engagement as a New and Contested Ritual*.

58 Bueno, *Community Engagement as a New and Contested Ritual*.

59 Pastor Marcos, Interview, 22 June 2011.

60 Pastor Marcos, Interview.

Church members from Pentecostal congregations actively engaged in community development initiatives also shared stories about the importance of new relationships with Catholic neighbours. Evelyn, a church member from *Santuario Bíblico* Church, talked about the importance of the new relationship with her Catholic neighbour, Luisa. She stated,

> I had never felt any reason to connect with her. She has a child with special needs. But when I realized her need for help, I offered to take care of her child.... That encouraged her to see that the church is now helping spiritually and economically. She saw the change in my family toward her family and how we provided help without needing anyone to know what we have done or us saying anything. Luisa is like an *hermana* (church sister). I would not want to lose communion with [Luisa and her family] because we always talk about God and the Bible... I also learn from them, and they from me.[61]

Like Pastor Marcos and Evelyn, church leaders and members have created new relational contexts that bridge networks and understandings with Catholic community members. Although not all church leaders and members extend the same degree of trust or solidarity to the new relationships, they generate spaces to engage in new discourses about community problems and collective action. Most still frame their engagement as opportunities to evangelise their neighbours, but they build relationships of trust that allow for new kinds of social interactions with Catholic neighbours. For many church members, these new relationships challenge their sense of interpersonal space with Catholics and their sense of civic engagement.

Catholics also described a change in their relationship with Pentecostal leaders. Dora, a Catholic community leader, described her new relationship with Pentecostal church members accordingly:

> Although I am not Evangelica (Pentecostal), I feel good working with the church (Pentecostal) because it is a friendship with the

---

61 Evelyn, Interview, 19 June 2012.

brothers and if they ask me to help them, I like to help the community because that is the way that you create friendships. This church is not like other churches that think that they are important. At least Pastor Marcos we know to be a great person. In the street he greets us and makes us feel as if we are friends.[62]

Ester, an active Catholic community leader, adds,

It used to be that when the church brothers would visit a home of a Catholic family they did not really want to welcome them into their houses, but now the communication has changed because they will open their doors to them (church brothers) because they know that when a church brother comes to their doors they come for two reasons: to share the Word of God and for some project that they are working on.[63]

Along with changes in relationships between Pentecostals and Catholics, the active participation in new forms of social engagement has also challenged how some Pentecostal leaders describe the mission of the church in their community. Tomas, another Pentecostal pastor, described how community engagement is an important practice for fulfilling the mission of the church. He stated,

The mission of the church is to solve society's problems. It is the hope of the world. We have the word of encouragement, God's message for the world that changes people's hearts. The church must first feel the burdens of our society. The list of needs is very long, but as we listen to God, he will give us solutions because God does not want us to be absent from or indifferent to the needs of our community. He wants us to feel what the community feels. Just like Jesus, when he saw the multitudes, he had compassion on them. Jesus showed unmerited love, like sheep without a shepherd.[64]

---

62 Dora, Interview, 16 March 2011.
63 Ester, Interview, 16 March 2011.
64 Pastor Tomas, Interview, 15 May 2010.

To Pastor Tomas, the mission of the church goes beyond the traditional Pentecostal focus upon self-reform or family reform to include community reform. The church must not be separate from but rather embedded in and a significant actor within the community.

The new practice of community engagement has created new spaces for relationships but also has challenged some Pentecostals' sense of identity, mission, and place in the world.[65] Some Pentecostal leaders and adherents do not see themselves as 'removed' from their communities with a mission to convert and recruit new members. Rather, there appears to be a shift among some adherents to understand themselves as being an active and important part of civic and community life. Moreover, to accomplish this goal, they see it as vital to befriend and collaborate with their Catholic neighbours. Pentecostals still believe that all Catholics need to be born again to experience personal transformation, but also recognise that they are an important part of the community and that friendship and effective partnership are the best ways to care for the physical needs of their communities.

FROM RETREAT TO COMMUNITY ENGAGEMENT

This chapter demonstrates how broader changes within political-economic orders and religious institutions in El Salvador have shaped the relationships that Catholic and Pentecostal Salvadorans created with one another in rural communities over the course of the twentieth century. Our focus on these 'background conditions' contextualises local Catholic-Pentecostal relationships in a number of important ways.[66] The transformation of the Catholic institutional church, the regular exercise of violence by state agents, the implementation of liberal and neoliberal economic policies, and the pluralisation of the local religious markets are all systemic realities that have profoundly shaped how Salvadoran Pentecostals worship and how they relate to their Catholic neighbours. Their dynamic patterns of social isolation and retreat, of proselytisation and recruitment, and of

---

65   Bueno, *Community Engagement as a New and Contested Ritual*.
66   Mintz, 'Food and Its Relationship to Concepts of Power'.

community engagement must be understood in relation to these larger conditioning factors.

Highlighting these dimensions of 'outside meaning' also enables a more nuanced understanding of what it means to be Pentecostal in places where the dominant Christian tradition has been Catholicism. We have argued that in order to elucidate the 'inside meanings' of being Pentecostal—which for many has entailed belonging to a religious minority that often experienced multiple forms of marginalisation—one must be attentive to the social relationships Pentecostals engage in at the local level. How Salvadoran Pentecostals routinely interacted with their Catholic neighbours and participated in catholicised community spaces is a window into how they made sense of their marginality.

Finally, our ethnographic research of rural Pentecostal congregations that actively participate in and create new practices of community engagement sheds light on the dynamic nature of the experience of marginalisation. Our analysis here suggests that the recent pluralisation of religious marketplaces—which has been facilitated in part by the neoliberal reordering of the state—has corresponded with the emergence of new local publics, where religious actors of various sorts compete for new converts and for local development resources. To be sure, the number of rural, Pentecostal congregations that participate in these publics remains small. Our ethnographic findings indicate, however, that regular participation in community development work affects how Pentecostals understand themselves, imagine and practise their mission, and interact with their Catholic neighbours in novel ways.

7

WHAT THEN SHALL WE SAY?
Responses of Tibetan Christians to Victimisation in a Time of Heightening Sinicisation

Gangri "Philip" Gobu

The Monument to the Peaceful Liberation of Tibet occupies the southern corner of the Potala Square. Its Chinese communal style stages a glaring juxtaposition to Potala Palace, the epitome of Tibetan architecture. To the (Han) Chinese government, it commemorates the expelling of 'imperialists' forces from Tibet in 1951, which led Tibet to 'advancement, prosperity, democracy . . . a new era', and the socio-economic development achieved since then.[1] To the Tibetan government in exile, however, it serves as a 'daily reminder of the humiliation of Tibetan people'.[2] Such diametrically opposite perspectives between the Han Chinese and the Tibetans are not solely historiographical. For Tibetans living under the Chinese Communist Party (CCP) since 1950, they extend to virtually all aspects of life.

This study looks at the CCP's sinicisation drive in Tibet and the Christian responses to it. Today there are Christians of Han, Tibetan, Hui, Salar, Mongolian, Tu, and other minority descents in Tibet. Here, I focus on Tibetan Christians' response to their increasingly sinicised homeland. By Tibet, I mean the historical and cultural landmass encompassing Amdo,

---

[1] 'Monument Erected to Commemorate Tibet Liberation,' *People Daily,* 23 May 2002, www.peopledaily.com.cn (accessed 21 November 2022).
[2] 'Anger over Tibet monument,' *BBC News,* 5 February 2002, http://news.bbc.co.uk/2/hi/asia-pacific/1802368.stm (accessed 21 October 2022).

Khampa, and Ü-Tsang areas.³ Most Tibetans residing inside and outside of the People's Republic of China (PRC) and the Central Tibet Administration (CTA)—the Tibetan government in exile—identify the same area.⁴ My primary sources are interviews of Tibetan Christian families from the official church, house church, and non-churched groupings over a period of six months during our frequent citywide snap lockdowns.⁵ My secondary sources are books, articles, and news reports.

THE SINICISATION OF TIBET

By 1950, the People's Liberation Army (PLA) had incorporated Tibet into the PRC. The following year, the CCP coerced the Tibetan government into signing the Agreement of the Central People's Government and the Local Government of Tibet on Measures for the Peaceful Liberation of Tibet, which authorised the entry of Chinese forces into Tibet and empowered the CCP to control Tibet's external affairs.⁶ Beijing swiftly tightened its grip over the region and soon refused further negotiations. This move effectively excluded Tibetans and the Dalai Lama from determining the fate of their homeland and people. From then on, the whole world witnessed one of the biggest social engineering feats of the century. The CCP banned the promised autonomy and systematically flouted Tibetan tradition, culture, political system, economy, and religious beliefs. Scholars call this process the 'sinicisation of Tibet'.⁷

---

3   Philip Y. Poh, *Third-Wave Missionary Leaders in Contemporary Yakland: An Analysis of Six Malfeasance and Leadership Formation Cases Using a Maturity-Support Approach* (Oxford: Amri Connect, 2017), 67–71.

4   See CTA's official website https://tibet.net/about-tibet/map-of-tibet/; see also https://www.nationsonline.org/;   https://www.thetibetpost.com/en/more/topic/5790-where-is-tibet-located-on-map-of-world;   https://tibetnetwork.org/about-tibet/;   https://freetibet.org/freedom-for-tibet/history-of-tibet/where-is-tibet/.

5   March—September 2022. Interviews were held over meals whenever possible. Online calls and messages were also used.

6   It further guaranteed that the Chinese government would neither alter Tibet's existing political system nor interfere with Tibet's cultural and religious beliefs; instead, they would grand regional autonomy to Tibet.

7   See for example Dawa Burbu, *China's Tibet Policy* (Routledge: New York, 2001), 100–124; Lawrence Davidson, *Cultural Genocide* (Rutgers University

Broadly defined, 'sinicisation' is an intentional and institutionalised effort to transform a foreign entity into a Chinese one in essence, character, and/or form. A historical example of this process is Vietnam's adaptation of the Chinese writing system under the millennia-long Chinese rule. Cultural exports, such as the writing system, are efficacious vehicles for spreading Chinese influence to other countries in the sinosphere.[8] In this study, sinicisation refers specifically to an official campaign to reform a belief system or doctrine, and elements of a culture, into compliance with the CCP's creed and values. Hence, the sinicisation discussed here is primarily not a cultural but a politico-ideological transforming force. Just like in Xinjiang, the CCP focuses its sinicisation effort in key areas of Tibet's everyday life: ethnic makeup of the general population, religion, education, language, culture, and employment.

Chinese Settlements

Over the decades, Beijing has used economic development as a plank to transfer large numbers of Han Chinese into Tibet. In 1949, there were between 300 and 400 Han Chinese residents in Lhasa, accounting for 0.0003 percent of the population.[9] In 1985, the exiled Dalai Lama lamented that the area where he was born, the Kokonor region of Amdo Tibet, had changed from being a predominantly Tibetan area to a population of 2.5 million Chinese and only 700,000 Tibetans.[10] By 2021–2022, Han Chinese accounted for 27 percent and Tibetans 70 percent of Lhasa's population. Qinghai (the Dalai Lama's home province) was 52.29 percent Han Chinese and 24 percent Tibetan in the same years.[11] These historically

---

Press: New Brunswick, 2012), 89–111; Tseten Samdup, 'Chinese Population—Threat to Tibetan Identity', 1993, archived 5 February 2009 at the Wayback Machine.

8 Sinicization, Wikipedia, https://en.wikipedia.org/wiki/Sinicization, (accessed 10 September 2022).

9 Roland Barraux, *Histoire des Dalaï Lamas—Quatorze reflets sur le Lac des Visions* (Albin Michel, 1993), reprinted in 2002.

10 The Dalai Lama, "A Vast Sea of Chinese Threatens Tibet," *New York Times*, 9 August 1985, https://www.nytimes.com/1985/08/09/opinion/a-vast-sea-of-chinese-threatens-tibet.html (accessed 20 September 2022).

11 *Xizang zizhiqu diqici quanguorenkoupucha zhuyaoshujvgongbao, Xizangzizhiqu tongjijv* (Statistics Department of Tibet Autonomous Region, Major Data of

Tibetan homelands are called Ü-Tsang and Amdo, respectively. The CCP has also targeted the institution of marriage to create a Han majority in Tibet. In 2014, Chen Quanguo, then CCP secretary of Tibet Autonomous Region (TAR), said, 'the government must actively promote intermarriages' between Tibetans and Chinese in order to promote 'ethnic unity'.[12]

Religion

The CCP has maintained a steady history of sinicizing Tibetan Buddhism since early 1950s. At the height of the Cultural Revolution, Red Guards looted and destroyed more than six thousand monasteries. They coerced tens of thousands of monks and nuns to denounce their religion, to leave their monasteries, to 'live a normal life' (i.e., to be married), and to participate in commune menial labour. Those who resisted were thrown into prison, forced into hard labour, tortured, and executed. The Potala Palace would have been destroyed had Premier Zhou Enlai not intervened and restrained the Tibetan Red Guards.[13] The CCP fully realises the Dalai Lama's strong hold on Tibetans. Intending to replace it, the Chinese government has enforced a complete ban on images of and references to the spiritual leader since 1996.[14] In a *tour de force* of communist hubris, the CCP even announced that the Dalai Lama and the Panchen Lama (the highest

---

the 7th National Population Census of Tibet Autonomous Region), https://www.xizang.gov.cn/zwgk/zfsj/ndtjgb/202105/t20210520_202889.html (accessed 22 September 2022); *Qinghai renkouzongshu tongjibiao* (Population Statistics of Qinghai), https://www.jinchutou.com/shtml/view-278193341.html. See also Claude Arpi, 'Lhasa Invaded Again. . .by Han Chinese', *Indian Defence Review*, 19 September 2022, http://www.indiandefencereview.com/spotlights/lhasa-invaded-again-by-han-chinese/ (accessed 19 September 2022).

12   Yeshi Dorje, 'Rights Groups Slam Xi's Latest Calls to 'Sinicize' Tibetan Buddhism', *Voice of America*, 3 September 2020, https://www.voanews.com/a/east-asia-pacific_rights-groups-slam-xis-latest-calls-sinicize-tibetan-buddhism/6195382.html (accessed 20 September 2022).

13   Dan Southerland, 'After 50 Years, Tibetans Recall the Cultural Revolution', *Radio Free Asia*, 9 August 2016, archived from the original on 10 July 2019, retrieved 31 October 2022.

14   See https://tibetpolicy.net/ccp-and-sinicization-of-tibet/, (accessed 4 September 2022).

and second highest-ranking living Buddhas in the dominant Gelugpa sect) would bend to its will by reincarnating in the form, shape, time, and place of its choosing.[15]

Schools sternly warn parents against allowing their children to attend classes at monasteries or to engage in any religious activity. Punishments for perpetrators include loss of government welfare and subsidies.[16] To demonstrate their resolution, the Chinese authorities demolished thousands of residences at the Yachen Gar Tibetan Buddhist centre in Sichuan Province, displacing as many as six thousand monks and nuns. They also closed the Larung Gar Buddhist Academy to new enrolment during the summer of 2019.[17]

Removal of Tibetan religious symbols, such as prayer flags, increased after 2010. The 'behavioural reform' program of summer 2020 in Amdo's Golog prefecture and Chamdo's Tengchen county entailed, *inter alia*, a sweeping destruction of prayer flags.[18] I personally witnessed such 'patriotic cleaning up' in Golog and Yushu (Jiekundo) Tibetan Autonomous Prefectures in the summers of 2021 and 2022. Surveillance teams from the Public Security Bureau (PSB, Chinese police forces) and National Security Bureau (NSB, Chinese equivalent of Homeland Security) move inside monasteries and villages to *weiwen* (maintain stability). They use state-of-the-art CCTV and facial-recognition software to 'protect' Tibetan residents (monitoring them for signs of opposition to the CCP's rule).[19] The most definitive confirmation of intention comes

---

15 Sean Silbert, 'Why the Dalai Lama Says Reincarnation Might Not Be for Him', *Los Angeles Times*, 20 December 2014; C. Buckley, 'China's Tensions with Dalai Lama Spill into the Afterlife', *New York Times*, 11 March, 2015, archived from the original on 31 January 2019, retrieved 30 November 2022.

16 Ben Halder, 'China Weaponises Education to Control Tibet', *Ozy*, 16 October 2019, archived from the original on 22 October 2019, retrieved 22 October 2019.

17 *IRF Annual Report*, www.uscirf.gov, archived from the original on 3 August 2020, retrieved 30 August 2020.

18 Lhuboom, 'China Orders Prayer Flags Taken Down in Tibet in an Assault on Culture, Faith', *Radio Free Asia*, 17 June 2020, archived from the original on 5 July 2020, retrieved 4 September 2022.

19 'China Expands Its Clampdown in Tibet: Report', *Radio Free Asia*, 16 June 2020, archived from the original on 1 September 2020, retrieved 5 September

straight from President Xi Jinping (Xi) in his August 2020 speech. This speech reiterated the imperative to 'actively guide Tibetan Buddhism to adapt to the socialist society and promote the *Sinicization of Tibetan Buddhism*' (italics mine).[20]

Education, Language, Culture, and Employment

The 1982 Chinese constitution paid lip service to the preservation of minority language in ethnic regions. There was short-lived enthusiasm in 2000 for Tibetanisation in Qinghai where schools were allowed to use Tibetan as the educational lingua franca.[21] This enthusiasm quickly evaporated when Xi became the CCP's head in 2013. Xi's vow to build a 'new modern socialist Tibet that is united, prosperous, culturally advanced, harmonious and beautiful' would be achieved primarily via secondary school reforms that 'plant the seeds of loving China deep in the heart of every youth' and by the 'sinicization of Tibetan Buddhism'.[22] Since then, the CCP has accelerated the sending of Tibetan children away from their families, religion, and culture into Tibetan-only boarding schools in China's many Han Chinese cities. Older students are allowed to leave the campus only if accompanied by a teacher. They are taught that. to get a job, they must

> support the CCP's leadership, resolutely implement the CCP's line and approach, policies, and the guiding ideology of Tibet work in the new era; align ideologically, politically, and in action with the Party Central Committee; oppose any splittist (division of Tibet from PRC) tendencies; expose and criticize the Dalai Lama;

2020; Tibetan Centre for Human Rights and Democracy, *Human Rights Situation in Tibet 2019 Annual Report*, tchrd.org, archived from the original on 5 July 2020, retrieved 5 September 2020.

20 'Tibetan Buddhism Must Be Tailored to Fit Chinese Society, Says Xi Jinping', *Apple Daily*, 30 August 2020. Apple Daily's website was permanently disabled after the Chinese government closed its headquarters and imprisoned its founder, Jimmy Lai.

21 Adrian Zenz, 'Beyond Assimilation: The Tibetanisation of Tibetan Education in Qinghai', *Inner Asia*. 12 no. 2 (2010): 293-315.

22 'Tibetan Buddhism must be tailored to fit Chinese society, says Xi Jinping'.

safeguard the unity of the motherland and ethnic unity and take a firm stand on political issues.[23]

In 2019, our schools for Tibetan girls (in Golog since 2007) were instructed to switch to Mandarin for all subjects. Schools in Ngaba Tibetan Autonomous Prefecture of Sichuan followed suit one year later. The government confiscated all the former textbooks in Tibetan and replaced them with ones in Mandarin heavily laden with the CCP doctrine. In Tibetan areas, official affairs are conducted primarily in Mandarin. Government officials are required to denounce Buddhism. Monasteries are ordered to end Tibetan classes, a millennium-long tradition.[24] Under the revised Regulations on Religious Affairs of 2018,[25] informal classes taught by Tibetan monks or other unapproved groups have been made illegal. Scholars and journalists have also reported on the CCP's use of forced re-education ('patriotic re-education'), detention, torture, and intimidation as tools to achieve 'stability' in Tibet, akin to their strategy in Xinjiang.[26] The next sections will show that sinicisation is not limited to Tibet and Tibetan Buddhism.

THE SINICISATION OF RELIGIONS

Since its first encounters with the West, Chinese society has tried to rid religious practices and foreign influence. Every foreign religious advance into China throughout its history has either been endorsed, tolerated,

---

23   Sutirtho Patranobis, 'Tibetan Graduates Need to "Expose and Criticise Dalai Lama" for Chinese Government Jobs', *Hindustan Times*, 19 October 2019, archived from the original on 20 October 2019, retrieved 22 October 2022.

24   Edward Wong, 'Tibetans Fight to Salvage Fading Culture in China,' *New York Times*, 28 November 2015, archived from the original on 31 January 2019, retrieved 30 September 2022.

25   'China (Includes Tibet, Xinjiang, Hong Kong and Macau)', International Religious Freedom Report for 2018, United States Department of State Bureau of Democracy, Human Rights, and Labor, https://www.state.gov/wp-content/uploads/2019/05/CHINA-INCLUSIVE-2018-INTERNATIONAL-RELIGIOUS-FREEDOM-REPORT.pdf.

26   'Tibetan Buddhism Must Be Tailored to Fit Chinese Society, Says Xi Jinping'; Dhanajay Sahai, 'CCP and Sinicization of Tibet', 16 March 2021, https://tibetpolicy.net/ccp-and-sinicization-of-tibet/ (accessed 20 October 2022).

modified, or proscribed depending on how it aligned with imperial objectives at the time.[27] To be accepted, non-Chinese beliefs and value systems have always undergone sinicisation. Examples are Indian Buddhism, which became Han Chinese Buddhism (*Hanchuan Fojiao*) and German Communism-turned-Maoism under Mao (*Maozedong Zhuyi*) and Socialism with Chinese characteristics (*Zhongguo Tese Shehuizhuyi*) under Xi.

Xi wants to control all aspects of Chinese society. Long before his enthronement in October 2022, his ambition to restrict religions and the civil society had already been revealed among foreign businesses, intellectuals, artists, religious leaders, and their institutions both in and beyond China.[28] Xi and cohorts blamed the implosion of the Soviet Union on its failure to champion Marxism and Leninism. They used this to justify the subjugation of their ideological rivals, many of whom lay hidden in religious vestments.

Thus the rise of religion, especially Christianity (and Islam), represents an existential threat to the CCP's political health. Xi is convinced that if the CCP is to survive as China's sole legitimate regime, it must instigate radical ideological renewal. Enter sinicisation as the necessary remedy.[29] Like the Maoist purges and incarceration of suspected political enemies in the 1950s, sinicisation is now the ideology and policy that put up to two million Uighur, Hui, and Kazakh Muslims in Xinjiang in re-education camps and detained and re-educated Chinese Christian pastors.[30]

Xi kick-started his version of religion sinicisation in a speech at the National Religious Work Conference in April 2016. Accordingly, in order to

---

27 Kerry Schottelkorb and Joann Pittman, 'China Tells Christianity to Be More Chinese,' *Christianity Today*, 20 March 2019, https://www.christianitytoday.com/news/2019/march/sinicization-china-wants-christianity-churches-more-chinese.html (accessed 17 November 2022).

28 Joann Pittman, 'The New Normal for Christianity in China', *Lausanne Global Analysis*, May 2019. https://lausanne.org/content/lga/2019-05/the-new-normal-for-christianity-in-china.

29 Thomas Harvey, 'The Sinicization of Religion in China: Will Enforced Conformity Work?' *Lausanne Global Analysis* 8 no. 5 (2019), https://lausanne.org/content/lga/2019-09/sinicization-religion-china (accessed 18 November 2022).

30 Harvey, 'The Sinicization of Religion in China'.

'actively guide the adaptation of religions to socialist society, an important task is supporting China's religions' persistence in the direction of sinicisation'.[31] His goal is to sinicise all five official religions—Daoism, Buddhism, Christianity, Catholicism, and Islam.[32] One might question why there is a need to sinicise the Chinese-origin Daoism. This paradox betrays the true intention behind Xi's religion sinicisation: he aims not to make all religions Chinese, but to make them 'Socialist with Chinese characteristics', which is in itself the fruit of sinicizing Marx and Engel's communism.

THE SINICISATION OF CHRISTIANITY

Upon declaring the founding of the PRC in 1949, Mao swiftly expelled foreign Christians and brought Chinese churches under party control through the Three-Self Patriotic Movement Committee (TSPM). The three-self principle is a brainchild of British Henry Venn and American Rufus Anderson in late nineteenth century.[33] Here is another illustration of how sinicisation works: by 1950, the CCP had modified the Venn-Anderson three-self principle to order Chinese churches to rid themselves of foreign influence (not in the original principle) and to be self-funding, self-propagating, and self-governing (all under the direction of the CCP). Registered churches in PRC are still today referred to as Three-Self Churches. 'Hostile foreign forces' hidden within non-Party associations, and especially within churches, deeply bedevilled Mao. He commissioned the United Front of Works Department (*Tongzhan Bu*, UFWD) to identify and eliminate such 'enemies' and to pressure religious leaders to submit to the CCP decree and embrace party ideology.[34] Subsequent presidents Deng, Jiang, and Hu

---

31 Julie Bowie and David Gitter, 'The CCP's Plan to 'Sinicize' Religions: Bureaucratic Changes Are Intended to Aid the CCP in Further Pressuring Religious Groups', *The Diplomat*, 14 June 2018, https://thediplomat.com/2018/06/the-ccps-plan-to-sinicize-religions/ (accessed 20 November 2022).

32 Schottelkorb and Pittman, 'China Tells Christianity to Be More Chinese'.

33 Madison Trammel, 'Marking Time in the Middle Kingdom', *Christianity Today Library*, 2017, https://www.christianitytoday.com/ctlibrary/41452; https://en.wikipedia.org/wiki/Three-self_formula (accessed 17 November 2022).

34 Harvey, 'The Sinicization of Religion in China'.

focused on nation building and pursuing economic prosperity; the UFWD was side-lined. Christianity blossomed under the ambiguous religious policies administration of these eras. Religious persecutions persisted, but churches were tolerated and even allowed to surface and expand. With Xi revisiting Mao-era themes by reigniting sinicisation and enlarging the jurisdiction of UFWD, the death bell of religious accommodation has tolled.

China Christian Council (CCC) and TSPM[35] were quick to applaud Xi's policy. According to these Protestant national committees, a historical failure of Christianity in China to overcome its 'foreign nature' has inhibited propagation of the faith. To correct that, they aim to transform 'Christians in China' into 'Chinese Christianity'.[36] To non-Chinese Christians unfamiliar with the track record and modus operandi of the CCP, this might look like 'indigenisation' and 'contextualisation' advocated by Western Christian missiology. A closer analysis reveals the contrary. The official 'Outline of the Five-Year Working Plan for Promoting the Sinicization of Christianity in our Country (2018–2022)' (Five-Year Working Plan) aims, *inter alia*, to

1. teach socialist values in classrooms, seminary schools and higher educational institutions, including theological colleges;

2. eliminate all non-Chinese source lyrics and music from church hymnal collections;

3. impose Chinese cultural motifs in church;

4. reinterpret the Bible to suit the context of socialism with Chinese characteristics; and

5. train preachers to preach from such "bible" messages that are in line with the CCP's message.[37]

---

35 Now subsumed under the powerful UFWD, these associations oversee registered Protestant churches in PRC.

36 *Tuijing woguo jidujiao zhongguohua wunian gongzuo guihuagangyao* (2018–2022) (Five years work keypoints of sinicization of Christianity 2018–2022), https://www.chinalawtranslate.com/outline-of-the-five-year-plan-for-promoting-the-sinification-of-christianity%EF%BC%882018-2022%EF%BC%89/ (accessed 12 October 2022).

37 'Five years work keypoints of sinicization of Christianity'.

Deciphering the document's convoluted and veiled wording yields a sinicised Christianity that entails

1. a communist-stylised church building (crosses to be removed; religious drawings and portraits to be replaced by Xi's portrait);

2. an eviscerated Bible (the gospel of Jesus to be replaced by the gospel of Xi Jinpin);

3. a distorted worldview (only parts of the Bible in harmony with the 'Core Socialist Values' to be introduced to Chinese devotees);

4. opportunistic hermeneutics (cherry-picked biblical stories should 'further the conscious identification of the Christians with the leadership of the CCP and the Socialist path');[38]

5. destruction of Chinese church history (all traditional hymns to disappear and be replaced with songs 'advancing Socialist culture');[39] and

6. an ideological clergy (all seminary graduates to be socialist, not Chinese).

The document should not be taken as mere rhetoric.[40] By 2018, the government banned exhibiting and selling the Bible on the biggest online shopping malls, such as Alibaba.com, Taobao.com, Pinduoduo.com, JD.com, Kongfz.com, Dangdang.com, and Amazon.cn. In September 2021, the Shaanxi Provincial Government officiated a grand opening of

---

38   See Chunhua Zhang, 'Sinicization of Christianity' in Full Speed after the 100th Anniversary: Christians Are Ordered to "Completely Get Rid of the Foreign Religion", "Sinicizing" Really Means "Identifying with the Leadership of the CCP".' *Bitter Winter* (20 July 2021). https://bitterwinter.org/sinicization-of-christianity-in-full-speed-after-the-100th-anniversary/.

39   Chunhua Zhang, "Sinicization of Christianity" in Full Speed After the 100th Anniversary: Christians are ordered to 'completely get rid of the foreign religion,' 'Sinicizing' really means 'identifying with the leadership of the CCP'", *Bitter Winter*, 20 July, 2021, accessed 20 Oct, 2021, https://bitterwinter.org/sinicization-of-christianity-in-full-speed-after-the-100th-anniversary/.

40   Compare with 'China tells Christianity to be more Chinese'.

Sinicization of Christianity Research Center.[41] In 2022, I saw a CCP textbook reinterpreting John 8:3–11 as Jesus admitting himself to be a fellow sinner after killing the adulteress to show that laws must be upheld at all costs.

The CCP and TSPM concluded their aforementioned first Five-Year Working Plan in October 2022. Currently they are formulating their next more problem-oriented (sic) Five-Year Plan for sinicizing Christianity.[42]

RESPONSES OF TIBETAN CHRISTIANS

It should be noted here that nobody has an authoritative say in the number of Tibetan Christians and churches in present-day Tibet. Depending on whom one asks, answers can range from tens of thousands to mere double digits. I personally know thirty Tibetan Christians from my eighteen years of living and working in Tibet. I am highly sceptical of any claims of tens of thousands Tibetan Buddhist Christians.[43] One can roughly divide Tibetan Christians into three sub-groups by their church affiliation: Three-Self churchgoers, house church attendees, and non-churched free agents. These distinctions become important in differentiating their responses to victimisation in a time of heightening sinicisation.

The Weaponisation of Zero-COVID Policy

Regardless of the subgrouping, all my interviewees were affected by Xi's zero-COVID policy. While the rest of the world opts to coexist with COVID-19 by prioritising people's livelihood and economic well-being, Xi-centred CCP

---

41   "We Continue to Develop Christianity in the Chinese Context: Chairman of CCC & TSPM," *International Christian Concerns*, 07 October 2022, https://www.persecution.org/2021/10/07/shaanxi-opens-sinicization-christianity-research-center/ (accessed 18 November 2022).

42   John Zhang, "We Continue to Develop Christianity in the Chinese Context: Chairman of CCC & TSPM", *China Christian Daily*, 25 October 2022, http://chinachristiandaily.com/news/china/2022-10-25/we-continue-to-develop-christianity-in-the-chinese-context—chairman-of-ccc-tspm_12072 (accessed 10 November 2022).

43   For an outlandish example, see https://believersportal.com/200000-tibetans-including-62-buddhist-monks-come-to-jesus/.

remains an outlier with its zero-COVID policy. This has devastated the civic society, livelihood, and economy. In order to bring the Chinese society to its knees, the CCP has created the following tools: (1) the aforementioned Five-Year Working Plan (2018), (2) Revised Regulations on Religious Affairs (2018), (3) *Sao Hei Chu E* (Anti-gang Crime) campaign (2018),[44] (4) Amended Counterterrorism Law (2018), and (5) Counterespionage Law (2021). The authorities decide what constitutes subversion and they spread rumours about who is a terrorist, gangster, or spy. Under 'gang crime' charges, at least fifty-one Tibetans were sentenced to up to nine years in prison for peacefully petitioning or protesting issues related to religion, environmental protection, land rights, official corruption, promotion of Tibetan language, folk traditions, and culture. Beijing instructed and commended such blatant abuse of law and campaign to crush any critics of government policy.[45]

The combination of these laws and regulations renders the following Christian activities illegal: (1) attending Christian conferences and seminaries outside of PRC in person or online, (2) having relationships with foreign churches and Christians, (3) hosting a foreign preacher or Bible teacher without a formal speaking/teaching permit, (4) gathering of a few Christians without UFWD's permission, (5) running or attending schools using unapproved curriculum (for example foreign Sunday school and Christian homeschool materials), (6) possessing unsanctioned Christian books and literature (including the Bible), and (7) sending and forwarding 'subversive' messages and 'rumours' on social media.

Pastor Wang Yi was arrested and sentenced to nine years in prison for 'incitement of subversion of state power'[46] and 'illegal business

---

44 "Sweep Away the Black and Eradicate Evil Forces", see Emily Feng, "How China's Massive Corruption Crackdown Snares Entrepreneurs across the Country", *NPR*, 04 March 2021, https://www.npr.org/2021/03/04/947943087/how-chinas-massive-corruption-crackdown-snares-entrepreneurs-across-the-country (accessed 11 November 2022); B. Hillman, "Law, Order and Social Control in Xi's China", *Issues and Studies* 57 no. 2 (2021).

45 "China: Tibet Anti-Crime Campaign Silences Dissent", *Human Rights Watch*, 14 May 2020, https://www.hrw.org/news/2020/05/14/china-tibet-anti-crime-campaign-silences-dissent (accessed 12 November 2022).

46 Wang led a blossoming church called *Qiuyu Zhifu* (Church of the Latter Rain) which held a remembrance service of 1989 Tiananmen crackdown. He wrote

operations'.[47] His congregants were detained and tortured soon after in 2019.[48] Having served in Tibet for sixteen years, in late 2022 a highly regarded Swiss husband-and-wife missionary doctor team were repatriated for being 'Taiwan agents'. Such terrorisation aimed to send a warning to all Christians: toe the Party line, or else. Fearing retribution and imprisonment, many Tibetan Christians have become silent and have severed ties with their foreign Christian friends and teachers.

The latest ammunition provided to the Party *apparatchiks* (members) to exert full control of the civic society and religious community is the zero-COVID policy. Originally designed to display Xi's mastery over the virus and superiority over the West's 'coexisting with COVID' approach, it has been conscripted by the UFWD as a weapon for religion sinicisation. Hence, the 'pandemic' became an umbrella 'reason' for banning Three-Self Churches (and mosques) after December 2021.[49] Dissenters of any government's sinicisation policy can be penalised with a red code in their mandatory health code app—a zero-COVID tool—even though they are not COVID-positive. This means no access to public transportation, supermarkets, malls, restaurants, shops, schools, hospitals, banks, parks, and other public amenities. The authorities use big data to track and incarcerate the red-coders in state institutions called *fangcang*.[50] These are makeshift lockups with questionable sanitation, bedding, and availability

---

essays critical of the CCP, one which said the CCP's ideology was 'morally incompatible with the Christian faith', a serious threat to the legitimacy of the sinicisation campaign.

47 Wang's church carried copies of the Bible and Christian publications not published in the PRC.

48 Eva Dou, "Activist Chinese Pastor Gets Nine-Year Prison Sentence", *The Wall Street Journal*, 30 December 2019, https://www.wsj.com/articles/activist-chinese-pastor-gets-nine-year-prison-sentence-11577698307 (accessed 17 November 2022).

49 Before that the church was allowed to congregate for a collective of two months between Jan 2020 to Dec 2021.

50 'Square berth'. For an example of experience in fangcang, see Serenitie Wang, 'Shanghai Surprise: How I Survived 70 days Confinement in the World's Strictest COVID Lockdown,' *CNN*, 17 June 2022, https://www.cnn.com/2022/06/17/asia/shanghai-covid-quarantine-lockdown-experience-dst-intl-hnk/index.html (accessed 12 November 2022).

of food and medicine that are custom-made to cage COVID-19–positive people. The red coders can be detained in *fangcang* for an indeterminate time because the authorities decide for how long the red code will remain. Such victimisation had increased significantly by 2022 to silence an explosion of protests over the destructive and disruptive zero-COVID policy.

Three-Self Churchgoers

In many ways, Three-Self churchgoers bear the brunt of Xi's sinicisation onslaught. Their pastors have little say beyond implementing the Five-Year Working Plan. Many whom I spoke to expressed indignation and helplessness. Caught in the crossroads of sinicisation of Tibet and Christianity, they are victimised for both their ethnicity and Christian faith. Sister Wangmo and husband brother Angzang[51] shared, 'Our family are already outcasts among our people. Now we are forced to be *Chinese* Christians! If there is one thing Tibetans hate more than Christians, it is the Han Chinese. If we continue this way, we will become neither Tibetan nor Christian, but socialists with Chinese characteristics!'

They were shaken by a recent incident: four local Christian families were banished to other provinces after the UFWD busted their summer camp and branded them 'gangsters', 'violators of pandemic measures', and 'colluders with foreign influence'. 'We need to lay low as this storm intensifies,' Wangmo confessed. They have responded to the sinicisation with resignation and passivity. They ignored their pastor's request, avoided 'Christians' with socialist fervour, stayed at home to read the Bible, and prayed by themselves. Tibetan Christians who have embraced the government's sinicisation drive saddened them. 'We don't think they know what they're getting into. They claim to be pragmatists and patriots, but to us they're ignorant traitors of both their people and faith! This pandemic is actually helping us; with constant lockdowns the Three-Self Church has been closed for three years now. We do not need to face those who try to convert us into being socialist with Chinese characteristics!' They are, however, worried about their future when the church takes them off its payroll for being 'insubordinate'.

---

51   I use pseudonyms to protect my interviewees' identities.

House Church Attendees

House church attendees are more affected by the sinicisation of Tibet than by the sinicisation of Christianity. Unregistered churches such as *Pa-wang Chimchok* (The Solid Rock Church) have long operated outside the mandate of TSPM. The all-controlling UFWD forces its will on them nonetheless. They commiserate with the first subgroup on persecution from their own community for being Christians. They know that their Tibetan-ness is being chipped away by the CCP. They watch with great alarm and wariness the next generation of Tibetans choosing Mandarin over their mother tongue and choosing 'soulless' Chinese pop music over Tibetan-themed songs.

Pastor-in-training Namjay is no stranger to persecution for his faith. In 2020, he was once again taken in by the *Guobao Dadui* (NSB). They offered him a way out by being their spy among the Tibetan Christians;[52] this job would entail reporting all the activities of foreign Christians. Namjay refused, and the UFWD promised to make his family suffer. They have since harassed him constantly at work (he works as a manager at a foreign-owned restaurant). Twice, without any reasons, his health code turned red for weeks, putting his family under tremendous trauma.

'As for me and my household, we will serve the Lord,'[53] a defiant Namjay commented. Their educational choice for their children embodies their life verse. They refuse to subject their children to further 'red-thought brainwashing' (sinicisation) at government schools, instead opting for home-schooling. They join our homeschool co-op, thereby risking arrest for 'colluding with foreign forces'[54] to 'subvert the government', because home-schooling is illegal. They are convinced, however, that the faith of their children is a weightier matter than their personal safety. 'This homeschool has been *cong* (interrogated and arrested) a few times already. They invited brothers Ganggo and Wang in for tea[55] numerous times. These

---

52   His interrogators were Tibetan CCP members who have supposedly denounced Tibetan Buddhism.
53   Joshua 24:15.
54   My wife is an American.
55   A Christian colloquia for being taken in for questioning, interrogation, detention, and sometimes torture.

cowards even harassed my wife. Still, we need to "train up a child in the way he should go: and when he is old, he will not depart from it,"[56] Namjay insists. His wife, sister Qianmu agrees, 'We can only stand on God's word when other grounds give way. If God is for us, who can be against us?'[57]

Non-Churched Free Agents

Sister Zaya, a entrepreneur, and her husband, brother Jashi, a high school teacher, ran a profitable cafe and Tibetan souvenir shop in Lhamosi until the Zero-COVID policy killed it. With three young children and a home mortgage, they were worried about how much longer they could last without income. 'The government forces our children to forsake our culture and ethnic identity. They took away textbooks in Tibetan and Mongolian and said from now on you speak *putonghua* (Mandarin). Then they try to take away our Lord's Prayer and say that from now on you recite core socialist values. Now they take away our livelihood and say zero-COVID is saving our lives!' Zaya uttered indignantly. They view the Three-Self Churches as government organs for brainwashing propaganda and sinicisation. They claim that the official church is completely insensitive and ignorant to their spiritual and cultural needs. They also shy away from Tibetan house churches because they have 'too much factional conflicts' and the pastors 'lack direction'.

The couple homeschool their children using a translated American curriculum. 'In the face of such ruthless sinicisation effort, we are the only guardians of our children's future. We won't allow the CCP to take our children away. We won't allow them to take our culture, language and faith away,' Jashi asserted. Zaya was very worried about the CCP feeding their future generations with bastardised bibles. The moment the government banned the online sale of the Bible in 2018, she secured two hundred Bibles through various channels and kept them in a secret storeroom. 'We need to counter the present evil with the biblical truth. We go astray without Jesus. All we need is His word, His unadulterated and infallible word. Isn't there a theological saying for *tambi zongrub jippu martuk mei* (Bible alone)? Zaya asked. 'Yes,' I replied, 'I believe it's *Sola Scriptura*.'

---

56   Proverbs 22:6.
57   Romans 8:31.

CONCLUSION

Xi's CCP has scorched the snowy land of Tibet with its unquenchable blaze of sinicisation. Riding stealthily under lofty slogans like 'China Dream' and 'The Great Rejuvenation of the Chinese Nation' is the sinister attempt by the state to homogenise ethnic minorities of the PRC. The expectation is not to change into Han Chineseness, but into socialism with Chinese characteristics. Tibetan Christians, a minority among minorities, find themselves in an epic fight for their very existence. Already alienated from their ethnic Buddhist community for being Christians, they face a new life-and-death battle to preserve their unique identity and faith. Cut off from the rest of the world, and barricaded in by discriminatory and unjust laws and campaigns, they face this seemingly insurmountable foe alone.

A surprising twist for all is how sinicisation and the zero-COVID victimisation are breaking down barriers among Tibetans. Resisting a common enemy who aims to strip *all* Tibetans of their cultural core, some Tibetan Buddhists are beginning to realise that they share more commonalities than differences with their Christian compatriots. Perhaps it is time to stop majoring in the minors, and to start working together on improving what make them collectively and uniquely Tibetan, be it as Buddhist or Christian.

Confronted with the confluence of sinicisation atrocities exacerbated by the weaponisation of the zero-COVID policy, Tibetan Christians now must choose conformity or civil disobedience. Those opting for the former might escape temporary persecution, but only at the cost of permanently losing their cultural and spiritual distinctiveness.

As for those choosing faithful defiance, what then shall we say? My interviewees and their families accept institutionalised victimisation as part of the cost of following Jesus. As Jashi summarises,

> Tibetans have traditionally fought injustice with violent retaliation or self-immolation; we have revered the Buddhist Sutra and our living buddhas' instructions as commands. Now that we are following Jesus, we have forsaken our former ways of fighting injustice, and elevated our reverence from the Sutra to the Living Word.

These Tibetan Christians freely confess their only hope in this and next life lie in their God, *jiamgun yeshi marherka*—Savior Messiah Lord Jesus—and his word. Their conviction of *Sola Scriptura* may seem defeatist and impractical to outside observers. Living through the travesty of Xi's sinicisation and zero-COVID policy, I concur with my fellow Tibetan Christians that it is the most proactive thing to do as a *yeshiqilipa* (Christ-follower). Here we will do well to remember what young David said to Goliath, 'You come to me with a sword, with a spear, and with a javelin. But I come to you in the name of the LORD of hosts, the God of the armies of Israel, whom you have defied',[58] and what happened thereafter.

---

58   1 Samuel 17:45.

8

AS IN HEAVEN, SO ON EARTH?
A Response to a Dominant Religious Ideology from a Mizo Christian Tribal Perspective

Marina Ngursangzeli Behera

The first Christians in the region called Mizoram today declared themselves to be *pathian mi* (God's people) and *vanram mi* (heavenly people/citizen). A Christian was no longer considered a citizen of this earthly world (*he lei ram mi*) but of the heavenly world (*van ram mi*). In the early period of the Mizo church, this drew the line between converts and those who were not (yet) Christians. When the majority of Mizo had become Christians, they began differentiating between allegiance to faith and church (the place to exert their heavenly citizenship while still on earth) and allegiance to the political and social community as citizens of a state called India.[1] In the multi-ethnic and multi-religious India of today, the Mizo are a minority in a triple way. They are Christians, they are a Scheduled Tribe (according to the constitution), and their history is outside the Aryan narratives of the subcontinent to which Hindus trace back their religion and culture. For the Mizo, allegations by Hindutva advocates that every Muslim or Christian is a convert and, hence, has Hindu ancestors does not make any sense.[2]

---

1   Marina Ngursangzeli Behera, 'Heavenly Citizenship: A Concept for Union and an Identity Marker for Mizo Christians', in *Studia Unversitatis Babeș-Bolyai. Theologia Orthodoxa* 63 no. 2 (December 2018): 75–90.
2   Suresh Upadhyay, a leader of the Vishva Hindu Parishad (Rajasthan), another Hindu nationalist organisation, for example, explains in an interview that

Outside of Mizoram, Mizo Christians may face discrimination and harassment, but this is probably due more to their appearance, because they differ visibly from what is considered the Indian physiognomy on the subcontinent.[3] They are, with the possible exception of few cases, not persecuted as Christians, but some of the missionaries the Mizo church sends to other parts of India have suffered martyrdom.[4] Being the majority in Mizoram they are, as an ethnic and religious minority in India, quite safe. The controversial Citizenship Amendment Act (CAA) and the proposed National Register of Citizens[5] predominantly target the Muslim minority in the Northeast of India and not the Christians in states with a majority or a major Christian population such as Mizoram, Nagaland, and Manipur. Nevertheless, with a citizenship in heaven they are challenged by a resurgent Hindu nationalism: Hindutva. The CAA questions the right to Indian citizenship of some minorities on the basis of an assumed history from time immemorial from which Mizo Christians are excluded.

---

whereas 'Hindu religion wishes for world's welfare', Muslims and Christians work for conversion. 'All present day Muslims and Christians were Hindus 3-4 generations ago'. https://dai.ly/x8hwtzz.

3   See Jelle Wouters's and Tanka Subba's metaphors of a 'face-scape' or a 'physiognomic map' that an 'Indian' may look like is the 'somatic embodiment that represents the Indian nation', quoted in Arkotong Longkumer, *The Greater India Experiment (South Asia in Motion)* (Stanford University Press, 2021, Kindle version), 55.

4   The Synod of the Presbyterian Church of India (Mizoram) runs a missionary training college in Aizwal. The college documents cases of former students killed while serving as missionaries, for example, Miss Lalbiakchhungi killed on 19 April 1989 in Manipur, and Miss Rohmingthangi killed on 23 September 1986 in Western Mizoram while working among the Chakma.

5   'The BJP had, in 2003, introduced a finer adjustment in the law governing citizenship when it stated that one acquires citizenship not simply by birth but by proving that either both parents are citizens or one parent is and the other is "not an illegal immigrant" at the time of one's birth'. David Emmanuel Singh, 'Emerging Cooperation among Minorities in Defense of Indian Secularism since the Adoption of the Citizenship Amendment Act under the BJP', in *World Christianity and Interfaith Relations*, ed. Richard F. Young (Minneapolis, MN: Fortress Press, 2022) 37-56, muse.jhu.edu/book/99712.

This paper is an attempt to analyse how the Mizo navigate the troubled spaces defined by their minority-majority status and how they negotiate their identity as citizens of heaven with the contestation of the Hindutva ideology that they are not rightful citizens of India.

RESURGENCE OF NATIONALISM

In 1992, the American Francis Fukuyama claimed that the history of humanity had reached its end. He did not predict the end of the world but that, with the global spread of Western liberal democracy, the history of ideological conflicts had come to its end.[6] In 1996, Samuel P. Huntingdon claimed, in response to Fukuyama's thesis, that after the end of the Cold War, peoples' cultural and religious identities would be the primary source of conflict and lead to the clash of civilisations.[7] Huntingdon's thesis has been heavily criticized not only because the expression 'the clash of civilisations' had been used in India to look at the Ayodhya incident in 1992,[8] but because it could act as a blueprint for the kind of conflicts that advocates of Hindutva attempt to provoke. Hindutva or Hindu-ness is a culturalized and politicized transformation of Hinduism based on a selection from the many streams within the Hindu religious and cultural milieu.[9] The long history of this ideology is well-known; its early story is part of the renaissance of Indian identity as the vantage point from which to argue for independence from colonialism.[10] Since the mid-1990s, the

---

6   Francis Fukuyama, *The End of History and the Last Man* (New York: Free Press, 1992).
7   Samuel P. Huntingdon, *The Clash of Civilizations and the Remaking of World Order* (New York: Schuster & Schuster, 1996).
8   For the use of this expression by Hindu revivalists, see Koenraad Elst 'Recollections with Sita Ram Goel: Part 3', *India Facts*, 2016, http://indiafacts.org/recollections-with-sita-ram-goel-part-3/.
9   Jyotirmaya Sharma, *Hindutva. Exploring the Idea of Hindu Nationalism* (New Delhi: Penguin/Viking, 2003): 156.
10 See, among other publications, Sharma, *Hindutva*; Thomas Blom Hansen, *The Saffron Wave. Democracy and Hindu Nationalism in Modern India* (Delhi: Oxford University Press; Princeton: Princeton University Press, 2001); Shashi Tharoor, 'Hinduism and the Politics of Hinduism', in *Why I Am a Hindu* (Victoria: Scribe Publications, 2018).

largest political wing of this broad movement, the Bharatiya Janata Party (BJP), has been successful in winning elections and in implementing its convictions through laws and by sanctioning practices of aggression and violence. As this is written, the BJP is currently in power as the federal government and is campaigning to win the 2024 general elections for Parliament. One of the few states where the party so far has not been successful is the northeast state of Mizoram.

Hindutva claims that Hindus form a nation defined by one history, one culture, and one language and, for some, by one blood or race. V. D. Savarkar and Madhav Sadashiv Golwalkar started to develop this ideology by transforming Hindu religious diversity into a hegemonic cultural concept in the first decades of the twentieth century.[11] The problem for Hindutva is not that others—Muslims and Christians—practise different religions but that their religion, history, culture, and language are rooted in a different *fatherland* (*pitribhu*) outside of 'Hindustan'. They are accused of having forcibly introduced their culture and religion into 'Hindustan' and of damaging the cultural unity and body of the Hindu nation. They may live in the same territory, but because of their allegiance to a civilisation other than the Hindu civilisation (Sarvarkar spoke of *sanskriti*[12]) they are enemies of the nation and have lost their right to dwell on the soil declared as Hindu.[13] K. N. Panikkar wrote in an article in 2004: 'Hindutva's cultural project, encoded in the slogan "nationalise and spiritualise", therefore is twofold. First, to retrieve and disseminate the cultural traditions of the "golden" Hindu past; and second, to eliminate all accretions that

---

11 V. D. Savarkar (1883-1966) wrote about this in his 1923 book *Hindutva: Who Is Hindu?*; see Sharma, *Hindutva*, 124-172. Madhav Sadashiv Golwalkar (1877-1958) wrote, in 1939, *We, Our Nationhood Defined*, in which he admired what he called the 'German Race-spirit'; see Hansen, *The Saffron Wave*. 80-84. On Golwalkar, see also Longkumer, *The Greater India Experiment*, 5-7.

12 Sharma, *Hindutva*, 163.

13 Siga Arles, 'India: Religious Polarisation in a Hindu Context', in *Freedom of Belief and Christian Mission*, Regnum Edinburgh Centenary Series 28, eds. Hans Aage Gravaas, Christof Sauer, Tormod Engelsviken, Maqsood Kamil, and Knud Jørgensen (Oxford: Regnum Publishing, 2015), 323, 329. Longkumer, *The Greater India Experiment*, 28.

had become part of the heritage.'¹⁴ In his widely known book, *Why I Am a Hindu*, Shashi Tharoor engages with the notion of the clash of civilisation and identifies the core of Hinduism as its tolerance and plurality. He states,

> Living with people of various kinds of faith, Hindus developed their tradition of acceptance of difference, but also understood that in both principle and practice, religion and politics should be divorced.... The idea of India is of one land embracing many.... The reason India has survived all the stresses and strains that have beset it for seventy years, and that led so many to predict its imminent disintegration, is that it maintained consensus on how to manage without consensus.¹⁵

RELIGION

Tharoor's argument that Hinduism developed a tolerant characteristic from its beginnings is itself a cultural construct, and the story of how the concept of a religion called Hinduism was created is well-known. One could say that tolerance of other religious practices is a possibility for some of the traditions grouped under Hinduism. Yet, like everywhere else, religions in India have been involved in politics and have instrumentalised or in turn have influenced politics. As well, in times of large kingdoms with a pronounced dominant religion, there were periods of suppressing other religions as well as periods of peaceful coexistence. Hindutva criticises Christianity as being the truly intolerant religion. In 2008 Dayanand Saraswathi, a Hindu *swami* (religious ascetic), argued in an article in an English daily newspaper published in Chennai, Southern India, that a Christian cannot help but convert others.¹⁶

---

14 K. N. Panikkar, 'In the Name of Nationalism', *Frontline*, 13 March 2004, 108, https://frontline.thehindu.com/cover-story/article30221708.ece.
15 Tharoor, *Why I Am a Hindu*, 106.
16 Dayananda Saraswathi, 'Conversion Destroys', *The New Indian Express*, 21 January 2008, 9.

Saraswathi is quoted here because his article was published in a newspaper and because he cites Hans Ucko as proof for the Christian compulsion (understood by Saraswathi as a vice) to proselytise. Acknowledging Ucko, whom he knows as an 'upright, outspoken gentleman', he scrutinises Ucko's statement that 'it is more important for us [Christians] to bear witness to Christ by our action of caring for people without any ulterior motive and by our exemplary living'. Whereas mission theologians find that the emphasis on bearing witness and caring is a step away from approaching others only for the sake of converting them, Saraswathi finds exactly this behind the words, because for him, conversion is in the DNA of Christians. 'So, given the theological compulsion to share the faith with a stranger, a serious Christian has no option except to exert and "save" the person, inevitably a non-Christian.' The ulterior motive of the Christian may be the fear that the other is lost and going to hell—the 'innocuous mandate "to bear witness" to Christ inheres the denigration of the "other"' and this leads to violence.[17]

Ucko and other theologians of the WCC dialogue program had been instrumental in organising a multi-religious consultation on the issue of conversion. At this Lariano Consultation, a statement was issued that 'religions should be a source of uniting and ennobling of humans. Religion, understood and practiced in the light of the core principles and ideals of each of our faiths, can be a reliable guide to meeting the many challenges before humankind'. Freedom of religion was agreed to be 'a fundamental, inviolable and non-negotiable right of every human being in every country in the world' including the right 'to practice one's own faith, freedom to propagate the teachings of one's faith to people of one's own and other faiths, and also the freedom to embrace another faith out of one's own free choice'. A remarkable agreement was that such an invitation 'should not be exercised by violating other's rights and religious sensibilities. At the same time, all should heal themselves from the obsession of converting others'.[18]

---

17   Saraswathi, 'Conversion Destroys', 9.
18   The Lariano statement is quoted by Ucko in Hans Ucko (Ed.), *Changing the Present, Dreaming the Future. A Critical Moment in Interreligious Dialogue* (Geneva: WCC Publications, 2006), 94–95.

While Ucko and other dialogue and mission theologians are accused of not being free from the obsession of converting others, Saraswathi himself adopted a patronising attitude, which suspected that the conversion of those who embrace the Christian faith could not be genuine. He believed the motives of those whom he accused of converting non-Christians was not genuine. Christians seeking to convert others to Christianity were presumed to have ulterior motives. We could interpret Saraswathi's argument as showing that details and differentiation are not important in the claimed and provoked eternal fight between constructed entities called Christianity, Hinduism, or Islam and the civilisations they inform. Koenraad Elst, in his book *Decolonizing the Hindu Mind*, sympathetically describes the perspective of Hindutva advocates on conversion. He explains that Christians' declared aim and hope of a rich harvest of converts from among the Hindus; the existence of well-developed apparatus, including educational institutions; and funding for their activities from outside of the country results in Hindu revivalists feeling they are 'under siege'. Elst states that revivalists, such as the advocates of Hindutva, feel drawn into 'a life-and-death struggle, besieged by enemies who are after its skin and who have already conquered quite a bit of territory, both geographically and psychologically'.[19]

This explains why declarations like the WCC's call for interfaith dialogue (Ucko) or a document like 'Christian witness in a multireligious world' (2011) are not able to dispel the suspicion that there is more at stake in a conversion than one person or family changing their religious creed.[20] The anti-conversion laws, which were introduced in several states in India as early as 1936, breathe this spirit of suspicion.[21] They seem to put anyone's wish to change his or her religious affiliation into the perspective that a conversion to Christianity is the result of pressure from Christians or that the converts have been lured by promises.[22] Because the BJP and other Hindutva organisations believe that conversion is the result not of faith

---

19   Koenraad Elst, *Decolonizing the Hindu Mind. Ideological Developments of Hindu Revivalism* (New Delhi: Rupa & Co., 2001), 270–271.
20   *Christian witness in a multireligious world*. World Council of Churches. 28 June 2011. http://tinyurl.com/ya69hx2e.
21   Arles, 'India: Religious Polarisation in a Hindu Context', 323.
22   Arles, 'India: Religious Polarisation in a Hindu Context', 324–325.

but of pressure, of luring and misleading with promises, they feel the need to restrict religious freedom, which the Indian constitution defines as an unalienable right of each and every one.[23]

MIZORAM

Far from such homogenizing and generalizing assumptions about Christianity and religion in general, the Christian fold in India is comprised of several diverse and distinct minority groups. The case of the Northeast states is but one of many special cases in this wide spectrum. Elst reports that Christians are the 'distant third' on the agenda of Hindu revivalists, after Islam and after Nehru's secularism. However, especially in the Mizo and Naga cases, Hindutva ideologists identify a cause-and-effect relation between Christian mission and separatist movements, which is proof to them that Christian conversion is an attack on the Hindu nation. Elst quotes a WCC document in which, next to religious freedom, the right of indigenous peoples to autonomy is emphasised; the advocates of Hindutva take this as a proof of the Christian threat to dismember the Indian nation.[24]

Arkotong Longkumer states in his recent study of Hindutva activists in the Northeast region that

> They engage primarily in social service (*seva*) and countering the hegemony of the 'Christian other' in the sphere of ideas and polemics, and in allying with non-Christian movements to pursue their agenda of Hindutva through cultural appropriation and assimilation with challenging consequences for intercommunity relations in the region. Hindutva actions may foment violence, but, importantly, they do so indirectly.[25]

---

23 Article 25 reads: 'religion. — (1) Subject to public order, morality and health and to the other provisions of this Part, all persons are equally entitled to freedom of conscience and the right freely to profess, practice and propagate religion.'
24 Elst, *Decolonizing the Hindu Mind*, 290.
25 Longkumer, *The Greater India Experiment*, 16.

Mizoram can be considered a Christian state, because it is one of the very few in which Christians form the absolute majority. There is widespread caution among the population in the state against the BJP and other Hindu nationalist organisations because of their Hindu chauvinist attitude. Despite this, the BJP has a presence in the state. The party's Mizo leader declared last summer that he hopes for more votes in future elections, because for him, the BJP is not a Hindu party but the party of development and progress, which he hopes more and more Mizo will come to understand.[26] In 2017, when the Indian Home Minister Rajnath Singh of the BJP visited Mizoram, a beef festival was celebrated on the day of his visit in Aizawl, the capital city. This was organised by an association named ZoLife. Zo is part of the name of the state Mi-zo-ram and designates the people.[27] Around three thousand people joined them and prepared and consumed beef in public as a way of expressing their protest against the beef ban.[28] The political centre run by the BJP has declared a ban on selling cows for slaughter in markets as well as several other regulations to be observed in order to save the cows, which are considered holy by Hindus. This is one of the many culturalised policies implemented by the proponents of Hindutva ideology and is commonly referred to as the beef ban. Besides what such a declaration of the centre means in a country formed by many states, one of the problems with this ban is that it is open to interpretation. This ambiguity has been used in some states by pressure groups to attack minorities and communities for whom beef is a way of either earning their living or a part of their diet.

With slogans like 'For God's sake, let's eat beef' or declaring on posters the beef ban to be an expression of religious arrogance, historical

---

26   Amrita Madhukalya, 'BJP Making Inroads in Mizoram Ahead of 2023 Assembly Elections', in *Deccan Herald*, 8 August 2022, https://www.deccanherald.com/national/bjp-making-inroads-in-mizoram-ahead-of-2023-assembly-elections-1116276.html (accessed 3 January 2023).

27   See the discussion of the concept of a Zomia region focusing on Asia's highland borderlands in Longkumer, *The Greater India Experiment*, 79.

28   See Manogya Loiwal, 'Beef Festival Organised in Aizawl as Rajnath Singh Visits Mizoram', *India Today*, 12 June 2017, https://www.indiatoday.in/india/story/beef-festival-aizawl-mizoram-rajnath-singh-982329-2017-06-12 (accessed 3 January 2023).

ignorance, and cultural fascism, the Mizo protesters made clear that they would not accept any policies that touch upon their culture, customs, and religion. The leader of the BJP in Mizoram, J. V. Hluna, attempted to clarify that the president of his party, Amit Shah, when asked about the ban, had declared that Mizo should follow their tradition because it allowed beef consumption as the Bible does.[29] It may sound comforting to hear this message, but it is ambivalent. The claim for exemption is based on a communal argument. The ban, in the same way, is based on a different tradition and religious custom in a region where the BJP claims this religion to be the majority. This is aligned with the situation in India where customs and even laws are related to communities, which are defined by their tradition, culture, and religion.[30]

The tradition and dietary customs of the Mizo ancestors knew a brand of bovines, the *mithan* or *gayal*. Slaughtering and eating these animals was an integral part of the many festivals celebrated in the village community. Killing the wild roving *mithan* was one of the deeds a man needed to perform to achieve the status of a *ram thangchhuah*, a kind of a cultural hero.[31] Eating beef has a long history and tradition among the Mizo, to the extent that they incorporated it into their brand of Christianity.[32] It would be more correct to claim that the Bible did not oblige Mizo to refrain from eating beef when they became Christians than to claim that the Bible allowed it.

---

29   Sujit Nath, '"Bible Allows Us to Eat Beef": Mizoram BJP Chief on New Cattle Rules', in *News 18*, 7 June 2017, https://www.news18.com/news/politics/bible-allows-us-to-eat-beef-says-mizoram-bjp-chief-on-new-cattle-rules-1425653.html (accessed 3 January 2023).
30   See Behera, 'Heavenly Citizenship', 86.
31   Behera, 'Heavenly Citizenship', 81, Footnote 17.
32   Joy L.K. Pachuau and Willem van Schendel, *The Camera as Witness. A Social History of Mizoram, Northeast India* (Cambridge: Cambridge University Press, 2015), 77–79: 'So Mizos proceeded to incorporate gayal sacrifice and feasting into their Christian moral code. Those who could afford it slayed a gayal for the main Christian feast, Christmas, or at weddings (Figures 4.21–4.23). They also killed gayals to celebrate when missionaries returned from furlough in Britain. Finally, Christian-inspired "revival" feasts also required the sharing of gayal meat.'

The issue here is that a Hindu nationalist ideology fights to extend its power and to establish political hegemony by using cultural and in part religious symbols as identity markers and make them obligatory for all. One of the main effects of the implementation of such policies is to mark the dividing line between those who claim their roots in the *pitribhu* as Hindus and those who are declared as its enemies. The culturised argument is that others may have other customs but, by observing these customs, they exclude themselves from the fold of the true citizens. Grounding the resistance in these differing customs and religion makes sense, but the danger on the level of opposing ideologies is that it confirms the argument of the aggressor: they truly are the others.

HINDUTVA NATIONALISM AND INDIAN SECULARISM

In my article 'Heavenly Citizenship', I analysed the concept of heavenly citizenship (Phil 3:20) among the Mizo Christians.[33] As explained, the first Christians in the region declared themselves to now be *pathian mi* (God's people) and *vanram mi* (heavenly people/citizens). As a Christian, one is no longer a citizen of this earthly world (*he lei ram mi*) but of the heavenly world (*van ram mi*).[34] Interestingly, the Mizo did not use this distinction to distinguish between themselves and the British colonial power or missionaries, because they too were considered to have heavenly citizenship. Heavenly citizenship is used to differentiate between a Mizo identity as a Christian and the identity of being a citizen of India. As I have already mentioned, the Indian constitution confirms the right to have and practise a religion and to promote and propagate it. It is formulated as an individual right for every Indian citizen. In India, religion, however, works on the basis of a communal understanding. This is clearly visible if one explores the concept of secularism in the constitution and in India.

---

33   I build here on Marina Ngursangzeli Behera, 'Perspectives from the Global South: Europe the Exceptional Case?', in *Mission in Secularised Contexts of Europe: Contemporary Narratives and Experiences*, eds. Marina Ngursangzeli Behera, Michael Biehl, and Knud Jørgensen (Oxford: Regnum Books International, 2018), 195–205.

34   Behera, 'Heavenly Citizenship', 76.

Talal Asad argues in his book *Formations of the Secular*, in which he studies secular formations outside of the Western sphere, that one could easily conceive of secularisation as the separation of religious from secular institutions of government and then observe how that has been implemented in various societies in history. However, modern 'secularism' is the result of secularisation processes and it introduced new concepts of 'religion', 'ethics', and 'politics' and brought new imperatives with it.[35] Asad highlights that the discourse on secularism is a political and cultural strategy that affects the understanding of both religion and politics. An elaborated and contemporary secularism discourse is not about enhancing the dividing line between the newer or modern secular and the sacred remnants of earlier times. The discourse on the secular shifts the distinguishing line and, with that shift, the realms of the secular and the religious are transformed. Asad opines that secularism today mediates different images of what a society is perceived to be, mediates how a society designs and implements power, and mediates in how far a society is imagined to have a transcendent background.[36]

India is by its constitution a 'Sovereign, Socialist, Secular, Democratic Republic'. Paulose Mar Gregorios states that 'Socialist' does not in any way reflect the present socio-economic reality and is in danger of heavy erosion.[37] Secular means that no religious community receives preferential treatment by the state. Democratic means power in the hands of the people that is exercised mainly through the vote. In politics, and especially in Hindutva politics, the appeal for votes is based on regionalism, communalism, and religion, against which the constitution does not provide much safeguard.[38]

According to the Indian constitution, citizenship is the legal status of an individual, independent of ethnicity, descent, or religion. It is defined by a set of privileges, rights, and responsibilities. It is important to remember that this understanding of citizenship in the Indian constitution has a

---

35   Talal Asad, *Formations of the Secular: Christianity, Islam and Modernity* (Stanford: The University of California Press, 2003), 1–2.
36   Asad, *Formations of the Secular*, 2003, 5.
37   Paulose Mar Gregorios, *The Secular Ideology: An Impotent Remedy for India's Communal Problem* (ISPCK/Mar Gregorios Foundation [OTS], 1998), 33.
38   Gregorios, *The Secular Ideology*, 34.

link to its colonial past and, in a complex way, to Western democratic traditions. Freedom of religion and worship are constitutional fundamental rights of the citizens of India. The state is expected to guarantee individual and corporate religious freedom and deal with an individual as its citizen irrespective of his or her religious faith. Secularism functions, however, more as claim of equality between the different religions and religious communities, many of which have not only their different customs and practices of life but also sets of laws that are valid only for them. Secularism in India is more an attitude that does not encourage intolerance among followers of different religions.

Today, secularism is under attack.[39] In multicultural, pluralistic Indian society, communalism and religious fervour have contributed to the rise of Hindutva or majoritarian militancy in electoral politics. Its consequences are being felt in the judiciary and in wider society. Secularism is attacked by Hindutva because it allows for a diversity of 'India', allowing multiple 'nations' and diversity on its territory and, thus, fragments the one country, one nation, and one language discourse.

AS IN HEAVEN—SO ON EARTH

The Mizo case in the Hindutva setting can be seen as one example in which a clash of civilisations actually occurs.[40] It is a conflict on earth but the arguments with religious undertones or religious legitimisation make it also a conflict in heaven. Religious figures and gods like Ram and Krishna invoked by Hindutva advocates make the Christian god look like a despot demanding that his followers on earth convert all others. That they seem to have no right to their religion is criticized by those who consider themselves to be 'true Hindus'. In this, a liberal Hindu like Tharoor and Hindutva seem to agree. Whereas it seems that, for Tharoor, Christians and Hindutva ideologists should learn from Hindu tolerance, for Hindutva activists, Christians are the enemies of the Hindu nation, even if they are

---

39 David E. Singh in his recent article writes about movements of protest against the Citizenship Amendment Act, which attacks the notion of secularism in the Indian constitution. See Singh, 'Emerging Cooperation,' 37–55.

40 Adapted from Behera, 'Heavenly Citizenship', 85–89.

not the first on their long list. For Hindutva activists, the encounter on earth is a life-and-death fight over the right way of living ordered by the gods.

The Mizo by origin, history, culture, and acquired religion are different from the sanskritised civilisation of Hindutva advocates. The Mizo also have a casteless society.[41] Their different history is the basis for the protest against the beef ban: 'We are Christians and this is part of our culture given to us by our God.' The concomitant Christian and Hindutva clash is an ideological battle of contesting constructions of mythical maps and stories and of differing times immemorial that span a mythological sky over the region. Arkatong Longkumer analyses how activists of the Hindutva ideology in the Northeast, mainly in Assam, spur a concept of a greater India spanning from the western coasts of the Indian subcontinent to Myanmar/Burma, Thailand, and even parts of China sharing Indian civilisation (*sanskriti*). They do this by speaking about a civilizing mission of Hindu saints and sages travelling and spreading their great tradition and by 'mapping' the ground covered by them by placing events and persons mentioned in the tradition—Vedas, Mahabharata, Ramayana, Puranas, and others—in the region, thus defining the region as Indian. Anyone living in the area thus mapped can be considered as belonging to the Indian soil, emptying it at the same time of contrasting indigenous identities.[42]

It seems to me that the beef-ban protest, the Christian legitimisation of beef eating, and the Mizoram BJP's reaction to the Mizo protest indicate that it may be possible to keep the Christian Mizo identity under the roof of the political ideology of Hindutva. Longkumer gives several examples of Hindutva activists in Assam who gave up their vegetarian diet in order to assimilate and fit in with the people there and consider this as their sacrifice for the greater cause of Hindutva. These were persons coming from mainland India who brought a vegetarian diet with them.[43] In the

---

41 Hrangkhuma Fanai, 'Christianity in North-East India', in *Witnessing to Christ in North East India*, Regnum Edinburgh Centenary Series 31, eds. Marina Ngursangzeli and Michael Biehl (Oxford: Regnum Publishing, 2016), 22.

42 See his discussion of these concepts in chapter 2, 'The Northeast and Time's Relentless Melt', in Longkumer, *The Greater India Experiment*, 49–89.

43 'The choice of food, as basic sustenance, is part and parcel of their sacrifice for working for the nation, where these categories—meat eater and

case of the Mizo members of the BJP in Mizoram, they obviously did not convert from their ancestral diet to vegetarianism, as the words of their leader shows.

In the neighbouring Northeast states with larger Christian populations (such as Assam, Tripura, Manipur, and Nagaland), the BJP has been able to forge political alliances. Mizoram has so far never had a BJP government or a government party in alliance with the BJP. However, the Mizoram branch of the BJP is not worried. As one leader explains, 'We are showing the people the benefits of PM Modi's schemes, and the development in eight years. People are beginning to be convinced that we mean progress.'[44] As a political party, the BJP seems to be able to suspend some of its foundational ideology and negotiate politics in order to win the voters in the state.[45] Suspending dimensions of its ideology for the time being is a political strategy. It is, however, evident that the BJP has taken root in tribal communities in Mizoram who are minorities in the Christian state, such as the Bru, of whom many are Muslims, and the Ma, of whom many are Buddhists. They can be assimilated, at least ideologically, to the greater India concept or an assumed Hindu civilisation. By accentuating the attempts of the Mizo Christian mission among them as attempts to break these tribal communities out of the Hindu fold, the Christians can be identified again as people with allegiance outside of the *pitribhu* (fatherland), or, metaphorically speaking, to cut them off from the body of mother India. This brings the risk that existing fault lines will be used to stir conflicts in the name of minorities against the majority in the state a clash of civilisations.

Mizoram as a majority Christian state will not agree to merging into the imagined history of a Hindu civilisation. Their story—where they come from and the traditions they developed while living in the region and

---

vegetarian—fade into the background.' Longkumer, *The Greater India Experiment*, 26.

44 Madhukalya, 'BJP Making Inroads', https://www.deccanherald.com/national/bjp-making-inroads-in-mizoram-ahead-of-2023-assembly-elections-1116276.html. (accessed 03 February 2023).

45 Henry L. Kohjol, 'Mizoram BJP Gets New Chief', *The Telegraph*, 7 January 2020, https://www.telegraphindia.com/north-east/mizoram-bharatiya-janata-party-gets-new-chief-in-vanlalhmuaka/cid/1733834, (accessed 3 February 2023).

becoming Christians—gives them a strong sense of identity as one people, one country, and one language anchoring their identity in their heavenly citizenship. This mirrors, in a way, the arguments of the Hindutva ideology. It had been a long process in which the evolving identity rooted in heavenly citizenship and the movement of the various tribes toward becoming one people formed a distinct identity of being Mizo. It seems to me that the Mizo in this complex situation need to stick to their identity as tribal Christians and as heavenly citizens. Their attitude, however, shown at the contact zones with marginalised groups within the state is a type of mission that has been criticised within the church as being too Mizo in its character and emphasis.[46] In a minority-majority situation like in Mizoram and within the larger context of Indian politics, it may become exclusive.

The BJP attempts to get a foot into Mizoram demonstrate how the Mizo union as a body on earth is set today in an India in which the Hindutva ideology attempts to impose the contours of a different body with a distinct physiognomy. The equation of religion with culture on both sides defines and magnifies the difference between imagined 'others'.

It seems to me that the relation between the heavenly citizenship, the community on earth, and the citizenship in India need to be renegotiated. The Mizo explored this tension on the basis of a reformed theological tradition. It assumed a close relationship and overlap of community and church congregation. This was undergirded by their tribal heritage, which was not proposing to differentiate between the community, its practices and customs, and its faith. At the same time, heavenly citizenship and the ensuing unity as a body of faith are a gift from God and thus are given, not earned. To be a Christian, in this perspective, means to be or to become part of a larger community that includes people from all tribes and nations. The emphasis on heavenly citizenship anchors Mizo Christians as Indian citizens; it unites them with Christians in other countries without losing a sense of being Indian. In Mizoram, this awareness expects Christians to live in solidarity with and serve those who are not. Their mission

---

46 Lawmsanga, 'Theology of Mission: The Mizo Perspective', in *Witnessing to Christ in North East India*, Regnum Edinburgh Centenary Series 31, eds. Marina Ngursangzeli and Michael Biehl (Oxford: Regnum Publishing, 2016), 51–52, 55.

and evangelism should not impose the Mizo identity or Mizo culture on those they reach out to. Heavenly citizenship is a gift. It is able to bridge a gap between the dominant cultural expression of Mizo Christianity and the Christian faith. In the national context, the theological argument of heavenly citizenship should encourage Mizo Christians to advocate together with others for secularism according to the understanding of the Indian constitution: equality of all religions and equality before the law. This could be a means of resisting the Hindutva advance. The motivation for striving for earthly and political citizenship should not be the wish for one's own rights alone. It should be the expression of all Christians being in solidarity with their compatriots.

9

FEAR AND INWARDNESS
An Examination of the Responses of Church of Pakistan and Full Gospel Assemblies Churches in Modern Pakistan

Gloria Calib

According to estimates, the Christian population in Pakistan varies between three and five million. Approximately 80 percent of the Christian community is clustered in the province of Punjab, with less in Sindh.[1] Pakistani Christians live in a complex context of poverty, discrimination, illiteracy, persecution, religious extremism, corruption, instability, terrorism, and energy crisis. Much of the country's population is in 'multi-dimensional poverty'.[2] According to a recent estimate of the World Bank, in Pakistan poverty increased from 4.4 percent to 5.4 percent in 2020, which means an additional two million people fell

---

1   'Population by Religion'. *Pakistan Bureau of Statistics,* 8 March 2023, https://www.pbs.gov.pk/sites/default/files/tables/population/POPULATION%20BY%20RELIGION.pdf. In 1998, one estimate was that 1.9% of the population is Christian, i.e., 2.8 million. Mano Rumalshah, *Being a Christian in Pakistan* (Peshawar: Peshawar Diocese, 1998), 30. Taking into account the national population growth rate of 3 percent annually, this would take the Christian population to nearly four million by 2009. There is a strong feeling among Christians that there has been a consistent under-enumeration of the Christian community in official census-taking.
2   'Half of Pakistan lives in Poverty,' The News, 3 June 2014, http://www.thenews.com.pk/todays-news-2-273911-half-of-pakistan-population-lives-in-poverty-un-report.

below the poverty line.³ Sultan, a Pakistani missiologist, writes, 'Christians are among the poorest of the poor . . . therefore, a ghetto mentality has emerged among them . . . the search for ways to play a significant role in witnessing contextually to the gospel values . . . is challenging for Christianity in Pakistan'.⁴ In 1976, Bishop of Sialkot wrote, 'It cannot be denied that most of the time and energy and personnel of the Church is spent on building up and maintaining Church structures rather on outreach.'⁵ The situation has not changed much since that time. Recently Carey, a British missionary in Pakistan for more than three decades, identified that 'with a few exceptions, the Pakistani Church is still not self-propagating, with growth almost entirely biological. . . . The main reason for a lack of growth is not the small number of Christians, however, but the nominalism that is so prevalent'.⁶

The question is whether this state of being inwardly oriented is changing. Based on a variety of primary sources from The Church of Pakistan (CoP) and the Full Gospel Assemblies (FGA) from two different geographical locations (Punjab and Sindh), I explore in this chapter two specific responses of Pakistani Christians.⁷ I first identify fear of persecution as a key perceived restriction contributing to the absence of outward action. Then I discuss self-centredness, personal ambitions, and internal politics that have contributed to the lack of mission engagement of the Pakistani Church. Through a selection of testimonies, I highlight evidence of the often-negative intra-church activism.

---

3   'Poverty in Pakistan rises to over 5% in 2020, estimates World Bank', *Business Standard*, 21 June 2021, https://www.business-standard.com/article/international/poverty-in-pakistan-rises-to-over-5-in-2020-estimates-world-bank-121062200084_1.html.

4   Pervaiz Sultan, *Small but Significant: Pakistan Praxis of Modern Mission,* (Karachi: FACT Publication, 2010), 19.

5   William Young, 'Selfhood and Mission', in *Struggle for Selfhood: A Consultation between the Church of Pakistan and Her Partners from Abroad,* ed. Anwar Barkat (Lahore: The Institute of Political and Social Studies, FCC, 1976), 37.

6   Fareda Carey, "Edinburgh 1910 and Pakistan", *Al-Mushir* 52, no. 4 (2010): 137–168, here 139.

7   At consideration of potential risks, participants' confidentiality and anonymity are maintained by using participant identification numbers.

FEAR OF PERSECUTION

There is a great deal of worldwide reporting on the persecution of the Pakistani Church. The participants were asked if persecution was a major restriction for their mission work. A range of both clergy and laity said that persecution was not the strongest constraint for mission engagement. Rather they were overwhelmed with internal issues and problems within the church, such as internal politics, lack of resources, and vision. For many participants, persecution and fear of it were real but less significant issues. One respondent from CoP, with nearly thirty years ministry experience, said, 'The fear of persecution is exaggerated, and it does not have any strong foundations.'[8]

Those from relatively higher socio-economic status and closer connections with Muslims also expressed such a view. For them, fear of persecution was more perceived than real. Some respondents, however, noted, 'When I think of engaging in mission, I am fearful because of Islamic extremism and 295 C law.'[9] 'The situation is getting difficult because of 295 C law. The consequences of mission engagement can be very dangerous.'[10] Some of the respondents were concerned for the whole community or church, for those who could be put in danger as a result of engaging in mission: 'You can't put the whole church in trouble just because of one lost sheep. If you have converted one non-Christian to Christ, it can generate a great trouble for him as well for the whole church which has accepted him.'[11] Another

---

[8] Participant identification no_S.M_1.12, in discussion with the author, Lahore, Pakistan, 2015. Section 295C to the Pakistan Penal Code to provide the death penalty or life imprisonment for the criminal offence of defiling the name of the Prophet Mohammad. Under 295 C untrue accusations and fabrication of blasphemy cases have become a quite common trend in order to threaten and assault individuals for personal and business reasons. To make the matter even worse, many Christian villages and communities have been attacked by angry Muslim mobs.

[9] Participant identification no_FGA_FG2_Q7_A2, in discussion with the author, Lahore, Pakistan, 2015.

[10] Participant identification no_IG_2.5, in discussion with the author, Hyderabad, Pakistan, 2015.

[11] Participant identification no_LQ_3.1, in discussion with the author, Lahore, Pakistan, 2015.

respondent said, 'Exaggerating things is a part of our culture that makes me afraid. What if I say or do something for Christ and someone would exaggerate it in a negative way—then me and my community could be all in trouble.'[12] Many felt that the blasphemy law enhanced the sense of fear:

> At the moment the biggest challenge is the blasphemy law. People are very scared. We can't preach openly because society has become so much radicalized and they don't want to hear the Christian message. The message I am receiving is that the majority community out there is saying that, it's fine you can preach in your own Church compound but not in the public square.[13]

With these mixed responses, the fear of persecution was added to the list of perceived restrictions identified by quantitative research. The overall results of responses are shown in Table 9.1.

About 65 percent of people in the sample population considered fear of persecution the highest restriction out of the list of sixteen restrictions. If we add the percentage of respondents who considered it moderately significant, then the percentage escalates to 83 percent, which is a matter of grave concern. The comparative analysis of quantitative research showed that both CoP and FGA equally considered persecution to be the highest restriction.

In the qualitative research, the Lahore diocese and FGA both shared their own experiences and various incidents faced by their local churches or parishes in rural areas of Punjab. In comparison to other provinces, Punjab was highly affected by incidents of persecution. According to the 1998 census, the province of Punjab is home to 81 percent of the Christians in Pakistan.[14] This clustering in Punjab is why Punjabi churches are at high risk of persecution, which is not the case in Sindh. One respondent said, 'We don't have many cases reported in Sindh under blasphemy law, it's mainly

---

12   Participant identification no_FGA_FG1_Q7_A4, in discussion with the author, Lahore, Pakistan, 2015.

13   Participant identification no_AM_1.2, in discussion with the author, Lahore, Pakistan, 2015.

14   'Population by Religion', *Pakistan Bureau of Statistics*, April 2015, www.pbs.gov.pk/sites/default/files/other/. . ./Population/16-16.pdf.

Table 9.1. Fear of Persecution.

Denomination	Fear of persecution because of certain laws. E.g. 295 C etc.					Total
	Not a restriction	Insignificant	Significant	Moderately Significant	Highly Significant	
CoP (Lahore & Hyderabad Dioceses)	3	16	29	47	164	259
FGA	4	15	21	49	170	259
Total	7	31	50	96	334	518

because we are very tolerant people. Sindhis are not bothered much with the religious affiliation; they respect the beliefs of all religions.'[15] Respondents of Sindhi origin in a focus group of Mirpur Khas region agreed that

> We don't have this issue of persecution like Punjab has. Generally, we are people who mind our business. It does not matter whether we live in desert or in a village, we have less or more. Even under tough weather conditions we continue to do our own work and tolerate other religions.[16]

Thus, it is clear that fear of persecution across the two denominations was not as intense in the Hyderabad diocese as it was in Punjab. The question of why Pakistani Christians are so fearful cannot be answered in a vacuum. One needs to glance back on the historical developments that considerably contributed to this state of fear.

LEGISLATION

Under the leadership of Muhammad Ali Jinnah (1876–1948), Pakistan came into being in 1947. Jinnah based his argument for a separate state for Muslims on the 'two-nation theory'. There was strong antagonism between Hindus and Muslims. Muslims, being a minority in the subcontinent, felt a competitive pressure and thus were strongly convinced in favour of a separate

---

15   Participant identification no_DF_2.3, in discussion with the author, Hyderabad, Pakistan, 2015.
16   Focus Group, Mirpur Khas at St. John's, Hyderabad, 11 April 2015.

Muslim nation. G. W. Choudhury observes, 'Pakistan was, in a sense, itself the product of minority problems.'[17] Although religion played an important role in nationalism, Jinnah famously declared in his speech on 11 August 1947:

> You are free; you are free to go to your temples, you are free to go to your mosques or to any other places of worship in the State of Pakistan. You may belong to any religion or caste or creed—that has nothing to do with the business of the State ... We are starting with this fundamental principle that we are all citizens and equal citizens of one State.[18]

Thus, Jinnah's speech makes it clear that he envisioned Pakistan to be a secular, liberal, democratic, inclusive, and pluralistic society. Unfortunately, following Jinnah's death in 1948, a process of official Islamisation began. The Pakistani constitution, which preserves religious rights and freedom for all its citizens,[19] has been steadily undermined by decades of constitutional and legislative revisions. The most damaging change to the blasphemy law (sections 295 A, B, and C) came in 1980.

The blasphemy laws underlie a huge proportion of inter-communal strife in Pakistan. A striking fact is that the blasphemy laws are not an original product of Pakistani government but are based on laws relating to religion in the Indian Penal Code introduced by the British in 1860 to stop inter-religious conflicts in the religiously pluralistic Indian society. They prescribed a punishment of two years imprisonment, a fine, or both, for 'injuring or defiling a place of worship, with intent to insult the religion of any class'.[20] The blasphemy laws were further amended in October 1990, making the crime punishable only by death.[21] According to the Agenzia

---

17 Golam Choudhury, 'Religious Minorities in Pakistan', *The Muslim World*, 46 no. 4, (1956): n.p.
18 Muhammad Munir, *From Jinnah to Zia*, 2nd ed. (Lahore: Vanguard, 1980), 30.
19 'The Constitution of the Islamic Republic of Pakistan', *Pakistan National Assembly*, 8 March 2023, https://na.gov.pk/uploads/documents/1333523681_951.pdf.
20 'Pakistan Penal Code (Act XLV of 1860),' 8 March 2023, https://www.pakistani.org/pakistan/legislation/1860/actXLVof1860.html.
21 John O'Brien, *The Unconquered: The Liberation of an Oppressed Caste*, (Karachi: Oxford University Press 2012), 284.

Fides Information Service of the Pontifical Mission Societies, between 1927 and 1986, only seven cases of blasphemy were reported.[22] So, there were no strong reasons to add the death sentence.

The National Commission for Justice and Peace says that in the last 25 years, 1,058 cases of blasphemy have been registered. Of the accused, 456 were Ahmadis, 449 were Muslims, 132 were Christians, and 21 were Hindus.[23] Thus, the misuse of the law affects citizens of all religions, including Muslims themselves. However, minority communities are more vulnerable to non-legal violence. Furthermore, the discriminatory attitudes are well-rooted in society and also in the corrupt institutions that enforce law and order, making access to justice harder for minorities. A large number of incidents have taken place against Christians. Under 295 C, untrue accusations and fabrication of blasphemy cases have become a quite common trend in order to threaten and assault individuals for personal and business reasons. To make the matter even worse, many Christian villages and communities have been attacked by angry Muslim mobs.

With the passage of time, blasphemy laws have acquired a status of divine laws among Muslims. Some steps have been taken by the Pakistani government, led by the late Minister for Minorities Affairs Shahbaz Bhatti, to improve religious freedom and tolerance. However, the assassinations of Shahbaz Bhatti (January 2011) and Governor of Punjab Salman Taseer (March 2011) for supporting progressive amendments to the blasphemy law has left the situation unchanged. Consequently, the issue has become religiously and emotionally so sensitive that any suggestion to hold a rational debate to reform these laws generates serious threats from self-appointed defenders of Islam.

RESPONSES TO PERSECUTION

Christian responses to persecution may be divided into four categories. Firstly, following specific episodes of persecution, greater

---

22 'Pakistan Blasphemy Laws: A Fact Sheet', The Agenzia Fides Information Service of the Pontifical Mission Societies at http://www.fides.org.

23 Akthar Patel, 'Pakistan's Blasphemy Law', *The Express Tribune* 26 August 2012, http://tribune.com.pk/story/426498/pakistans-blasphemy-law/.

communication, networking, and partnership between the persecuted and non-persecuted have grown. Those who have not experienced persecution consistently come to help those persecuted through prayer, practical help, and counselling. Many Christian leaders, especially from the Lahore diocese, have appeared a number of times on primetime TV talk shows. They have expressed their views in favour of the victims and have also pleaded the case for the abrogation of the antagonistic laws. Secondly, anti-persecution protests in both peaceful and violent forms have become a typical response of Christians after the events of persecution.[24] For instance, protests following after the Youhanabad, Lahore, suicide bombing of churches in March 2015 gained immense attention worldwide.[25] Thirdly, some Christians think that the only solution to the problems Christians face is a demand for a separate homeland. Thus, some have suggested a Christian land known as *Takistan* (vineyard).[26] Fourthly, different initiatives by Christian political leaders have followed after almost every catastrophe.[27] Various advocacy agencies have also come forward in support of the persecuted Christians offering legal aid and representation in court trials, settlement,

---

24 A recent trend of violent protests are not only defaming Christian community nationwide but also creating many more difficulties for peaceful Christians, for instance, undue arrests, threatening of mob attacks, and hateful comments from the majority community.

25 See, for example, 'Lahore: Twin Blasts Near Church in Youhanabad', *Dunya News*, 15 March 2015, http://dunyanews.tv/index.php/en/Pakistan/267601-Lahore-Twin-blasts-near-church-in-Youhanabad-kill; 'One Killed, 12 Injured as Christians Protest Countrywide over Deadly Church Attacks', *Tribune Express*, 16 March 2015, http://tribune.com.pk/story/853983/two-separate-cases-registered-against-lahore-church-bombings/.

26 For example, Nazir S. Bhatti, the president of Christian Congress, demanded in a press conference that the Punjab to be divided into three parts, thus giving one part to Christians of Pakistan. *The News International*, 22 April 1992; Pakistan Christian Congress, March 2014, https://pakistanchristiancongress.org/contents.php?section_id=1.

27 For example, Federal Minister for Ports and Shipping Kamran Michael strongly condemned the terrorist attack. *SAMMA News*, March 2015, http://www.samaa.tv/pakistan/2015/03/task-force-needed-for-worship-places-security-minister/.

rehabilitation, shelter, and protection of victims of sexual abuses and domestic violence.[28]

Rarely have Pakistani churches engaged in much detail with the theology of suffering, persecution, and martyrdom for Christ and its significance for mission engagement. In most churches, theological reflection emerges orally right after the incident, reaches a climax at the next Sunday service and dies in the next couple of weeks until something happens again. This reflection is beneficial sometimes, through sermons, the believers are strengthened, and the witness of the believers becomes more effective. However, it cannot take the place of an organised and consistent theological reflection. An appropriate response should result in theologizing of persecution. Instead of accepting the pain and suffering passively, how can the Pakistani Church deal with its fear and actively seek opportunities to engage in society through presence, service, identification, dialogue, and proclamation?

SELF-CENTREDNESS AND PERSONAL AMBITIONS

Self-centredness and personal ambition within the churches is rated in the quantitative research as the second highest restriction. About 54.4 percent of people considered this a significant restriction for mission engagement. The results of the quantitative research are shown in Table 9.2.

The results in Table 9.2 show that 'self-centredness' is a significant issue in both denominations. Rather than engaging with society, there is a tendency in churches to be consumed with self-gain and self-serving. Bishop Jiwan said,

> Today if we are selfish and self-centered, it is because we are all the time looking inward. Dennis Clark in this book, "The Third World and Mission", has rightly said "Lawsuits, party strife, factions and

---

28   There are two prominent indigenous advocacy organisations; one is the National Commission for Justice and Peace (NCJP), which has worked since 1985. The second is the Centre for Legal Aid Assistance and Settlement (CLAAS), which originated in 1992.

Table 9.2. Self-Centredness in the Church.

Denomination	Trends of self-centredness and personal gain in churches					Total
	Not a restriction	Insignificant	Significant	Moderately Significant	Highly Significant	
CoP (Lahore & Hyderabad Dioceses)	8	7	45	51	148	259
FGA	4	17	31	73	134	259
Total	12	24	76	124	282	518

jockeying for the assets of church property have drained Churches of spiritual power and evangelism vigor"... The Pakistani Church is disobedient to the Great Commission. How can a Church grow spiritually if it is disobedient to God's commandment? We mature in faith when we share and participate in the missionary vision of God ... if there is friction and dishonesty, it is because we are inward-looking and not outward looking.[29]

Evaluating Self-Centredness

The data generated from the qualitative research showed that self-centredness and personal ambitions in the church can be seen from three perspectives: (1) the self-centredness of the ordained clergy pointed out by the congregants; (2) the self-centredness pointed out among ordained clergy in hierarchal terms, which included issues with the top leadership and subordinate leadership, both pointing at each other; and (3) the self-centredness of the congregants pointed out by the ordained clergy. The statements of the respondents suggested that churchgoers from all walks of life placed their welfare above everything else. This made it difficult for them to reach out to engage in society as Christians.

The awkwardness surrounding the theme of self-centredness in the church did not stop respondents from speaking straightforwardly. For instance, some mentioned greed-based, wealth-consuming, self-promoting

---

29 Bashir Jiwan, 'Mission and Selfhood', in *Struggle for Selfhood: A Consultation Between the Church of Pakistan and Her Partners from Abroad*, Anwar Barkat (ed.) (Lahore: The Institute of Political and Social Studies, FCC, 1976), 30.

leadership. They pointed to people in the church who were self-absorbed and ego-driven. These reflections reveal that a great deal of mistrust exists inside Christian communities.

The Lahore diocese was seen to be more stable. The respondents here did not express any significant mistrust against the leadership. If any controversial issues emerged out of the conversations, they defended each other. This can be counted as a strength. However, in both the Hyderabad diocese and FGA, ordained clergy and the congregants highlighted grievances within the church involving issues of self-centredness and selfish ambitions. The importance of healthy relationships was considered highly valuable among CoP's pioneers:

> During the discussion we realised that we could not talk of relationships with others unless we set our own house in order. We should first look at our own Church. It is Church here that needs to change for the sake of its mission in order to establish healthy and meaningful relationships.[30]

While defining 'selfhood' for a newly founded church, A. Barkat stressed that

> Surely, selfishness, self-centeredness, and narrow-minded arrogance are concepts which are associated with selfhood... Selfhood is not to be understood in its individualistic or atomized sense, but in pluralistic sense. We cannot think of selfhood in its separateness, but rather in terms of its relationship.[31]

A wide variety of issues related to self-centredness came out in the qualitative research. It included authoritative leadership that did not listen, land grabbing, and lack of pastoral care for both clergy and laity. One participant of CoP said:

> A hierarchical church structure with the seeking of unquestioned obedience by Church leadership further constipates innovative

---

30 J. V. Samuel "Opening Keynote Address" in *Struggle*, 13.
31 Anwar Barkat, 'Introduction', in *Struggle*, 5.

and creative ideas. Pastors need to be engaged into applied missions studies and subjects such as conflict resolutions and community development need to be incorporated.[32]

A respondent from FGA said,

> FGA is a hugely well-known and recognized denomination in Pakistan. But certain people in executive leadership have their own feudal system, they want to keep everyone under their own control and command. In my understanding that's the major challenge for missional engagement. Feudalism should be brought down, and the specific leadership should repent and seek true repentance of their ungodly behaviors. It is an essential step for the denominational future.[33]

Several serious property-related issues both in CoP and FGA were raised. There were people from within and outside of the church who were seen to be directly or indirectly involved in grabbing diocesan or denominational properties. There was a consensus in both denominations that there is significant financial strain on the churches' annual budgets due to court cases. Thus, in some cases, in the churches there was more money needed for safe-guarding church property then for doing what churches should do in society: 'Lahore Diocese has been engaged with legal battles with regard to the number of cases related to land grabbing and illegal occupations on the church property. This has implication for financial resources that negatively affects the working on other dimensions of the church.'[34] Many leaders from Hyderabad mentioned issues of land-grabbing in the Hyderabad diocese. One commented,

> We are facing property issues from many years. There are so many illegal occupancies in the parish compounds by the people who

---

32   Participant identification no_Al_1. 10, in discussion with the author, Lahore, Pakistan, 2015.
33   Participant identification no_GT_3. 5, in discussion with the author, Lahore, Pakistan, 2015.
34   Participant identification no_Al_1.10, in discussion with the author, Lahore, Pakistan, 2015.

once used to work for the diocese. We are spending so much money in the court cases that we could have saved and used for mission work.[35]

One leader from FGA said that

> We face various challenges related to property at the local church level. Sometimes the local pastor raises funds, on top of that he gets financial help from the center for the church building. Then, he legally allots that property in his own name. Then there are illegal occupancies in some of our properties and we have to spend a lot of money and energy to get those properties.[36]

Another issue, lack of pastoral care, was also raised. Some leaders in both the denominations shared their stories about when they needed help but their senior leaders did not give it. Some junior leaders were ignored by the senior leadership to teach them a lesson or because they failed to please the senior leader. This significantly contributed to mounting mistrust and fragmentation. It was evident in both the denominations. One respondent of CoP said,

> My father has been sick. While I was caring for him, I reflected on the mounting strife in the diocese and I decided that I would resign. So, I sent a text message to my leader saying that 'I can't continue my service therefore I am resigning'. His response was just one word 'ok', he did not even say that you come back to your parish and then we can discuss the issues and resolve the conflict. After two days my father died and he did not even call me for condolences.[37]

---

35 Participant identification no_KJ_2.1, in discussion with the author, Hyderabad, Pakistan, 2015.
36 Participant identification no_SS_3.2, in discussion with the author, Lahore, Pakistan, 2015.
37 Participant identification no_MB_2.8, in discussion with the author, Hyderabad, Pakistan, 2015.

In a focus group in FGA, most of the respondents agreed:

> We have never been visited or asked that how are we doing in our ministries. Only favorites ones are being followed-up.[38] There is a need to give attention to the mission workers. We are doing things on our own initiative. We are left without any help like orphans.[39]

A board member from FGA defended the centre in this way:

> As a centre we could not teach our local churches to be self-sufficient. So, financially they are not independent. Many times, they have an unjustified expectation that the center should be doing something more to support them. Another challenge is that we have a weaker link with the local churches, although our interaction is polite but sometimes we can't be there for them at their time of need. We have a lot of financial issues which means we can't travel much to meet pastors even when we should be there for them.[40]

Poverty and Dependency

The issue of dependency needs highlighting. Those in authority can often become a target of people's anger when their needs are not fully met. There are congregants who expect the church to help them in kind or cash when need arises. For instance, they expect financial assistance for their own needs or help to find a job, or provision of a letter to support their refugee status in applying for immigration.[41] If the church denies them help, they

---

38   Participant identification no_FGA_Focus Group no 4, Lahore, Pakistan, 2015.
39   Participant identification no_LS_3.6, in discussion with the author, Lahore, Pakistan, 2015.
40   Participant identification no_KC_3.8, in discussion with the author, Lahore, Pakistan, 2015.
41   A significant number of the Christian community migrate to economically wealthy countries because of the fear of persecution, discrimination, and lack of opportunities. So, it is not uncommon that many Christians craft

feel frustrated and consider it deliberate discrimination and disloyalty. This may be traced to the reality of landlessness. Christians often come from poor families dependent often on their Hindu or Muslim *zamindars* (landowners). This has lingered among them and has created what John O'Brien calls a 'chronic dependency syndrome'. It was caused by years of subjugation and oppression. He quotes the adage *'Tussi Sadhe Ma-bap o'* (You are our father and mother), through which he notes that 'historically, the dependency on the *zamindar* was transferred onto the church: here was a benevolent ma-bap [mother and father] who could provide, forgive and accept'.[42]

The Pakistani Church's context is largely that of poverty. Azeem Rehmat, a Bible teacher at FGA Bible College, writes,

> Many pastors live lives of poverty. They don't have a good house to live in. Their children cannot attend a good school. They live miserable lives; even their basic needs are not being met. All this badly affects their ministries and above all pastors themselves become mentally distressed and sick . . . unfortunately many churches keep their pastors under financial strain, they only pay them 5000 Rupees (approximately 15 pounds sterling) monthly income . . . there are many church councils who use their pastors like puppets, they do not let their pastor work part-time at some other place to supplement his income and don't pay him enough. This gives rise to hatred, fragmentation and hard heartedness.[43]

Azeem compares a congregational system with a diocesan or episcopal system and considers the diocesan system to be better and well-structured. It facilitates its clergy with better salaries, transportation, medical needs, and housing. He concludes that they can have a better lifestyle and can be effectively engaged in mission.[44]

---

false cases of persecution in order to get refugee status in a desired country. Some expect the leaders to support them in their fake cases of persecution.

42 O'Brien, *The Unconquered*, 140.
43 Azeem Rehmat, 'Is My Church Part of Body of Christ? Part II', *Satoon-e-Haq*, 26 no. 6 (June 2012): 17, 19, and 20.
44 Rehmat, 'Is My Church, Part II,' 11.

Azeem in his judgement is right to some extent, for CoP has carefully crafted rules on financial matters. such as loans and provident fund.[45] Even then, some key informants in CoP think that the vision of most local priests is very poor, for they are often worried about paying the assessment to the diocesan office.[46] A respondent said the following: 'I tell you 90 percent of my problems are administrative and funds related. I am so overwhelmed that I can't even think of mission'.[47]

INTERNAL POLITICS

Internal politics within the churches featured prominently in responses. About 53 percent of the sample population considered it to be a highly significant factor. There was a strong connection between politicking and self-centredness. Politicking is an activity directed toward acquiring power and influence, achieving one's own goals. It also facilitates an unavoidable slide toward fragmentation. The survey results are illustrated in Table 9.3.

These survey findings, which are supported by qualitative interviews, reveal the destructive existence of politics and fragmentation within the churches. In the context of CoP, Sultan notes,

> Many Christians . . . have formed opposition groups which are called 'partibazzi' (groups formed to oppose each other). It has become a characteristic of the Christians in big villages to relate to one group or another, based on kinship, leadership or other factors . . . The influential people . . . adopt the old formula of 'divide and rule' to hold the influence on people. . . Church elections are also heavily affected by partibazi.[48]

---

45 For example, see The Constitution and Bylaws of the Hyderabad Diocesan Council, 47–54.
46 The salary of each clergy is given by the diocesan office but, in return, each parish must raise funds equivalent to the salary and submit them regularly to the diocesan office; this is known as assessment in CoP.
47 Participant identification no_KJ_2., in discussion with the author, Hyderabad, Pakistan, 2015.
48 Pervaiz Sultan, *Church and Development: A Case Study from Pakistan* (Karachi: FACT Publication 2001), 175 and 203.

Table 9.3. Internal Politics within the Churches.

Denomination	Internal Politics within the Churches					Total
	Not a restriction	Insignificant	Significant	Moderately Significant	Highly Significant	
CoP (Lahore & Hyderabad Dioceses)	7	15	19	70	148	259
FGA	14	13	30	71	131	259
Total	21	28	49	141	279	518

Similarly, Rehmat highlights negative politics within FGA:

> Today the Pakistani churches have the biggest danger from within which is consuming it. Church is not always threatened from outside but from inside . . . today the Pakistani churches are divided from within, different groups are formed, sometimes pastor himself is involved in politicking. . . at times politicking is involved for forming Church councils. A pastor wants his people to be part of the council whereas the opposite group seeks to bring their own people. Sometimes this hatred is so escalated that people fight and they may even physically attack each other.[49]

The issue of politics is specifically related to elections in the churches. One key respondent of CoP said, 'Elections have become a very dirty game within CoP.'[50] In the context of congregational elections, Rehmat writes,

> Today in churches, we have election system, this is human invention . . . Church elections for pastors, church council or executive leaders is a political election. Due to which the churches are standing at the brink of destruction . . . for sometimes due to elections wrong people come in the position of authority who are necessarily committed to.[51]

---

49 Azeem Rehmat, 'Is My Church Part of Body of Christ? Part 13', *Satoon-e-Haq*, 24 no. 8 (August 2012): 17.

50 Participant identification no_MR_1.5, in discussion with the author, Lahore, Pakistan, 2015.

51 Azeem Rehmat, 'Is My Church Part of Body of Christ? Part 12', *Satoon-e-Haq*, 23 no. 5 (2011): 6.

Reportedly, while some leaders were noted for forgiving opponents, many just carried on with the destructive tactics of lobbying and revenge. One confessed,

> I was very much involved in a bishop's election in a certain period. I was supporting my brother-in-law who was one of the candidates for bishop's elections. We worked day and night but, in the end, he lost because the selected bishop of that time had more power, influence and money. However, I knew that it was not all well behind the elections. So, when he won, I gave him a very tough time and in return he gave me even tougher time.[52]

Some leaders stressed the necessity of such politics for survival, 'If we wouldn't do politics how can we survive? The congregations will simply throw us out.'[53] The need for gaining *izzat* (respect) was cited often in relation to politics in the church. One respondent said, 'Instead of building team for engagement in society, many people in position of power are spending all their energy to secure their status, position and authority.'[54] Another said,

> Only a few are trusted, and they have surrounded the leader, rest of the people are at periphery. It does not count if you can do the job better. There is one, who is doing everything, the other one is waiting for a task to be delegated to him. If someone fails to fulfill the drive of *izzat* (respect) of a person in authority, he can be in real trouble.[55]

One of the key respondents said,

> I know they don't respect me. They just want me to be a problem solver. They want some extra favors from me. I know when they

---

52 Participant identification no_IG_2.5, in discussion with the author, Lahore, Pakistan, 2015.
53 Participant identification no_MA_0.2, in discussion with the author, Lahore, Pakistan, 2015.
54 Participant identification no_AM_2.6, in discussion with the author, Hyderabad, Pakistan, 2015.
55 Participant identification no_SM_1.6, in discussion with the author, Lahore, Pakistan, 2015.

meet me, they pretend they respect me but, on my back, they say nasty things about me. This situation is so intense that we can't think of anything else.[56]

A respondent of FGA mentioned, 'Favoritism hinders FGA from engaging in mission. Some leaders preach more but it cannot be seen in their own lives. They only think about themselves, they know how to demand *izzat* (respect) but they don't know how to give *izzat* to the other people as well.'[57]

In the light of the above statements, the Pakistani Church context can be described as that of internal fragmentation and conflict. It also demonstrates that some relationships within the church need healing and reconciliation before the church will be taken seriously outside its boundaries.

When analysing intra-church fragmentation, one can notice two important factors: desire for power and impact of culture. Khan describes this as follows:

> The powerless people dream of having power. Only a few are able to have power in society.... In a country like Pakistan the churches and Christian institutions offer an opportunity to assume positions of power. Tragically, people make use of these organizations as a springboard to rise to positions of power.... Politics has become a pastime for people who have leadership qualities. These people normally do not have any other civic or national political forum where they can exercise their skills as a politician. The result is that they make the church into a body which is divided into different parties. This can easily start a court case. These are often about property of the church, positions, constitutional matters, illegal occupation of church buildings etc.... This is rather a common... phenomenon... Church after church suffers from it.[58]

---

56   Participant identification no_KJ_2.1, in discussion with the author, Hyderabad, Pakistan, 2015.
57   Participant identification no_LS_3.6, in discussion with the author, Lahore, Pakistan and Pakistan' Al-Mushir 52 (April 2010): 137–168, 163–164.
58   Ashkenaz Asif Khan, 'Fate or Call?' quoted in F. Carey, *Edinburgh 1910*, 163–164.

In the light of Khan's observation, powerless people, in search of power, are accused of causing fragmentation. People seek power because they need the wider affirmation within their own community; this is because they often experience exclusion in the wider society. Christians mostly survive on the margins of society as a minority. Gaining power and influence in their own community, denied in the society at large, fulfills a deeply felt need.

It is also worthwhile to investigate cultural factors and the possible influence they can have on the fragmentation of the Christian community. As noted above, 80 percent of Pakistani Christians live in Punjab; therefore, the Pakistani Church is 'strongly influenced by the worldview, beliefs, values, social institutions, and patterns of behavior of Punjabi society'.[59] The *biradari* system dominates the Punjabi worldview. A *biradari* is a kinship group that is larger than the extended family and involves a complex system of favours and obligations.[60]

There are several disadvantages of *biradari*. The loyalty demanded from the *biradari* can make it difficult to be loyal to others. Yusaf, a Catholic bishop, has done intensive work on the *biradari* system, and he points out that the Punjabi culture requires that a man must belong to a *biradari* or he is nothing. *Biradari* demands the highest loyalty. Often individual conscience and personal initiative are crushed. Disagreements between *biradaris* often end in violence, and the spirit of revenge lasts for generations.[61]

Another disadvantage of *biradari* is nepotism. Some have investigated the concept of *biradari* and have mentioned that the complex system of favours and obligations within the *biradari* leads to a situation where Christian leaders in places of position and authority are expected to use their influence to provide economic and political support for their own *biradari* members. If requests for jobs are not fulfilled within the *biradari*, the relationships can become very strained, even if those requesting are

---

59 Wayne McClintock, 'A Sociological Profile of the Christian Minority in Pakistan,' *Missiology: An International Review*, 20, no. 3 (July 1992): 347.
60 McClintock, 'A Sociological Profile', 349.
61 Patras Yusaf, 'The Biradari System in Punjabi Society', *Al- Mushir*, 22 no. 4 (1980): 155, 158–159.

not competent to fulfil the job. Yet, complying in providing help will result in heavy criticism of nepotism from other church members. Ironically, those critics would do the same in securing benefits for their *biradari* if they were in a position to do so.[62]

Another issue connected to the topic in view is that of *izzat*. *Izzat* is a foundational value of the Punjabi culture and is used as a psychological tool for controlling society and ensuring conformance with social, cultural, religious, and moral values. *Izzat* can be described as honour, prestige, respect, personal pride, self-esteem, or worth. The opposite of *izzat is be-izzat*, which brings shame not only to an individual but to whole *biradari*.[63]

Once lost, *izzat* can never be fully regained. It can be partially restored, however, either by avenging the original offence by an act of violence or, in the case of minor offences, by seeking reconciliation. In order to preserve one's *izzat,* one must be loyal to the family, clan, and its traditions.[64] The notion of *izzat* influences the behaviour of Christians within the church. The longing for *izzat* and personal recognition in a relational society where the *biradari* has deep influence on all aspects of life often leads to scheming, fragmentation, and manipulation.[65]

CONCLUSION

Much of the discourse on Christianity in Pakistan focuses on its persecution. This often characterises Pakistani Christians as mere victims lacking agency or choice. It also paints a rather static picture of a homogenous minority stunned by the sustained hostility of an Islamic republic. While

---

62   McClintock, 'A Sociological Profile', 349–350; Domnic Moghal, *Human Person in Punjabi Society: A Tension between Religion and Culture* (Rawalpindi: Christian Study Center, 1997), 66; Patrick Sookhdeo, *A People Betrayed*, 309.

63   McClintock, 'A Sociological Profile', 350; P. Yusaf, 'The Principle of Izzat: Its Role in the Spiritual Formation of Punjabi Religions', *Al-Mushir,* 22 no. 1 (1980): 17–28, 18.

64   Wayne McClintock, 'A Sociological Profile', 350.

65   See John Charles Heinrich, *Psychology of Oppressed People* (London: Allen and Unwin, 1937), 15–42.

such descriptions deserve space, their narrow characterisations of Pakistani Christians often miss details only a participant observer can offer.

In this chapter, I showed that, internally, both CoP and FGA choose not to engage in wider society because of their sense of fear and powerlessness—both of which come from their history of deprivation. I also highlighted the hidden states of these churches as exemplified by two sites. These states I described will likely be seen by some to be signs of a failing or missionally drifting church lacking the impetus to 'witness to the world' and, thus, denying 'the gospel of his [Christ's] transforming grace' to Muslims in Pakistan;[66] however, the value of the picture I paint in this chapter is in drawing readers in to view these churches' inner states as I see them. These churches may be inwardly oriented, but they are far from being a passive minority incapable of choice or agency.

I identified the fear of persecution as the main factor responsible for the churches' supposed inaction. A selection of the qualitative testimonies of my respondents also highlighted factors other than fear that show their internal activism even if, theologically, these would be deemed unworthy of their Christian calling or mission: (1) self-centredness and (2) internal politics. The discussion of these two responses to fear showed that the Pakistani churches' most important 'battles' are fought largely within and not in external engagement in society.

---

66   See Christopher Wright, *The Mission of God's People: A Biblical Theology of Church's Mission* (Grand Rapids: Zondervan 2010), 283.

10

CHRISTIAN-MUSLIM DIALOGUE AS SOCIO-POLITICAL ACTION IN EGYPT

Toby Kan and Henrik Lindberg Hansen

This chapter describes Egyptian society as a clientelist system, where religious affiliation helps delineate belonging and opens possibilities to secure life through social networks for both Muslims and Christians. We then discuss a growing decentralizing tendency after the 2011 Revolution, where people individually engage with the public sphere using a humanist discourse rather than the more traditional and institutionalised religious discourse. Since the Arab conquest in 640 CE, Christians[1] and Muslims in Egypt have lived side by side. On the one hand, the two communities suffered historically under the same rulers and were united in resisting British imperialism; on the other hand, Muslims, as part of the state religion, enjoy freedoms, while Christians suffer from discrimination. In order to

---

[1] In this chapter, 'Egyptian Christian' and 'Copts' are identical in meaning. The Coptic Orthodox Church makes up the majority of the Egyptian Christian community. The Arabic word *al-qibṭ* for Copt means 'the inhabitants of the Nile valley' and its original Greek word, *aigyptos*, simply means 'Egyptian'. The percentage of Christians among the Egyptian population has been a politically sensitive topic for decades. Nowadays, the highest estimation from the Coptic Church is around 20 percent, and the lowest estimation from the government is 6 percent. Scholars believe that a realistic number should be between 8 to 12 percent. For more details, please refer to Sana Hassan, *Christians versus Muslims in Modern Egypt: The Century-Long Struggle for Coptic Equality* (Oxford, New York: Oxford University Press, 2003), 17-21.

understand the complex dynamics between the two faiths in contemporary Egypt, understanding their social and political context is crucial.

We examine interfaith relations through the lens of clientelism, through which the regime shares power and offers protection to social groups. These groups offer allegiance to the system in exchange. The major religious groups and organisations function as social groups in this system. They act as brokers of the central authority and ensure 'proper behaviour' of their members. This socio-political context has dominated the interfaith dialogue in Egypt at large. However, with the 2011 Revolution, grassroots interfaith movements have also thrived and the voices critical of the clientelist and religious representation has gained momentum. To date, some movements continue under restrictions and the agenda of social solidarity blessed by the current regime, although much of the pre-revolutionary discourses, such as national unity, are again in place, as will be obvious in the chapter.

CLIENTELISM IN EGYPT

According to Hansen,[2] clientelism can be outlined as follows:

> Fundamental to clientelism is the patron-client relationship, whereby a patron earns the allegiance of clients by somehow improving their lives through favours, and the client secures the patronage by somehow backing the patron in society, thus enhancing their status, political influence, etc. The favours involved might have pecuniary value, but this is rarely the case. Clientelism only thrives in places where power and/or wealth is unevenly distributed, making it possible for few to become the personal distributors of this power and wealth. This in turn increase the power of the patron, as he or she can build a large following that can be mobilized for elections, riots, protection, etc. [. . .] Clientelism is not a system of governance on its own, but arises as part of systems

---

2   Henrik L. Hansen, *Christian-Muslim Relations in Egypt: Politics, Society and Interfaith Encounters*, Library of Modern Religion, vol. 43 (London: I.B. Tauris & Co. Ltd, 2015).

whenever gaps between the rulers and the ruled arise. People seek to fill these gaps by seeking favours from those who have access to power in the country, in order to gain access to the distribution of the wealth [or other favours] of said country.

In the early formation of clientelist theory, scholars emphasised the 'instrumental friendship' in the ties between a patron, who has higher socioeconomic status, and a client with lower status. The patron promises favours to the client as an exchange for the client supporting the patron. In other words, 'a patron is the superior and a client the inferior in an unequal, vertical, and reciprocal relationship'.[3] The hierarchical structure between patron and client(s) is 'not only in terms of money and relative inequality, but also in terms of access (to decision makers, to bureaucracy, to judges, to all sorts of authorities and service providers) and absolute inequality (i.e. inclusion/exclusion, access/no access)'.[4]

In later development of the concept, scholars focussed more on the broker's chain of the patron-client relationship and researched its impact on the society.[5] Normally, the brokers are those 'who have standing in the community and are deeply embedded in local networks'.[6] The main broker is an intermediary between the lower level's brokers or clients and the top-level patron. According to the survey of Allen Hicken,[7] there is no generally accepted definition of clientelism, but it usually includes several key

---

3 Sharon Kettering, 'The Historical Development of Political Clientelism', *The Journal of Interdisciplinary History*, 18 no. 3 (1988): 425, https://doi.org/10.2307/203895.

4 Sina Birkholz, 'Multi-Layered Dependency: Understanding the Transnational Dimension of Favouritism in the Middle East', in *Clientelism and Patronage in the Middle East and North Africa: Networks of Dependency*, eds. Laura Ruiz de Elvira, Christoph H. Schwarz, and Irene Weipert-Fenner, Routledge Studies in Middle Eastern Democratization and Government 22 (London ; New York: Routledge, Taylor & Francis Group, 2019), 23.

5 Susan C. Stokes, 'Political Clientelism', in *The Oxford Handbook of Comparative Politics*, ed. Carles Boix, The Oxford Handbooks of Political Science 1 (Oxford: Oxford University Press, 2009), 604–627.

6 Allen Hicken, 'Clientelism', *Annual Review of Political Science*, 14 no. 1 (2011): 291, https://doi.org/10.1146/annurev.polisci.031908.220508.

7 Hicken, 'Clientelism'.

elements: the dyadic relationship between patron and the main broker, the contingent or reciprocal nature of the patron-client exchange, their hierarchical positions, the ongoing nature of the relationship, and the freedom to exit the relationship if dissatisfied.

In Egypt, clientelism was an integral part of the social system before the 1952 revolution. The patron-client position between state and church had been formed long before President Gamal Abdel Nasser (the founder of the current political system) came to power, as was obvious in the interactions between the patriarchs of the Christian community and the regime.[8]

From Nasser, the pact between the patriarch and the president guarantees benefits for both sides. Egyptian presidents 'ensured the security of the community and the status of the Patriarch as the Copts' legitimate representative and spokesperson' while the Coptic community publicly supported the regime.[9] By showing loyalty to the authority, the church gained autonomous powers, such as administrative rights, permission to build or renovate a certain number of church buildings, permission to approve or disapprove the marriage status of their members, and support for the governing member's religious as well as family affairs. Moreover, as a non-Muslim minority in an Islamic society, peace is negotiated by acting 'correctly' before the patron. Some scholars call this relationship a 'neo-millet system' with an exclusive focus on the relation between state and church.[10] However, clientelism adds to the understanding of this relationship, because it places the relation between state and church among general socio-political dynamics in Egyptian society. The nuance between millet system and clientelism is mainly that the former is an official tool in the political system to govern the *dhimmi* or the protected non-Muslim people, while the latter is an analytic tool of the social phenomenon. Moreover, clientelism exists

---

8   Adel Guindy, *A Sword over the Nile: A Brief History of the Copts under Islamic Rule* (New York: Austin Macauley Publishers LLC, 2020).

9   Paul Sedra, 'Class Cleavages and Ethnic Conflict: Coptic Christian Communities in Modern Egyptian Politics', *Islam and Christian–Muslim Relations*, 10 no. 2 (July 1999): 226, https://doi.org/10.1080/09596419908721181.

10 Paul S. Rowe, 'The Church and the Street: Copts and Interest Representation from Mubarak to Sisi', *Religion, State and Society*, 48 no. 5 (19 October 2020): 346. https://doi.org/10.1080/09637494.2020.1849894.

as an unofficial but customary practice between the authorities and social groups and not as an official policy of the regime.

DISCRIMINATION AND THE CLIENTELIST SYSTEM

In Egypt, a discourse on persecution is commonplace among Christians who face discrimination. The discourse builds on a historic narrative of suffering for Christ and martyrdom in the Coptic Orthodox tradition. However, the definition of persecution by the Coptic Church does not necessarily align with the Western understanding, where the term builds on, for example, the persecution during the Roman time, where the regime hunted down Christians. The Coptic Orthodox Church partakes in politics and aligns with the regime to overcome the difficulties of heavy discrimination against it. Thus, in this chapter, we prefer to use 'discrimination' rather than 'persecution'.[11]

Various forms of social inequality exist in a hierarchical society like Egypt. Religious identity adds another reason for some Muslims to legitimise discrimination against Coptic neighbours. The Copts are not homogeneous and, therefore, not everyone feels the same degree of discrimination. Among them, there are for example wealthy and poor, educated and illiterate, rural and city-dwellers. The affluent Copts hardly ever experience discrimination. However, the ordinary Copts experience discrimination in various ways. In summary, there are two kinds of discrimination: systemic and personal. Examples of systemic discrimination include the state's emphasis on *shari'a*, Islamic teaching in public schools, and the permeation of Islamism in Egyptian society. Personal discrimination consists of negative stereotypes of Copts in general, disadvantages in different social situations, distrust in relationships, and so on.[12] Besides these, intergroup conflicts happen over wealth, church building, and the rumours of religious conversion or interreligious love affairs, especially in poorer areas where radical Islamism is more active. However, at the same time, most Christians also talk about positive relations with many of their

---

[11] See also Hansen, *Christian-Muslim Relations in Egypt*, 110.
[12] Hansen, *Christian-Muslim Relations in Egypt*, 113–25.

Muslim neighbours. Muslim groups differ as much as the Christian groups. In this chapter, we describe some of the different political and social roles that Christians take in defining relations between different Muslims groups. This is to say, it is highly simplified to talk about 'Christian-Muslim relations' as a duality.

The discrimination is obvious and present, but there is reluctance to admit its existence. As part of the patron-client relationship, the church is obliged to reaffirm national unity when sectarian incidents happen. In many cases, complaining about discrimination or sectarian violence is problematic for the president, who can be seen as not providing for or too weak to protect his clients. It can also have a negative effect for the interests of other stakeholders, such as the Islamists or Nationalists. By taking the client position, the church has less bargaining power. Historically, the native church had to preserve an image of peaceful coexistence between Muslims and Christians and by this show loyalty to the patron. The options are either to function outside the clientelist system or to deny any discrimination. The obvious choice for the church has been to remain in the sheltered position within the clientelist system.

Another problem of the clientelist state-church relation is that the enemy of the regime is an enemy of the whole clientelist system, including the church. A clear example is the threat from radical Islamists. Copts become scapegoats of the tension between the regime and Islamist groups.[13] Since 1970s, extremists have provoked the government by making numerous terrorist attacks targeting Christians and tourists, who are supposed to be protected by the regime. The attackers aim to create internal tension in society and to draw international attention to the regime. For the radical Islamist, 'to assault the Copts is to assault the state' and they see the sectarian attack as a 'substitute for its inability to strike directly at the state'.[14]

---

13 Peter E. Makari, 'Conflict and Cooperation among Christians and Muslims in Egypt: Communal Relations, Toleration, and Civil Society' (PhD thesis, New York University, 2003), 58, https://search.proquest.com/docview/305314516/abstract/36D8181574D64635PQ/1.

14 Gilles Kepel, *Muslim Extremism in Egypt: The Prophet and Pharaoh* (Berkeley: University of California Press, 1985), 240.

THE COERCIVE FOUNDATION OF THE CLIENTELIST SYSTEM

The state apparatus is crucial to guarantee the operation of clientelism in Egypt. The coercive forces at its disposal are the police and the army. The police force (regular and secret police) grew vastly during the time of Hosni Mubarak. The police are feared for their brutality. They are the chief arm of the state, aggregating the functions of several agencies. This also affects the public, in that many people believe that the secret police constantly monitor them in everyday life. The police thus influence all aspects of Egyptian life, if not by direct surveillance, then through the fear of being watched. On the other hand, their experience also leads to their growing dissatisfaction, resulting in events such as the 2011 uprising.

Another coercive agency is the military, which has played a role in Egyptian politics and the economy since Nasser's time. With the exception of President Morsi, all other Egyptian presidents have had a military background. Traditionally, the youth in the army are treated as 'our sons'. During the bread shortages under Mubarak, the military bakeries baked bread and distributed it among ordinary people. This was a symbol of the state's benevolence. This explains why people were clapping when they saw the military tanks moving into the Tahrir square during the 2011 Revolution. After the ouster of Mubarak, the army acted as the sole regulator of political transition, which enhanced their prestige. However, in critical moments, the regime still uses soldiers to control the crowd. The incidents of the Maspero TV building in 2011 and Rabi'a Square in 2013 both exemplify the military's formidable power over the citizens.

While the coercive forces can be used to repress people who act against the regime, the police and army are under the same system of patronage as well. For instance, with the blessing of the authoritarian regime, the army has become 'a formidable stakeholder of Egypt's national economy', owning 'business enterprises, running hotels, constructing tollways, and so on'.[15] By obeying the order of the patron, the police and army are able

---

15 Mehmet Hecan and Fouad Farhaoui, 'The Coercive Power and Democratic Transition in the Post-Uprising Middle East and North Africa', *Democratization*, 28 no. 6 (18 August 2021): 1162, https://doi.org/10.1080/13510347.2021.1897788.

to obtain all necessities for their living, education for their children, and presidentially appointed posts after their retirement, but the army is also part of the foundation of the power of the president. Those in the army, however, are also composed of citizens with different ideologies, including the extremists. Examples have been noted of police officers who engaged in violence against the Copts in the past.[16] However, for a Copt, obtaining a higher position in police or military is impossible. This is evidently discriminatory toward the Copts.

OFFICIAL DIALOGUE UNDER THE CLIENTELIST SYSTEM

As part of the clientelist system, official dialogue emerges as a major means of negotiating Christian-Muslim relation in Egyptian society.[17] On the local level, some religious leaders cultivate good rapport with each other and resolve conflict using the discourse of national unity. On the national level, Muslim and Christian leaders greet each other during feasts like Christmas and Ramadan. Regular meetings between representatives of both faiths, such as the Grand Imam of Al-Azhar and the heads of different Christian denominations, are organised to discuss issues of mutual interest, especially during periods of sectarian attacks and unrest.

This official dialogue builds on the earlier-mentioned discourse of national unity, claiming that in Egypt there is no difference between Muslims and Christians. Even Christians and Muslims, who might not agree with the discourse, often deny the existence of sectarianism in Egypt—although they later detail discrimination against Christians. This view seems to be embedded in Egyptian identity, because it is rooted in the official narrative about government being the protector.

After sectarian violence, the clergies and government officials usually display their unity by appearing together before the media. Although

---

16 United States Government (Ed.), *Religious Persecution in the Middle East: Faces of the Persecuted*, Senate. Hearing 105-352 (Washington: U.S. Government Printing Office, 1998), 114–115.

17 Henrik L Hansen, 'Interreligious Dialogue and Politics in Revolutionary Egypt', *Journal of Islamic Research*, 9 no. 2 (2015): 4–27, https://doi.org/10.7146/tifo.v9i2.25350.

official dialogue ventures to demonstrate harmony between faiths, many in the grassroots have lost faith in this. Some feel that this is merely a show, and many intellectuals from both faiths argue that it is a political illusion. Because religious institutions act as representatives of their community, the type of interfaith dialogue dominating relations is top-down in nature.

During Mubarak's time, another predominant issue impacting Christian-Muslim relation was the sectarian conflicts targeting Copts. Christians were treated as 'soft targets' of attacks. According to Alaa Al-Din Arafat,[18] the sectarian conflict against the Copts escalated during the years leading up to the 2011 Revolution. In many cases, no legal action was taken to uphold justice. This contributed to growing tensions among Christians, Muslims, and Mubarak's government. It threatened the clientelist system as Christians began to question the determination of the government to protect them. Despite internal opposition against this, the Pope continued his supportive gestures toward Mubarak's regime until the end of the 2011 Revolution.

After the revolution, many Egyptians, Muslims and Christians, were eager to rebuild their nation. However, nation building as a joint focus faced a setback just after it started. In 2012, Mohammed Morsi won the presidential election. Morsi, an ex-chairman of the Freedom and Justice Party, promoted the idea of establishing an Islamic state with 'fundamental religious functions'. He subsequently emphasised 'the Qur'an is our Constitution' and ignored the demands of Christians in the constitutional amendment. All our Christian interviewees negatively portray this period as being 'very difficult', 'a disaster', 'reaching the boiling point', and one said that 'the 2011 Revolution was kidnapped by the Islamists'. Many Christians felt that they suddenly became second-class citizens and were further marginalised in society under an Islamist regime. Indeed, the voice of radical Islamists became louder. Many radical groups publicly promoted their extreme points of view, which fuelled religious fanaticism. In this period, the relation between Christians and Muslims quickly deteriorated.

However, the Muslim Brotherhood did not pay homage to the Supreme Council of the Armed Forces in their power struggle, and many

---

18   Alaa Al-Din Arafat, *The Rise of Islamism in Egypt* (Cham, Switzerland: Palgrave Macmillan, 2017), https://doi.org/10.1007/978-3-319-53712-2.

Egyptians felt that they were ruling with a hidden agenda, which resulted in a re-revolution. A Muslim respondent, who is a leader of an interfaith network, explained why he chose to join the re-revolution of 2013 together with Christians:

> First, I think a religious government is actually even worse than a dictatorship because you cannot criticize them as everything comes from God and they are always representing God. You can still criticize a dictatorship government in some ways. Second, we want a secular government, which treat people in a more equal manner. Third, there were some indications and rumours about emerging of many radical Islamic groups in the time of Morsi [in Egypt]. We don't really know if it was true, but some news also talked about it. Therefore, we were willing to protest with our Christian neighbours.[19]

The respondent also saw Muslims protesting together with Christians in 2013 as healing for Christian communities after their fears under Morsi. After the overthrow of the Muslim Brotherhood regime, Abdel Fattah al-Sisi, a general in Egyptian army, seized power. Sisi continued the style of government of Mubarak, also based on the discourse of national unity. At the same time, his Copt-friendly gestures restarted interfaith relations. As something new, he was the first president to attend Coptic Christmas mass since 2014. During the pandemic, he also sent greetings to Christians over Christmas and Easter. He urged Muslims and Christians together to renew the religious discourse in order to create a more peaceful atmosphere between both faiths. He advocated building the New Administrative Capital's cathedral and promised to build a mosque and a church in every new city. In addition, many licences for church buildings were granted.

Under his national security consideration, President Sisi openly declared war with radicalism and showed his support for an interfaith friendly society. In a speech during Ramadan in 2019, Sisi stated that:

---

19   Interview with a male Muslim interfaith practitioner who is a main leader of an interfaith network in Egypt.

> We have been killed by our people for years and we spent a huge amount of money on our security [to be protected] from this [extremist] ideology...We need to monitor ourselves', and he continued to say 'When we wish our Christian brothers a happy feast or [congratulate them] on building new churches, we represent our religion.[20]

In some mosques, the regime also began to monitor the preaching to avoid religious hate speech. For many Christians, this was seen as a sign of improvement in inter-religious relations at the political level. In Sisi's era, the interfaith activities mostly attempted to bring people with different faith backgrounds together to work on the common good in society. In other words, the church again partook in clientelist politics, which is showcased by Pope Tawadros II standing next to President Sisi during public announcements. Under clientelism, every denomination is presumed to engage in the official dialogue as a religious institution and the Coptic Orthodox Church, being the largest church in Egypt, always acts publicly as a representative of all Egyptian Christians.

GROWING HUMANIST DISCOURSE

Around 2011, many grassroots movements flourished. For example, following the tragedy of Coptic Christmas Eve on 6 January 2011, thousands of moderate Muslims made a 'human shield' in front of churches to fight the threat of Islamic militants against Christians. Their action was not organised by any religious institution but was self-motivated. This not only proved that Muslim-Christian relations were amicable in some groups but also showed that many moderate Egyptian Muslims wanted peaceful coexistence of the two religions. This mentality eventually grew into a humanist movement after the 2011 Revolution. The history of Egyptian humanist discourse can be traced back to the time after the World War II. According

---

20   Samar Samir, 'Sisi: Religions Can Be Weakened by Their Believers' Practices', EgyptToday, 2 June 2019, http://www.egypttoday.com/Article/1/71139/Sisi-religions-can-be-weakened-by-their-believers'-practices.

to the *Minimum Statement on Humanism*, which can be found on Humanist International's website,

> Humanism is a democratic and ethical life stance, which affirms that human beings have the right and responsibility to give meaning and shape to their own lives. It stands for the building of a more humane society through an ethic based on human and other natural values in the spirit of reason and free inquiry through human capabilities. It is not theistic, and it does not accept supernatural views of reality.

This understanding of human rights, freedom, ethic, naturalism, atheism, civil society, and democracy is closely related to the Western concept of humanism. In 1948, many Western countries adopted the Universal Declaration of Human Rights (UDHR), which was a crucial international document. This document was criticised by some Arabic countries as 'an ethnocentric document' based on Western culture and philosophy. This became clear during the drafting process of UDHR, where the Egyptian delegation questioned the universal standards of religious freedom and discrimination in the discussion. In Egypt, although some intellectuals agreed with human equality as a global standard after the war, many Arabs saw the spreading of Western humanism as a new kind of 'cultural imperialism' echoing their painful memories of colonialism.[21] Therefore, humanism gained a negative connotation among many Egyptians.

Later development of humanism in Egypt was overshadowed by the Egyptian nationalist discourse. In the time of Nasser, the regime focused more on social-economic establishment under the advocacy of the Arab nationalism than on human rights.[22] Under the flag of socialism, Nasser stressed the urgency of national solidarity and played down any discussion of humanism in Egypt, which became the approach of the successive

---

21 Dalia Vitkauskaitė-Meurice, 'The Arab Charter on Human Rights: The Naissance of New Regional Human Rights System or a Challenge to the Universality of Human Rights?', *Jurisprudence*, 1 no. 119 (2010): 168.
22 Bosmat Yefet, *The Politics of Human Rights in Egypt and Jordan* (Boulder, Colorado: Lynne Rienner Publishers, Inc., 2015), 18–19.

rulers. After Nasser's defeat in the 1967 Arab-Israeli War, Islamist discourse replaced Arab nationalism. While the resulting state Islamism was not radical, it left space for radical Islamism to develop reaching alarming levels by the end of the reign of President Sadat.

After the assassination of President Sadat, the development of radical Islamism was suppressed. By emphasizing national unity and security, President Mubarak again built his ideology on nationalism and employed strong-arm policies to monitor the Egyptian people. Mubarak also attempted to nationalise the non-governmental organisations (NGOs) to control the human rights discourse and save face among the international alliances. Although different ideological currents used humanism as a part of their rationale, the humanist discourse has become marginalised in Egypt. However, with the help of globalisation and communication technology, the seeds of humanism are taking roots among the youth.

The plethora of human dignity slogans during the 2011 Revolution highlighted demands for human equality and rights. Real social justice and human rights were discussed and the number of human rights organisations increased shortly after the revolution. People with different backgrounds engaged in discussions about building a 'new' Egypt. The general atmosphere of society became more welcoming to differing opinions and ideas. It became possible to discuss some topics that had been sensitive in the past, such as workable models of civil society and equal rights for all citizens regardless of religion, belief, gender, and so on.[23] Many people who were a part of the revolution agreed that everyone should be equally treated, albeit there were various interpretations on the meaning of 'human equality' in practice. Although this process was reversed later, it gave people a chance to open their hearts and build new relations with different communities.

Next to this resuscitation of the humanist discourse, the youth also inject fresh energy into the debate. For instance, a few years prior to the 2011 Revolution, some young Muslims and Copts wanted to deal with social issues in their homeland. One of the movements was called *Kefaya*

---

23   Limor Lavie, 'The Idea of the Civil State in Egypt: Its Evolution and Political Impact Following the 2011 Revolution', *The Middle East Journal*, 71 no. 1 (Winter 2017): 23–44, https://doi.org/10.3751/71.1.12.

(enough) established in 2004 and became prominent during the Arab Spring. Similar to the *Wafd* party's model used in the 1900s, the founding leadership of *Kefaya* included both Copts and Muslims. The movement engaged in peaceful activism to demand 'real political change, end to economic inequality and corruption, and reorientation of Egypt's dependent foreign policy', regardless of the religious identity of the members. Many Copts supported the movement and joined their protests against the Mubarak's regime.[24]

In 2011, the overthrow of Mubarak's regime paused the clientelist system and allowed civil society to discuss the future of the country. People from all occupations no longer feared expressing their opinions and wanted to contribute to the nation. Many NGOs were established to build society. Due to the success of the bottom-up nature of the revolution, more interfaith movements or activities, such as the *Salmīyah* network and the Gusour Cultural Centre, began their work from the grassroots level as well, especially targetting the youth. Other existing organisations, like *Misriyati*, which promotes principles of peaceful living through community education, have expanded their projects since the 2011 uprising.

Among Egyptians, the flourishing of the humanist discourse gave more space for the work of interfaith activity. A Muslim peace-building facilitator depicts the phenomenon as a 'natural development' and states that

> During the Revolution of 2011, that [Egyptian humanism] was pretty evident because it was the motif of the Revolution. People cried for *'aīsh, hurriyya, 'adāla igtimā'iyya* [Bread, freedom and social justice]. People want social justice and human rights. The number of human rights organisations was even increasing during that time.[25]

Another Christian interfaith worker in the church setting also found that Egyptian people have been, in general, more receptive to humanism since the 2011 Revolution. The discourse of human equality bridges

---

24 A. Z. Gökpinar, 'Coptic Ethnopolitical Mobilization on the Road to and beyond the January 25 Revolution', (master's thesis, Sosyal Bilimler Enstitüsü, 2012), 80, 103.

25 Interview with a male Muslim leader in the international team of an NGO.

the social gap between Christians and Muslims. As a result, it helps their religion-friendly activities among the public. Encouraged by the revolution, the youth managed their fear and began to engage with religious others. It is, as an interfaith peace-building NGO's leader points out,

> One of the significant impacts of the Revolution, which lasted only I think two or three years [after the 2011 Revolution], was that many of the young people who have been very confined in their religious community ... went out and reached out to other young people from other communities. ... It's especially for Christians because they are the minority, right? But I think the Revolution was the momentum that encouraged this to happen.[26]

Thus, many young Christians and Muslims oppose the clientelist nation building that relies on their religious institutions to represent them. In the church, some of the youth want to become a more visible part of Egyptian society, even following the setback after the 2011 Revolution. Unsurprisingly, the new common ground between this group of 'outgoing' Christians and Muslims is largely based on humanism and national unity. The *Kefaya* movement exemplifies the political involvement of the revolutionary Egyptians from both faiths. A leader of a prominent peace-making network, considered a moderate Muslim, discusses the impact of the 2011 Revolution:

> [The Revolution] has made a huge difference in the whole dynamic [of the interfaith relations] that Christians were saying that 'Let's go out of the walls of our churches!' Before the Revolution, we have been living inside the walls of the churches. And after the Revolution we go out of it! ... They enjoy the fact that there are people who are Muslims but share with them the same values, the same feeling, the same fear and the same hopes. ... So they want to act. ... And some of them are very courageous and they criticize the church and the religious leaders ... on the other side we as Muslims also do the same![27]

---

26 Interview with a female Muslim interfaith organisation leader and scholar.
27 Interview with a male Muslim interfaith practitioner who is a main leader of an interfaith network in Egypt.

A similar phenomenon has also happened in the mosques. Many Muslims are questioning the norms about social separation and are looking to work with Christians to build a more harmonious society. Based on the discourse of Egyptian humanism, Christians and Muslims are finding a common language in the public space.

EXAMPLES OF CURRENT INTERFAITH ACTIVITIES

Given that the national and humanist discourses have been employed in various situations as mentioned, today the interfaith relations are progressing in a way that mixes them.

In the Coptic Orthodox Church, while the Pope continues his leading role in the official dialogue, more cooperations among the members of Islamic and Christian institutions can be found. For example, the churches have been working together in the project called The Egyptian Family House (*bayt al-'ay'la al-maṣraya*) under the umbrella of Al-Azhar. Its aim is to cultivate peace through moral and intellectual education among the youth and to spread the culture of peace by rejecting hatred, violence, and stereotypes against religious others. Under this, the initiative named 'Together for Egypt' was established. In the beginning, it was simply an imam-priest exchange project visiting famous Christian and Muslim sites and serving local communities. . According to a Coptic cleric who is involved in various interfaith dialogues, the focus of their interfaith activities is to build 'unity in society' and 'harmony between different faith groups and denominational groups'. He explains that The Egyptian Family House is

> a great invention and it has a committee that has branches in every city of Egypt. And this is working on harmonizing the situation between Christians and Muslims. They're working on different kinds of conflict resolutions and it has been a great help. Whatever kind of situation that can arise and hurt the harmony, they intervene and we work together. The cooperation actually is very much supported by the government . . . the government will have a very strong role to help this process on developing towards [Egyptian] openness.[28]

---

28   Interview with a highly positioned male clergy of Coptic Orthodox Church.

Despite official dialogue still dominating religious discourse as part of the clientelist system, various churches have adjusted their interfaith activities to include ordinary people on the ground. For example, the Gusour Cultural Centre in Anglican Church was founded after the 2011 Revolution. As the name shows ('Gusour' means a small bridge), the centre wants to provide opportunities for all society members of all cultural backgrounds to build bridges of understanding, acceptance, and cooperation through art, music, education, and cultural activities. It not only works among Christians and Muslims in a casual setting but also uses indirect ways to push for a culture of peace in Egyptian society. They learned from the revolution that interfaith dialogue should involve ordinary Egyptians, not only high-level religious and political leaders. A high-level Anglican cleric who has been involved in both the high-level and grassroots dialogues before and after the Revolution reflects on his lifelong experiences as follows:

> Until 2011, I found that the dialogue between the religious leaders was good, But! it's not influencing the grassroots. So, I thought a lot about how we can bring the influence of Christian-Muslim dialogue from the level of the religious leaders to the grassroots level. And I thought of this Culture Centre. That's one reason. The other reason is ... in 2011 and before some people [a suspicion in some Muslim circles that Christians are planning to take over part of Egypt as their own and are wanting to establish a Christian state within Egypt] thought that the churches are full of weapons. ... So, I thought that when we start the Culture Centre, we will bring people to see what's going on in the church and to see that there are no weapons in the church. And experience a warm welcome and love inside the church.[29]

To many like him, grassroots activities effectively carry the ideas of interfaith harmony and peaceful coexistence to ordinary Egyptian people by removing misunderstandings between the two faith communities. Shortly after the 2011 Revolution, this cleric successfully shifted the focus of his

---

29   Interview with a highly positioned male clergy of the Anglican Church in Egypt.

interfaith ministry from official dialogue to grassroots interaction in art. According to him, they prefer simultaneously to run the interfaith ministry in two paths: official and grassroots dialogue.

Another good example is the Coptic Evangelical Organization for Social Service (CEOSS). Founded by Samuel Habib in 1950, CEOSS has been a pioneer of social service. CEOSS is a long-established development NGO in Egypt and one of the major partners of the Egyptian government. Regardless of the religious background of beneficiaries, CEOSS runs numerous development initiatives, such as inter-religious dialogue as well as aid programs throughout the country. In the past, Habib was criticised 'for being too conciliatory with regard to the Muslim community'.[30] Nevertheless, more and more local evangelical leaders have begun to agree with Habib's vision since the 2011 Revolution and have even founded their own ministry to serve all Egyptians, Christians and Muslims alike, based on the aforementioned humanist thought. The intense discussion in Egyptian civil society during the 2011 Revolution helped the evolution of developmental ministries in the Christian community.

CONCLUSION

In Egypt, clientelism fills the gap between the rulers and different social groups. It also dictates religious interactions based on clientelist relations between church leaders and the regime. This system experienced uncertainties around the 2011 Revolution, which opened a new discussion on the foundation of interfaith dialogue where some interfaith practitioners pushed for human rights and humanism-based arguments for dialogue. After the 2011 Revolution, many social movements emerged in Egypt building on this discussion. It affected interfaith relations as the growing humanist discourse nurtured religious dialogue among the grassroots. Seeing religious others primarily as human beings provided a space for discussing issues of equality, citizenship, discrimination, and the like facing Egyptian society.

---

30 Makari, 'Conflict and Cooperation among Christians and Muslims in Egypt', 111–114.

As before the 2011 Revolution, the predominant type of interfaith 'official dialogue' still takes place among top-ranking religious leadership, negotiating their clientelist ties. However, since the 2011 Revolution, an increasing number of people have been using humanist thought for mediating conversations and common actions. This is especially true among the educated people, the middle-class, and the youth. Although the reinstallation of clientelism as the dominant environment for social and religious discourse continues, Egyptian humanism continues too to develop in society as it pushes for reformation in interfaith relations, where the revolution failed.

11

LIVING AS FOLLOWERS OF JESUS IN DISFAVOURED COMMUNITIES
Perspectives from the Northern Nigerian Context

Uchenna D. Anyanwu

This chapter explores what it means to live as a follower of Jesus in the northern Nigerian context. It first highlights the demographics of Nigeria and focusses on the demographic differences between Christians and Muslims in the states and the Federal Capital territory (Abuja) of Nigeria. Based on demographic data from the *World Christian Database* and qualitative data collected from ethnographic research in northern Nigeria, the chapter engages in a critical analysis of the states with higher Muslim and lower Christian demographics. Finally, the chapter offers a theological discussion arising out of a range of Christian experience across the states of northern Nigeria and posits that Jesus's *staurocentric* pathway remains the model *par excellence* for Jesus's followers to adopt if they must triumph over death, evil, sin, and violence.

DISFAVOURED CONTEXT OF JESUS'S FOLLOWERS

Jesus's followers during the early Christian centuries lived out their faith within disfavoured contexts. They were the demographic minority in the Greco-Roman world in which they found themselves. There is an overwhelming consensus among church historians and sociologists that the number of those who identified themselves as Jesus's followers between the first and third Christian centuries remained under 10% of the population of the time. Robert Wilken, for example, asserts that

> at the end of the first century there were fewer than ten thousand Christians in the Roman Empire. The population at the time numbered some sixty million, which meant that Christians made up one-hundredth of one percent, or 0.0017 percent according to the figures of a contemporary sociologist. By the year 200, the number may have increased to a little more than two hundred thousand, still a tiny minority, under one percent (0.36).[1]

After the resurrection and ascension of Jesus, his followers were persecuted in Jerusalem. One of the seven deacons, Stephen, was the first to die for his testimony concerning Jesus the Messiah (Acts 7). He was stoned outside the city of Jerusalem just as Jesus was crucified outside the city. Stephen's death orchestrated the dispersion of many followers of Jesus in view of 'a great persecution' (Acts 8:1) and certainly in view of coercive polities exerted on all those who were followers of the Way.[2] Following Stephen was James the brother of John—one of the sons of Zebedee—whom Herod the king killed with the sword (Acts 12:2). From Luke's account in Acts 12, we obtain some data of coercive polities against Jesus's followers at that time: 'About that time Herod the king laid violent hands to harm those who belonged to the church.'

The expression of interest here is the Greek expression translated as 'laid violent hands to harm'. This expression connotes casting or throwing something (in this context, *tas cheirsas* the hands) over someone in a violent manner. The same expression is used in Mark 14:37 to express the violence of the waves breaking into the boat in which Jesus and his disciples

---

[1] Robert Louis Wilken, *The First Thousand Years: A Global History of Christianity* (New Haven, CT: Yale University Press, 2012), 65; see also Rodney Stark, *The Triumph of Christianity: How the Jesus Movement Became the World's Largest Religion* (New York: HarperOne, 2011), 156.

[2] Jesus's followers during the first Christian century identified themselves as people belonging to the Way (see Acts 9:2; 19:9, 23; 24:14, 22; and 22:4).

were when crossing the Sea of Galilee. Herod violently cast his hands over some who were followers of Jesus (members of the *ecclesia*—that is, the community of called-out-ones, called out of darkness and of sin to become God's own redeemed community). The aorist active infinitive verb, *kakōsai* (to physically harm, to hurt, to cause injury, to mistreat, to ill-treat, to morally embitter),[3] conveys the intensity of the violence meted out against Jesus's followers. One need not go far reading the text to see the degree of this intense violence and physical harm against the followers of the Way.

> [Herod] killed James the brother of John with the sword, and when he saw that it pleased the Jews, he proceeded to arrest Peter also.... And when he [Herod] had seized him [Peter], he put him in prison, delivering him over to four squads of soldiers to guard him, intending after the Passover to bring him out to the people. (Acts 12: 2–4)[4]

What was the response of the early community of Jesus's followers given their context? Acts 12:5 points to one of their responses: 'So Peter was kept in prison, but earnest prayer for him [Peter] was made to God by the church.' The church's response was first to pray. The continued violence led to the dispersion of many of them from Jerusalem to the neighbouring regions. In their dispersion, they continued to testify to their faith in and following of Jesus. Eminent church historians Dale Irvin and Scott Sunquist note that, although they were 'dispersed from Jerusalem by persecution, a number [of Jesus's followers] took refuge in other cities of the region where they continued to spread the message of the risen Messiah'.[5] The harm meted out to them was not restricted geographically to Jerusalem alone where the Jesus movement began. They maintain that the 'persecution of the Jesus movement outside the land of Israel was in the hands of civil authorities of the Gentiles'.[6]

---

3   Gerhard Kittel and Gerhard Friedrich (Eds.), *Theological Dictionary of the New Testament*, Vol. III, trans. Geoffrey W Bromiley (Grand Rapids, MI: W. B. Eerdmans, 1982), 484.
4   All Bible citations in this chapter, unless otherwise indicated, are taken from *The ESV Study Bible* (Wheaton, IL: Crossway, 2008).
5   Dale T. Irvin and Scott Sunquist, *History of the World Christian Movement: Earliest Christianity to 1453*, vol. I (Maryknoll, NY: Orbis, 2001), 1.
6   Irvin and Sunquist, 26.

During the early second century of the Jesus movement, assemblies of Christ's followers continued to face persecution. Ignatius (the bishop of Antioch in Syria), for example, was arrested and later martyred. Wilken observed that Ignatius 'was to become one of the most celebrated martyrs in the Church's early history'.[7] A few decades later, the bishop of Smyrna[8], Polycarp, was burned for his refusal to recant his faith in Jesus and his 'death was . . . celebrated annually'.[9] Jesus's followers at the time made it a custom 'to gather together in joy and gladness to celebrate the day of [his] martyrdom as a birthday, in memory of those athletes who have gone before, and to train and make ready those who are to come hereafter'.[10]

It was not only during the first Christian century that Jesus's followers found themselves in demographic minorities. Before I focus on the northern Nigerian context, however, I point an investigative flashlight toward an early Muslim context in the time of John of Damascus, who lived in an era of Muslim rule. Damascus was, until the invasion of the Arab Muslim armies in 635 CE, one of the major Christian theological centres. John of Damascus—born Mansur Ibn Sarjun—was the son of Sarjun son of Mansur. John's grandfather, Mansur Ibn Sarjun,[11] was one of the prominent officials in Damascus and 'was the financial governor of Damascus when the Arabs besieged the city in 635'.[12] John of Damascus lived in a context where the Arab Muslims had taken over Syria and were governing his native city of Damascus. 'It was common for sons to follow in their fathers' professions'[13] and, thus, John

---

7   Wilken, *The First Thousand Years*, 29.
8   Smyrna was an ancient Greek city. It was renamed Izmir in about 1930 in today's Turkey.
9   Wilken, *The First Thousand Years*, 28, 48.
10 Cyril C. Richardson (Ed.), *Early Christian Fathers* (New York: Touchstone, 1996), 156; See also Kirsopp Lake (Ed.), *The Apostolic Fathers* (New York: G. P. Putnam's Sons, 1919), 337.
11 The Arabs knew John of Damascus as Mansur ibn Sarjun, exactly the same name as his grandfather. Much later, he was known as Yuhanna ibn Mansur ibn Sarjun. Daniel J. Janosik, *John of Damascus, First Apologist to the Muslims: The Trinity and Christian Apologetics in the Early Islamic Period* (Eugene: Pickwick, 2016), 26.
12 Janosik, *John of Damascus*, 25.
13 Peter Schadler, *John of Damascus and Islam: Christian Heresiology and the Intellectual Background to Earliest Christian-Muslim Relations* (Carol Stream, IL: Brill, 2017), 99.

'followed his father as an official in the Muslim government in Damascus until the caliph sought to islamicize his administration, at which point [he] became a monk, spending the rest of his life in a monastery'.[14]

It was customary for Muslim rulers to impose the *jizya*—a tax on non-Muslims living under their rule. Christians and other non-Muslims living during the time of the Muslim caliphs were obliged to pay this tax, while Muslims were exempt. The economic strain that such a fiscal burden brought upon non-Muslims often led many to declare their allegiance to Islam to unyoke themselves from paying the burdensome taxes. Besides the tax, Christians were also not permitted to 'build new churches or repair old ones if they were in Arab quarters'.[15] This practice of restraining Christians from developing or renovating their places of worship remains in force in many domains today where Muslims are in demographic majority.

Scholars suggest that John's life would have spanned a total of about 75 years between 675-750 and would have included familiarity with the following Umayyad Caliphs: Mu'awiyah I (661-680), Yazid I (680-683), Mu'awiyah II (683), Marwan I (684), 'Abd al- Malik (685-705), al-Walid I (705-715), and possibly up through Sulayman ibn Abd al-Malik (715-717) and Umar II (717-720).[16] Among all these caliphs, Umar II was reputed to have been the most intolerant toward Christians. Some scholars suggest that such intolerance may have been one of the underlying factors that made John of Damascus withdraw to the monastery where his apologetic writings were produced. John's response to the coercive policies of Muslim authorities was intellectual. Janosik asserts that John's 'two works on Islam, the *Heresy of the Ishmaelites* and the *Disputation between a Christian and a Saracen*, were written in response to the religious and political pressure of this new form of monotheism, which John viewed as a Christian heresy'.[17] These two volumes sought to counter Islam. His other work, *Orthodox Faith,* was a systematic theological basis for countering the Islamic teaching that he

---

14   Ian A. McFarland et al. (Eds.), *The Cambridge Dictionary of Christian Theology* (Cambridge, UK: Cambridge University Press, 2011), 251.
15   Janosik, *John of Damascus,* 27.
16   Janosik, *John of Damascus,* 25; Ibn Warraq, *The Quest for the Historical Muhammad* (Amherst, NY: Prometheus Books, 2000), 550.
17   Janosik, *John of Damascus,* xiii.

considered a heretic form of monotheism of his time. John of Damascus is reputed to have been the first to employ the term *perichoresis* to explain 'the relationship among the Persons of the Trinity'.[18] In sum, John of Damascus and followers of Jesus of his time did not respond to persecution of Christians with violence. Instead, John employed both a spiritual approach (indicated by his withdrawal to live as a monk) and an intellectual tool of apologetic writings.

DISFAVOURED COMMUNITIES IN NORTHERN NIGERIA

Modern-day Nigeria has thirty-six states and the Federal Capital Territory (FCT). FCT (of which Abuja is the Federal capital city) in itself does not possess the status of a state, just as Washington DC in the USA is not a state. The thirty-six states (and FCT) in Nigeria are further grouped into six geopolitical zones as follows:

1. North-Central consisting of six states: Benue, Kogi, Kwara, Nassarawa, Niger, Plateau, and the Federal Capital Territory (Abuja);

2. North-East consisting of six states: Adamawa, Bauchi, Borno, Gombe, Taraba, and Yobe;

3. North-West consisting of seven states: Jigawa, Kaduna, Kano, Katsina, Kebbi, Sokoto, and Zamfara;

4. South-East consisting of five states: Abia, Anambra, Ebonyi, Enugu, and Imo;

5. South-South consisting of six states: Akwa Ibom, Bayelsa, Cross River, Delta, Edo, and Rivers; and lastly,

6. South-West consisting of six states: Ekiti, Lagos, Ogun, Ondo, Osun, and Oyo.

Figure 11.1 shows Nigeria's six geopolitical zones.

---

18 McFarland et al., *The Cambridge Dictionary of Christian Theology*, 251.

FOLLOWERS OF JESUS IN DISFAVOURED COMMUNITIES   225

Figure 11.1. Nigeria's Six Geopolitical Zones.[19]

Data from the *World Christian Database*[20] show the following demographic distribution of Christians and Muslims by state for the year 2020. I present here only the data for three of the six geopolitical zones that are the focus of my discussion: the North-Central, the North-East, and the North-West geopolitical zones.

In order to illustrate explicitly, I highlight particularly the data for the North-East and North-West geopolitical zones in the form of pie and bar charts.[21] These two geopolitical zones form the locus of our discussion

---

19 Shapefile is obtained from GADM.ORG. 'GADM license makes data freely available for academic use and other non-commercial use.' https://gadm.org/license.html (accessed 23 December 2022).
20 Todd M. Johnson and Gina A. Zurlo, *World Christian Database*, Center for the Study of Global Christianity, 2022.
21 Peter Crossing, of the Center for the Study of Global Christianity, helped me to prepare these charts.

Table 11.1. Christian-Muslim Demographics for North-Central Geopolitical Zone—2020.

Geopolitical Zone	State	State Population	Christians	Christian %	Muslims	Muslim %
North-Central	Benue	6,117,000	4,588,000	75%	612,000	10%
North-Central	Kogi	4,766,000	2,383,000	50%	1,954,000	41%
North-Central	Kwara	3,401,000	1,531,000	45%	1,701,000	50%
North-Central	Nasarawa	2,688,000	1,210,000	45%	1,075,000	40%
North-Central	Niger	5,919,000	1,480,000	25%	4,143,000	70%
North-Central	Plateau	4,475,000	2,685,000	60%	761,000	17%
North-Central	Abuja (FCT)	3,797,000	1,898,000	50%	1,139,000	30%
	Total	31,163,000	15,775,000	51%	11,385,000	37%

Table 11.2. Christian-Muslim Demographics for North-East Geopolitical Zone—2020.

Geopolitical Zone	State	State Population	Christians	Christian %	Muslims	Muslim %
North-East	Adamawa	4,526,000	1,358,000	30%	2,942,000	65%
North-East	Bauchi	6,964,000	1,045,000	15%	5,571,000	80%
North-East	Borno	6,243,000	1,249,000	20%	3,746,000	60%
North-East	Gombe	3,470,000	1,041,000	30%	1,908,000	55%
North-East	Taraba	3,267,000	980,000	30%	1,797,000	55%
North-East	Yobe	3,509,000	351,000	10%	3,053,000	87%
	Total	27,979,000	6,024,000	22%	19,017,000	68%

Table 11.3. Christian-Muslim Demographics for North-West Geopolitical Zone—2020.

Geopolitical Zone	State	State Population	Christians	Christian %	Muslims	Muslim %
North-West	Jigawa	6,209,000	621,000	10%	5,464,000	88%
North-West	Kaduna	8,791,000	3,077,000	35%	4,396,000	50%
North-West	Kano	13,931,000	1,254,000	9%	12,677,000	91%
North-West	Katsina	8,343,000	584,000	7%	7,592,000	91%
North-West	Kebbi	4,730,000	473,000	10%	4,162,000	88%
North-West	Sokoto	5,325,000	266,000	5%	5,005,000	94%
North-West	Zamfara	4,810,000	241,000	5%	4,522,000	94%
	Total	52,139,000	6,516,000	12.5%	43,818,000	84.04%

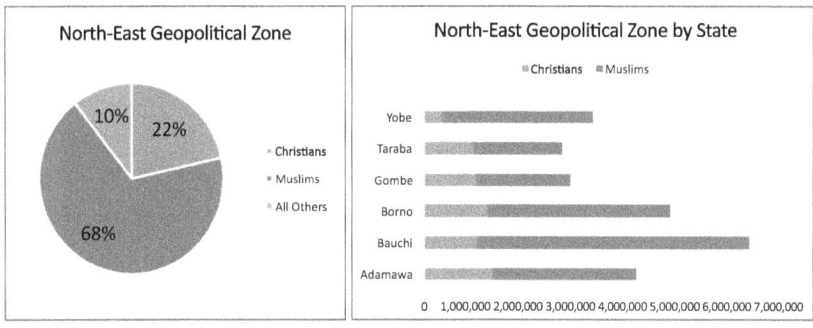

Figure 11.2. North-East Geopolitical Zone.

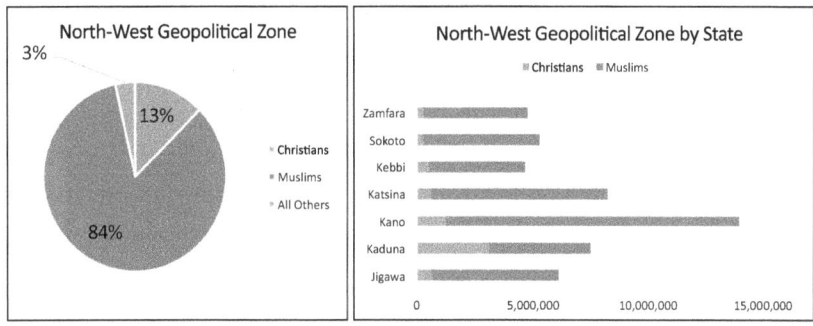

Figure 11.3. North-West Geopolitical Zone.

because, as can be observed in Figures 11.2 and 11.3, the Christian population is in the minority in these states.

The 2020 data show that the six states in the North-East geopolitical zone have a total of 27.98 million out of which 22 percent are Christians and 68 percent are Muslims. The population of adherents of all other religions (mostly ethno-religion) accounts for the remaining 10 percent of the population of the North-East zone. The data also show that the North-West zone (with seven states) had a total population of 52.14 million in 2020, out of which about 13 percent are Christians, 84 percent are Muslims, and 3 percent are adherents to all other religions (mostly ethno-religion).

The incidents of Islamist acute violence, often perpetrated by groups such as Boko Haram, in Nigeria have been numerous in (but not limited to) the two geopolitical zones with the highest population of Muslims (North-East and North-West). Islamist acute violence is defined as 'acts of violence undertaken by militant Islamic extremists. . . . a phenomenon of violence encompassing human bloodshed, suicide bombing, destruction of properties, burning of villages, kidnapping/abduction of people et cetera'.[22] These acts characterise many of the states, particularly in northern Nigeria, where acute violence is prevalent. This includes kidnapping and abductions. Fulani herdsmen and bandits who kidnap and abduct people often demand outrageous amounts of money for ransom. Many people have been killed even after ransoms were paid.

Although the Islamist groups like Boko Haram and Muslim Fulani herdsmen appear to be non-state actors, the Shari'a legal system in some states creates ambiguities in a society that is not entirely Muslim and a country that is constitutionally a secular state. I have noted elsewhere that 'twelve states in northern Nigeria . . . adopted the Shari'a legal system . . . , and the issue continues to generate debate and remains a potential source of conflict'.[23] It is not surprising, therefore, that the twelve states that subscribe to the Shari'a legal system are all within the North-East and North-West geopolitical zones where Islamist acute violence is most prevalent. States within these two zones that have not adopted Shari'a are Adamawa and Taraba—where the percentage of Christian population in 2020 was 30 percent in both states and the Muslim population was 65 and 55 percent respectively.

On the other hand, Niger state in the North-Central geopolitical zone is among the Shari'a states and has a population of 5.92 million out of which 25 percent are Christians and 70 percent are Muslims (see bar chart in Figure 11.4). From the works of some researchers who have highlighted the incidents of acute violence in Nigeria,[24] we deduce that states worst hit by the Islamists are primarily those with greater Muslim population or their neighbouring states, or states where there appears to be parity between the Christian-Muslim demographics.

---

22 Uchenna D. Anyanwu, *Pathways to Peacebuilding: Staurocentric Theology in Nigeria's Context of Acute Violence*, American Society of Missiology Scholarly Monograph Series 61 (Eugene, OR: Pickwick, 2022), 11.

23 Anyanwu, *Pathways to Peacebuilding*, 37.

24 Toyin Falola, *Violence in Nigeria: The Crisis of Religious Politics and Secular Ideologies* (New York: University of Rochester Press, 2009); Richard Bourne, *Nigeria: A New History of a Turbulent Century* (London: Zed, 2015); Ioannis Mantzikos, 'Boko Haram Attacks in Nigeria and Neighbouring Countries: A Chronology of Attacks', *Perspectives on Terrorism*, 8 no. 6 (2014).

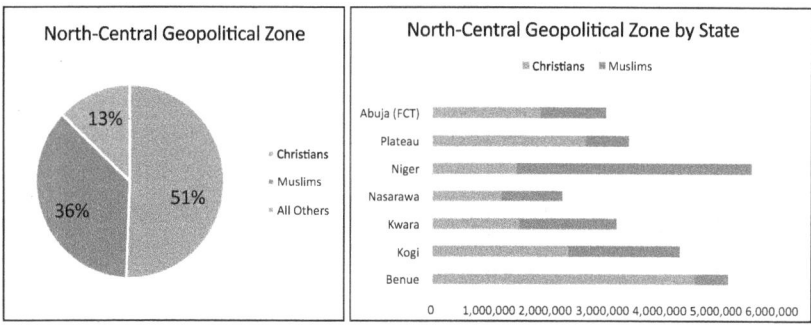

Figure 11.4. North-Central Geopolitical Zone.

What do all these data suggest? It is an undeniable fact that the incidents of acute violence in northern Nigeria have led to the death of many followers of Jesus and non-followers of Jesus alike. To be clear, it is not only Christians who suffer the consequences of acute violence in northern Nigeria, even though, *prima facie*, the violent attacks are aimed at Christians. Acute violence in Nigeria worsened during Muhammad Buhari's tenure as president (2015–2023). Bishop Matthew Hassan Kukah (Catholic Bishop of Sokoto Diocese) put it bluntly in his homily during the funeral mass of a seminarian (Michael Nnadi) killed by Islamists on 31 January 2020. Kukah, in the homily he delivered on 11 February 2020, maintained that although Buhari campaigned for the presidential ticket on the grounds of integrity and probity, yet, his [Buhari's] northern Nigeria 'has become one large grave yard, a valley of dry bones, the nastiest and most brutish part of our dear country'.[25] Kukah went further to state that

> the persecution of Christians in northern Nigeria is as old as the modern Nigerian state ... the northern Muslim elite has not developed a moral basis for adequate power sharing with their Christian

---

25   Matthew Hassan Kukah, 'Homily at Funeral Mass of Seminarian Michael Nnadi in Kaduna', Catholic for Life, 11 February 2020, https://www.catholicforlife.com/homily-at-the-funeral-mass-of-seminarian-michael-nnadi/. Michael Nnadi was an 18-year-old student at the Good Shepherd Seminary in Kaduna. He was abducted on January 8, 2020, with three other seminarians who were released after payment of ransom. The Muslim abductors, despite the payment of ransom, killed Michael.

co-regionalists. We deny at our own expense. By denying Christians lands for places of worship across most of the northern states, ignoring the systematic destruction of churches all these years, denying Christians adequate recruitment, representation and promotions in the State civil services, denying their indigenous children scholarships, marrying Christian women or converting Christians while threatening Muslim women and prospective converts with death, they make building a harmonious community impossible. Nation building cannot happen without adequate representation and a deliberate effort at creating for all members a sense, a feeling, of belonging, and freedom to make their contributions. This is the window that the killers of Boko Haram have exploited and turned into a door to death. It is why killing Christians and destroying Christianity is seen as one of their key missions.[26]

I previously alluded to the Muslim practice of restraining Christians from developing or renovating places of worship. Bishop Kukah, in his homily cited above, points this out as it pertains to the Nigerian context, where Christians across most northern Nigerian states are denied lands to erect their places of worship. Existing places of worship are systematically destroyed and burned down with tacit support from Muslim authorities. During my undergraduate studies at Ahmadu Bello University Zaria, in Kaduna State (in the North-Central geopolitical zone), about 102 Christian places of worship were burned down by Muslims across the state. Boko Haram Islamists, considered non-state actors, continue to destroy Christian places of worship in northern Nigeria. Boko Haram activists have destroyed over two thousand places of worship of Ekklesiyar Yan'uwa a Nigeria (EYN, Church of the Brethren). Other church denominations all over northern Nigeria attest to the same level of destruction of their places of worship. Local state actors tacitly support similar acts under the guise of enforcing the Shari'a legal system despite the constitutional provisions that bar the federal and state governments from adopting a state religion and that prohibit religious discrimination.

Given the various ways that non-Muslims in majority Muslim northern Nigerian states (and indeed across the entire country) have

---

26   Kukah, 'Homily at Funeral Mass'.

experienced terror in its different facets, the United States 'Secretary of State, [on December 2, 2020], designated Nigeria a "Country of Particular Concern" for having engaged in or tolerated particularly severe violations of religious freedom'.[27] Millions of villagers—Christians, Muslims, and ethno-religionists alike—are displaced from their homes, villages, and farmlands and live in internally displaced persons' (IDP) camps.

The psychological trauma that such incidents of violence engender is enormous. Patience M. Ahmed, in her PhD research, investigated the impact that such incidents of terror produce in internally displaced persons in Nigeria. The conclusion from the study (involving both quantitative and qualitative analyses) adequately shows

> a high rate of depression and PTSD [Post-Traumatic Stress Disorder] in the population. [And] the unique features of terrorism, such as concern for survival, disruption of a sociocultural landscape, worries about the future, somatic symptoms, and physical injuries may have impacted the population beyond the expected psychological responses to trauma.[28]

Ahmed further underscores the fact that 'the overwhelming clinical symptoms resulting from terror indicate that terror is a significant risk factor for psychological problems'.[29] In a similar mixed-methods study, Andrea K. Canales in her PhD research sought to understand the complication of grief in the light of traumatic losses occasioned by terror. Canales's research gives 'a glimpse of the horrific realities and traumatic losses due to Boko Haram terrorism'.[30]

---

27   U.S. Department of State, 'Nigeria: International Religious Freedom Report for 2020', Office of International Religious Freedom, 12 May 2021, https://www.state.gov/reports/2020-report-on-international-religious-freedom/nigeria/.

28   Patience M. Ahmed, 'Impact of Terror on Internally Displaced Persons in Nigeria' (PhD thesis, Fuller Theological Seminary, 2019), 71.

29   Ahmed, 'Impact of Terror', 39.

30   Andrea K. Canales, 'Understanding Complicated Grief in the Face of Traumatic Losses Due to Terrorism: A Mixed-Methods Study in an Internally Displaced People's Camp in Nigeria', (PhD thesis, Fuller Theological Seminary, 2019), 79.

Thus, the impact of terror orchestrated by Islamists goes beyond physical harm and destruction of properties. Individuals bereaved of their loved ones or acquaintances are subjected to deprivation of different sorts. What is more excruciating for the survivors is the psychological trauma through losing a family member and not having the privilege to see the dead body or to give one's dead a befitting burial.

CHRISTIAN RESPONSES TO ACUTE VIOLENCE IN NORTHERN NIGERIA

I draw here from individual and focus group interviews in ethnographic research I conducted in north-eastern Nigeria between September and November 2018 to shed some light on the responses of Jesus's followers living as disfavoured communities within the northern Nigerian context. In the study, I interviewed thirteen participants from three church denominations (ECWA, EYN, and COCIN)[31] and five participants from other denominations. In addition, I conducted three different focus group interviews with twenty-eight participants.[32]

One of the questions I asked participants during the ethnographic research was "How has your church denomination responded to the type of violence caused by Boko Haram?" One participant, Salamatu,[33] said their denomination

> has been hit very hard with the effect of the insurgency, because the church was left with nothing and it couldn't help itself so we were left at the mercy of sister organizations that bring aids to

---

[31] ECWA—Evangelical Church Winning All (formerly Evangelical Church of West Africa); COCIN—Church of Christ in Nations (formerly, Church of Christ in Nigeria); and EYN—Ekklesiyar Yan'uwa a Nigeria (Church of the Brethren in Nigeria).

[32] For more details on the research methodology employed for the study, see Anyanwu, *Pathways to Peacebuilding*, 17–22.

[33] In conformity with the informed consent signed by participants in my research and the document approved by the Institutional Review Board (IRB) that approved the ethnographic research protocol, pseudonyms are used for interviewed participants for the purpose of security.

the church because there was no cloth, no food, nothing, medical assistance, nothing for the church. So, the church has not really responded in too deep directly to the violence. But the church tries to heal, because a lot of killings, a lot of looting so the church was traumatized, . . .the church tries to build resilience. . .tries to heal trauma among the people that were traumatized. The church tries to rebuild communities, rebuild church [buildings that were burned down], rebuild homes for the returnees. The church tries to promote peaceful co-existence among the communities.[34]

'The church' here refers to a church denomination (not just a local church). The particular denomination referred to above, at the time the research was conducted in 2018, had had about two thousand local places of worship located in northeastern Nigeria burned down and had about the same number of church members in various locations killed by the Islamists. Themes that emerged from the interviews across denominations included trauma and trauma healing; rebuilding their communities, places of worship, and homes that had been burned down; and relief in IDP camps. In addition to these, the hard work of peacebuilding remained at the core of their responses.

The participants also identified pragmatic ways that the church denomination referred to above (hereafter EYN) is engaging in some of these responses. Salamatu pointed out that their church is 'a peaceful church from the beginning. So, we are not violent people, the church through the peace program has been promoting peaceful co-existing through creating a platform for Christians and Muslims to come and dialogue together to talk about the issues that bring about conflict'.[35] EYN created what they call CAMPI—Christian and Muslim Peaceful Initiative—a community

---

[34] Salamatu D3#2:89-97. Individual interviews are referenced according to a participant's church denomination, interview order, and line numbers of the transcribed text. 'Salamatu D3#2:89-97' refers to an individual interview with Salamatu (a pseudonym); D3 indicates that this participant is from the denomination coded as 3; #2 indicates that the individual is the second participant interviewed from denomination 3. 89-97 refer to the line numbers of the transcribed text of the interview.

[35] Salamatu D3#2:102-105.

engagement platform that facilitates Christians and Muslims engaging in dialogue together to promote peaceful co-existence.

Another participant from EYN described their church's response to the acts of violence against them, saying,

> because EYN is a peace church, we responded by non-violence. Instead of retaliating, the church organized what is called Trauma Healing and Peacebuilding.... we are going to communities both Muslims and Christians, we are bringing them together, telling them this is what we believe in. We can only conquer this world through peace, so we did not retaliate, fighting back or go and preach, go and fight, we did not do that.[36]

Asked how EYN is doing this, Ayuba's response was

> we have a peace department... that carries on with this work. The peace department will go to a certain community, will get names of Christians and Muslims for a two- or three-day workshop, telling them the importance of living together and the importance of peace.... In spite of all these troubles, we are also using our resources.... we need to live together with them [Muslims]. So, at no time [has our denomination] ever preached that we should go and fight. We only preach the peace of Jesus Christ and that is what is sustaining us so even you go to these communities, Muslims can tell you that surely [our church denomination] is a peace church.[37]

EYN formed three IDP camps through their Disaster Relief Ministry (DRM), providing people with food, clothing, temporary shelter, and some medical assistance. They are working hard to empower their women— some of whom have been widowed— to rebuild their lives. As I was curious about what must have been the theological impetus driving EYN to respond to such acute violence in the manner they are doing, I probed further by asking, 'What is pushing your church denomination to respond in

---

36   Ayuba D3#1:53–60.
37   Ayuba D3#1:64–73.

such a peaceful way?' The response was 'As a member and as a pastor in this denomination, Jesus said: "My peace I give unto you, my peace I leave in this world." So, without Jesus, no peace, without understanding each other, no peace. So our foundation is the word of God and Jesus Christ.'[38]

Responses from participants in a different church denomination (COCIN)[39] revealed ambivalent positions. One participant said,

> Rev. Dr. Obed Dashan [formerly the Vice President of COCIN] has been championing peacebuilding and seminars on how to make our peacebuilding biblically-based and never to respond to the violence by violence, but [instead] by peaceful means, following the biblical principles. But we do not only champion these seminars here on the Plateau, but back to where the thing is happening, back-to-base so to say, the base of the Boko Haram, which is Borno, either in Maiduguri city or the surrounding areas where there is relatively peace and the people could still listen and respond to seminars and workshops, so the church is into that training leaders and pastors and mobilizing them for them to go back to their areas, and to always talk to Christians to respond as Christians not to respond with violence.[40]

COCIN as a denomination sustains its effort in organizing seminars and workshops on peacebuilding. They do not wait for incidents of violence to occur before they do so; instead, they consistently assure that their members are well informed and prepared to respond appropriately to incidents of violence in their contexts. On the one side within COCIN,

> there are those who are Mennonites and in response to this insurgency, [and on the other side, there are] those who are evangelicals . . . saying, look oh, let's buy weapons and respond fire-by-fire. . . . So COCIN has not yet made a definite [theological] position in response to violence. But then she has been

---

38 Ayuba D3#1:84–87.
39 COCIN—Church of Christ in Nations (formerly, Church of Christ in Nigeria).
40 Andraus D2#1:269–277.

preaching peace and trying to maintain peace and respond biblically to violence.[41]

I asked the participants to express their views on how Jesus would guide members of their church denomination to respond to violence, were he to be physically present as one of COCIN leaders. Ishaya's response was 'Jesus would encourage the believers to respond by showing love. I remember the Bible said: 'Vengeance is mine, says the Lord' and that Jesus will never ask the believer to go and retaliate. Jesus will only ask us to be patient and repay evil with good'.[42] This response echoes Miroslav Volf's words, who 'maintains that for evil "to triumph fully, [it] needs two victories, not one. The first victory happens when an evil deed is perpetrated; the second victory, when evil is returned. After the first victory, evil would die if the second victory did not infuse it with new life"'.[43] Responding to violence with violence, blood with blood, tit-for-tat only makes evil continue in an unbroken chain—as Gregory Boyd asserts, 'Tit for tat, eye for an eye, tooth for a tooth . . . is what makes the bloody kingdom of the world go around'.[44] In order to undo the chain of violence, Jesus's followers in disfavoured communities can follow Jesus's approach of overcoming evil with good, thus disarming evil and making it impossible for it to obtain its triumph.

Responses from my interview participants from ECWA also demonstrated a *staurocentric*[45] approach. A regional leader, Jibreel, answering to the question about ECWA's response to the Boko Haram violent attacks, said,

---

41 Andraus D2#1:304–309.
42 Ishaya D2#3:280–283.
43 Miroslav Volf, *The End of Memory: Remembering Rightly in a Violent World* (Grand Rapids, MI: W. B. Eerdmans, 2006), 9; cited in Anyanwu, *Pathways to Peacebuilding*, 64.
44 Gregory A. Boyd, *The Myth of a Christian Nation: How the Quest for Political Power Is Destroying the Church* (Grand Rapids, MI: Zondervan, 2006), 24; cited in Anyanwu, *Pathways to Peacebuilding*, 89.
45 Simply, *staurocentric* means 'cross-centred'. The term is derived from the Greek word *stauros*. Staurocentric approaches, therefore, point to 'postures and actions that [are in coherence] with Jesus's attitude when he faced the cross-event'. Anyanwu, *Pathways to Peacebuilding*, 9.

One of the ways we responded was by asking church members to *pray and fast* for peace in Nigeria. We also had to raise funds and foodstuffs to help the Internally Displaced Persons (IDPs), also clothes, especially in Yola/Jimeta[46] where most of the IDPs settled in the homes of some church members. I remember a sister who had about 30 or more people in her home, some were seen sleeping in her car. In my own compound we had to accommodate about 20 people and gave them refuge.[47]

Jibreel went further to underscore the *staurocentric* response of Jesus's followers in their denomination, stating,

The attackers are like warriors with guns and bombs out to kill and destroy as stated in John 10:10; and all we can do is pray for them. However, other Muslims who have also been displaced came to us to request for food and stood afar off because of fear. But when their message got to me as [one of the regional leaders] I encouraged that they be brought in because hospitality is one way of sharing the gospel so *we prayed* together and I talked about peace and coexistence against such menace that has befallen us all, even [including] them [the Muslims]. So we gave them [to the Muslims] food and clothes. The news spread and others [Muslims] came as well. What we did was to announce through churches that we had relief materials and people came. . . Some of us have relatives that are of the Muslim faith and not all of them are in support [of the violence]. So, the gospel of love has to be shared because love brings peace.[48]

Two themes are of importance from the excerpt above. The first is *response through prayer*. In my earlier discussion in this chapter, I pointed out that

---

46 Yola is the capital city of Adamawa State in the North-East geopolitical zone in Nigeria. The city is among the cities/regions worst-hit by Boko Haram acute violence attacks.
47 Jibreel D1#2:53–58. Emphasis in italics is mine.
48 Jibreel D1#2:69–79. Emphasis in italics is mine.

Jesus's followers responded first in prayer when Herod 'threw his violent hand to harm' them (Acts 12:5). In a focus group interview, one participant further affirmed that *response through prayer* is one way their church has responded to the violence, saying,

> I see the church responding to [violence] peacefully in the aspect of prayers. . . . Some of our churches hold all nights,[49] individuals [are] having prayers. Recently, Dr. M[50] was telling us that ECWA as a church is calling attention on all of her members to be [involved] in three-days prayers and fasting for our dear sister Leah [Sharibu].[51] So it is another way I see the church actively doing that with the hope and faith that God is going to work, whether in the political level or at other levels.[52]

The second important theme is the *staurocentric pathway* of loving the enemy—responding to evil with good, overcoming violence through the cross. Jibreel (an interview participant) highlighted this theme. Their church's provision of hospitality and relief was extended to Muslims who were also displaced due to acute violence orchestrated by Islamists. It is one thing to love those who are benevolent toward you. Indeed, it is common among humans to love those who love them and do good to them; but it is uncommon to love those who are hateful or violent.

Indeed, it is incomprehensible to the natural human mind. It is *staurocentric* to do so. It is the path of Jesus when he was physically in our midst and that he taught others to follow. Although it is a less-travelled road, yet it leads to life and it defeats evil. Bishop Matthew Kukah made the same point in his homily at the funeral of Michael Nnadi—the 18-year-old seminarian killed by Muslim Islamists whom I earlier mentioned. In that homily, Bishop Kukah told his audience,

---

49 'All nights' in churches in Nigeria are nights of vigil in prayer and praise that usually start around 9:00 p.m. and go on until dawn.
50 'Dr. M' is a professor in the theological seminary where the focus group was conducted.
51 Leah Sharibu is one of the girls abducted by Boko Haram.
52 Anyanwu, *Pathways to Peacebuilding*, 273. Focus Group #1:379–383.

> Anger, the quest for vengeance, are a legitimate inheritance of the condition of unredeemed human being . . . Through violence, you can murder the murderer, but you cannot murder murder. Through violence, you can kill the liar, but you cannot kill lies or install truth. Through violence, you can murder the terrorist, but you cannot end terrorism. Through violence, you can murder the violent, but you cannot end violence. Through violence, you can murder the hater, but you cannot end hatred. Unredeemed man sees vengeance as power, strength and the best means to teach the offender a lesson. These are the ways of the flesh.[53]

Kukah further told his Christian listeners at the funeral that

> Others believe in an eye for an eye, a tooth for a tooth, . . . [but], for us Christians, Jesus stands right in the middle with a message that is the opposite of all that is sensible to us as human beings. Put back your sword (Mt. 26:52). Turn the other cheek (Mt. 5:38). Pray for your enemy (Mt. 5: 44). Give the thief your cloak (Lk. 6:29). None of these makes sense to the human mind without faith. This is why Jesus said the only solution is for us to be born again (Jn. 3:3). The challenge before us is to behold the face of Jesus and ask the question: Are we born against hatred, anger, violence and vengeance?[54]

Those whom Jesus Christ redeemed through his death on the cross (and implicitly through his resurrection from the dead) are called to walk the less-travelled road that Jesus walked—the Calvary road. That road, understandably, is incomprehensible and foolish to the natural human mind. It is otherworldly. It is not from below. Instead, it is heavenly and divine. Jesus modelled this way for those who would follow him. This was Jesus's method for triumphing over death, evil, sin, and violence. It is the *staurocentric* pathway. To the degree that Jesus's followers in the northern Nigeria context (and indeed in all other global contexts) adopt this pathway in their responses to evil and violence meted against them, to that degree their triumph in Christ is assured.

---

53 Kukah, 'Homily at Funeral Mass'.
54 KKukah, 'Homily at Funeral Mass'.

PART III

STATES AND CHRISTIAN MAJORITY

12

PERSECUTION IN A LAND OF RELIGIOUS FREEDOM
The Jehovah's Witnesses' Experience in Malawi 1964–1993

Klaus Fiedler and Kenneth R. Ross

By the time Malawi became an independent country in 1964, the majority of its population were Christians. It prided itself on its strong public morality and on the freedom of religion that its citizens purportedly enjoyed. Yet during the three decades that followed, one particular religious community was subjected to sustained persecution. This was the Jehovah's Witnesses, who had a long history in Malawi and numbered around seventeen thousand at the time of independence in 1964. The Malawi government strongly identified with Christianity but chose to victimize the Jehovah's Witnesses—a minority religious community with which it had some differences. It was also a case of complicity on the part of the wider society, including the influential Christian churches—both passively by not doing anything to oppose the persecution and actively by taking part in it. The terror and violence inflicted on the Jehovah's Witnesses is even more striking because Malawi is largely a peaceful country. There have been incidents of violence at moments of high political tension, but these have been on a small scale. At both local and national levels, most of the time Malawians have been able to resolve divisive issues by peaceful and constitutional means. Why then did Malawi's Jehovah's Witnesses suffer egregious abuse of their human rights between 1964 and 1993?

MALAWI CONGRESS PARTY

For our purposes, there are two important points to note about the Malawi Congress Party (MCP) government that ruled Malawi from independence in 1964 until the introduction of multi-party democracy in 1994. The first is that it was born out of the struggle against colonialism. In Malawi's case, colonial rule took a particularly sinister turn in 1953 when, against the wishes of almost its entire African population, Nyasaland (as it was then called) was incorporated into the Federation of Rhodesia and Nyasaland.[1] This brought together the three territories of Southern Rhodesia, Northern Rhodesia, and Nyasaland under a White settler government in Salisbury (now Harare).

Peaceful protests in Nyasaland were to no avail and its people faced a future where it was clear that they would become second-class citizens in their own country. The African Nyasaland Congress, formed as a national body in 1944, had envisaged a gradual process of power transfer from the British colonial regime to steadily maturing political institutions of the African people. These hopes were suddenly shattered in 1953 and the Congress faced a situation where hopes of any meaningful self-government were fast disappearing.

Initially, the Congress movement was stunned but soon realised that it had to change its strategy and confront the Federation head-on. With this in view, it took the portentous decision to recall a long-absent medical doctor, Hastings Kamuzu Banda, to return to his homeland to spearhead the political struggle. Banda duly returned in July 1958 to embark on something of a David-and-Goliath battle with the Federation. It was an unequal struggle because power and resources were in the hands of the Federation, which enjoyed the support of the British Empire. All that Banda had at his disposal was the unity of the people of Malawi in their determination to get out of the Federation and take control of their own destiny. Through an intense struggle in the late 1950s, the Congress movement finally prevailed, the British government changed its policy, and Malawi was on course to become an independent nation. In the heat of the struggle, unity was seen as paramount because any divisions in the ranks were likely to be exploited

---

[1] See John McCracken, *A History of Malawi 1859–1966*, (Woodbridge: James Currey and Mzuzu: Mzuni Press, 2021 [2012]), 336–365.

by the Federation. This meant that there was little or no tolerance of dissent. For example, when Chester Katsonga founded another pro-independence party, the Christian Democratic Party in 1960, it was quickly crushed and the Congress did not hesitate to unleash violence against Katsonga and his supporters.[2] The unity, moreover, was expressed in terms of personal loyalty to Kamuzu Banda as leader on the understanding that the greater the unanimity of the support for Banda, the stronger would be his hand in negotiating Malawi's independence from Britain. What began as a tactic in the anti-colonial struggle became the defining feature of political life in independent Malawi as Banda demanded the unquestioning loyalty and support of all citizens. Even his own cabinet ministers were ruthlessly treated if they were anything less than 100 percent behind the *Ngwazi* (conqueror).[3] For those like the Jehovah's Witnesses, who placed limits on the loyalty they could offer, this became a life-and-death issue.

The second important point to note is that the MCP was, largely, a product of the Christian missions in the country. It was Christian not in the confessional sense but in the sense that the great majority of its leaders and members were practising Christians. Three religious traditions are substantially present in Malawi: African Traditional Religion (ATR), Islam, and Christianity. Prior to independence, adherents of ATR and Islam tended to keep a distance from Western education and the modern economy to which it granted access. This meant that the great majority of those who advanced educationally and entered employment with the government or in commerce and industry were those who had been educated at the Christian missions and, in most cases, had become practising Christians.

In particular, the Scottish Presbyterian Missions of Livingstonia and Blantyre had offered a high level of education, and it was from among their 'graduates' that the leadership of the Congress was largely drawn. As Nyamayaro Mufuka observed, 'As late as 1960 these graduates of Scottish missions so dominated the political life of the country that a meeting of

---

2   Matthew Schoffeleers, *In Search of Truth and Justice: Confrontations between Church and State in Malawi 1960–1994* (Blantyre: CLAIM-Kachere, 1999), 86–90.

3   See Andrew C. Ross, *Colonialism to Cabinet Crisis: A Political History of Malawi* (Zomba: Kachere, 2009).

the African Congress Party was barely distinguishable from a synod of the Church of Scotland'.[4] As a result, when the MCP came to power with independence in 1964, those who entered office were almost invariably Christians. The same applied to the civil service, the army, the police, and all organs of the state. Banda himself often asserted his Christian identity. He had been educated at the Livingstonia Mission and, while living in Scotland in the 1930s, had been ordained as an elder in his local Church of Scotland congregation—a status to which he often appealed as ideologically bolstering his authority in a strongly Christian country.[5] The regime, while not formally Christian, was composed largely of people who professed to be Christians.

THE JEHOVAH'S WITNESSES

The Jehovah's Witnesses are an international religious organisation, started in the USA by Charles Taze Russel in 1881 as the Zion's Watch Tower Tract Society. It was Russel's aim not to start a new denomination but a new movement of Bible students preparing for the end soon to come. He believed that Christ would return to earth in 1914, which did turn out to be a momentous year in world history but did not include the return of Christ. Russel died in 1916, somewhat bewildered, but the organisation he had started lived on, consolidated, and spread. No precise date for Christ's return was ever set again, though the date of the beginning of his invisible presence was moved to 1914. The event of 1914 was now seen as a heavenly event, marking the beginning of the final stage in world history, which would not take longer than one generation. The Watchtower Movement then developed from a somewhat loosely structured organisation into a tightly controlled religious group, centrally directed from headquarters in Brooklyn, New York. The Jehovah's Witnesses do not see themselves as one church among others. They see themselves as the Theocratic

---

4 K. Nyamayaro Mufuka, *Missions and Politics in Malawi* (Kingston, ON: Limestone Press, 1977), 169.

5 See Kenneth R. Ross, *Here Comes Your King! Christ, Church and Nation in Malawi* (Mzuzu: Luviri Press, 2020), 137-138 (Blantyre: CLAIM–Kachere, 1998). This is a Malawi convention used for Kachere Series books published with CLAIM.

Organization, whose members will be saved in the final battle of Armageddon. They have no fellowship with Christian churches but are represented in most countries of the world, counting presently more than eight million members worldwide, many of them in Africa. Their organisation is strictly centralised. Their Bible studies, magazines, and books are the same everywhere, usually translated from English, and display a style strongly identified with an American religious subculture.

Worldwide, the Jehovah's Witnesses are distinguished by their determination to keep their distance from the state. During their first decades, they saw the state as evil in principle. Later, they received 'newer light' so that the state came to be seen, according to Romans 13, as not bad in itself. Even before this change in teaching, Jehovah's Witnesses were law-abiding citizens, but the 'newer light' removed any doubts about such matters as the propriety of paying taxes or sending their children to state schools. On the other hand, Jehovah's Witnesses continue to decline to do any military service, and they refuse to take any part in politics. The latter proved to be the point on which they came into collision with the one-party state in Malawi.

The Jehovah's Witnesses (then Watchtower Society) originally came to Malawi in 1908 through the preaching of Elliot Kenan Kamwana, a disillusioned product of the Presbyterian Livingstonia Mission.[6] The link to Russel in the USA was Joseph Booth in Cape Town, a controversial anti-colonial Baptist missionary who had been barred from entering Malawi by the colonial government, to which he had been a thorn in the side since his arrival in 1892.[7] After a visit to Russel in 1906, Booth returned to Cape Town as a Watchtower representative. There he was joined by Kamwana, whom he trained as a Watchtower missionary. In this capacity, Kamwana returned to his native Malawi, where he had great success among his own Tonga people, baptizing more than nine thousand within three months in 1908. Kamwana preached the coming of the millennium in 1914, adding some anticolonial

---

6   See J. C. Chakanza, *Voices of Preachers in Protest: The Ministry of Two Malawian Prophets: Elliot Kamwana and Wilfred Gudu* (Blantyre: CLAIM-Kachere, 1998).

7   See Harry Langworthy, *Africa for the African: The Life of Joseph Booth* (Blantyre: CLAIM-Kachere, 2002).

touches to the general Watchtower message about the millennium and becoming a focus for an accessible version of the Christian faith and for a protest against colonial rule.[8] Both the Livingstonia Mission and the British colonial government regarded Kamwana's ministry as a threat to public order, and he was deported to Mauritius, not returning to Malawi until 1937.

In 1934, the international Watchtower Society, now under the name Jehovah's Witnesses, sent a representative to check on the state of affairs in the Watchtower movement in Malawi. He declared almost all Watchtower members to be heretical, because they had departed from official teaching about the millennium. Only thirty were accepted as genuine Jehovah's Witnesses. Starting with this small group, the international Jehovah's Witnesses built up their organisation in Malawi, until at the time of independence it had about seventeen thousand members. The expelled Watchtower adherents continued as Watchtower Mission (Native Controlled). When Kamwana finally was allowed to return in 1937, his branch became the Watchman Healing Mission. Though the two movements have a common root, they do not recognise each other, and in this chapter the name Jehovah's Witnesses applies only to those who belong to the international organisation under that name.[9]

VICTIMISATION

Persecution of Jehovah's Witnesses started in 1963 in the run up to the elections that led to independence.[10] By this time, it was becoming clear that the incoming Congress government would have little tolerance for dissenting views on political matters. The murder of Gilbert Pondeponde,

---

8   See Wiseman Chijere Chirwa, 'Msokwa Elliot Kamwana Chirwa: His Religious and Political Activities and Impact in Nkhata Bay, 1908-1958', in *Christianity in Malawi: A Reader*, eds. Klaus Fiedler and Kenneth R. Ross (Mzuzu: Mzuni Press, 2021), 137-169.

9   See Chakanza, *Voices of Preachers in Protest*, 27-38; H.-J. Greschat, 'Kitawala: The Origins, Expansion and Religious Beliefs of the Watch Tower Movement in Central Africa', (PhD thesis, University of Marburg, 1967).

10 This perpetration of human rights abuse was eventually acknowledged by the Malawi government in *History and Hope in Malawi: Repression, Suffering and Human Rights under Dr Kamuzu Banda 1964-1994* (Blantyre: National Compensation Tribunal, Government of Malawi, 2005).

Secretary General of the Mbadwa party and staunch advocate of political pluralism, on Christmas Eve 1963 was a grim indication of what lay ahead.[11] For the Jehovah's Witnesses, the point of collision with the state was the MCP's requirement that every citizen should buy a party card. The financial cost was small and the vast majority of the population complied for the sake of a quiet life. For the Jehovah's Witnesses, however, a crucial point of principle was at stake. To buy the card, and thereby join a political party, would be a betrayal of their faith.[12] Some other religious groups, such as the Seventh-Day Adventists and Providence Industrial Mission, initially shared this concern but eventually relented on the basis that having a party card was no more than a formality that was required to continue living peacefully in Malawi. For the Jehovah's Witnesses, there could be no such compromise. They were prepared to resist the requirement to buy a party card at any cost. This brought them into collision with the full force of the totalitarian state.[13]

Already, before independence, the Jehovah's Witnesses had been targeted. Kingdom Halls were burned down, children were barred from attending primary school because their parents did not have a party card, houses were burned, and crops were uprooted.[14] Things calmed down after independence and there was even judicial redress in favour of Jehovah's Witnesses who had suffered injustice.[15] However, when the 1967 MCP Convention was held at Mzuzu, it recommended strongly 'that the Jehovah's

---

11   Matthew Schoffeleers, *In Search of Truth and Justice*, 86–90.
12   See further Klaus Fiedler, 'Power at the Receiving End: The Jehovah's Witnesses Experience in One-Party Malawi', in *God, People and Power in Malawi: Democratisation in Theological Perspective*, ed. Kenneth R. Ross (Blantyre: CLAIM-Kachere, 1996), 149–176.
13   Members of the Watchman Healing Mission, which had split from the Jehovah's Witnesses in the 1930s, also suffered severe persecution at the hands of the state. Interview Fletcher Kaiya, 10 August 2022.
14   Interview Faison S. Chimphepo, 14 April 1995, by Ashanie Gawa; Interview Macdonald Simoni, 14 April 1995, by Charles Eliyasi. All the interviews cited here as primary data were conducted by students at Chancellor College, University of Malawi, during their Easter vacation in 1995. Eight Jehovah's Witnesses were killed (*Watchtower* 68, 2/1, 73).
15   Acting Judge L. M. E. Emejulu sentenced eight men to death for the murder of Elton Mwachande in Mulanje. *Watchtower* 68, 2/1, 75 and *Glasgow Herald*, 29 October 1964.

Witnesses denomination be declared illegal in this country as the attitude of its adherents is not only inimical to the progress of this country, but also negative in every way that it endangers the stability and peace and calm which is essential for the smooth running of our state'.[16] This recommendation was heartily endorsed by President Kamuzu Banda in his closing address, in which he alleged that the Jehovah's Witnesses were 'causing trouble everywhere'.[17] Within a month, Parliament duly passed a law banning the Jehovah's Witnesses and introducing a prison sentence of fourteen years for anyone found guilty of promoting the movement.[18]

Long before the bill was passed, however, the MCP had taken the law into its own hands and launched a ferocious onslaught on the Jehovah's Witnesses. In this onslaught the youth wing of the party, and in some areas the (paramilitary) Malawi Young Pioneers, were prominent, obviously acting under the direction of higher party officials. At Gowoka, in Mzimba District, the area chairman told the youth leaguers to hunt down all Jehovah's Witnesses. One was Mr. Phiri.

> The Youths surrounded his house at night, ordered Mr Phiri out, then entered the house and threw his sleeping wife out and started to beat both of them. Their books were torn to pieces and scattered on the way. Then they pushed them to walk, while singing a mocking song. After arriving at a school, both were undressed (except underwear) and were forced to run around the school blocs so that the Youth Leaguers, encircling the bloc, could beat them. Soon others were brought in and were subjected to similar treatment. Torture of women was discontinued in the morning, for men it continued till midday, with sticks with sharpened metal pieces being used in the exercise. Some were left for dead, but they had only fainted. None could be taken to hospital, because the Jehovah's Witnesses were not allowed to use 'Kamuzu's hospitals'.[19]

---

16 *Malawi News*, September 19, 1967.
17 *Malawi News*, September 19, 1967.
18 "Malawi Bans 'Danger' Sect," *Daily Times*, October 23, 1967, p. 1.
19 Interview Syton E. F. Mumba for Amosi Phiri, 20 April 1995, by Munthali.

Such sickening scenes became all too familiar. Major methods of persecution were the burning of houses (preferably with the inhabitants inside), the slashing of crops in the fields, confiscation of property, general beatings, and more exquisite forms of torture. Sometimes the torture led to the death of the victim, while others were deliberately assassinated. An eyewitness recalled seeing a Jehovah's Witness killed on the spot for refusing to buy a party card: 'He was cut into pieces as a demonstration to others to scare them but they were not.'[20] In spite of this severe persecution, most Jehovah's Witnesses continued to refuse to buy party cards, and they would meet at night in private houses in smaller groups or even in the bush. Despite many Witnesses fleeing to neighbouring countries, their numbers did not decrease, because their faith continued to be attractive.

It seemed for a time that the persecution was becoming less intense and, for example, at Chitawira in Blantyre, Jehovah's Witnesses were able to meet openly in 1969/70 and even to build a large Kingdom Hall. This, however, was the lull before the storm—a fresh wave of persecution was unleashed by the 1972 MCP Convention held at Zomba. Highly inflammatory language was used as party officials were encouraged to drive out Jehovah's Witnesses.[21] Once again, President Banda strongly endorsed the resolutions of the convention. William Clark, the expatriate national leader of the Jehovah's Witnesses, was given twenty-four hours to leave the country; his departure was soon followed by the looting of his house in Blantyre.[22] A much worse fate awaited his Malawian co-religionists. Any civil servant found to be a Jehovah's Witness was dismissed; private employers were expected to follow this example. In 1972, Professor Ted Binney, Principal of Bunda College of Agriculture, was deported after he refused to dismiss three members of staff who were Jehovah's Witnesses. As historian John Lwanda explains, 'The three members of his staff had their houses burned to the ground; two were killed and a third had his hands cut off. After the killings the

---

20   Interview Stewart Kumbanyiwa, 2 May 1995, by Charles Eliyasi.
21   *Malawi News*, 19 September 1972.
22   Interview Michael Kovuluva, 15 April 1995, by Hanna Bonzo.

MCP youths stopped a bus carrying children of the College staff and made the children look at the bodies.'[23]

In rural Malawi, according to one observer, 'They were not regarded as human beings but animals, for example, they were not allowed to visit hospitals, buy food at the markets, cross bridges, go to the maize millers. They lived in the bush.'[24] The 1972 persecution surpassed in cruelty and scope the persecution of 1967. Most Jehovah's Witnesses seem to have left Malawi at this time to find refuge in neighbouring countries, usually Mozambique or Zambia. Some managed to remain by giving up their faith or by somehow compromising it; others remained without doing either. Meanwhile, as John Lwanda observed, 'by September 1975, beatings, torture and deaths of Jehovah's Witnesses were commonplace'.[25] He cites a particularly gruesome episode when Harry Kampango and Aizeki Zoyaya were denounced for refusing to buy party cards: 'The Local Youth League Chairman, Kachoka, had them beaten and tortured for three days before killing them by cutting off their genitals. Kachoka was never brought to trial.'[26]

By this time there was an even more systematic attempt to target the Jehovah's Witnesses as now the judicial system became officially involved. A regular pattern was established: Jehovah's Witnesses would be brought to court at Dowa to be accused of treason and plotting to overthrow the MCP government. The judge was always Muhango, who would always find them guilty and sentence them to two years imprisonment with hard labour. They would serve their prison term at Dzaleka, a detention camp specially constructed for political offenders. Conditions were harsh:

> At Dzaleka ... they were given hoes and were told to level down a hill which was nearby. They were forced to work all day long whether under intense sunlight or rainfall. They were not allowed

---

23   Africa Watch, *Where Silence Rules: The Suppression of Dissent in Malawi* (London: Human Rights Watch, 1990), 65, cited in John Lloyd Chipembere Lwanda, *Kamuzu Banda of Malawi: A Study in Promise, Power and Legacy. Malawi under Dr Banda 1961–1994* (Zomba: Kachere, 2009), 328–329.
24   Interview Aaron Mkandawire, no date, by Mirriam Chipeta Banda (1995).
25   John Lloyd Chipembere Lwanda, *Kamuzu Banda of Malawi*, 329.
26   Africa Watch, *Where Silence Rules*, 66, cited in John Lloyd Chipembere Lwanda, *Kamuzu Banda of Malawi*, 329.

to rest and were constantly being beaten at the back while working. Many people were dying, in a week six to ten people could die. They were working from 6:00 a.m. to 7:00 p.m. They ate at 12 midnight without washing hands. They could stay for two or three months without taking a shower.[27]

The only mitigating factor was that the prison term was regulated and after two years the inmate would be given a warrant to travel home, and there was an understanding that the party was not to trouble them unduly.

By 1978, the persecution began to relent. It was still illegal to be a Jehovah's Witness. There was still periodic harassment by the MCP Youth League over the issue of the party card, sometimes involving the confiscation of property equivalent in value to the cost of a party card. But the extreme violence of the 1960s and 1970s was no longer evident in the 1980s. Finally, with Malawi under intense pressure to demonstrate respect for human rights in the post–Cold War period, in September 1993 Parliament rescinded all restrictions on the Jehovah's Witnesses. Finally, their victimisation was brought to a close, at least so far as the state was concerned.

In reviewing the persecution experienced by the Jehovah's Witnesses in Malawi between 1964 and 1993, a number of features stand out. The first is its public character. During Malawi's one-party era, persecution of opponents was often a hidden activity, with anonymous hit squads claiming their victims at night, the criminals covering up their steps. Such clandestine actions were undertaken at times by organs of the state in Malawi. However, it was not the favoured method when it came to dealing with the Jehovah's Witnesses. Their persecution was public and deliberately so. It was intended to have a deterrent effect.

A second feature to note is the extrajudicial character of most of the persecution. During the first peak of the persecution in 1963–1964, there was no shred of legal basis for persecution. In 1967, a legal pretence for persecution was produced, providing for a ban and for prison sentences for those who contravened the ban. However, the persecution started as soon as Kamuzu had made his remarks at the MCP Convention and did not wait for legal niceties to be completed. Even once legal provisions were put in

---

27   Interview Michael H. Nambera, 11 April 1995, by Charles Eliyasi.

place, they were disregarded. The beatings, paradings, killings, destruction of crops, humiliations, and expulsions were carried out without any reference to the legal system until 1975. The extrajudicial character of the persecution was officially emphasised at the Zomba 1972 convention, which appealed to government 'to give maximum possible protection to members of the party who deal with the adherents of those sects'.[28] This protection was given to the maximum. The party was taken to be the highest legal authority; its members could act freely as investigators, accusers, judges, and executioners.

Thirdly, the persecution was marked by extreme cruelty on a large scale. Taking the situation for what it was, some of the persecution of the Jehovah's Witnesses could be taken as lawful because there was some kind of legal basis for it. By government order, the Jehovah's Witnesses were banned, and by the same order clandestine activities were threatened with punishment by up to fourteen years in prison. In 1972, by party resolution, expulsion and expropriation of property were added. Local MCP leaders may have seen this as a legal basis for persecution. But in most cases the sufferings inflicted went far beyond what was provided for in this questionable "legal" basis. There was no provision in it for torture, public parading of victims, slashing of crops, burning of houses, or murder. These were actions of extreme cruelty, executed with intensity and delight and with random crowds participating in the show. Harris Nakhumwa describes his experience:

> One Youth Leaguer held an extended piece of the rope in one hand. The other was busy blowing on his whistle. By the time we had reached Chitakale, about 3 km from Mulanje boma, a crowd followed behind me. The whistling Youth Leaguer prompted the group into a song: *Wopanda card sachidya, sachidya, uyo chimubvundira* (The one without the card will not eat food, will not eat food, that one, it will rot for him).[29]

Fourthly, the persecution was marked by the use of shame and sexual violence. In Malawi, proper behaviour in order not to be shamed is

---

28   *Malawi News*, September 19, 1972.
29   Interview Harris Nakhumwa, 11 April 1995, by Peter Mitunda.

considered of high value. Kamuzu Banda prided himself on the high public morality that prevailed in regard to such matters as dress and hairstyle, a combination of his own Chewa tradition with the Victorian values he had imbibed while living in Britain. However, in the persecution the party members were obviously encouraged to break the taboos of decency. One account, for example, records, 'Arrived at Gowoka 7 p.m. in June 1972 and here they were told to buy cards but they declined. . . . So, they were stripped of their clothes and put outside their houses for all to see. Stayed outside from 9 p.m. to 2 a.m. without clothes. They were six of them i.e. him, his wife, and the founder Mr. Amosi and his wife and some other two ladies'.[30]

Sexual taboos are even stronger in Malawi than those of shame, with the incest taboo being the strictest. Attempts to force Jehovah's Witnesses to publicly violate this taboo were a frequent aspect of torture inflicted. One account indicates that '[After having been paraded round the village naked] they were put in lines and fathers were forced to face their daughters while naked, similarly mothers were asked to face their sons while naked'.[31] Another records, 'They undressed us completely men as well as women and our children. After undressing us they could take a man and his daughter to have sex. When we refused, they could whip us like cows.'[32] Even pregnant women were spared neither shame nor abuse: 'By then, she was pregnant (7 months), but when the Youthmen came to her home, they got hold of her and beat her severely. Thereafter they raped her in her own house all five of them. After that they let her go while crying bitterly. When she came out of the house, she found her father literally naked having been beaten heavily.'[33]

COMPLICITY

Surveying Malawi's social landscape during the period in question, it is clear from the demographics that many of those perpetrating the atrocities

---

30 Interview Winston S. B. Neba, 18 April 1995, by Munthali.
31 Interview Frank Homela, 11 April 1995, by Charles Eliyasi.
32 Interview Mchima Msuku, 10 April 1995, by Esnat Mdolo.
33 Interview Alabia Bernard, 18 April 1995, by Rosemary T. Muhuwo.

described above must have been practising Christians. It is therefore an inescapable question to ask how they reconciled their Christian faith with their conduct in relation to the Jehovah's Witnesses. Unsurprisingly, those who were directly involved have not been keen to explain themselves, so answers to this question can only be speculative. To put the best possible construction on their behaviour, Malawi was a young nation and its best chance of success seemed to be for everyone to rally behind the Congress Party that had led the struggle for independence. Those who failed to comply could be seen as a threat to the integrity and progress of the new nation and therefore harsh treatment to bring them into line could be justified. It may be that some rationalised the infliction of severe and degrading punishment along these lines.

The social hierarchies that shaped the life of the young nation might have reinforced any such rationalisation. The elite group that inherited the colonial state belonged to the mainstream churches (predominantly Presbyterian, with an Anglican minority and a growing Catholic component) and comprised staunch card-carrying members of the MCP. They set the standards and expectations for what was expected of a loyal citizen. Minority groups who chose not to comply with these standards and expectations could easily come to be regarded as dangerous deviants. When the all-powerful President, 'Father and Founder of the Nation,' roundly condemned the Jehovah's Witnesses, it might have been natural to place them in this category and to conclude that they deserved all the punishment that they suffered. The fact that they were also "deviant" in their understanding of Christian doctrine might have been another factor in the equation that convinced practising Christians that it was justifiable to persecute the Jehovah's Witnesses. Furthermore, it is not possible to exclude consideration of the human capacity for sadism and cruelty, particularly since the extreme punishments that were inflicted went far beyond what was required by the legislation.

Another important aspect of the context is that the use of violence to achieve political ends was to a great extent normalised during the Banda dictatorship.[34] The oft-repeated four cornerstones of the MCP—unity,

---

34   See T. D. Williams, *Malawi: The Politics of Despair* (Ithaca: Cornell University Press, 1978); John Lloyd Chipembere Lwanda, *Kamuzu Banda of Malawi*;

loyalty, discipline, and obedience—could be interpreted as positive values but they carried a dark undertone of intolerance and violence. In his speeches, Banda did not hesitate to threaten those who had crossed him politically with a grisly fate—his claim that his opponents became meat for the crocodiles was not metaphorical.[35] Individuals who fell foul of the party could be picked up by the security forces. They might never be heard from again or might spend many years as political prisoners. What was unusual about the Jehovah's Witnesses was that an entire religious community was targeted. They were not the only group to be singled out for persecution. When Masauko Chipembere, a member of Malawi's first cabinet, fell out with Banda and sought to challenge him, the village from which he originated was subjected to collective punishment. The entire village was set on fire and many of its inhabitants detained without trial.[36] While the treatment of the Jehovah's Witnesses was an extreme case, it represented a wider pattern whereby the state felt justified in inflicting violence upon citizens who were perceived to be disloyal. As people grew accustomed to life in such a society, it may be that at the time the atrocities perpetrated against the Jehovah's Witnesses did not seem as strange and disturbing as they do from a later vantage point.

There is no evidence that the police (colonial or independent) did anything to stop the forced selling of party cards. This suggests that the police colluded in the persecution. The police also seem to have shared in it in other ways, like keeping detained Jehovah's Witnesses and, on occasion, beating them. On the other hand, it is clear from the records that often the police protected the Jehovah's Witnesses or assisted them. Sometimes police cars ferried them to safety. In one instance the police, in a night action witnessed by the District Commissioner of Nsanje, Harry Ghabu, ferried Jehovah's Witnesses back to safety in Mozambique, from where they had been taken previously by the MCP. The police had an

---

Africa Watch, *Where Silence Rules*; *Malawi: Human Rights Violations 25 Years after Independence* (London: Amnesty International, 1989); *Malawi: Prison Conditions, Cruel Punishment and Detention without Trial* (London: Amnesty International, 1992).

35 See Jack Mapanje, *And Crocodiles Are Hungry at Night* (London: Ayebia Clarke, 2012).

36 See John Lloyd Chipembere Lwanda, *Kamuzu Banda of Malawi*, 353–355.

equivocal role, both participating in the persecution and assisting Jehovah's Witnesses against their persecutors. It is understandable that Banda preferred that the MCP and its para-military wing the Malawi Young Pioneers (MYP) deal with them. In the available material, there is no evidence that the army shared in the persecution, except that it provided some of the vehicles used for the forced repatriation from Zambia. On the other hand, there is evidence that they helped transport fleeing Witnesses to safety. Prisoners from Dzaleka, who had to serve part of their sentence working for the army, were treated very well.

Despite the egregious and extensive persecution suffered by the Jehovah's Witnesses, none of the churches in Malawi ever raised any public voice of protest. This is where the issue of complicity is most acute. By their silence, it appeared that the mainstream churches approved of what was taking place. Again, there is a wider context to consider. It was not only on the issue of the persecution of Jehovah's Witnesses that the churches were silent.[37] It was on every issue that might be considered 'political'. Part of Malawi's self-image as a highly ethical country was the claim that its people enjoyed freedom of worship. This claim was echoed repeatedly in the rhetoric of the ruling regime. To some extent, it was true. People could gather for worship unmolested and the various churches could run their affairs in accordance with their own traditions without any state interference. There was, however, a tacit understanding that there was a *quid pro quo*. In return for the freedom they enjoyed, the churches were expected to refrain from any comment that might be considered critical of the government and to provide ideological support for the ruling regime.

Church leaders were prominent on national occasions and were expected to give their blessing to the Life President and the ruling party. In 1974, for example, the Catholic Archbishop of Blantyre and the General Secretary of the Presbyterian Blantyre Synod released a joint statement:

---

[37] See Grenna Kaiya, 'The Role of the Churches in Human Rights Advocacy: The Case of Malawian Members of Jehovah's Witnesses, Their Accounts of Stories and Memories as Victims of Religious Persecution from 1964 to 1994' (master's thesis, Diakonhjemmet University College, 2013), 48–60.

> What has been achieved during this period in all fields is so unbelievable that it confounds even the most optimistic expectations of most of us and there is no doubt that all of this achievement is due to the untiring efforts, dedicated, selfless and responsible leadership of His Excellency, the Life President Ngwazi Dr H. Kamuzu Banda. If this country has grown from the ranks of the poor nations into a nation with a viable booming economy, with a healthy educated people, it is due to His Excellency's own dynamic leadership and the stable and peaceful conditions that leadership has created.[38]

This kind of laudatory language was expected and required, but it should be noted that this statement was made at the very time when the persecution of the Jehovah's Witnesses was at its most intense. The churches had little choice, in a context of surveillance and intimidation, but to echo the rhetoric of the regime, and if their leaders privately entertained any misgivings, they were well-advised to keep these to themselves. At local levels, no service was complete without a sycophantic prayer for the long life and prosperity of the Life President.

Some exceptional church leaders found ways to open up some critical distance between the church and the state.[39] The general picture, however, was that the churches were silent on matters that the government deemed to fall within its domain. With the benefit of hindsight, the churches could see that they had been too complicit. The Presbyterian Blantyre Synod, for example, confessed in 1993 that

> If we look at our own history as the CCAP during the time of the struggle for Independence, we will see that Blantyre Synod was very much in support of the Nyasaland African Congress (later

---

38 *Joint Message from the Churches of Malawi on 10th Anniversary of Independence*, 6 July 1974, signed by Most Reverend James Chiona, Archbishop of Blantyre, and Very Reverend J.D. Sangaya, General Secretary, CCAP Synod of Blantyre, 2.

39 See, for example, Kenneth R. Ross, "Where Were the Prophets and Martyrs in Banda's Malawi? Four Presbyterian Ministers," *Missionalia*, 24 no. 2 (1996): 113–128.

called the MCP). Because of this very verbal stance on the side of the MCP, after Independence, the CCAP was aligned closely with the government and became so assimilated with the government's activities that the Synod was often invited to pray and participate as a Church at various government functions. However, because of this assimilation and alignment with the MCP, the Church gradually lost its ability to admonish or speak pastorally to the government.[40]

Among the matters on which the church was unable to admonish or speak pastorally to the government was the treatment of the Jehovah's Witnesses during this period.

The only known exception is that, in the early 1970s, a group of church leaders, including Archbishop James Chiona of Blantyre and Bishop Matthias Chimole of Zomba, met President Banda in private to raise their concerns about the harsh treatment of the Jehovah's Witnesses. They believed that, as a result, the president ordered an end to the atrocities being perpetrated at that time.[41] There is little evidence that this actually happened and the imprisonment of Jehovah's Witnesses at Dzaleka started soon afterwards. Occasionally, an individual missionary, such as the Anglican priest Jack Biggers, spoke out publicly on behalf of the Jehovah's Witnesses and was deported as a result.[42]

There were also episodes where the churches, at a local level, offered support to Jehovah's Witnesses in time of trouble. For example, priests from Thunga Parish and the nearby Nantipwiri Pastoral Centre helped to protect Jehovah's Witnesses who were under attack, as did their neighbour, the Italian Mr. Dondi. After the Young Pioneers had attacked the Jehovah's Witnesses congregation at Chitawira Kingdom Hall in Blantyre in June 1972 and beaten and scattered the worshippers, some Catholic and CCAP

---

40 'A Statement on the Role of the Church in the Transformation of Malawi in the Context of Justice and Peace,' Produced by the Administrators Conference, Blantyre Synod CCAP, 22–23 January 1994, 4.

41 Interview Very Rev. Prof. Silas S. Ncozana, 8 May 2020 and personal communication from Bishop Kalilombe to Klaus Fiedler, 2008.

42 James Tengatenga, *Church, State and Society in Malawi: The Anglican Case* (Zomba: Kachere, 2006), 114.

Christians hid them in their houses, warning them when the MYPs were coming and providing them with food. Such cases seem to be the exception rather than the rule. There were also sympathetic local chiefs who were often Christians. Chief Chiendausiku 'ordered that in his territory no house was to be set on fire and nobody was to be harassed'.[43] Since he could not keep the Witnesses safe, he advised them to flee to Mozambique. Other chiefs did not reveal that there were Jehovah's Witnesses in their villages.[44] On Chisi Island in Lake Chirwa, the Jehovah's Witnesses were never molested.[45]

CONCLUSION

For those with religious freedom at heart, the story of the Jehovah's Witnesses in Malawi between 1964 and 1993 is a sobering one. Here is a country that proudly took the title 'the warm heart of Africa'. Its people are famous for their friendliness and good nature. It is known for its peaceful history. It is a strongly Christian country, its public morality shaped by biblical teaching and a large majority of its population professing to be Christians. It is proud of its tradition of freedom of worship. Relations between different faith communities are largely cordial. Yet it was here that the Jehovah's Witnesses suffered the horrifying persecution that has been outlined above. They were law-abiding, tax-paying citizens but were victimised by the one-party regime simply because their faith required them to abstain from active participation in politics. The lack of any public protest from the mainline churches gave the impression that they condoned the actions of the state against the Jehovah's Witnesses. Worse still, many of those who perpetrated the atrocities were practising Christians. The Malawi case serves as a warning note in regard to the power of propaganda and the danger of complacency. The machinery of the one-party state created a plausibility structure in which extremely harsh treatment of Jehovah's Witnesses appeared to be justified. With few exceptions, Malawi's citizens

---

43   Interview L. Chipoka, 9 April 1995, by Peter Kalawa.
44   Interview Mr. Banda, no date, by Bernadette S. Banda [1995].
45   Interview Joseph de Gabriele, formerly priest at Sitima Catholic Parish, 15 May 1995.

complied and became complicit in the persecution. Even more troubling is the evidence that many of those who inflicted the persecution chose to impose extreme and violent punishments that went beyond even what was required by the state. The human capacity for cruelty and sadism can never be underestimated. From the Malawi case, we can learn that freedom of religion can only be upheld through constant vigilance and that the litmus test might well be provided by a dissident minority.

13

REHASHING THE ALLIANCES OF THRONE AND ALTAR
On the Instrumentalisation of Religion in Contemporary Central and Eastern Europe and Building Resilience

Pavol Bargár

INTRODUCTION

Recently, there has been a clear tendency in many Central and Eastern European countries, including such secularised contexts as the Czech Republic, to use religious discourse and religious capital in general. Its purpose has been to reinforce nationalism, fundamentalism, and a lack of trust in the West, the European Union, and liberal democracy.[1] In such discourse, then, the reference to so-called Christian values is employed to control and exclude from public life those considered 'the other' because of ethnicity, gender, culture, sexuality, and political view, but also because of religious conviction and affiliation. As such, Christianity here plays the role of both a victimiser and a victim. The former mode can be found in the examples of 'unholy alliances' between political parties, movements, and figures and certain churches and/or church representatives seeking

---

[1] This text is an output of the research project on 'The Misuse of Religion in Post-Communist Countries and Building Resilience', supported by the Porticus and Renovabis foundations and the Charles University's research programme no. UNCE/24/SSH/019.

to claim their place in the public arena. The latter becomes apparent not only through the bad image Christianity gets but also through the lives of actual Christians being marginalised or suffering on account of the public expression of their faith.

Roman Catholicism and Orthodoxy are often the dominant actors here, but there is yet another perspective to be added to the overall picture. The alliances are often made not along religious denominational lines but rather along the 'conservatives' and 'liberals' divide. The primary objective of these alliances, it seems, does not consist in spreading the Christian faith. This is underlined, *inter alia*, by diminishing church attendance. For example, the data from the 2021 EU census confirm this trend in countries with such differing attitudes toward religion as the Czech Republic and Slovakia, respectively.[2] Similarly, a recent report on the Hungarian situation affirms the image of a rapidly secularizing society, with a tiny minority of the citizens (12 percent) regularly attending church, while a majority of them still identifying as Catholic. The report concludes: 'Less than 15 percent of Hungarians say religion is "very important" in their lives. Christmas markets, generous public subsidies to religious schools, and beautifully preserved churches have done little to arrest this steady decline.'[3] Therefore, one can argue that the objective pursued by the actors in this alliance is a reinforcement of the political, cultural, and social status quo by way of fostering a 'fortress mindset' and keeping the other on the outside.[4]

---

[2] For statistics on religious belief in the Czech Republic, see https://www.czso.cz/csu/scitani2021/religious-beliefs (accessed 27 March 2023). For statistics on religious belief in Slovakia, see https://www.scitanie.sk/en/population/basic-results/structure-of-population-by-religious-belief/SR/SK0/SR (accessed on 27 March 2023).

[3] Will Collins, 'The Myth of a Christian Revival in Eastern Europe', *The American Conservative* (7 January 2019), https://www.theamericanconservative.com/the-myth-of-a-christian-revival-in-eastern-europe/ (accessed 27 March 2023).

[4] Otherness is here understood in not only confessional or religious but also political, ethnic, and cultural terms. See more in Joseph Sverker, 'Confessing Christ in "Christian Europe": The Death of the Church as a Theological Response to Populism', in *The Spirit of Populism: Political Theologies in*

This chapter will explore the complex dynamics between religion (particularly Christianity) and politics and the instrumentalisation of religion in contemporary Central and Eastern Europe (CEE), with a particular focus on the Czech Republic. I argue that the willingness on the part of Christians to support the alliances of 'throne and altar' harms the church's credibility and creative potential vis-à-vis its witness in society. The chapter proceeds in three major steps. First, I will discuss various aspects of the multivalent relationship between religion and populist politics. I will next examine the role religion plays in the CEE context, giving special attention to the Czech Republic. The final part of the chapter is a theological reflection on how Christianity can become more faithful to its public vocation, thus—at the same time—developing immunity to various attempts at political instrumentalisation.

THEORIZING RELIGION, OTHERNESS, AND POPULISM

While attempts at a definition have remained elusive, it is fair to assert that religion represents a way of life and accounts for an essential element of human identity. Encompassing spiritual, ideological, behavioural, and ethical dimensions, it goes far beyond the level of a mere opinion. Paul Ricoeur and his hermeneutics of the self can help one better understand religion as a factor of identity formation. His hermeneutics of self-distinguishing sameness (*idem*) and selfhood (*ipse*) are an effort to avoid the absolutisation of the self (i.e., the self serving as its own foundation).[5] This understanding is rooted in the positive acknowledgment of otherness. Otherness is seen as desirable. The other does not represent a mere negative background against which the 'radiance' of one's own identity shines. Rather, the other is the necessary counterpart of the self. Without the other, one cannot

---

Polarized Times, eds. Ulrich Schmiedel and Joshua Ralston (Leiden: Brill, 2022), 263–264.

[5] See Paul Ricoeur, *Oneself as Another*, trans. Kathleen Blamey (Chicago: The University of Chicago Press, 1992), 4–6. See also Sturla J. Stålsett, 'The Other in the Ecclesial Self: The Church and the Populist Challenge', in *The Spirit of Populism: Political Theologies in Polarized Times*, eds. Ulrich Schmiedel and Joshua Ralston (Leiden: Brill, 2022), 278–293, especially 281–284.

become truly oneself. The alterity of the other is to be appreciated and cherished because it helps one to come to terms with and pursue one's own self more fully.

However, it is no less important that one relating to the other recognises how much they have in common. To put it in other words, my neighbour who might differ from me in terms of gender, education, profession, political views, and religion can expand, through their otherness, my understanding of the various facets of my own identity. At the same time, the encounter with the other makes me aware of our common story, values, and humanity. As such, one needs the other to become truly oneself rooted in a broader humanity.

This argument is based on the understanding of human identity in terms of the fundamental interconnectedness of self and other. I am because you are; I am because we are. These ideas give rise to a relational theological anthropology that views human existence as inseparably connected with a complex and multi-layered web of relationships that includes human beings, non-human beings, creation at large, and the reality that transcends the world we live in. In biblical tradition, the latter is referred to as God. One needs to be part of this web in order to become truly oneself.

Still, there is also another aspect to this issue. Since religion touches upon the core of humanity, it can easily fall prey to instrumentalisation and violence. Populism, like religion, has to do with the relationality of human existence. Populism is characterised as the idea of a uniform 'people' pitted against another people. Importantly, that 'other people' is construed and promoted as a threat to the integrity and, indeed, existence of 'the people' that populists claim to represent.[6] In populist rhetoric, then, religion can serve as 'a protective shield of sameness against otherness'.[7] In such an understanding, religion effectively represents a national identifier that provides a basis for creating an opposition between a certain country (or Europe as a whole) against other countries, continents, or cultures—and other religions. This arrangement poses a lure also for religion, because faith communities may in turn receive from political players 'their share of

---

6 See Sverker, 'Confessing Christ', 264. See also Jan Werner Müller, *What Is Populism?* (London: Penguin, 2017).

7 Stålsett, 'The Other', 285.

privilege and power'.[8] Following this logic, alliance between religion and populist politics represents both 'a threat and temptation for churches'.[9] To make sense of this potential, the term *Christianism* has been coined in contrast to *Christian faith*.[10] The former fosters 'secularised' references to the Christian faith, so that the cultural or civilisational aspect of 'belonging rather than believing' gains the upper hand. Spirituality, reading and interpretation of sacred scriptures, and participation in worship services are considered of minor significance. To put it briefly, in Christianism, religion becomes a force for shaping identity.

This force entails an intentional effort to foreground, and even absolutise, one or several of the complex human identity markers, such as race, gender, sexuality, ethnicity, culture, or—with particular relevance to our topic—religion and nation, at the expense of the balance with the other identity markers. The declared objective is to shape an identity that enables a group to reassert its self-assurance. However, the actual outcome frequently represents an imaginary construct that pits itself in a stark opposition, or even open hostility, against an undefined 'other'. Speaking from and on the CEE context, András Máté-Tóth refers to this dynamic as 'tribalism', arguing that it stands for, in essence, 'a cry because of the wounded collective identity'.[11] For him, the notion of the wounded collective identity represents a way to come to terms with 'all the complex problematics of societal communication in the [Central and Eastern European] region'.[12] Whether one uses the term tribalism, Christianism, or 'identitary' temptations, the main point is that the fear of the unknown (*xenophobia*) and an undue regard for one's identity can produce a volatile mix that appeals to the 'baser instincts' of humanity and leads to hateful attitudes/actions. While, originally, it might have been a mechanism to protect or to provide

---

8   Stålsett, 'The Other', 285.
9   Stålsett, 'The Other', 285.
10 See Rogers Brubaker, 'Between Nationalism and Civilizationism: The European Populist Moment in Comparative Perspective', *Ethnic and Racial Studies* 40, no. 8 (2017): 1191–1226, here at 1199.
11 András Máté-Tóth, 'Wounded Words in a Wounded World: Opportunities for Mission in Central and Eastern Europe Today', *Mission Studies* 37, no. 3 (2020): 365.
12 Máté-Tóth, 'Wounded Words', 360.

guidance for living in a complicated world, it easily turns into rhetoric and a practice of hatred and even violence.

Mattias Martinson provides a complementary perspective. He maintains that Christianity is in populist rhetoric reduced to a monument, even a 'museum' or a 'mausoleum'.[13] The political power of such an understanding of Christianity as a 'monument' lies in the reductionist contrast that it establishes between 'people' and 'non-people'. Ulrich Schmiedel perceives the implications of this political move as follows: 'Once Christianity is monumentalized, the populists can weaponize their concept of Christianity. Hence, when churches advocate for conversations with Islam, they can be criticized for a sell-out of Christian identity, charged with desecrating and destroying the monument.'[14]

In this context, the concept of 'Christian Europe' is used to exclude others. This situation then poses a theological question for Christians to reflect on what confessing Christ means today in CEE (and elsewhere), where the church stands for an institution with immediate cultural and national connections. In other words, the challenge for a theologically reflective Christian consists in the need to respond constructively to the instrumentalisation of Christianity against the other. The core of the issue can largely be located in the way one interprets sacred scriptures. As Hannah Strømmen observes, populist engagement with scriptures is not so much about the 'reading' of holy texts as it is about appealing to them as to 'cultural symbols' and 'material and affective artefacts'.[15] In *Embodied Existence*, I discuss the exclusivist versus inclusivist stances adopted by certain

---

[13] See Mattias Martinson, 'Towards a "Theology" of Christian Monumentality: Post-Secular Reflections on Grace and Nature', in *Monument and Memory*, eds. Jonna Bornemark, Mattias Martinson, and Jayne Svenungsson (Berlin: LIT, 2015), 21–42.

[14] Ulrich Schmiedel, 'Introduction: Political Theology in the Spirit of Populism—Methods and Metaphors', in *The Spirit of Populism: Political Theologies in Polarized Times*, eds. Ulrich Schmiedel and Joshua Ralston (Leiden: Brill, 2022), 13.

[15] See Hannah M. Strømmen, 'Sacred Scripts of Populism: Scripture-Practices in the European Far Right', in *The Spirit of Populism: Political Theologies in Polarized Times*, eds. Ulrich Schmiedel and Joshua Ralston (Leiden: Brill, 2022), 92.

groups of people toward those who differ from them in terms of 'dreaming' and 'struggling' for a future that challenges the status quo. While such a dream propelled by an exclusivist vision can be a 'nightmare' for those who do not belong, I have highlighted the potential of inclusivist images, such as feasting, that in the biblical imagination and practice represent God's hospitality as embodied in God's reign.[16] The latter provides an example of a theologically constructive potential to counter the instrumentalisation of religion, in particular Christianity, as a shield against the other in the context of (Central and Eastern) Europe. Before I embark on exploring such a potential in the last part of this chapter, however, I will take a closer look at the religious landscape of CEE, and specifically that of the Czech Republic.

THE CONTEXT OF CENTRAL AND EASTERN EUROPE: RELIGION AND SOCIETY

The notion of CEE is contested. Identifying CEE as one of the geographical sub-regions of Europe, EuroVoc identifies the following countries as part of it: Albania, Armenia, Azerbaijan, Belarus, Bosnia and Herzegovina, Bulgaria, Croatia, the Czech Republic, Georgia, Hungary, Moldova, Montenegro, North Macedonia, Poland, Romania, Russia, Serbia, Slovakia, Slovenia, and Ukraine.[17] In contrast, the Organisation for Economic Co-operation and Development (OECD) maintains that CEE comprises Albania, Bulgaria, Croatia, the Czech Republic, Estonia, Hungary, Latvia, Lithuania, Poland, Romania, Slovakia, and Slovenia.[18] For the purpose of this chapter, I consider the term CEE to include the European countries

---

16 See Pavol Bargár, *Embodied Existence: Our Common Life in God* (Eugene, OR: Cascade Books, 2023), 144–145.

17 See Publications Office of the EU, *EuroVoc*, 'Concept 914: Central and Eastern Europe', available at https://op.europa.eu/en/web/eu-vocabularies/concept/-/resource?uri=http://eurovoc.europa.eu/914 (accessed 27 March 2023). EuroVoc is a multilingual thesaurus maintained by the Publications Office of the European Union.

18 See Directorate, OECD Statistics, 'OECD Glossary of Statistical Terms—Central and Eastern European Countries (CEECs) Definition', available at https://stats.oecd.org/ (accessed 27 March 2023).

with experience of communist (socialist) regimes during the period following the end of the Second World War until the dissolution of the Soviet Union in 1991. There are scholars who call for a moratorium on the use of the term 'post-communist' because they believe this concept evokes the ghosts of the past by constantly coming back to the party state times as the frame of reference for interpreting contemporary events and trends.[19] Nevertheless, I maintain that a shared heritage of life 'in the shadows' of the past plays a significant role in the dynamics of political and social life, including religion, in the region.

As I have already suggested, a trend toward the exploitation of religious traditions for political ends have acquired a distinct flavour in the CEE context due to its particular history and context. This development is related to an ideological vacuum that emerged after the end of the Cold War and the disintegration of the communist empire in the 1990s. Typically, collective identity in the post-communist countries came to be reinforced through nationalism and various appeals to 'return' to cultural-religious roots (of the pre-communist era). Religion and nation emerged as the two most powerful symbols of collective identity to design a framework for a shared 'us', only too often—sadly—negotiated against a certain 'them'. Recently, this process has been intensified by the intertwined processes of globalisation, migration, and 'euro-integration', implying a sense of uncertainty and a perceived threat allegedly posed by such phenomena as migration, the 'decadent West', and Brussels' 'bureaucratic machinery'. This process has resulted in what Zygmunt Bauman calls 'liquid fear', that is, a state of constant anxiety about the various and unexpected dangers that people living in the late modern age face at any time.[20] Such fear can then result in similarly 'liquid' resentment toward the groups of people, systems, and structures that one feels prevent one from living a full and dignified existence. Although it is notoriously difficult to pinpoint, this tendency is largely nourished by religious sentiments and resources. As such, religious rhetoric and religious capital in general are, in the CEE context, exploited to fan and reinforce nationalism, fundamentalism,

---

19 See, for example, Anne-Marie Kool, 'Trends and Challenges in Mission and Missiology in "Post-Communist" Europe', *Mission Studies* 25, no. 1 (2008): 24.
20 See Zygmunt Bauman, *Liquid Fear* (Cambridge, UK: Polity Press, 2006).

xenophobia, and a lack of trust in the West, the European Union, and liberal democracy.

As our discussion on Christianism and identitary temptations above has shown, this exploitation is usually done by turning Christianity into a reservoir of cultural symbols and artefacts, sometimes even without any direct link to lived religion. The Hungarian case illustrates this point very clearly. In 2018, starting his fourth term as prime minister, Viktor Orbán declared liberal democracy a 'shipwrecked' project to be replaced by what he called 'Christian democracy'. While he equates the former with mass migration, international capitalism, and cultural decay, the latter guarantees, in his view, 'people's freedom [and] security' and 'supports the traditional family model of one man and one woman, keeps anti-Semitism at bay, and gives a chance for growth'.[21] Orbán's idea is readily apparent, for example, in the following excerpt from the interview that he gave with regard to the election of the new president of the European Commission in 2019:

> At any rate, I know what is in Hungary's interest. I'm enough of an old fox in the Brussels jungle—or in the Brussels forest—to know what kind of President of the Commission would serve Hungary's interests. What's more, I have a very clear mandate from the people: I must support a candidate who is opposed to immigration, who has national feelings, and who therefore respects European nations. And I must support a person who personally sees the importance of Christian culture, and who is prepared to protect it. This mandate comes with fixed conditions: I believe that the people have said that I must stand by only such a candidate.[22]

---

21   Viktor Orbán cited in Darko Janjevic with Reuters, 'Orban: Era of "Liberal Democracy" Is Over', 10 May 2018, https://www.dw.com/en/viktor-orban-era-of-liberal-democracy-is-over/a-43732540 (accessed 27 March 2023).

22   Viktor Orbán, 'Interview with Prime Minister Viktor Orbán on the Kossuth Radio Programme "Good Morning Hungary"', 31 May 2019, https://2015-2019.kormany.hu/en/the-prime-minister/the-prime-minister-s-speeches/interview-with-prime-minister-viktor-orban-on-the-kossuth-radio-programme-good-morning-hungary20190602 (accessed 27 March 2023).

As this quotation shows, Orbán identifies himself as a champion of the people, acting on their behalf and knowing what is best for them. He equates Christian culture with 'national feelings' against the immigrants, the outsiders. I would suggest that it is of significance that the term *Christian culture* is employed, rather than *Christian faith*, because what is at play here has more to do with a symbolic frame of reference (Christianism) than with everyday religious practice (Christianity). Martinson puts it in terms of 'the fictional *post-Christian* narrative about a strong and profound Christian identity among the people of Hungary and elsewhere' that is notoriously difficult to counter.[23] Evidence for this claim can be found, *inter alia*, in various decisions made by Orbán's government, such as the ban of the homeless from public spaces, 'a move that has more to do with making Budapest palatable to foreign tourists than building a genuinely Christian society'.[24]

It is worth paying attention to the stance Hungarian churches adopt vis-à-vis this situation. Even though their research affirms the religious indifference of populist voters, Zoltán Ádám and András Bozóki argue that the two main Christian denominations in Hungary, Roman Catholic and Reformed, play a propaganda and ideological role for the regime by supporting Orbán's idea of Hungary as a sacred Christian entity. In return, they get financial benefits, as they have become major players in publicly funded education and social services.[25] In this way, the alliance of throne and altar is rehashed without either the church or the state having to pay much regard to everyday lived faith and religious practice.[26]

---

23   Mattias Martinson, 'Populism, Christianity, and the Role of the Theologian', in *The Spirit of Populism: Political Theologies in Polarized Times*, eds. Ulrich Schmiedel and Joshua Ralston (Leiden: Brill, 2022), 141, emphasis in the original.
24   Collins, 'The Myth of a Christian Revival'.
25   See Zoltán Ádám and András Bozóki, 'State and Faith: Right-Wing Populism and Nationalized Religion in Hungary', *Intersection: East European Journal of Society and Politics* 2, no. 1 (2016): 98–122, here at 113.
26   Nevertheless, it is fair to add, as Ádám and Bozóki's research shows, that Orbán has won over Christian voters by establishing a 'strategic alliance' with the Christian Democratic People's Party (*Kereszténydemokrata Néppárt—* KDNP). See Ádám and Bozóki, 'State and Faith', 111.

Another example of such rehashing of the alliances of throne and altar can be found in the phenomenon of unaffiliated religiosity. Stefan Huber and Alexander Yendell explore the nexus between religion and proclivity for far-right politics in another post-communist context, the eastern part of Germany. They build on Theodor Adorno's insight that people who foster an inclination to beliefs in supernatural powers independent of institutionalised religion (e.g., Christian churches) often show an affinity with ethnocentrism and authoritarian political views. This is, to an extent, similar to those for whom religion represents a factor of social status and security, devoid of content. Belief in the supernatural, as Huber and Yendell's sociological research indicates, is a factor for voting for the right-wing populist party, Alternative for Germany (*Alternative für Deutschland*—AfD).[27] We can conclude that even with respect to institutionally unaffiliated religiosity, one can speak of an alliance of throne and altar, even if this 'altar' is perhaps one dedicated to an 'unknown god' (compare to Acts 17:23).

ZOOMING IN ON THE CZECH RELIGIOUS LANDSCAPE

The phenomenon of institutionally unaffiliated religiosity is an appropriate point of connection for recalibrating our discussion on the context of the Czech Republic. In the 2021 EU census, circa 960,000 people living in the Czech Republic self-identified as 'believers, not belonging to a church or religious society'. This accounts for 9.1 percent of the population and represents the most numerous single religious grouping, followed by the Roman Catholic Church with some 741,000 adherents.[28] For many scholars of religion, this fact lays the basis for what they refer to as the shy or timid spirituality of the Czech people, a notion that gives an expression to the

---

27 See Stefan Huber and Alexander Yendell, 'Does Religiosity Matter? Explaining Right-Wing Extremist Attitudes and the Vote for the Alternative for Germany (AfD)', *Religion and Society in Central and Eastern Europe* 12, no. 1 (2020): 63–82, here at 68. See also Theodor W. Adorno, *Studien zum autoritären Charakter* (Frankfurt: Suhrkamp, 1999).

28 For the data, see https://www.czso.cz/csu/scitani2021/religious-beliefs (accessed 27 March 2023).

deep-rooted and long-term reluctance of the Czechs to discuss the matters of their faith and beliefs in public.[29] Furthermore, an important role in the movement of a significant part of the population toward institutionally unaffiliated religiosity is also played by strong Czech anti-clericalism and a distrust of institutions, including religious ones.[30]

Even in this setting, however, religion comprises a significant factor in political life. This probably became most apparent in the 2015 European migrant crisis. Evoking the fear of and hatred toward the refugees from the Middle East and North Africa, certain Czech politicians and activists appealed to presumably 'European' or, at times, explicitly 'Christian' values in their self-proclaimed 'crusade' to protect the European civilisation from the influx of 'barbarians'. In this discourse, the refugees were regarded, to all intents and purposes, as being Muslims. The argument then went that 'their' culture could never live side by side peacefully with 'ours' on account of its inherent differences. One of the most notorious—and influential—proponents of these anti-immigrant sentiments was Miloš Zeman, the president of the Czech Republic until March 2023. In a 2016 article in *The Economist*, Zeman is quoted as saying that 'Muslim refugees are "practically impossible" to integrate'.[31]

This voice has extended its impact well beyond the events connected to the 2015 situation because Zeman spread such ideas consistently throughout the whole period of his ten-year presidency. Notably, though a self-identified left-wing politician, Zeman kept very good relations and close links to Cardinal Dominik Duka, former archbishop of Prague. As

---

29 See Pavel Hošek, 'Discerning the Signs of the Times in the Post-Communist Czech Republic: A Historical, Sociological and Missiological Analysis of Contemporary Czech Culture', in *A Czech Perspective on Faith in A Secular Age*, eds. Tomáš Halík and Pavel Hošek (Washington, DC: The Council for Research in Values and Philosophy, 2015), 13–42, here at 27–28.

30 See, for example, Dana Hamplová and Zdeněk R. Nešpor, 'Invisible Religion in a "Non-Believing" Country: The Case of the Czech Republic', *Social Compass* 56, no. 4 (2009): 581–597 and Zdeněk R. Nešpor, 'Religious Processes in Contemporary Czech Society', *Sociologický časopis/Czech Sociological Review* 40, no. 3 (2004): 277–295.

31 'Big, Bad Visegrad', *The Economist* (28 January 2016), https://www.economist.com/europe/2016/01/28/big-bad-visegrad (accessed 27 March 2023).

they both repeatedly emphasised, the two were of the same mind on the issues of values and culture. Duka adopted an 'accommodating approach in the church-state dispute over the ownership of Prague's St Vitus Cathedral'. After he became archbishop of Prague in 2010, he celebrated the mass for state representatives in the president's summer seat in 2015. Zeman bestowed the Order of the White Lion, the top state award, on Duka in 2016 and intervened with Pope Francis to prolong Duka's mandate after the latter turned seventy-five in April 2020. This alliance provoked criticism not only from some believers but also from the public.[32]

Another key actor on the Czech political scene that since 2015 has used references to religion (specifically, Christianity) to pursue its anti-immigrant and anti-Islam agenda is the right-wing populist movement Freedom and Direct Democracy (*Svoboda a přímá demokracie*—SPD). Its political program says the following:

> The movement Freedom and Direct Democracy is a patriotic and democratic movement that will pursue a uncompromising political struggle for the independence and sovereignty of the Czech state. The current model of European integration is a faulty project striving to establish a European superstate. The project is linked with an effective weakening, and dissolution, of the nation-states and nations of Europe. We demand the right for the citizens to vote leave the EU in a referendum. In addition, the project of the current European integration poses a direct threat to freedom and democracy in Europe. Part and parcel of this process is an orchestrated Islamisation of Europe. The ongoing illegal immigration represents the first stage of the conflict that will ultimately

---

32 See ČTK, 'President Zeman's Alliance with Cardinal Duka Raises Questions', *Prague Business Journal* (16 February 2020), https://praguebusinessjournal.com/president-zemans-alliance-with-cardinal-duka-raises-questions/ (accessed 27 March 2023). For a critical outsider's commentary on Duka, see Robert Fisk, 'Europe's Catholic Leaders Are Undoing the Good Work of Pope Francis over the Migrant Crisis', *Independent* (15 May 2016), https://www.independent.co.uk/voices/europe-s-catholic-leaders-are-undoing-the-good-work-of-pope-francis-over-the-migrant-crisis-a7025526.html (accessed 27 March 2023).

endanger freedom, democracy, and the very existence of the Czech Republic and our nation. We do not proclaim hatred of any nation, race, culture, or religion. The national traditions of our society are rooted in Jewish, ancient [i.e., Greek and Roman], and Christian culture and civilization. We will protect these values. They represent the foundation stone of democracy, freedom, and human rights. The ongoing Islamisation of European countries is irreconcilable with these values. We therefore consistently reject the multicultural ideology which is a tool of Islamisation. We say out loud that it is not our duty to open our doors to anybody who seeks to settle in our territory but that it is a privilege for foreigners to be allowed to stay in our home. If someone wants to work and live here, they must respect our values and accommodate. Our homeland has been built by our ancestors for centuries. Let us be real masters in our land. Let us be good patriots.[33]

It is worth citing this rather lengthy passage in full here because it aptly shows how religion features in the rhetoric of populist political movements and parties, such as Freedom and Direct Democracy. At the core of the movement's political program is a brief but important reference to Christian (as well as Jewish and ancient Greek and Roman) *culture and civilisation*. In this understanding, Christianity is introduced not as a daily experienced religious faith, but as an artefact, a 'mausoleum', an ideology. This ideology then serves as a tool to back up nationalist sentiments and protect the purportedly endangered Czech nation—as well as freedom, democracy, and human rights—from the 'multicultural ideology' forced through by the EU. Although it is stated that those who respect Czech values are welcome to live and work in the country, the program makes unequivocally clear that the 'ongoing Islamisation of European countries' is irreconcilable with these values. In the view of Freedom and Direct Democracy, the Muslim as the ultimate other is thus made unacceptable for the Czech society, a society rooted in *Christianism*.

---

33 Svoboda a přímá demokracie, 'Politický dlouhodobý program SPD', https://www.spd.cz/program-vypis/ (accessed 27 March 2023); translation is mine.

The 2015 European migrant crisis disclosed yet another narrative in which religion features in the Czech society—in addition and in contrast to the 'Christianism narrative'. This narrative is built around the notion of solidarity that is perceived as lying at the heart of European civilisation. In an article written at the time when the discussion on accepting refugees from the Middle East peaked in 2016, Jan Škrob reminds Christians that humanity and unconditional solidarity represent the fundamental values that they share with all other people. Therefore, he argues, 'Christians ought to advocate the idea that the human being is first and foremost a human being, and a Muslim is not entitled to one's help any less than a Christian is'.[34] Similarly, analyzing the story of the last judgement from Matthew 25 and writing from the Czech context, Tim Noble shows that care for those in need represents an indissoluble part of Christian mission.[35] The care for those in need is not an optional extra, pursued in addition to proclamation; rather, it is a proclamation through action, the *kerygma* put into practice. Following Jesus means doing what Jesus did in both word and deed. For Christians, therefore, embracing the other is an essential element of their ecclesial 'agenda'. Christians are asked to call on those in the position of power to fulfil their duties when the latter stigmatise and exclude others as a threat.

Even though one must concede that the voices advocating the solidarity narrative represent a minority position and are not often found among politicians, they still represent an important part of the overall discourse on religion in the public space. Furthermore, they provide space for the hope that religion itself has the potential to play a role in building resilience against those who seek to instrumentalise it to exclude others.

TOWARD BUILDING RESILIENCE

This leads me to the final part of this chapter, in which I explore some ways for preventing political instrumentalisation of religion and for building

---

34 Jan Škrob, 'Křesťanštější než křesťané?', *Protestant* 27, no. 4 (2016): 1; translation is mine.
35 See Tim Noble, 'Misie jako pohostinnost vůči druhému', *Misiologické fórum* 2 (2016): 17–25, especially at 17–20.

resilience. Robert Schreiter suggests that resilience sensitises us to the fact that overcoming injustice and other consequences of sin, such as identitary temptations, does not mean that one's quest for the flourishing of humankind and creation would ever come to an end.[36] One can therefore argue from a theological perspective that resilience reminds us of our calling to relate to others, especially the marginalised and stigmatised, in solidarity and respect. Moreover, if to be Christian means becoming a part of God's story with creation, aimed at its transformation and consummation, then one is called to be profoundly and authentically involved in a rich meshwork of relationships with God and fellow human beings regardless of their religious, ethnic, cultural, and any other affiliations.[37]

Essentially, this discussion is centred on the understanding of what the church should be vis-à-vis the broader nature of humankind. In my previous work, I have suggested viewing the church in terms of 'comm/unity', which refers to 'a meshwork of multiple relationships by dignified individuals that appreciate the interdependence and essential unity of humankind based on their createdness in the image of God as well as human interconnection with the rest of creation'.[38] At the most rudimentary and yet powerful level, comm/unity is attained in everyday situations through interpersonal encounter. It is pursued whenever people care for one another, relating to their fellow human beings in acts of solidarity and carrying each other's burdens (compare to Gal 6:2). Of prime relevance in this respect are those deprived of the opportunities to benefit from the present socio-political system and those who do not belong due to their real or imagined otherness.[39] The church has a vital role to play in this process because it can invite people to *metanoia*, that is, the reorienting of the general mindset in society to make us all more sensitive to the needs of the marginalised and poor.[40] More significantly still, Christians are called—through their pursuit of comm/unity—to embody and enact what they

---

36   See Robert Schreiter, 'Locating European Mission in a Wounded World in Deep Transformation', *Mission Studies* 37, no. 3 (2020): 333–353, here at 342.
37   See Bargár, *Embodied Existence*, 113–114.
38   Bargár, *Embodied Existence*, 145.
39   See Schreiter, 'Locating European Mission', 348.
40   See Máté-Tóth, 'Wounded Words', 369.

believe and proclaim, thus contributing their share to the transformation of the world, including political life.

A critical test for the church then lies in addressing the excluded other, while preserving and promoting his or her dignity.[41] To give some guidance for how to put this imperative in practice, Stålsett refers to the gospel stories of the Good Samaritan (Luke 10:25–37) and the Syrophoenician woman (Mark 7:24–30), respectively. While Jesus speaks of the former in a way that turns a stranger into a role model for the followers of Jesus, the latter challenges the church (as it shows Jesus himself being challenged) by subverting ethnic, gender, and religious borderlines. Being much more than didactic devices, these stories may help the church 'to avoid their reduction to more of the same or a self-sufficient fellowship'.[42] The very being of the church, and the faithfulness to its calling, then, comprises the inclusion of the excluded other. However, one needs to add in the same breath that the otherness of the other must not get lost in the inclusion but should be preserved even when embraced.[43] With regard to the theme of this chapter, it means that the church must resist the identitary temptations to present its story in an exclusivist mode, which becomes a 'nightmare' for those who do not fit in. The church is not called to be the custodian of a museum but rather an agent of the good news in the everyday life of society.

Sociological research discloses, interestingly, that church attendance has the potential to serve as an antidote against right-wing populism.[44] Huber and Yendell explain this phenomenon by pointing out that 'the Christian doctrine of universal love and the idea of "Christian Humanitas" grants minorities the same rights as majorities' and 'the emphasis on "spirit" tends to prohibit natural characteristics such as "racial traits"'.[45] Similarly, the teachings on the love of neighbour, translated into practical endeavours pursued by churches, such as welcoming refugees in one's churches and homes and showing other forms of hospitality and acceptance toward

---

41 See Stålsett, 'The Other', 290.
42 Stålsett, 'The Other', 291.
43 See Stålsett, 'The Other', 290–291.
44 See Huber and Yendell, 'Does Religiosity Matter?', 76.
45 Huber and Yendell, 'Does Religiosity Matter?', 68.

those who are other, might serve as 'immunizing factors' toward hatred and contribute to building resilience against the instrumentalisation of religion.[46] Furthermore, interestingly, research indicates that 'in spite of the aggressive use of religious themes by far-right movements, polls show that their supporters are actually disproportionately irreligious'.[47]

Negatively, and even more challengingly for Christian theology, one can construe the building of resilience in terms of 'the death of the church'. Joseph Sverker suggests that if one seeks to be a faithful follower of Jesus the Christ, who came and lived *for* the world, in the Europe that claims to be heir to 'Christian values', one might (should?) be led to call for the church to give up any privileged position it might have in European society. To put it in a radical language, what is at stake here is 'not a death of God, but a death of the church of "Christian Europe", a death that came about because Christians communally was *for* the world and thus witnessed what it means to be the body of Christ (1 Cor 15)'.[48]

Theologically, we can frame such *modus vivendi* of the community of Christ's followers in the world in terms of kenotic presence, which is rooted in a holistic and embodied understanding of Christian faith. Essential elements of such presence include unpresumptuous living together with fellow others (convivence), relational anthropology, interdependence in a rich web of being, and the common striving toward the consummation of God's reign.[49]

It remains to be seen whether the churches in CEE (and elsewhere) will be immune to the temptation to rehash the alliances of throne and altar, and to pursue a contextually relevant and sensitive kenotic presence *for* and *with* the world instead. There certainly are signs of hope to this end. During the presidential election campaign in the Czech Republic in

---

[46] See also Sverker, 'Confessing Christ', 270 and Joshua Ralston, 'Bearing Witness: Reframing Christian-Muslim Encounter in Light of the Refugee Crisis', *Theology Today* 74, no. 1 (2017): 22–35.

[47] Tobias Cremer, 'Defenders of the Faith: Why Right-Wing Populists Are Embracing Religion', *The New Statesman* (30 May 2018), https://www.newstatesman.com/politics/religion/2018/05/defenders-faith-0 (accessed 27 March 2023).

[48] Sverker, 'Confessing Christ', 277, emphasis in the original.

[49] For more details on kenotic presence, see Bargár, *Embodied Existence*, 123–128.

January 2023, for example, the Carmelite Order decided to close the doors of the Prague Church of Our Lady Victorious to presidential candidate Andrej Babiš. Babiš sought to visit the home of the world-famous Infant Jesus of Prague in what was perceived as an attempt to win over the believers. Pavel Pola, rector of the church, was quoted as saying that the Carmelite Order did not want to be part of Babiš's campaign, which they thought was led in 'a very aggressive and fear-inducing manner'.[50]

---

50   Daniela Lazarová, 'Carmelite Order Closes Church Doors to Presidential Candidate Andrej Babiš', *Radio Prague International* (17 January 2023), https://english.radio.cz/carmelite-order-closes-church-doors-presidential-candidate-andrej-babis-8772433 (accessed 27 March 2023).

14

THE ROMANIAN ORTHODOX CHURCH AND THE EVANGELICALS
Conflicts and Collaborations

Cristian-Sebastian Sonea and Teofil Stanciu

CONTEXT OF TENSIONS AND COLLABORATION

This chapter examines the conflict and collaborations between the Romanian Orthodox Church (ROC) and the Evangelical churches in Romania.

The history of the church in Romania dates back to the early Christian era. Orthodoxy is therefore considered to be part of the intrinsic character of the majority in Romanian Christianity. This is illustrated by some especially noteworthy events in its relatively recent history. In 1872, the ROC became autonomous—the Ungrovlachian and Moldavian Metropolitanates were released from canonical obedience to the Patriarchate of Constantinople. The Metropolitan of Ungrovlachia, who was also Archbishop of Bucharest, became the Metropolitan Primate of Romania. The Holy Synod of the ROC was officially constituted. After the Great Unification of 1918, on 23 April 1919 the Orthodox Church from Transylvania was united with the ROC. On 4 February 1925 the Holy Synod of the ROC decided to establish the Romanian Orthodox Patriarchate. Metropolitan Primate Miron Cristea was elected Patriarch of the ROC.[1] After the Second

---

1 Mircea Păcurariu, *Istoria Bisericii Ortodoxe Romane* (Galați, Editura Episcopiei Dunării de Jos, 1996), 383.

World War and Romania's entry into the sphere of influence of the USSR, the Orthodox Church experienced persecution. In 1948, church properties were expropriated, religious education in schools was abolished, and priests were dismissed from the army. In 1959, under Decree 410/1959 on monasteries, many monks and nuns were expelled from monasteries and convents and most religious houses were closed or had their purpose changed. In 1990, however, several dioceses of the ROC (abolished during the communist period) were re-established, and hierarchs were elected to vacant or reactivated episcopal and metropolitan sees. This period therefore saw a return of the church into the public sphere.

Evangelical Protestant Christianity has a relatively recent history in Eastern Europe. Like its Orthodox counterpart, during the Soviet domination, many communities were forced underground or suppressed. After the fall of communism in the late twentieth century, different Evangelical traditions among them experienced a resurgence in many Eastern European countries. In Romania, the Evangelicals have experienced steady growth in the last century and make up around 5 percent of the population. The Orthodox majority has indiscriminately applied derogatory labels, such as 'repenters' and 'sectarians', to the Evangelicals.

Early in their history, the Evangelicals experienced persecution led by the Romanian Orthodoxy clerics.[2] The first Baptist martyr is considered Ioan Lazăr, who was from Talpoș, a village now in Bihor County in the north-western part of Romania.[3] Despite this, the first Baptist community in Romania enjoyed 'maybe the best acceptance among all recorded in the continent of Europe'. The magistrate of Bucharest allowed them to keep their register of births, marriages, and deaths, which was a kind of official recognition.[4]

Although contested by some, the Romanian Pentecostal movement recently (in 2022) celebrated its centenary.[5] It has been said, 'The Romanian

---

2   See Dobrincu, 'Sub puterea Cezarului', in Dorin Dobrincu and Dănuț Mănăstireanu, Omul evanghelic. O explorare a comunităților protestante românești (Iași, Polirom, 2018), 121.
3   Dobrincu, 'Sub puterea Cezarului', 52.
4   Mihai Ciucă, Baptiștii din România: Pionierii vol. 1, (Oradea, Casa Cărții, 2023), 91–92.
5   Ciprian Bălăban, *Foc din cer. Un secol de penticostalism românesc* (București, Pleroma, 2022), 26.

Pentecostal movement, with its rich heritage, experienced wide and rapid growth after the beginning of WWI with a sudden, spontaneous eruption in all the provinces of the country. As a result, it is difficult to ascertain the exact time and place of the movement's inception.'[6] The interwar period was difficult for the newly formed Pentecostal communities because they were refused official recognition, which resulted in almost constant persecution.[7] For example, the local bishop Grigore Gheorghe Comșa[8]—a supporter of the Lord's Army Orthodox revivalist movement—was an inveterate adversary of the new "sectarian" movement. In this context, the first Romanian Pentecostal martyr, Partenie Pera, died in 1927. The 'Romanian Pentecostal movement crystallised into three different associations which obtained a temporary official recognition by the state'.[9] Their institutionalisation and state recognition came, however, at a price: the three major groups disputing their legitimacy and supremacy had to unite into a single organisation.[10]

The Brethren communities began their existence in the Romanian-speaking lands in 1899 and over the turn of the twentieth century. They received a disproportionate amount of attention from both the police and the Orthodox majority. As early as 1908–1909, so less than a decade after their first gatherings, the Orthodox hierarchy requested and obtained the expulsion of a Brethren missionary (Francis Berney), followed in subsequent years by the expulsion of all their foreign missionaries. It seems that the doctrinal distinctions between the Brethren and the Baptists were not very clear-cut at the outset, but gradually they acquired more distinctive features. As of today, the Brethren remain the smallest denomination of the three discussed here. The Brethren gained their largest

---

6   Stanley M. Burgess (Ed.), *The New International Dictionary of Pentecostal and Charismatic Movements: Revised and Expanded Edition* (Grand Rapids, Zondervan. Kindle Edition) Kindle Locations 9104–9106.
7   Bălăban, *Foc din cer*, 57. See also Ciprian Bălăban, *Istoria Bisericii Penticostale din România (1922–1989). Instituție și harisme* (Oradea / București, Scriptum / Pleroma), 41–80.
8   See the case study in Bălăban, *Istoria Bisericii Penticostale*, 32–40.
9   Ciprian Bălăban, *Labirintul oglinzilor. Șase ipostaze ale pionierului penticostal Eugen Bodor* (București, Pleroma, 2022), 51.
10 Bălăban, *Istoria Bisericii Penticostale*, 87–96.

number of adherents in Muntenia, southern Transylvania, and Moldavia.[11] They received official recognition as a religious association in 1933, but in 1939, two independent groups, 'Christians according to Scripture' (gathered around the 'Tudorists') and 'Christians according to the Gospel', were forced by the authorities to merge into a single official denomination. The most significant difference between them was that the 'Tudorists' practised child-baptism, while the latter group, today's Brethren, did not. After the fall of communism, the two branches parted again and remained separate.[12]

EVANGELICALS AND ORTHODOX RELATIONS

Evangelical historians agree almost unanimously that the relationships of these communities with the Orthodox majority were somewhat complicated and almost constantly impeded by various forms of oppression from the Orthodox side, especially in the interwar period but also in the first decades after the fall of the communist regime.[13] Because of their teachings, which emphasised an individual's 'conscious choice to accept Jesus's offer of eternal life', most Evangelicals rejected child baptism. They also contested the requirement for confession of sin to be mediated by a priest, along with the church's claim to be the authorised interpreter of the scriptures. Icons and saints were not just seen as unnecessary; they started to be dismissed as a form of idolatry. All this resulted in a distinctiveness that became instrumental for Evangelical withdrawal from a purportedly 'Christian' society that was, at best, indifferent (if not actually favourable) to sinful behaviour.[14]

---

11   Dobrincu, 'Sub puterea Cezarului,' 64–70.
12   See their official history: http://www.bcev.ro/despre-noi/istoria-miscarii-fratesti-din-romania_c_53_ro.html (accessed 12 January 2023).
13   See, especially, George Hancock-Stefan and Sara Grace Stefan, 'From the Ivory Tower to the Grass Roots: Ending Orthodox Oppression of Evangelicals, and Beginning Grassroots Fellowship', *Religions* 12 no. 601 (2021): 43–58. https://doi.org/10.3390/rel12080601; Dobrincu, 'Sub puterea Cezarului', 119–122; Bălăban, *Istoria Bisericii Penticostale*, 41–80; Ciucă, *Baptiștii din România*, vol. 1, 625–631.
14   Ronald Clark, *Sectarianism and Renewal in 1920s Romania: The Limits of Orthodoxy and Nation-Building* (London: Bloomsbury, 2021), 103.

The usual allegations against Evangelicals were that they belonged to strange sects, were hypocritical, compromised national unity and identity, accepted money from abroad and had extraterritorial loyalties, were divided and nurtured division, were dangerous for society and for humanity, etc.[15] Some of these accusations were used as grounds to suppress them.[16] In 1942, the government banned all Evangelical denominations. This ban offered baptism to those prepared to become Orthodox.[17] A few years earlier, the Pentecostals in the Arad region faced fierce persecution, and they decided to become Baptist instead because Baptists were still legal at the time. This was not received well.[18]

Soon after the communist takeover, the authorities decided to set up a Federation of Evangelical Denominations (*Federația Cultelor Evanghelice*) that included the Baptists, the Pentecostals, the Brethren, and the Adventists. This was meant to facilitate state surveillance. This federation never worked according to the state's plan.[19]

The communist period was especially difficult for the Evangelicals. There are in their stories both heroes and cowards; there are stories of triumph and tragedy. The official files reveal different types of compromises and betrayal used by Christians to gain power and influence.[20] After 1989, in the new context of freedom, the Evangelicals started to step out of their church buildings and display their activist spirit in various ways (stadium preaching, marches, TV channels, radio stations, etc.). Their interaction with the Orthodox majority was often still problematic, although some ecumenical spirit was evident in the first years. Tensions persisted on both

---

15 See, for example, Grigore Gh. Comșa, 'Cheia sectelor religioase din România,' *Biserica și școala* 54 no. 38, Arad, (21 September 1930): 1–7.
16 Dobrincu, 'Sub puterea Cezarului', 124.
17 Alexa Popovici, *Istoria baptiștilor din România 1856–1989*, 637–640. Bălăban, *Foc din cer*, 87–89.
18 Bălăban, *Istoria Bisericii Penticostale*, 75–78.
19 Bălăban, *Istoria Bisericii Penticostale*, 97–100.
20 For example, *Pigmei și uriași* [Pygmies and Giants], by Daniel Mitrofan (Oradea, Christianus, 2007) was 'strategically launched' before a Baptist congress. See the response of Petru Dugulescu (a Baptist pastor accused of being a Securitate informer): https://prologos.ro/uncategorized/petru-dugulescu-despre-pigmei-si-uriasi/ (accessed 10 January 2023).

sides. The causes ranged from old memories of the interwar period when the Evangelicals had faced the oppression mounted by the state in alliance with the Orthodox to unfortunate personal experiences. There was also the exclusivist and arrogant mentality among the Evangelicals; they considered all Orthodox as 'non-Christian' or 'pagans'. Missionary efforts with support from abroad increased, which hardened negative views among the Orthodox. The old caricatures describing the Evangelicals as the 'repenters', if not aliens and even agents of foreign powers, re-emerged. This was nothing new, but it gained fresh impetus because of religious freedom.[21] A more substantive allegation was that Evangelicals proselytise, which in many ways has been 'the main burden for the Orthodox–Evangelical relationships'.[22]

In some cases, the tensions escalated and took a violent form, as in Ruginoasa, when the Orthodox parishioners beat up nine Baptists.[23] Another incident between the Orthodox and Pentecostal believers took place in Tudora.[24] These appear to have been isolated cases, but they are evidence of an underlying tension that remained for more than a decade after the fall of communism. More recently, however, the Orthodox and Evangelicals have been collaborating on issues and values both consider fundamental.[25] This creates solidarity between them. Some of the issues

---

21 Radu Preda, Radu, *Biserica în Stat. O invitație la dezbatere*, București, Scripta, 1999, 53–54.

22 Daniel Buda, 'Orthodoxy and Evangelicalism: An Overview of Their Relationship from the Perspective of Moral Values', *Religions*, 12 no. 6 (2021): 383, https://doi.org/10.3390/rel12060383. From an evangelical perspective, see Dănuț Mănăstireanu, 'Response 1: Ethical Witness, Absolutely! Proselytizing, Hopefully Not!' in *The Mission of God. Studies in Orthodox and Evangelical Mission*, eds. Mark Oxbrow and Tim Grass (Eugene: Wipf & Stock, 2015), 135–142. See also Miroslav Volf, 'Fishing in the Neighbor's Pond: Mission and Proselytism in Eastern Europe,' *International Bulletin of Missionary Research*, 1996, 20.

23 The Baptist Pastor, Petru Dugulescu, a member of Parliament, addressed this incident in a speech before the Chamber of Deputies. https://dezvaluiri.wordpress.com/petre-dugulescu/dugulescu-1/ (accessed 5 January 2023).

24 'Razboi intre ortodocsi si penticostali la Tudora', *Ziarul de Iași*, 24 March 2000, https://www.ziaruldeiasi.ro/botosani/razboi-intre-ortodocsi-si-penticostali-la-tudora~ni18bm (accessed 5 January 2023).

25 See Buda, 'Orthodoxy and Evangelicalism', 61–63.

that have made this collaboration possible are abortion, same-sex marriage, and the definition of the family. They share similar positions on these issues even if they use different arguments. We are therefore witnessing a paradoxical situation. However, there is no official and/or institutional theological dialogue between the Orthodox and Evangelicals. A common ethical ground, therefore, holds the best promise for the future of their relations. To illustrate their emerging collaboration, we present below three cases: teaching of religion in public schools, the Bodnariu family, and the 2018 referendum on the family.

RELIGION IN PUBLIC SCHOOLS

The issue of religious education in public schools came to the fore shortly after the events of 1989. In Romania, until the adoption of the *Law on Public Education* (25 November/7 December 1864), education had been almost exclusively provided by the church. Under this law, the subject of religion occupied an essential place in primary, secondary, and higher education. In 1948, a communist decree on educational reform removed religion from school curricula. After the fall of communism in 1989, 'moral and religious education' was reintroduced into primary and secondary schools in 1990–1991 based on a protocol signed in 1990 between the Ministry of Education and Science and the State Secretariat for Religious Affairs. In this context, the Romanian Constitution, approved by a national referendum on 8 December 1991, stipulates that 'the State guarantees freedom of religious instruction following the specific requirements of each religion'. In public schools, religious instruction must be organised and this is guaranteed by law (art. 32, para. 7).[26] Later, Education Law no. 84/1995 introduced the subject of religion into public schools at all levels as part of the standard curriculum that was compulsory for all students. However, an exception was stipulated in the law: parents or legal guardians who did not want their children to receive religious instruction could apply to withdraw them from religion classes. The New Law of National Education, no. 1/2011, maintained the same status for the subject of religion.

26　Daniel, Patriarhul BOR, 'Educația religioasă—formarea tinerilor pentru viață', Basilica.ro, 4 September 2016, https://basilica.ro/educatia-religioasa-formarea-tinerilor-pentru-viata/.

On 12 November 2014, after several petitions from secular NGOs, a plenary session of the Constitutional Court decided that the requirements of Article 18(2) of the New Law of National Education no. 1/2011 were unconstitutional.[27]

From a legal point of view, it has been argued that the opportunity to study religion in public schools is a right and not an obligation. Therefore, those who want their children to have religious education should have it on demand and not as part of the compulsory school curriculum. It mentions how participation in religion classes should be organised:

> A person cannot be put *ab initio* in the position of defending or protecting his freedom of conscience, because such an approach would contravene the negative obligation of the state, which, under this obligation, cannot impose the study of religion. Thus, it is only after the expression of the wish of the pupil of full age, or of the parents or legal guardian of the minor pupil, for the pupil to learn through study the precepts specific to a particular religious faith that the positive obligation of the State to provide the necessary framework comes into play.[28]

Vasile Crețu, a professor of Orthodox theology in Bucharest and a supporter of keeping the subject of religion in public schools, has pointed out that the subject of religion itself is not optional; however, participation in religion classes is optional.[29] The Constitutional Court's decision preserved the status of religion.

Beyond the legal provisions and the alignment of the education law with constitutional principles, the secular NGOs aimed to remove religion from public education and consequently limit the presence of faith in the public space. The bureaucratisation of access to religious education

---

27 Vasile Crețu, 'Criza educației religioase în învățământul românesc de astăzi. Cauze, provocări și perspective', in *Repere ale educației creștine în teologia sfântului Ioan Gură de Aur, actualizate în relația biserică-familie-școală din contextul contemporan*, ed. Adrian Nicolae Lemeni (București: Basilica, 2015), 142.
28 Augustin Zegrean et al., 'DECIZIA Nr.669', *Monitorul Oficial* no. 59 (23 January 2015): l. 19.
29 Crețu, 'Criza educației religioase' 2015, 142.

would contribute toward removing religious discourse from the public sphere. Proponents of this approach based their argument on the claim that neither trust in religious institutions nor the percentage of those who believe in God is as high in Romania as statistics suggest. We may recall that in 2010, according to a European Commission assessment, Romania ranked third of European countries where belief in God was widespread, with a percentage of 92%, behind only Malta and Turkey.[30] Then, as an opinion, it is possible that the secular NGOs were also counting on the passivity of Romanians regarding exercising their constitutional rights, knowing as they did that even in local and general elections, the level of participation is usually meagre. Thus, following the same logic, only a few Romanians would ask to fill in forms to request religion classes for their children.

To raise awareness of the importance of religion in public schools, the Consultative Council of Religious Denominations in Romania[31] held a working session on 28 February 2015. It noted that the Constitutional Court had upheld the status of religion as a school subject, including it in the standard curriculum and the educational offer of the school, and that the court had modified only one aspect—that concerning the procedure for a student's participation in religion classes, namely the completion of an application form. Based on their shared conviction that the teaching of religion promotes eternal spiritual values and peaceful and responsible human behaviour in the family and society, the Consultative Council of Religious Denominations in Romania adopted the joint appeal *Light for Life*. The importance of religious instruction for the education of children and young people was underlined here, and a request was made to the Romanian Parliament when it adopted the legal provisions to implement the Constitutional Court's decision no. 669/2014, to include Article 18 paragraph 1/2011 of the Law of National Education, to consider the following proposal:

---

30 'Eurobarometer 73.1' (European Commission, 2010), 204, https://web.archive.org/web/20130425025156/http://ec.europa.eu/public_opinion/archives/ebs/ebs_341_en.pdf.

31 The 'Consultative Council of Religious Denominations in Romania' is nonprofit ecumenical organisation.

The enrolment or re-enrolment of the pupil to attend religious education shall be made by a written request of the pupil of full age, or the parent or legal guardian appointed for the minor pupil; a written request shall also be made to change this option or to withdraw from Religion, by the pupil of full age, or by the parent or legal guardian of the minor pupil."[32]

Following the provisions suggested by the Constitutional Court and the recommendation of the Consultative Council of Religious Denominations in Romania, the methodology for organising the teaching of religion was modified as follows: 'The parents/legal guardians of minors and adult pupils who wish to exercise their right to participate in Religion classes shall express their choice in writing, in a request addressed to the educational establishment, specifying the name of the religion requested.'[33]

This defence of religious education generated strong support from parents, who organised themselves into the Parents for Religious Education Association (APOR),[34] represented by the journalist Liana Stanciu, with members drawn from all denominations and religious communities in most of the counties of Romania. All the religious communities worked together for the same purpose. Each parish and congregation encouraged members to fill in the forms to ask for religious education in schools.

It is vital to mention that the teaching of religion in schools is confessional in nature. Each community issued a curriculum approved by the Minister of Education, and its contents are taught in schools according to the number of students who belong to a specific community. As a result of joint efforts at the beginning of 2015, 2,167,485 applications were registered

---

[32] Basilica.ro, 'Consiliul Consultativ al Cultelor din România reafirmă importanța orei de Religie pentru educația copiilor și tinerilor', Basilica.ro, 28 February 2015, https://basilica.ro/consiliul-consultativ-al-cultelor-din-romania-reafirma-importanta-orei-de-religie-pentru-educatia-copiilor-si-tinerilor/.

[33] 'Metodologia de organizare a predării disciplinei Religie în învățământul preuniversitar 14.09.2015 actualizat 2023', Pub. L. No. 5 (2015), art. 3, https://lege5.ro/Gratuit/g44danjugq/metodologia-de-organizare-a-predarii-disciplinei-religie-in-invatamantul-preuniversitar-14092015.

[34] 'Asociația „Părinți pentru Ora de Religie" (APOR)', APOR (blog), accessed 24 January 2023, https://www.oradereligie.ro/despre-noi/.

in the Romanian Integrated Education Information System out of a reporting base of 2,371,697 students, which equates to 91.39%.

What was the outcome of this campaign to keep religion in public schools? It was the first time in the recent history of Romania that all faiths and beliefs had fought for a common goal. Every religious community considered it essential that religion should retain its place in public schools and acted accordingly, each at its level. This was one of the joint ecumenical exercises involving all denominations to which there were no significant objections within the religious communities. By fulfilling parents' wishes, the discipline of religion gained a popular legitimacy that could not quickly be challenged by those who were against the presence of religion in public schools. Encouraging believers with children to apply in writing for religious education in schools was interpreted as a 'democratic exercise' in which all the religious denominations in Romania participated.

The high percentage of applications for religious education was a moment of reinterpretation of the relationship between the state and the churches. Although there is a constitutional separation in Romania between state and church, it was found that there could be no clear-cut separation between the believers in the churches and the citizens of the state. They are the same people. The state, as the custodian of citizens' tax money, is obliged to extend its use to the religious education of their children at the request of believing citizens.

FAMILY SOLIDARITY

In November 2015, the children of Marius and Ruth Bodnariu, a Romanian-Norwegian Pentecostal couple living in Norway, were taken into the custody of the Child Protection Agency because the principal of the school in the village of Vevring notified the authorities about possible child abuse in the Bodnariu family. The parents acknowledged that they applied corporal punishment to discipline their children. The following month, the local agency of the Barnevernet started a Termination of Parental Rights process against Marius and Ruth Bodnariu.[35] The case was

---

35 See a chronology in Cristian Pantazi, 'Cazul Bodnariu, exemplu de ciocnire a civilizatiilor. Autoritatile norvegiene au luat cei cinci copii in custodie pe motiv de violenta fizica, parintii recunosc «palme la fund», dar reclama masuri

controversial and complicated legally and politically. This incident became widely known and it attracted the attention of national and international media. As early as January 2016, the Romanian national television station (TVR) broadcast a fifty-minute coverage of this case, inviting the Bodnariu family and a wide range of guests for interviews.[36] In the same period, similar cases started to show up in families belonging to other denominations, especially Orthodox, who were also part of the Romanian diaspora; one of them was the case of Nan.[37]

The Pentecostal community was the first to react in this case, because the Bodnarius are Pentecostals. An equally important factor was that Marius's brother was a member of a Pentecostal church in Chicago, a community that was gaining visibility in the Evangelical media and in the new media because of its vocal pastor, Cristian Ionescu. Soon, other Romanian denominations took up the cause. In November 2015, Pastor Viorel Iuga, the president of the Union of Romanian Christian Baptist Churches, appealed to his brothers and sisters to pray for the Bodnariu family. An online petition was already available for everyone who wanted to express their support. In January 2016, the Press Office of the Romanian Patriarchate issued a short press release announcing (in Romanian and English) that it 'has taken note with concern of the critical situation of the Bodnariu family in Norway due to the forced separation of the five children from their parents, following the decision of the Norwegian local authorities'.[38]

The result was that in many cities around the globe, not just in Romania, protest demonstrations were organised that brought together participants from different denominations. In Oradea, for example,

---

disproportionate. Cronologia evenimentelor,' *Hotnews*, 06 January 2016, https://www.hotnews.ro/stiri-esential-20708995-cazul-bodnariu-exemplu-ciocnire-civilizatiilor-autoritatile-norvegiene-luat-cei-cinci-copii-custodie-motiv-violenta-fizica-parintii-recunosc-palme-fund-dar-reclama-masuri-disproportionate-cronologia-e.htm (accessed 5 January 2023).

36 'În numele copilului—totul despre povestea norvegiană a familiei Bodnariu' https://www.youtube.com/watch?v=QKIrwo8jEfc (accessed 5 January 2023).
37 An Orthodox family also living in Norway. See, for example, https://tribuna.us/cosmarul-familiei-nan-in-norvegia-continua/ (accessed 5 January 2023).
38 'Solidarity with the Bodnariu Family', https://patriarhia.ro/solidarity-with-the-bodnariu-family-8550-en.html (accessed 12 January 2023).

although the public gathering was organised by the Pentecostals and Baptists, the Orthodox, Catholic, Greek Catholic, and Reformed traditions joined. The top leaders represented their denominations.[39] They were invited to make a speech to the crowd and a Christian TV channel broadcast the entire event.[40] This was not a unique case, but it was a significant one because the Oradea protest was perhaps the largest that took place for this specific cause.[41]

In the end, the president and the prime minister took notice of the case and had to issue an official position. Some members of Parliament were monitoring the situation, and they even initiated official procedures. After more than two hundred days, the Bodnariu family was reunited, and later they managed to leave Norway and moved to Romania.

The real gain for the Romanian Christianity—at least as it seemed at that time—was the capacity to show solidarity and a shared compassion for a cause that transcended denominational boundaries. This emphasised common values and a common ground that were not incidental but a direct outcome of their Christian beliefs. At a more personal level, this was a chance for Christian leaders and ordinary believers to speak to each other and achieve something considered almost impossible. The Evangelicals gained significant visibility on a common cause considered good even by the Orthodox.

REFERENDUM FOR THE FAMILY

Another issue that brought the two communities together was the highly controversial 'referendum for the family', a national referendum on the definition of family and marriage held in Romania on 6–7 October 2018. This was the first civil society initiative since the fall of communism in

---

39 As reported by the National Radio broadcaster: https://www.romania-actualitati.ro/stiri/romania/mitinguri-de-solidaritate-in-tara-cu-familia-bodnariu-id80134.html (accessed 12 January 2023).

40 See *Bihoreanul*, 23 January 2016: https://www.ebihoreanul.ro/stiri/destramarea-unei-familii-a-unit-bisericile-in-premiera-pe-aceeasi-scena-liderii-cultelor-oradene-au-transmis-un-mesaj-comun-de-iubire-si-solidaritate-125214.html (accessed 12 January 2023).

41 Estimates ranged from 2,500 to 10,000 people.

1989, promoted by the 'Coalition for the Family', which included 44 conservative NGOs, the Orthodox Church, the Evangelical Alliance in Romania, and other religious and socially conservative groups. The referendum aimed to change the definition of family in the Romanian Constitution to define it as the union between one man and one woman, effectively preventing same-sex marriage.

This initiative was seen as a distinctive form of Christian ecumenism and inter-religious dialogue in Romania, because different religious denominations and groups came together to promote traditional family values and defend the traditional definition of marriage, regarded as core values and a fundamental basis for Romanian society. During 2016, the Coalition for the Family collected over three million signatures in support of their legislative initiative. The referendum was held in October 2018, but participation in the vote was below the threshold needed for the result to be considered valid. The objective was to revise article 48, paragraph 1 of the Romanian Constitution, which states, 'the family is based on the freely consented marriage . . . between spouses'.

At the time of the referendum, same-sex marriage had already been legalised in over 25 countries around the world, including some Orthodox countries (Cyprus and Greece). The conservative definition of marriage as a union between a man and a woman (as promoted by the Coalition for the Family) had been adopted in some other countries, such as Croatia and Hungary, which imposed this definition through referendums in 2012–2013.

The agreement of religious denominations was a case of ecumenical collaboration. Their source of authority was the Bible: Genesis 1:27–28 and Matthew 19:4–5.

The supporters of the referendum were described as 'intolerant and religious fanatics'.[42] With a single exception (discussed below), every Christian denomination—and other monotheistic religions as well—aligned themselves with the view that the family was designed by God and was based on the union between a man and a woman. In what follows,

---

42   *Iohannis despre revizuirea Constituției în privința definirii căsătoriei: Este greșit să mergem pe calea fanatismului religios,* Mediafax.ro, https://www.mediafax.ro/politic/iohannis-despre-revizuirea-constitutiei-in-privinta-definirii-casatoriei-este-gresit-sa-mergem-pe-calea-fanatismului-religios-15831478 (accessed 25 January 2023).

we will explore the official positioning of different religious organisations concerning this perspective.

The Consultative Council of Religious Denominations expressed the belief that participating in the referendum was a profoundly democratic act, supported by the religious denominations, together with the affirmation of the family as a human institution created and blessed by God, the Creator of the universe and man, according to the teachings of the monotheistic religions of Judaism, Christianity, and Islam.[43] The National Ecclesiastical Assembly of the ROC (BOR) stated on 29 September 2018, shortly before the referendum, that the traditional family based on marriage between a man and a woman is sanctified by God and should be protected in the constitution. Participating in the referendum was considered an act of professing faith in God's love for the family and the sanctity of human life born from the conjugal love between a man and a woman.[44]

On 20 September 2018, the Catholic Church in Romania issued a declaration that followed the message expressed by Pope Francis in 2016 in *Amoris Laetitia*. He had encouraged Catholics to protect marriage between a man and a woman as the foundation of a natural family. He told them not to be afraid to promote it, even if this went against current trends or popular thinking. The declaration called on all Roman Catholic and Greek-Catholic bishops in Romania to support the modification of Article 48 of the constitution by participating in the referendum.[45]

---

43   *Consiliul Consultativ al Cultelor din România susține referendumul pentru definirea căsătoriei ca uniune între un bărbat și o femeie*, https://ziarullumina.ro/actualitate-religioasa/stiri/consiliul-consultativ-al-cultelor-din-romania-sustine-referendumul-pentru-definirea-casatoriei-ca-uniune-intre-un-barbat-si-o-femeie-137661.html (accessed 25 January 2023).

44   *Campanie BOR: Patriarhul Daniel îi îndeamnă pe români să voteze DA la referendumul pentru familia tradițională pe motiv că ar fi un act patriotic și național / El denunță 'acțiunile agresive' de boicotare*, https://www.hotnews.ro/stiri-esential-22728189-campanie-bor-patriarhul-daniel-ndeamn-rom-voteze-referendumul-pentru-familia-tradi-ional-motiv-act-patriotic-ional-denuniunile-agresive-boicotare.htm (accessed 25 January 2023).

45   Redacția B1TV, 'Biserica Catolică îndeamnă preoții și credincioșii să voteze la referendum și să promoveze familia tradițională', *B1TV.ro* (blog), 20 September 2018, https://www.b1tv.ro/eveniment/catolici-vot-referendum-familia-traditionala-241099.html.

Viorel Iuga, pastor and former president of the Baptist Union, said that he believed that a small group of people were attempting to teach the Romanian nation that there was a different lord of life and a different standard of normality for family life. He implied that this group was promoting alternative family forms, such as same-sex families, which he believed were not in line with the traditional and biblical definition of the family. This statement aligned the Baptist community with the above-expressed position favouring a traditional and Christian view of marriage. Several press releases expressed the official stance of the Baptist Union.[46]

Cristian Ionescu (a controversial Pentecostal pastor) said, 'We are ready to obey God rather than men, even if we have to break their laws, which violate our principles and conscience.'[47] He made this statement in a video posted on YouTube on April 15, 2017. In this quote, he expresses his willingness to listen to God more than to people and suggests that laws that promote alternative forms of family, such as same-sex families, conflict with his community's religious beliefs and that they are ready to act according to those beliefs, even if it means breaking the law. Moise Ardelean, president of the Pentecostal Community,[48] and Virgil Achihai, president of the Brethren Union,[49] also adopted positions in line with that expressed above. They were also highly active in promoting the referendum via various public gatherings held all over Romania.

The statement issued by the leadership of the Evangelical Church of Augustan Confession in Romania emphasised that, as a German-speaking church, they were an integral part of the German minority in Romania and supported belief in God, freedom, and tolerance toward minorities. Each individual was free to participate or not participate in the referendum

---

46 See, for example, this one, from November 2017: https://stiripentruviata.ro/comunicat-uniunea-bisericilor-crestine-baptiste-din-romania-isi-reafirma-sustinerea-pentru-familia-naturala-si-cere-organizarea-referendumului-pentru-familie/ (accessed January 25, 2023).

47 *Cristian Ionescu—Dreptul de a fi normali într-o țară normală*, 2017, min. 3:05, https://www.youtube.com/watch?v=seaLPxJ-cbE.

48 *Moise Ardelean—Marșul Pentru Viață 2017—Arad*, 2017, https://www.youtube.com/watch?v=bjfxw-cyF2s.

49 *Virgil Achihai—Marșul Pentru Viață 2017—București*, 2017, https://www.youtube.com/watch?v=Qh92w6Yroac.

according to his or her own beliefs and conscience.[50] Their declaration reflects the perspective that individuals should be free to make their own choices and that the church as an institution should not impose its views on the congregation. It also highlights the importance of tolerance and respect for minorities and their beliefs.[51]

As already stated, the referendum did not reach the validation threshold of 30% of those entitled to vote, with only 21.1% of the population participating. Of those who did participate, 91.56% voted in favour of defining marriage as between a man and a woman. The reasons for the low voter turnout were attributed to several factors, including an aggressive media counter-campaign, the supposedly political motivations behind the government preparation of the referendum, a lack of solid support from the political parties, and the general indifference of the population. Additionally, some citizens may have perceived the referendum as a project of the Social Democratic Party (PSD),[52] leading to a negative image and apathy toward participation in the referendum.[53] The information we have suggests that voter turnout was relatively high in areas with major Orthodox monasteries and communities or with large Evangelical communities. These communities were likely motivated to vote because they shared the religious and conservative values—i.e., the strong support for the traditional definition of family and marriage—promoted in the referendum.[54]

---

50 Reinhart Guib, Daniel Zikeli, and Friedrich Philippi, 'Cuvântul Prezidiului B.E.C.A.R. La Referendumul Din 6–7 Octombrie a.c.', https://www.evang.ro/ro/noutate/artikel/auf-ein-wort-anstelle-eines-aufrufs/ (accessed 25 January 2023).

51 'Cuvântul Prezidiului B.E.C.A.R. la Referendumul din 6–7 octombrire a.c.' Biserica Evaghelica C.A. din România, https://www.evang.ro/ro/noutate/artikel/auf-ein-wort-anstelle-eines-aufrufs/ (accessed January 25, 2023).

52 In that period, the party was caught up in a major socio-political fight and was led by a highly controversial figure. The referendum was interpreted by some to gain popular support for the party and for the government.

53 Vasile Crețu, 'Referendumul pentru limpezirea definiției constituționale a căsătoriei din 2018. Cauzele unui eșec surprinzător. Interogații catehetice', *Teologie și Viață* no. 1–4 (April 2022): 47–48.

54 Dana Humoreanu, *'Peste 170.000 de suceveni au votat „Da", 7.500 au votat „Nu" și peste 2.800 și-au anulat votul la referendum',* Monitorul de Suceava, 9 October 2018, https://www.monitorulsv.ro/Local/2018-10-09/Peste-170000-

The statement of the ROC following the non-validation of the 2018 national referendum is generally seen from inside the church as showing maturity, pragmatism, and discernment. The ROC acknowledged that the referendum had failed to achieve its goal. Still, it also recognised the importance of respecting and analysing the attitudes of Romanian citizens as shown through their participation or absence thereof in the voting process. The statement also considers the high degree of secularisation and desacralisation of Romanian society and the need for more education and information concerning traditional values and the family based on faith in God. This communique by the Orthodox Church has been judged to be an excellent example of how a religious institution can respond to a situation in a way that is respectful of democracy and the freedom of citizens to express their opinions while also recognising the importance of values based on faith. The statement emphasised the importance of continuing dialogue on the topic and the need to work on educating and informing society on the issue.[55] The referendum represented a significant opportunity for communication and ecumenical consensus among the Christian denominations in Romania and for interfaith dialogue. It was a form of ecumenism.

LOOKING INTO THE FUTURE

This chapter emphasises some pivotal moments in the history of the relationships between Evangelical communities and the Orthodox majority in Romania. This helps to imagine a shared future. As we have tried to show, the tensions between these groups persisted for decades, which were followed by an abrupt and forcible intervention from outside—the imposition of a communist government by the Soviets. While that period deserves a chronicle of its own, we focussed on the post-communist period, when religious freedom became the kind of reality that was unprecedented in Romanian history. The first decade of the new era was characterised by

---

de-suceveni-au-votat-Da-7500-au-votat-Nu-si-peste-2800-si-au-anulat-votul-la-referendum.

55 Crețu, 'Referendumul pentru limpezirea definiției constituționale a căsătoriei din 2018. Cauzele unui eșec surprinzător. Interogații catehetice', 59.

mutual suspicions and dormant tensions, with a few moments of climactic outbreak. Later, however, the religious climate began to change when the different denominations started to 'feel' the impact of secularisation and other contemporary processes perceived as menaces. In this context, such events as the support campaign for the Bodnariu family and the Referendum for the Family became an occasion for Evangelicals and Orthodox to come together and act together.

Suppose such opportunities are not to remain a merely circumstantial form of alliance. In that case, they should be extended to a permanent dialogue that capitalises upon the existing common ground, especially in this last decade. The convergence and solidarity, the shared values and jointly undertaken campaigns should be kept actively in memory and referred to as critical elements of a different way forward. There is also an academic dialogue transposed into terms that would communicate to non-academics in such a way as to favour fraternal interaction between the religious majority and religious minorities.

Some actions or symbolic gestures of reconciliation would be expected for us to come to terms with our tormented past. The question of who initiates them should be settled at the appropriate moment, but the idea should be retained and promoted within religious interaction. One should not underestimate the power of mutual forgiveness in a world constantly being polarised and antagonised for the sake of ideologies and the benefit of demagogues and populists. A common Christian witness—not destroying denominational boundaries but crossing them in respect and mutual benevolence—is a powerful 'weapon' in a society ready to criticise anything religious.

15

CHRISTIANITY IN KENYA
When Would-Be Liberators Are Marginalised in a Country Where They Are a Majority

Oliver Kisaka Simiyu

> So they departed from the presence of the council, rejoicing that they were counted worthy to suffer shame for His name.
>
> Acts 5:41 NKJV

In July 2021, Evangelical Christians in Kenya organised their first ecumenical 'Church and Politics' conference. This was attended by over four thousand Christians worldwide, three hundred of them physically present at the venue in Nairobi. The organisers, Hesabika Movement, Kenya Church, FOCUS Kenya, and Catalead Associates, together with facilitators from the Evangelical Alliance of Kenya, the National Council of Churches of Kenya (NCCK), the Kenya Conference of Catholic Bishops (KCCB), Tear Fund, and CORAT Africa, among others, desired to create an opportunity for Christians to reflect on their role in the political governance of Kenya. Concerned about bad governance in Kenya and the decreasing influence of Christians, the intention of the organisers was to create room for serious reflection on how the quality of leadership could be improved and the role they could play. Such concerns about the socio-economic and political governance of Kenya are not new to Christians. They sometimes consider themselves deliberately marginalized by the political class and by Muslims (a minority religious group) despite being in majority in Kenya.

This paper focuses on the narratives that accuse Christians of collaboration with the state against Muslims and on the emerging reality of the exclusion of Christians in Muslim-dominated polities of some counties in Kenya.

MARGINALISATION: CONCEPT AND NARRATIVES

Concept

Adam Oloo, a senior lecturer and chair of the Department of Political Science and Public Administration, University of Nairobi,[1] traced the term 'marginalisation' to Park and Stonequist, who used it 'to describe the immigration of second generation Americans and their assimilation into the dominant political culture'. He added that it was then 'generalised to refer to status-based social attributes afforded to the elite relative to that of the impoverished ... conventionally ... distinguished by experiences that cause economic or political oppression/segregation of individuals or groups over an extended period of time'. He further noted that it includes 'a process through which persons are *peripheralised* on the basis of identities, association, experience and environments'. In his view, therefore, 'the enduring marginalised personality results from the longstanding misappropriation of individuals into a binding subordinate social or economic stratum within which the realization of their full self is prohibited and from which they are unable to ascend'. The term *marginalisation* was first used in Kenya in the 1920s 'to describe the experience of living between two asymmetrically disproportionate worlds'.[2] It described the disadvantaged status of underrepresented communities, especially those in the northern three-fifths of Kenya, where a significant part are Muslims. Marginalisation remained such an important reality that Kenyans, in the period from 1990 to 2010, defined it in their new Constitution of Kenya 2010, Article 260:

---

[1] Adam Oloo in Friedrich-Ebert-Stiftung. *Regional Disparities and Marginalization in Kenya* (Nairobi: Friedrich-Ebert-Stiftung, 2012), 30.
[2] Oloo, *Regional Disparities*.

> Marginalised community is (a) a community that, because of its relatively small population or for any other reason, has been unable to fully participate in the integrated social and economic life of Kenya as a whole; (b) a traditional community that, out of a need or desire to preserve its unique culture and identity from assimilation, has remained outside the integrated social and economic life of Kenya as a whole; (c) an indigenous community that has retained and maintained a traditional lifestyle and livelihood based on a hunter or gatherer economy; or (d) pastoral persons and communities, whether they are—(i) nomadic; or (ii) a settled community that, because of its relative geographic isolation, has experienced only marginal participation in the integrated social and economic life of Kenya as a whole; "marginalised group" means a group of people who, because of laws or practices before, on, or after the effective date, were or are disadvantaged by discrimination on one or more of the grounds in Article 27 (4) 10.

Article 27 (4) of the Constitution of Kenya states the following on equality and freedom from discrimination:

> The State shall not discriminate directly or indirectly against any person on any ground, including race, sex, pregnancy, marital status, health status, ethnic or social origin, colour, age, disability, religion, conscience, belief, culture, dress, language or birth.

Narratives in Kenya

Marginalisation narratives are rife in Kenya. They focus on gender, persons with disability, youth, and religion, each needing its own critique. In its survey report of 2018, the National Gender and Equality Commission (NGEC) traced the norms and standards on minority and marginalised groups (conventions, laws, and policies) put in place at the UN agencies' level, regional continental level, and Kenya national level to contextualise its research. A key paragraph for this paper reads:

Despite Kenya's politico-legal development guaranteeing inclusion of minority and marginalized communities by the new constitution ushering in devolution, concerns still persist. There is now need to shift focus to addressing intra-regional and intra-ethnic inequalities, disparities and marginalization. Kenya's engagement with marginalized and minority issues is informed by its constitutional commitment as the national instrument, which determines Kenya's compliance with participatory and inclusive governance system that is expected to ultimately deal with socio-economic inequalities in Kenya. The Constitution recognizes the primacy of respecting minority and marginalized rights and makes substantive provisions for the affirmative action in favor of these groups.[3]

Since this paper focuses on Christians, its discussion is located in the context of religious marginalisation, where religion drives coercion. For a long time, scholars addressed marginalisation in terms of the plight of the people groups who live in the Arid and Semi-Arid Lands (ASAL) of Kenya. These include counties like Wajir, Mandera, Garissa, Isiolo, Marsabit, Tana River, Lamu, Samburu, Baringo, and Turkana in the north and Kajiado in the south. The fact that a significant percentage of the people groups of some of these counties are Muslims focuses this paper on Muslim-Christian interaction. The main narrative is that Christian colonial and post-colonial governments marginalised Muslims. Writers like Odhiambo date the discussion on the marginalisation of Muslims as follows:

> Back to colonial times when government policy was informed by imperatives of containment which saw much of areas designated closed districts, movement in and out of which was strictly regulated. The colonial government used laws such as the Outlying Districts Ordinance, 1902 and the Special Districts (Administration) Ordinance, 1934 to restrict movement into and out of the territory that now constitutes the counties of Wajir, Mandera, Garissa, Isiolo, Marsabit, Tana River, Lamu, Samburu, and Kajiado . . . Indeed, for ASALs that lie within North Eastern Province, the situation

---

3   The National Gender and Equality Commission, 2018, 2-13.

worsened with independence, as the new government introduced measures to counter the threat of Somali secession. The measures included declaration of a state of emergency, which would last for nearly three decades, providing an excuse for pervasive violation of human rights, marginalization and underdevelopment.... Post-colonial marginalization of the ASALs was institutionalized in Sessional Paper No. 10 of 1965 on African Socialism and its Application to Planning in Kenya, which focused on national economic development strategies towards agriculture, investing resources in the so-called high potential areas.[4]

Today however, after the promulgation of the Kenya Constitution 2010, marginalisation parameters have shifted. Those who suffered marginalisation as minorities in the centralised national government system have become majorities in the context of devolved governments at the county level. Scholars like Ndzovu detect a mentality that exacerbates rather than alleviates marginalisation. Those who cried foul as victims of marginalisation now marginalise the minorities in their counties and demonstrate an inability to face their realities and find solutions. In some cases, they continue to complain even when they are accessing greater resources and opportunities than their compatriots. Take the serious matter of terrorism, for example, that Ndzovu writes about:

> In this context, there has arisen two theories of why we do have jihadist Islam in Kenya, and, for that matter, in other parts of the world. The one argument is that it is due to the social and economic marginalization and exclusion of Muslims from the dominant and governing hegemony of the mainly Christian-affiliated parties in the country. This causes discontent and dissatisfaction among Muslims, especially among the poor and underprivileged, with the result of their radicalisation, attraction and exposure to, the jihadi groups. The other argument, and this coming from the

---

4   Michael O Odhiambo. 'The ASAL Policy of Kenya: Releasing the Full Potential of Arid and Semi-Arid Lands—an Analytical Review', *Nomadic Peoples* 17 no. 1 (2013), June 5.

Christian side, is that Muslims are not the only ones economically marginalized in the country. For them, one of the main factors for the radicalisation of some Muslims and their joining of jihadi groups, is the indoctrination by charismatic Muslim leaders (imams).[5]

In my field research on this topic, one respondent asked me, 'Who told Muslims that Christians and others do not have problems or complaints?' The narratives that identify Christianity with the state and power have done a lot to undermine what should have been a cordial relationship between fellow citizens who belong to different religions. Another respondent observed that whenever marginalisation happens in a country with a Christian majority, the tendency is to blame Christians. On the flipside, few highlight the matter when Christians are marginalised in regions where other religions are dominant. To provide a more nuanced critique to this entrenched narrative, the question must be asked, 'Who marginalized whom?' It seems to me that such a question could receive different answers depending on the historical point of departure. For those who focus on the politics of British colonialism and of the first 50 years of independent Kenya, Muslims were the marginalised peoples of Kenya. For those who look further into the history of East Africa, however, the Muslim Arabs were the original colonisers. In their time, they marginalised Africans and exploited them through slavery and slave trade. Later, the British collaborated with the Zanzibari and Mombasa Arabs and Somali and Kenyan Somalis, who were predominantly Muslim in faith; the British afforded them certain privileges because these Muslims ruled over the Africans around them. Another of my respondents stated as an example that 'the British are responsible for elevating many Muslims to positions in their colonial government. This [sic] why the Isaack Community of Muslims are spread across Kenya, originally from Somaliland that had been colonized by the British'.

---

5   Hassan J. Ndzovu, 'Religious Indoctrination or Marginalization Theory? Muslim-Christian Public Discourses and Perceptions on Religious Violence in Kenya', *Journal for the Study of Religion* 30 no. 2 (2017): 154-177, https://www.jstor.org/stable/26489068.

Three things are, therefore, important in this discussion: a critique of existing narratives, a consideration of some statistical facts, and an appreciation of the similarities and differences of how Christianity and Islam approach society.

First, the narratives that take British colonialism as their point of reference refer to the determination of the colonial state to marginalise the Northern Frontier districts of Kenya, through legislation and policies, which declared the arid or semi-arid north of Kenya unproductive and of little development priority. To some scholars, the fact that the colonisers were British and White implicates Christianity. In the review of literature for my research,[6] I found that history has somewhat been misread. Scholars have highlighted the fact that Britain initially acquired the East Africa Protectorate (EAP) to secure Lake Victoria, the source of the River Nile, from German aggression.[7] They did not suggest that they did so to develop or promote Christian missions.[8] The British at that time were focused on Mombasa Port and Lake Victoria, since there were no viable minerals worth exploiting for economic advantage. They, therefore, chartered the Imperial British East Africa Company (IBEAC) in 1888 as a private investor to manage it. The IBEAC prioritised the areas it thought productive for its return on investment but ran bankrupt. The British government was forced to set up the EAP in 1894/1895 under Commissioner Sir Arthur Hardinge soon after the IBEAC gave a notice to quit. Commissioner Hardinge set up the colonial state, based on prior demarcation work done by the IBEAC, and acquired a loan of 5.5 million British pounds to construct a railway line from Mombasa to Lake Victoria between 1897 and 1901. Its purpose was

---

6 Oliver K. Simiyu, *Christians and Citizenship: A Critical Study of the Contribution of Ecumenical Protestants to the Citizenship of Africans in Kenya from 1918 to 1982* (Middlesex University, OCMS, 2016).

7 D. A. Low, 'Settlers and politics in Kenya. British East Africa: The Establishment of British rule 1895-1912', in *History of East Africa*, eds. Vincent Harlow, E. M. Chilver, and Mergery Perham (Oxford: Clarendon Press; 1965), 1–56; C W. Hobley, *Kenya from a Chartered Company to Crown Colony: Thirty Years of Exploration and Administration in British East Africa* (London: H F & G Witherby, 1929).

8 Kendall Ward, *The Kenya Land Question: The History of African and European Land Settlement.* (London: The Voice of Kenya. 1952), i.

to provide the infrastructure necessary for the rapid transfer of soldiers from Mombasa to Lake Victoria, in case the Germans decided to block the outflow of the river Nile.

Charles Elliot succeeded Hardinge. He had the great burden of keeping Lake Victoria secure and repaying the huge railway loan. He, therefore, asked the British government to allow him to demarcate agriculturally productive lands that were temperate enough for White settlement. This productive land for the settlers ranged from Voi near Mombasa to Mount Kenya and Mount Kilimanjaro, the Aberdare ranges, the Ngong Hills and Longonot areas, and the Rift Valley all the way to the Cherengani Hills and Mount Elgon. This land was all within one hundred miles on either side of the railway line. In addition, he proposed to recruit White settlers from the British Commonwealth to engage in commercial agriculture as a way of generating business for the railway line, profits for themselves, and revenue for the colonial state.[9] Once he got the green light, he demarcated the fertile lands mentioned above, dispossessed Africans of it, relocated them to crowded areas known as Reserves, and recruited White farmers with a promise of fertile land and cheap labour. The demarcated lands became known as the White Highlands. Consequently, the railway that ran from Mombasa to Western Kenya facilitated all the myriad developments that accompanied the new ease of communication, including trade, common Swahili language, education, Africans' integration, and even security. This entire effort exploited Africans and their lands in the southern two-fifths of Kenya, leaving the northern three-fifths of Kenya untouched.

I have argued in my previous research that the missions and churches welcomed the colonial state's governance benefits.[10] They had laboured at the Coast from 1844 to 1890 and found it difficult to expand their work into the interior due to poor security and travel infrastructure. They used the new railway and improved security to travel farther inland. The state took advantage of their interests to avoid spending money on Africans, because the missions were building schools and hospitals in addition to spreading Christianity. The missionaries introduced Africans to education, which

---

9   Krishan M. Maini, *Land Law in East Africa* (Nairobi: Oxford University Press, 1967), 21–27.
10 Simiyu, *Christians and Citizenship*.

the Hindu Indian traders, the Muslim Arabs, and the Christian British colonists had not done; the missionaries worked against the enslavement and exploitation of Africans and later worked to improve race relations. Thus, the narrative that the missions were part of the state has no supporting evidence.

In one of my interviews, a respondent asks, 'Why doesn't anyone point out that the mission work that they as Coastal and Northern Kenya Muslims rejected, is what flourished in the interior southern parts of Kenya?' It is worth noting just a few specific places in the interior that benefitted by the relocation of missions: Fort Portal (present-day Murang'a), Kikuyu (the present-day ecumenical Alliance School), Kijabe and Chogoria (home of famous hospitals and schools), Maua in Meru, Maseno (home of Maseno School and hospital), Kaimosi (home of Friends Schools, East Africa's referral hospital, and Teachers College), and Lugulu and Kamusinga stations (home of the best schools in Bungoma). To achieve this level of outreach in the interior of Kenya, the missions took advantage of the railway line.

The discussion above shows that Muslim narratives on marginalisation conveniently begin with White colonialism. Objectivity, however, requires a more comprehensive look at history. Consider the following questions.

A respondent asks, 'Why doesn't anyone question why the Muslim Omani Arabs, who ruled the East Coast of Africa for close to a millennium, left East Africa impoverished?'[11] Records show that the Omani Arabs, who began operations on the east coast of Africa about 1000 CE, did nothing for the benefit of Africans. They enslaved and exploited them for slave labour instead. Their main success was in establishing small townships along the East Coast and spreading Islam as they progressed, wherever they desired. There is little evidence that they supported development, whether infrastructural, educational, or medical, for Africans. Hardly any schools, hospitals, training centres, industries, or any form of noteworthy developments were established in the approximately thousand years they colonized the territory. They did not even educate the Muslim coastal or northern

---

11   See also Shaheen Ayubi and Sakina, 'Mohyuddin Muslims in Kenya: An Overview', *Institute of Muslim Minority Affairs Journal* 15 (1994): 1–2, 144–156.

Kenya ethnic groups. Is this not why communities that converted to Islam very early on are the ones that today point fingers at Christian missions for ignoring them? In the light of this, one might ask, 'Who marginalised whom?'

Second, in terms of statistics, the 2019 population census of Kenya identified the Muslim population at about 5.2 million.[12] This population lives in the northern and coastal regions of Kenya, with significant presence in almost all urban areas, chiefly Mombasa and Nairobi. Religion and ethnicity are often linked. Most members of each ethnic group adhere to the same religious beliefs. Sources that have a Muslim background, including writers, activists, and political leaders, tend to count them at between 25 to 33 percent of Kenya's population. They do so and accuse the state of understating their population to deny them development funding. Sources that have a Christian background count Muslims at between 7 and 11 percent of Kenya's population, making them an even smaller minority. Research on behalf of the NCCK, for example, counted Christians at 53 percent of Kenyans in 1962 and 66 percent in 1972.[13] The 2009 population census showed that there were 4.3 million Muslims and 31.8 million Christians representing 11 per cent and 82.6 percent of Kenya's population respectively. In his thesis focused on Christian perceptions of Islam in Kenya, Brislen found that non-partisan studies placed the population of Muslims between 7 and 11 percent, with ethnic Somalis forming 50 percent of them.[14]

One respondent pointed out, however, that despite their minority status, Muslim activism has ensured representation of 10 to 16 percent in national and senate levels of Parliament,[15] and significant numbers in the

---

12 Population data from 'Islam in Kenya', Wikipedia. http://tinyurl.com/mvtwxww8.
13 David B. Barret, George K. Mambo, Janice McLaughlin, and Malcolm J. McVeigh (Eds.). *Kenya Churches Handbook: The Development of Kenyan Christianity, 1498-1873* (Kisumu: Evangel Publishing House, 1973), 165-166.
14 Michael D. Brislen, 'Christian Perceptions of Islam in Kenya: As Expressed in Written Sources from 1998 To 2010', (PhD thesis, University of Birmingham, 2013).
15 Interpreted using the statistics compiled by Florence Wanjiru, '2022 Election Results per County in Kenya: Which Party Won in the Most Counties?'

civil service, security forces, and business enterprises. Proportionally, they are more advantaged than other Kenyans. Another respondent indicated that, based on statistics, northerners including Christians and Muslims have an opportunity to redress the disadvantages they suffered in the past, but their recovery does not have to be at the expense of fellow citizens in the south. While Muslims have their own internal ethnic or sect divisions, the unity they display to the observer is admirable.[16] They do not apply the arguments they use to gain inclusion and advantage at national level to either help their rural folk or to include the minority non-Muslims in their counties. It is on this latter point that Christians suffer coercive marginalisation in Muslim-controlled areas.

Third, the perception of marginalisation also depends on how Islam and Christianity approach society. Muslims talk more about marginalisation than do Christians, Hindus, and the other faiths combined. It reflects the fact that, in the Muslim faith, there is no separation between religion, politics, and business. Consequently, they operate in solidarity and tend to exclude non-Muslims, except when they see an advantage in inclusion. It is believed that Muslims seek positions of authority if it serves a 'praiseworthy' objective as, for example, if it helps to spread Islam. One source indicated, for example, that 'seeking leadership for power and personal gain is strongly discouraged, but seeking leadership for legitimate reasons is praiseworthy. It may be obligatory for individuals who have the qualifications to fulfill those roles competently'.[17] This view reflects a discussion in my previous research, which noted that, in 1923, the Muslim community reacted negatively when Governor Coryndon chose Dr. Arthur, a Presbyterian minister, to represent Africans in London in the discussions that preserved Kenya for Africans in the Devonshire White Paper.[18]

Tuko Digital News, 30 August 2022, https://www.tuko.co.ke/facts-lifehacks/guides/470246-2022-election-results-county-kenya-party-won-counties/ (accessed 15 December 2022).

16 David E. Reed, *Islam in Kenya: General Observations.* Letter to Walter S. Rogers of Institute of Current World Affairs, 1954.

17 Shaykh I. Sedick, 'Is it recommended to seek political leadership?' *SeekersGuidance,* 4 January 2022. https://seekersguidance.org/answers/general-counsel/is-it-recommended-to-seek-political-leadership/.

18 Simiyu, *Christians and Citizenship,* 91–95.

On the flipside, the dominant Christian approach does not seek to secure opportunities because Christians expect to be given their rightful position without undue influence on processes. This approach separates church and state and focusses on evangelism, services to the needy, justice and righteousness, prayer for government, responsible citizenship to hold government accountable, and seeks the good of all. Consequently, Christians do not have the collective mind to aggressively seek positions and use them to exclude those of other faiths. The result is that society thinks Muslims are disadvantaged and others are not. Evidence in Kenya shows that one is more likely to find a Muslim elected to represent a constituency that is predominantly Christian than to find a Christian elected, or even nominated, to represent a predominantly Muslim constituency.

MARGINALISERS OR LIBERATORS?

In his paper titled 'The Criticism of the Church,'[19] Sorensen used the quote 'if you say that the history of the Church is a long succession of scandals, you are telling the truth, though if that is all you say, you are distorting the truth'.[20] Hasan Ndzovu, a scholar who has written a lot on issues that concern Muslims, pointed out that in much of the discussions that concern religious groups, information is presented selectively to present the writer's faith in positive light. He captured the following sentiment:

> If one engages a Muslim in a discussion about the condition of Muslims, the conversation will likely include the following points: educationally, there is low enrolment of Muslim children in schools; economically, the majority of Muslims are jobless or low-income earners and generally poor; and politically, Muslims

---

19 The word 'church' is a translation of the Greek *ekklesia*, which means 'the assembly of the called' and the Hebrew *qahal*, which stands for 'gathering', 'assembly', or 'congregation' (Deut. 9:10; 18:16; 1 Sam. 17:47; 1 Chron. 13:2). Among Christians the church is 'the body of Christ, a community of faith of which Christ Himself is the Head'.

20 Richard B. Sorrensen, 'Criticism of the Church', 1 November 2010, updated 23 November 2020, rich@westernwww.richardsorensen.com.

do not have sufficient clout to influence policy making. As a result, Muslims have come to perceive their situation as collective discrimination, punishment and marginalization of the community.[21]

The root of Christian-Muslim differences is historical, doctrinal, and missionary. Both faiths are fundamentalist (uphold their scriptures), absolutist (hold theirs as the only true faith), and expansionist (actively seek to convert the whole world) in the teachings they hold dear. This is problematic because each obviously has some irreconcilable differences with other faiths in their doctrine and the methodologies of expansion. In history, especially in the period 900 CE to 1200 CE, European Christians and Arab Muslims took up arms against each other in what Christians called the Crusades and Muslims called the Jihads. While speaking to a Muslim-Christian inter-faith session in 2014, I pleaded with participants, saying,

> Our problem is one. All you Muslims are seeking by all means possible to convert us Christians, me included, to become Muslims. And I, speaking to you, I am openly seeking to convert all of you to be Christians. Since both of us are missionary and expansionist, why don't we create an atmosphere in which you can share the truths of your faith for our consideration and we can share the truths of our faith for your consideration. No one has to force anyone, or attack anyone and if anyone opens up to the other faith, let their choice be respected.[22]

Paustian highlights post-colonial discourse on missions, suggesting that these were 'the benign mask of empire, the enemy of African cultures and freedoms'.[23] Such perspectives, though based on the visible relationship

---

21 Ndzovu, 'Muslims in Kenya Politics: Political Involvement, Marginalization and Minority Status (Evanston: Northwestern University Press, 2014), 3.
22 Oliver Kisaka Simiyu, Deputy General Secretary, NCCK. Remarks at a one-day Interfaith Symposium held by the Cultural Centre of the Iranian Embassy at the Louis Leakey Auditorium, Nairobi National Museum, 25 November 2014.
23 Megan C Paustian, '"A Real Heaven on Their Own Earth': Religious Missions, African Writers, and the Anticolonial Imagination', *Research in African Literatures* 45 no. 2 (2014): 1–25. https://doi.org/10.2979/reseafrilite.45.2.1.

that the missions had with the colonial state, are not always accurate. Windel captured the narrative thus:

> In Southern Rhodesia the economic attractions of gold and cattle and potentially cheap labour encouraged white settlement beginning in the last years of the nineteenth century. To gain access to the territory required violence wielded by the British South Africa Company, but settlers knew they could not rely on coercion alone to secure labour and peaceful cooperation from the people of Mashonaland and Matabeleland. The resolution of this dilemma produced an uneasy marriage between European missions, primarily in search of souls, and settlers out for fortune—a collaboration that was duplicated in Kenya where the earliest missions were set up near the first company stations created by the Imperial British East Africa Company in the East African interior. In both Kenya and Southern Rhodesia, settler needs required a civilizing mission that would convert Africans, through what was recognized as a long process, into proto-Europeans who would peacefully co-exist with their tutors in civilization while inclining them toward the economic practices of modern capitalism—i.e., individuated labor that was free enough from the obligations to land and community to be sold cheaply on the market.[24]

The findings of my research do not corroborate the narrative of missions' and churches' collusion in the marginalisation of Kenya's people groups. Evidence presents them as organisations that invested in the conversion, education, development, and representation of Africans.[25] In their mind, their greatest act of inclusion was to introduce the communities to Christianity and its benefits. Christianity, for example, teaches its adherents to respect those in authority over them and at the same time to hold them accountable when need arises. To amplify this, let me focus on three areas,

---

24   Aaron Windel, 'British Colonial Education in Africa: Policy and Practice in the Era of Trusteeship', *Compilation of History Compass* 7 no. 1 (2008): 1–21. http://on linelibrary .wiley.com/
25   Simiyu, *Christians and Citizenship*.

namely, development, political representation, and education in that order.

First, Odhiambo pointed out that the colonial state adopted a policy through sessional paper number 10 of 1965 of 'non-development' of the north and even restricted entry into or out of it.[26] The missions and churches were not consulted in adopting this policy. The resulting marginalisation was therefore not a missions' matter. On the contrary, Ludwig Krapf had initially invested a lot of time in north Kenya as he worked to access the Oromo people of southern Ethiopia. It was after the Oromo and their neighbouring Somali people on the Kenya side rejected his effort that Krapf returned to set up the first mission station at Rabai Mpya near Mombasa. Here, he and his colleague Rebmann set up the first Anglican Church and mission station, developed the first English-Swahili dictionary, set up education classes, and began the work of translating the Bible into Swahili. Despite the resistance they faced from Muslim groups, the few people from the Miji Kenda group, where their station was located, were converted to Christianity; they learned how to read and write and developed new ways of life. Those first converts formed the more progressive families among the Miji Kenda and were prominent in the development of Kenya.

Second, the colonial state maintained a policy of segregation not just of the northerners, but of all Africans. Indeed, it was the clash between the White settlers and the Indian community, the former seeking to make Kenya a Whiteman's country like South Africa and Rhodesia (present-day Zimbabwe) and the latter seeking to turn Kenya into the first Indian colony, that necessitated major conflict resolutions in London. Unbeknown to those who view Christians as agents of marginalisation, Protestant missions sent Dr. Arthur to the discussions as advisor to Governor Coryndon. Dr. Arthur networked with Dr. J. Oldham of the International Missionary Council to originate a draft statement that the Devonshire White Paper of 1923 adopted. This declares, 'Primarily, Kenya is an African territory, and His Majesty's Government think it necessary definitely to record their considered opinion that the interests of the African native must be paramount, and that if, and when, those interests and the interests of the immigrant races should conflict, the former should

---

26 Odhiambo, 'The ASAL Policy of Kenya', 5.

prevail.'[27] Politically, both Europeans and Indians were ahead. The former had demanded political representation as early as 1905, leading to the formation of the Legislative Council (LegCo) in 1907. The Hindu Indians managed to gain representation on the LegCo through the appointment of Jeevanjee in 1909. The first Muslim Arab was, however, appointed in 1924. At that time, Africans gained representation through Governor Coryndon's appointment of the Presbyterian missionary, Dr. Arthur, as their representative. This was because the missions were the only ones that from time to time intervened for Africans against the excesses of the colonial state and the other groups.

Third, in terms of education, I have already shown that the missionaries initiated and led the efforts at educating Africans, even if at a basic primary level.[28] The missions went on to initiate the first Africans' secondary school, the Alliance Boys in 1926. They later allowed Rev. Beecher to chair the committee that proposed the expansion of Africans' education in 1950. At the time of independence, the Kenyatta government realised that the missions and churches owned about 64 percent of all the schools in Kenya. The government, therefore, entered an arrangement with the churches to allow the government to run the schools under the ministry of education, on condition that the state would recognise the churches as sponsors, allow them to run chaplaincies, and allow them to have majority representation on the boards of governors. The churches, organised as the National Council of Churches of Kenya, constructed the first national primary and secondary schools in northern Kenya, known as Garba Tulla National School, in 1973. Individual churches, like the Anglicans, Quakers, Methodists, Roman Catholics, Presbyterians, and African Inland Missions, did the same. These efforts show that the missions and the churches engaged in efforts to include the north rather than to exclude them.

MARGINALISATION OF LIBERATORS

In light of the above, it is a matter of concern that Christians should experience marginalisation in Muslim-dominated counties in Kenya. With

---

27 Simiyu, *Christians and Citizenship*, 100–101.
28 Simiyu, *Christians and Citizenship*.

regard to development, Christians living and working in the north are increasingly marginalised in Muslim-dominated counties. Increasingly, Christians and their churches are denied opportunity to acquire property for homes and churches or even to set up schools and hospitals. A Christian respondent highlighted a most disturbing matter when he said that they are even denied opportunity and land to bury their dead. He indicated that whenever a Christian dies in those regions (and many are killed by undisclosed terrorists), the relatives must struggle hard to find a way of transporting the body back to their original home in southern Kenya. While Christians in counties where they are dominant have not hindered their Muslim fellow citizens from acquiring property for business, construction of worship centres, or cemeteries, they are shocked by the deliberate marginalisation they experience at the hands of their fellow citizens. A key Muslim scholar called Ndzovu writes;

> The numerous killings of non-Muslims by Muslim jihadi groups in Kenya, have fueled ethno-religious tensions manifested in hatred and anger against the entire Muslim community. Though anti-jihadi Muslims have rightly condemned the targeting of their non-Muslim countrymen by the jihadists, the Christian leaders have not been satisfied by their counterpart's internal self-criticism. There are suspicions from Christians, even when anti-jihadi Muslims disassociate themselves from the heinous criminal acts of the jihadists, that all Muslims are the same, and posing a threat to peace in the country. In this context, there has arisen two theories of why we do have jihadist Islam in Kenya, and, for that matter, in other parts of the world.[29]

With regard to politics, Christians hardly have an opportunity to offer themselves for political office in Muslim-dominated areas. This is in contrast to the Christian-dominated counties where, in at least three cases, the local citizens have elected Muslims from northeastern backgrounds to represent them in Parliament. This is what the Constitution of Kenya 2010 reads in part:

---

29   Ndzovu, "Religious Indoctrination', 154.

Article 39 on Freedom of movement and residence. (1) Every person has the right to freedom of movement. (2) Every person has the right to leave Kenya. (3) Every citizen has the right to enter, remain in and reside anywhere in Kenya.

Article 40. On Protection of right to property. (1) Subject to Article 65, every person has the right, either individually or in association with others, to acquire and own property— (a) of any description; and (b) in any part of Kenya.

Article 197 on County assembly gender balance and diversity reads;

(1) Not more than two-thirds of the members of any county assembly or county executive committee shall be of the same gender. (2) Parliament shall enact legislation to—(a) ensure that the community and cultural diversity of a county is reflected in its county assembly and county executive committee; and (b) prescribe mechanisms to protect minorities within counties.

One respondent indicated that, despite the constitutional provision as stated above, Christians are marginalised in the following ways:

1. Christians in Muslim-dominated areas are not allowed to own, keep, read, watch, listen to any other materials except Islamic; Muslims often also interfere with private Christian worship.

2. Should a person convert to Christianity, they are ostracised/divorced or put under house arrest; access is denied or restricted altogether to water and social amenities (schools, medical facilities, etc.).

3. Christian congregational worship is also often restricted or disrupted.

4. At the national level, Muslims are disproportionately advantaged in the life of the country including key appointments, policies that favor Islamic practices, economic and political caucusing, and participating in national processes.

He opined that a full commitment to follow the constitution highlighted above would go a long way in fostering true nationhood and common citizenship.

With regard to education, Muslims have deliberately undermined Christians' engagement. During the years that the NCCK ran the Garba Tulla schools cited above, they were top performing and were responsible for the education of key leaders in the north, many of them Muslims. When governance shifted to the counties, Muslim groups in Isiolo began to quarrel with the NCCK and the Methodist church over their operations. Today the schools are a pale shadow of their former glory. Christians willing to serve in Muslim-dominated areas are troubled by the level of insecurity that has on occasion cost them their lives.[30] The worst form of educational marginalisation happened when 147 university students studying at Garrissa University were brutally murdered.[31] Furthermore, the main suspect, believed to have joined Al Shabab, was formerly a head teacher of a primary school in that same Garrissa County. Christians sometimes think that the attacks that Christians experience are aimed at discouraging them from operating in Muslim counties. As my respondents ended their discussions, they said, 'Christians mean well and desire the best for the people of the north. They must not fear converting to Christianity, for it is a great equalizer.'

The discussion above highlights that there is a significant shift in marginalisation parameters. It cannot be denied that, previously, the north did suffer. The fact, however, is that Muslims, who complain a lot about marginalisation, themselves marginalise non-Muslims. This reveals deep fissures in Kenya where Muslims, and Islam as a minority religion of Kenya, are becoming the main facilitators of marginalisation.

---

30 Fredrick Nzwili, 'Mass Exodus of Teachers Triggers Education Crisis in North East Kenya', https:// www.worldwatchmonitor.org/2020/03/mass-exodus-of-teachers-triggers-education-crisis-in-north-east-kenya/.

31 'Kenya attack: 147 dead in Garissa University assault,' *BBC World News*, 3 April 2015, https://www.bbc.com/news/ world-africa-32169080.

16

ORTHODOX CHRISTIANITY IN ETHIOPIA
The Shifting Influence of a Religious Majority

Ralph Lee

Less than a century ago, if one had travelled to Ethiopia's capital, Addis Ababa, or to many parts of the nation, but perhaps especially in its northern regions, it would have been apparent that the Ethiopian Orthodox *Täwaḥədo*[1] Church (EOTC) dominated the nation's religious, social, and political life. It had done so since the conversion to Christianity of King Ezana in the second quarter of the fourth century. Orthodox churches would have been prominent in cities, towns, villages, and remote rural areas. The peaceful Yaredic[2] chant would have been heard throughout the night in preparation for the liturgy. There would have been other religions, but their physical presence would have been less apparent and their influence limited. There would have been a significant number of Muslims, especially in regions in the path taken by Ahmed Gragn's Islamic *jihad* in the sixteenth century, but mosques would have been modest constructions and probably not on main streets. Protestant Christianity was at its inception, but associated church buildings would have been inconspicuous or even hidden. Catholics were very few in number, having been regarded

---

1 This word means 'fused' and is an expression of the staunch Miaphysite Christology of the EOTC.
2 See Antonella Brita, 'Yared,' in *The Encyclopaedia Aethiopica*, ed. Siegbert Uhlig (Wiesbaden: Harrassowitz, 2014).

with heavy suspicion since the country's encounter with Jesuit missionaries in the sixteenth and seventeenth centuries.³

A century on, the strong presence of the EOTC and its influence on every part of life is still very much evident, but, especially in the major cities, one encounters a much more diverse religious and social environment. There are still prominent Orthodox churches, and their now amplified chants fill the air at night, but nowadays they compete with the Islamic *adhan* (call to prayer) and with the lively sounds of Pentecostal popular worship. The century that has passed was punctuated by two critical events that marked shifts in the way in which the EOTC influenced the nation and its religious, social, and political environment: (1) the Ethiopian Revolution of 1974 initiated eighteen years of communist rule by the Derg regime,⁴ with significant persecution and subjugation of religious groups, and (2) the overthrow of that regime by the Ethiopian People's Revolutionary Democratic Front (EPRDF) led by Meles Zenawi in 1991 ended Ethiopia's experiment with communism and ushered in an age of religious freedom.

For Orthodox churches in general and very much for the EOTC specifically, history is very important. Events that occurred centuries ago have strong contemporary relevance. A brief excursus, therefore, into historical encounters between the EOTC and other religions lays a foundation for understanding the complexities of the contemporary situation.

BACKGROUND

Ethiopia's conversion to Christianity is a complex story, but it is certain that the conversion of King Ezana in the fourth century was a powerful force for Christian influence in the region, lying as it did at the southern limit of the strong early expansion of Christianity. Before the rise of Islam, Jewish presence and opposition to Christianity in Arabia was strongly felt

---

3   Jesuits first came to Ethiopia in the sixteenth century; their strong influence came in the seventeenth. Ines G. Županov and Festo Mkenda, 'Jesuit Involvement in Africa, 1548–2017,' in *The Oxford Handbook of the Jesuits* (Oxford University Press, 2018).

4   From the Amharic word for 'committee' or 'council'.

in Ethiopia,[5] and early in the sixth century, Ethiopia's King Caleb (r. 514–542) mounted an international expedition across the Red Sea to Najran to attack Jewish rulers who had displaced Christian kings, leading to an Ethiopian presence there for 50 years.[6] Later, in the early seventh century, Mohammed's followers were persecuted in Mecca and found refuge in Ethiopia,[7] marking the beginning of a long and complex relationship between Ethiopia, the EOTC, and Islam, in which Islam has thrived in many regions of the nation but, until recently, most definitely under the watchful eye of the Orthodox Christian rulers. A legendary tenth-century conqueror of Aksum, Ǝsato (Gudit), apparently fought to overthrow Christian rulers but ultimately failed.[8] Gudit's unlikely portrayal as being Jewish is a mark of the tension there was with Jewish aspirations in Ethiopia. She possibly sought to overthrow Ethiopia's Zagwe rulers, who rose to their zenith with King Lalibela and his renowned rock-carved churches.[9]

The establishment of the 'Solomonic dynasty' in 1270 is validated by *Kebra Nagast, The Glory of Kings*, Ethiopia's national epic, which narrates the story of how Ethiopians believe the Ark of the Covenant came to Ethiopia and the nation became Jewish, and indeed God's chosen nation, which is an unusual way of cementing Ethiopia's strong Christian identity.[10] *Kebra Nagast* is a complex work, but it firmly plants the EOTC as underpinning the authority of Ethiopia's rulers. A further Jewish presence

---

5 Irfan Shahid, *The Martyrs of Najran: New Documents* (Brussels: Societe des Bollandistes, 1971), 7.
6 Irfan Shahid, 'The Book of the Himyarites: Authorship and Authenticity,' *Le Muséon*, 76 (1963); Ian Gillman and Hans-Joachim Klimkeit, *Christians in Asia before 1500* (Richmond: Curzon Press, 1999), 79–80; Shahid, *The Martyrs of Najran*. See also a brief reference in the Ethiopian national epic, Kebra Nagast in E. A. Wallis Budge, *The Kebra Nagast* (New York: Cosimo Books Inc., 2004).
7 Spencer J. Trimingham, *Islam in Ethiopia* (London: Oxford University Press, 1952), 44–48.
8 Steven Kaplan, 'Ǝsato', in *Encyclopaedia Aethiopica*, ed. Siegbert Uhlig (Wiesbade: Harrassowitz Verlag, 2005).
9 Gianfranco Fiaccadori, 'Zagʷe,' in *Encyclopaedia Aethiopica*, ed. Alessandro Bausi and Siegbert Uhlig (Wiesbaden: Harrassowitz Verlag, 2014).
10 For an extended discussion of this, see Ralph Lee, *Symbolic Interpretations in Ethiopic and Early Syriac Literature*, vol. 24, Eastern Christian Studies (Leuven: Peeters, 2017).

is seen in this epoch with the emergence, at least in the historical records, of Ethiopia's enigmatic Beta Israel Jewish community—who may indeed have emerged in part from a converted Judaizing group of Christians.[11] It also points to the complex relationship that Ethiopian Christianity has had with Judaism—although it would be a mistake to describe Ethopian Christianity as 'Jewish'.[12]

The EOTC continued to develop an ever closer relationship with the Ethiopian state, perhaps reaching its peak during the reign of Zera Yaqob (r. 1434-1468), who strengthened monastic institutions and the associated missionary project of the church.[13] However, the church did not accommodate itself well at this time to the challenge of the diverse peoples, languages, and cultures of Ethiopia. As territories were added in the southern part of what is now the nation of Ethiopia, speakers of non-semitic languages found the ancient language of Gə'əz more challenging than did their northern Amharic- and Tigrigna-speaking compatriots, and Orthodoxy was less firmly established in these regions.

Later, in the sixteenth century, Ethiopian Christianity was confronted by two major challenges to its authority and existence in the form of Roman Catholic mission and Islamic *jihad*. The Portuguese Jesuits who first encountered Ethiopian Christianity were horrified by what they considered its 'judaising', but, in an unusual and important document, King Claudius (r. 1540-1559) graciously defends the Ethiopian expression of Christianity, making a clear distinction between their practice and Jewish customs. This defence was sensitive because, at that time, Ethiopia was facing the onslaught of Ahmed Gragn's (c. 1506-1553) *jihad* unleashed

---

[11] Steven Kaplan, *The Beta Israel (Falasha) in Ethiopia* (New York and London: New York University Press, 1992); Steven Kaplan, 'Betä Ǝsra'el,' in *Encylopaedia Aethiopica Vol. 1: A-C*, ed. Siegbert Uhlig (Wiesbaden: Harrassowitz Verlag, 2003).

[12] For a detailed discussion of the EOTC's so-called Jewish elements, especially its interpretation of the Ark of the Covenant, see Lee, *Symbolic Interpretations*, 24.

[13] Tibebe Eshete, 'Ethiopia, Eritrea, Somalia and Djibout', in *Christianity in Sub-Saharan Africa*, eds. Kenneth R. Ross, J. Kwabena Asamoah-Gyadu, and Todd M. Johnson, Edinburgh Companions to Global Christianity (Edinburgh: Edinburgh University Press, 2017), 144.

on Ethiopia and sought Portuguese assistance in the military defence of the nation. Notwithstanding this need, Claudius produced a gracious but unyielding defence, especially of the apparent judaising elements of Ethiopian Christianity.[14] Ahmed Gragn's campaign was a challenge to the very existence of the nation, seeking to impose Islam as the nation's religion, and the combination of Ethiopian zeal and skill and Portuguese military support thwarted his aims.[15]

This event prompted the further development of an uncomfortable interaction with Catholicism in the seventeenth century through the missionary efforts of Pedro Paez (1564-1622) and Alfonsus Mendes (1579-1656).[16] Paez took a humble approach and gained favour with Emperor Susenyos (r. 1607-1632), who made a public confession of Catholic faith, although the monks were not persuaded.[17] Paez died shortly after this, and his successor, Mendes, took a confrontational approach, excommunicating clergy and insisting on rebaptism. His harsh approach was rebuffed by Susenyos' successor Fasilides (r. 1632-1667), who expelled the Jesuits; no Catholic clergy were permitted to enter Ethiopia for over a century.[18]

Much later, in the nineteenth century, Menelik II (r.1890-1913) embarked on a unification project that brought the diverse cultural groups together under the strong influence of the EOTC, leading to a political cohesion under the influence of the EOTC that had previously been lacking, although at the same time he allowed Lutheran missionaries from Sweden to start their work.[19] It was in the twentieth century, under the reign of Ethiopia's last emperor, Haile Selassie (r. 1930-1974), that Protestant

---

14   Edward Ullendorff, 'The Confessio Fidei of King Claudius of Ethiopia', *Journal of Semitic Studies* 32 no. 1 (1987).
15   Franz-Christoph Muth, 'Aḥmad b. Ibrāhim al-Ġāzī', in *Encylopaedia Aethiopica*, ed. Siegbert Uhlig (Wiesbaden: Harrassowitz Verlag, 2003).
16   They were driven somewhat by the 'successes' of activities in India, culminating with the disastrous (for Indian Christians) Synod of Diamper in 1500 CE. See Gillman and Klimkeit, *Christians in Asia before 1500*, 188-201.
17   Leonardo Cohen, 'Susənyos', in *The Encyclopaedia Aethiopica*, ed. Siegbert Uhlig (Wiesbaden: Harrassowitz Verlag, 2010).
18   Ines G. Županov and Festo Mkenda, 'Jesuit Involvement in Africa, 1548-2017', in *The Oxford Handbook of the Jesuits*.
19   Eshete, 'Ethiopia, Eritrea, Somalia and Djibout.

mission began to thrive. Perhaps the most important of the Protestant missions was SIM,[20] whose work led to the establishment of the largest Protestant denomination in Ethiopia, the Kale Hiwot Church.[21] Lutherans arrived, first from Sweden and later from the USA, associated with the Mekane Yesus Church, which is the largest single church in the Lutheran World Federation. It is important to stress, however, that the prospering of these Christian expressions was often built on the legacy of the EOTC's involvement across the nation, and that this laid the foundation for tensions between the EOTC and other groups that it came to regard as 'sheep stealers'.[22]

THE TWENTIETH CENTURY

An attempt at colonizing Ethiopia was made in 1896, when the Italians were routed by Ethiopian forces at Adwa, an event that inspired independent, African-led Ethiopianist Christian movements in South Africa and other parts of the continent.[23] This also perhaps gave momentum to Ethiopian efforts at religious independence, with the EOTC still being formally under the authority of the Patriarchate in Alexandria. Italy tried again and occupied Ethiopia in 1935, which led to a push toward autocephaly in the EOTC, which was finally realised in 1959, breaking the formal connection between Alexandria and the appointment of Ethiopian bishops. While this connection has been perceived by some as restrictive, in reality the EOTC had expressed its indigenous theological ideas in its own language for many centuries before 1959. The move did, however, allow the appointment of a patriarch and senior bishops, which gave the EOTC a new public face nationally and internationally. The Italian occupation also allowed

---

20 Then the Sudan Interior Mission, but working today in Ethiopia and elsewhere under the title Serving in Mission.
21 See Raymond J. Davis, *Fire on the Mountains: The Story of a Miracle—the Church in Ethiopia* (Sudan Interior Mission, 1981).
22 Tibebe Eshete, *The Evangelical Movement in Ethiopia: Resistance and Resilience* (Waco, Texas: Baylor University Press, 2017).
23 See J. Mutero Chirenje, *Ethiopianism and Afro-Americans in Southern Africa, 1883–1916 / J. Mutero Chirenje* (Baton Rouge: Louisiana State University Press, 1987).

significant growth in Protestant and Pentecostal expressions but without the need for foreign missionaries.

Although there were positive outcomes from the Italian occupation for many religious groups, progressive movements within the nation remained discontent and a significant intellectual struggle with the conservatism of Orthodoxy slowly fermented.[24] This struggle led ultimately to the Communist Revolution of 1974 and the formation of the Derg[25] regime that governed Ethiopia until 1991. The revolution came for many reasons, but it was clear that a major impetus came from the wide discontent of Ethiopia's poorer classes expressed toward wealthy landowners, including the church, which owned about one-third of the nation's land.[26]

Religion came under attack by the Derg but, in this deeply religious nation, religion fared well in some ways under oppressive rule. Perhaps too, while to keep their Soviet Union backers content the Derg needed to be seen to suppress religion, they understood that driving this oppression too hard would backfire and create resistance, because Ethiopians would not give up their religion easily—what they wanted was to wrest it from the hands of the ruling elite. One indicator of this was the lifting of the strict curfew imposed on the citizens of Addis Ababa throughout the communist years for the Christmas and Easter vigils, perhaps feeling that people would just have defied it anyway.

All religious groups suffered during this period, including the EOTC. The restructuring of religious organisations that came about under the Derg led to robust organisations that could persevere for a time and were poised to exploit new freedoms when they came in 1991. Muslims remained relatively inconspicuous in many parts of the country, although communist ideals of equality meant that Muslim festivals became national holidays in addition to the existing Christian ones.

The nationalisation of all land by the Derg regime dealt a severe blow to the EOTC, because the loss of her estates also meant the loss of income derived from them. The church's feudal approach to land and income had

---

24 See Zewde Bahru, *A History of Modern Ethiopia, 1855–1991*, 2nd ed. (Oxford: James Curry, 2001); Zewde Bahru, *Pioneers of Change in Ethiopia: The Reformist Intellectuals of the Early Twentieth Century* (Oxford: James Currey, 2002).
25 Derg is an Amharic word for 'committee'.
26 Eshete, *The Evangelical Movement in Ethiopia*.

limited development, and the changes became the stimulus for reform and reorganisation of parishes in an unprecedented form of devolution and democratisation. The Derg regime pressured the church in the appointment of a new Patriarch, Abuna Täklä Haymanot, in place of Abuna Tewoflos whom they had murdered. There was a certain naivety on the part of the Derg in this appointment. Abuna Täklä Haymanot seemed an unthreatening figure, with his life shaped by monastic simplicity. He went barefoot and gave his salary to projects for the poor, and had no previous experience of church administration—and so was perhaps perceived by the Derg as someone whom they could manipulate. He was, nevertheless, very popular, and his monastic piety was an inspiration to many in their own struggle with the vicissitudes of the communist era. Following the loss of land, one of the most important changes that he instigated was the promotion of parish councils, which were formalised with the constitution of the General Assembly of Parish Councils in 1983.[27] These flourished, promoting the building and renovation of churches and monasteries.[28] In these ways, the EOTC thrived not in collusion with the state but by focussing on things that directly affected most of the laity. This response strengthened the church further, because a main impetus of the revolution had been the poor's resentment of the rich and powerful. Under the reforms, local clergy and others had significant control over their churches, and priests often became champions of the poor.[29]

Evangelical churches established themselves strongly in the southern parts of Ethiopia in the 1920s and then through the Italian occupation, during which missionaries were expelled. Churches like the Kale Heywot Church, connected to the work of SIM and now Ethiopia's largest single Protestant denomination, grew very strongly without any missionary presence. Under communism, the Evangelical expression spread more widely from its southern and largely rural base. As Evangelical Christianity spread, and with strong indigenous influences, the churches became more charismatic in their expression—a process that also led to significant breaking down of barriers between different Evangelical and the newer Pentecostal churches, creating a strong ecumenical community. Evangelicals were

---

27 John Binns, *The Orthodox Church of Ethiopia: A History* (London: I.B. Tauris, 2017), 238–240.
28 Binns, *The Orthodox Church of Ethiopia*, 240.
29 Binns, *The Orthodox Church of Ethiopia*, 239.

certainly persecuted, but this drove the formation of identity that would endure and strengthen the church through strong lay leadership that developed partly through necessity following the exile of prominent leaders. In this sense, some of the developments in these communities paralleled those in the EOTC in generating a robust church that was focussed on the needs of the majority of Ethiopians.[30] Importantly, however, neither Evangelicals nor Orthodox were well versed in reflecting on social and political matters. Although their emphasis on local and lay leaders was the root cause of them not only surviving but thriving under the Derg, it did not prepare either group well for the challenge in the public sphere that would come after the overthrow of the Derg.

Although today many Evangelical and Pentecostal churches are virtually indistinguishable in their praxis, Ethiopia's Pentecostal churches have a followed a slightly different path that is important to note. Pentecostalism in Ethiopia emerged in the 1950s from Scandinavian roots, with the first church, the Mulu Wongel Church (Full Gospel Believers' Church) established in 1967, although official registration was refused, forcing the Pentecostal church underground much like Evangelicals were forced to behave under communism. Initially, under communism, Pentecostals were free, but they were soon strongly opposed and faced prison sentences, torture, closure of meeting places, and confiscation of land. They were now like the Evangelicals.[31] Under lay leadership and without the strong conservative influence of foreign missionaries, many Evangelical churches adopted Pentecostal/Charismatic worship styles.[32] In parallel, Pentecostalism, which is often an urban religious phenomenon, moved into the rural areas of Ethiopia.[33]

---

30 Eshete, *The Evangelical Movement in Ethiopia*, 301–304.
31 Jörg Haustein and Emanuele Fantini, 'Introduction: The Ethiopian Pentecostal Movement—History, Identity and Current Socio-Political Dynamics', *PentecoStudies: An Interdisciplinary Journal for Research on the Pentecostal and Charismatic Movements* 12 no. 2 (2013).
32 Tibebe Eshete, 'The Early Charismatic Movement in the Ethiopian Kale Heywet Church'; *PentecoStudies: An Interdisciplinary Journal for Research on the Pentecostal and Charismatic Movements* 12 no. 2 (2013), https://doi.org/10.1558/ptcs.v12i2.162.
33 Dena Freeman, 'Pentecostalism in a Rural Context: Dynamics of Religion and Development in Southwest Ethiopia', *PentecoStudies: An Interdisciplinary*

The end of communism in Ethiopia was an extraordinary event. In the turbulent days before the Derg's final demise, Ethiopian President Mengistu Hailemariam fled to Zimbabwe. In his place, Tesfay Gabra Kidan became the acting communist leader of Ethiopia. In extraordinary events, one of his first actions during his week of office was to declare a national day of prayer and fasting for peace, and on 23 May 1991, Christians of all expressions and Muslims spent the day in their places of worship in prayer.[34] It was as though a communist outlook on religion had evaporated. The prayers of many were answered, and the fight for Addis Ababa on the 28 of May following was a remarkably short affair, with few clashes and minimal casualties.

THE AGE OF RELIGIOUS FREEDOM AFTER 1991

Soon after these events, Meles Zenawi returned from exile to lead the nation as the leader of the EPRDF and quickly instigated a new age of freedom both in religion and in economics. The EPRDF had previously boasted a liking for Enver Hoxha's Albanian socialism, but Meles Zenawi understood well Ethiopia's need for support, and the West's victory in the Cold War turned the EPRDF quickly to a revolutionary democratic outlook.[35] The leading party remained intolerant toward political opposition, but oversaw remarkable economic growth, maintaining growth rates of above 10% for almost a decade from 2004. Religious freedom came quickly, and the new constitution of 1995 affirmed separated of state and religion, affirmed no interference of government in religious affairs, and guaranteed freedom of belief, expression, and association[36].

In the decades after the downfall of the Derg, Orthodoxy remained the largest religious group, followed closely by Islam, but Protestant Christianity grew rapidly and carved out a place in the nation's northern

---

Journal for Research on the Pentecostal and Charismatic Movements 12 no. 2 (2013), https://doi.org/10.1558/ptcs.v12i2.231.

34 I witnessed these events, but have not yet found any published accounts.
35 Tefera N. Gebregziabher, 'Ideology and Power in TPLF's Ethiopia: A Historic Reversal in the Making?' *African Affairs* 118 no. 472 (2019), https://doi.org/10.1093/afraf/adz005.
36 Jörg Haustein and Emanuele Fantini. 'Introduction: The Ethiopian Pentecostal Movement'.

Orthodox heartlands. The weakness of this new administration was, however, its close association with the heartland that in the past bred its opposition to the Derg regime, Tigray. Many accusations of nepotism have been made, with many senior positions across Ethiopian public and private organisations being given to Tigrayans. This association was used by some against the Patriarch, Abuna Pawlos, appointed at the inception of this new age of religious freedom. Abuna Pawlos had been appointed a bishop early in the revolution and had served time in prison. He was made Patriarch in 1991 to replace Abuna Merkorios, who had been appointed in 1988 but was dethroned, leading to a damaging split in the church, with Abuna Merkorios operating a rival synod from the USA. This split did not feature strongly within Ethiopia, but it caused harmful breakdown in relationships among the diaspora communities, especially in the USA. Abuna Pawlos was considered by some to be too close to the Tigray-led administration of Meles Zenawi—a position that Abuna Pawlos undoubtedly took because he felt it best served the church. In the emerging ethnic tensions in the nation, this possibility interfered with the authority of the Orthodox Church for some. The EOTC responded with the robust development of lay-led activities in discipleship and community practice. These activities created some very important connections between highly skilled urban communities and those in rural areas needing support in what might be termed an 'Orthodox work ethic' that has focussed more on mutual assistance and support than on economic growth.[37]

As far as religious influence was concerned, the crucial difference after the fall of communism among Orthodox churches, other churches with a broadly Evangelical base, and the Pentecostal churches was their vision for political and social action. Pentecostal and Charismatic groups specifically sought an active presence in the public sphere and sought to undermine secular influences in the nation. Following the death of Meles Zenawi in 2012, Pentecostals were catapulted to the highest political offices. Prime Minister Hailemariam Desalegn became Ethiopia's first

---

37 Ralph Lee, '"Modernism" and the Ethiopian Orthodox Sunday School Movement: Indigenous Movements and their International Connections', *The Journal of Ecclesiastical History* (2022), https://doi.org/10.1017/s0022046921001391.

non-Orthodox ruler in 2012, even if his Oneness expression of Pentecostalism is suspicious for some, especially the staunchly trinitarian Orthodox.[38] Other groups were ill-prepared for a presence in the public sphere and even eschewed it. Indeed, the Pentecostal outlook has encroached into what is often described as 'prosperity' gospel, with the ruling EPRDF changing their party name to the Prosperity Party, but their role in driving Ethiopia's startling economic growth has been extremely important.[39]

The new age of freedom quickly brought visible changes in public spaces. During the communist era, and before, Muslims were reticent to identify themselves publicly, although their names would have often betrayed their religious roots. With the proclamation of new religious freedoms, Muslims gained a new public confidence, and by the early twenty-first century Muslims would, for instance, happily perform their prayer rituals in public spaces—restaurants or cafés. Major new mosques were commissioned and have become very prominent in the skyline of Addis Ababa and other major cities. Islamic dress, such as the skull cap or the hijab, are now commonplace.[40] The confidence of Muslims grew in other ways, with some Muslim groups, notably Oromo ethnic groups, seeking to portray Orthodoxy as the religion of their Amahara oppressors. This has led recently to previously unheard-of attacks on Orthodox Churches in Oromo regions, and bold claims were made of the Islamisation of important cities, including Bahir Dar in the northern Orthodox heartlands of Gojjam.[41] The historical good relations between Muslims and Orthodox Christians have been significantly undermined.

---

38 Jörg Haustein, 'The New Prime Minister's Faith: A Look at Oneness Pentecostalism in Ethiopia', *PentecoStudies: An Interdisciplinary Journal for Research on the Pentecostal and Charismatic Movements* 12 no. 2 (2013), https://doi.org/10.1558/ptcs.v12i2.183.

39 Haustein and Fantini, 'Introduction: The Ethiopian Pentecostal Movement'.

40 Jörg Haustein and Terje Østebø, 'EPRDF's Revolutionary Democracy and Religious Plurality: Islam and Christianity in Post-Derg Ethiopia,' *Journal of Eastern African Studies* 5 no. 4 (2011), https://doi.org/10.1080/17531055.2011.642539.

41 'Three Killed in Attacks on Ethiopian Orthodox Church, According to Report', *VOANEWS*, 2023, https://www.voanews.com/a/three-killed-in-attacks-on-ethiopian-orthodox-church-report-/6948447.html#:~:text=The%20

At the same time as the public confidence of Muslims developed, Protestant churches also gained new energy. Not only could they now worship freely, but previous restrictions from the Imperial government and then later from the communists on work in the northern Orthodox regions were lifted, and Protestant missionary activity was allowed to develop. In the diversity of Addis Ababa, this was perhaps simply another voice in the multi-ethnic, religiously diverse city, but in the Orthodox heartlands it was seen as a threat. Significant tensions have persisted since that time, primarily through Protestant assumptions that the Orthodox are truly pagans, and then in turn the Orthodox condemn the Protestants as heretics—identifying them primarily with the fourth-century arch-heretic Arius because of the language they have chosen to use about Jesus Christ. Some of this may also be put down to poor mutual understanding, rooted on the Protestant part at least by their early growth in regions without a strong Orthodox presence, allowing them to grow while mistakenly considering Orthodoxy irrelevant, perhaps encouraged by the Western missionaries who served them and shared their ignorance of Orthodoxy.

On the Orthodox part, they consider the Protestants in all their expressions as imposters and often conflate the Protestant renewalist outlook with problems arising from secularisation and globalisation. Protestants and Pentecostals have targeted the Orthodox, insisting that Orthodox belief and praxis are heretical. This has led to deep tensions even within families, with what seem superficial matters, such as Pentecostal avoidance of alcohol, dividing family gatherings. 'Renewal' movements in the Orthodox Church have also formed and have mostly split from the church—primarily over their Pentecostal worship forms, which jar against Orthodox sensitivities. Nevertheless, there have also been some formal moves toward better mutual understanding. The formation of the Inter-Religious Council of Ethiopia in 2010 marks a significant change. It reflects a change from the condescension of the Orthodox toward other groups to a genuine approach to cooperation, associated with a general acceptance on the part of Orthodox Christians that the Protestants are 'here to stay'.

TMC%20said%20two%20Orthodox,miles)%20south%20of%20Addis%20Ababa (accessed 15 March 2023).

WHAT LIES AHEAD

There is another chapter to be written in the tensions between Orthodox and Protestant and Pentecostal groups. The rapid economic growth of the nation under its new Pentecostal political masters gave that Christian expression an undoubted precedence—it was new, fresh, and could demonstrably show benefit to the nation. There have been accusations of nepotism and corruption—but still, many have benefitted from increased economic prosperity. Then, in 2020, the nation was plunged into civil conflict. The leaders of the Tigray region were unsettled by attempts to postpone elections due to the global pandemic, causing strong disagreement between the federal government and that of the Tigray region. This conflict took the focus off the economic growth that underpinned the outlook of the current administration. The current Prime Minister Abiy Ahmed was awarded the Noble Peace Prize for the rapprochement with Eritrea that had so seriously undermined stability, but the conflict that developed with Tigray is in some ways more insidious and has led to major divisions in the nation that will take many years to reconcile. Different religious groups have responded differently to the conflict—with Pentecostals reluctant to speak out in ways that would undermine their newfound influence. Patriarch Abuna Mattyas has spoken out, but because of deep ethnic tensions, his voice calling for peace has been compromised because of his Tigrayan roots.[42] As this chapter is being written, a new peace agreement has been put into place, but it is in the very early stages of implementation, and many are cautious about its prospects.[43] Nevertheless, as this process plays out over the coming years, it may be that the war in Tigray marks another significant point in the shifting influences within the nation.

In January 2023, an unprecedented event took place in southern Ethiopia that challenged and ultimately affirmed the EOTC's enduring strong

---

42   'Ethiopian Orthodox Church Patriarch Condemns Tigray "Genocide",' *CNN*, 2021, https://edition.cnn.com/2021/05/08/africa/orthodox-church-tigray-ethiopia-intl/index.html (accessed 15/03/2023).

43   'Blinken to Visit Ethiopia as Progress under Tigray Peace Deal Slows,' *Washington Post*, updated 13 March 2023, https://edition.cnn.com/2021/05/08/africa/orthodox-church-tigray-ethiopia-intl/index.html (accessed 15 March 2023).

influence. On 26 January, Abuna Sawiros, the archbishop of South West Shoa Diocese, with two other archbishops, appointed twenty-six bishops specifically for people from the Oromo ethnic group. These appointments were justified on the basis that the EOTC had not looked after the needs of this group by not allowing the use of Oromifa language in the church and by imposing a different culture on them. This was a bold schismatic act, taking place without the Synod of the EOTC. This act was quickly condemned by Patriarch Abuna Mathias I and by the Synod, and the bishops responsible were excommunicated. The event was extraordinary because the bishops must have known that this would be the response. Within the Orthodox Churches, no other response would have been possible, which points to a likely political motivation for the act, most likely aimed at promoting the Oromo independence cause.[44]

In a remarkable response from the central government, pressure was applied to the Synod to recognise the breakaway group. Although by early February Prime Minister Abiy Ahmed was promoting dialogue, there was a strong impression that he and his government supported the schism.[45] The government, for instance, forbade people from wearing black in government offices and some other public spaces. These events took place during a fasting period, but unconventionally EOTC laity and clergy took to wearing black in a national (and international) act of mourning over the split in the church.[46] Although there appears to have

---

44 'What's Behind the Crisis in Ethiopia's Orthodox Tewahedo Church?' *Al Jazeera*, 12 February 2023, https://www.aljazeera.com/program/inside-story/2023/2/12/whats-behind-the-crisis-in-ethiopias-orthodox-tewahedo-church (accessed 10 March 2023).

45 'Analysis: PM Abiy Weighs in with Call for Dialogue in the Deepening Crisis within Orthodox Church as Accusations of State Interference Grow Louder', *Addis Standard*, 1 February 2023, https://addisstandard.com/analysis-pm-abiy-weighs-on-deepening-crisis-within-orthodox-church-with-call-for-dialogue-as-accusations-of-state-interference-grow-louder/ (accessed 10 March 2023).

46 'News: Orthodox Synod Declares Faithful to Wear Black for Fast of Nineveh to Protest against "Illegal Group"', *Addis Standard*, updated 3 February 2023, https://addisstandard.com/news-orthodox-synod-declares-faithful-to-wear-black-for-fast-of-nineveh-to-protest-against-illegal-group/ (accessed 15 March 2023).

been a rapprochement, this event is remarkable in the way that it galvanised the Orthodox Christians of Ethiopia into a national act that largely rode above ethnic identity. This brought the EOTC into a very public confrontation with the government, showing that the EOTC remains a very powerful institution even as it struggles to find its place in the current pluralistic age in Ethiopia.

17

BETWEEN POLITICS AND RELIGION IN EASTERN EUROPE
Eastern Orthodoxy, State, and Religions in Contemporary Bulgaria

Valentin Kozhuharov

THE BULGARIAN ORTHODOX CHURCH SINCE THE 1990S

Bulgaria was in turmoil after the fall of the Berlin Wall in November 1989. As an unfortunate addition, the Bulgarian Orthodox Church (BOC) split into two bodies; each claimed to be the rightful Orthodox church of Bulgaria. The schism lasted twenty years, 1992 through 2012, and led to further divisions and hostilities between clergy and ordinary believers. Bulgarians realised that they could be Christians of other traditions (mostly Pentecostal), not only of the Eastern Orthodox church. It has been noted, though, that 'the mass influx after 1989 of religious emissaries and evangelizers from different denominations did not lead to the realization of expectations of the emergence of a "free market of religions". The majority have instead preferred to return to traditional religious denominations'.[1]

In such circumstances, it is no wonder that BOC tried to convince Bulgarians that they are Orthodox by tradition and that only this religious

---

[1] Simeon Evstatiev, Plamen Makariev, and Daniela Kalkandjieva, 'Christianity, Islam, and Human Rights in Bulgaria', in *Religion and Human Rights: An International Perspective*, eds. Hans-Georg Ziebertz and Gordan Črpić (Switzerland: Springer International, 2015), 2.

tradition could give people security and hope for a better future. Not being able to provide such security, BOC turned to the government for support and for help in its efforts to counter non-Orthodox churches in favour of 'the right faith' in BOC. This involved an emphasis on being Bulgarian (conflated with being Orthodox), nationalistic language, and theological conservatism. Consequently, BOC was culpable in the suppression of other religions and especially other Christian traditions.[2]

The first couple of years in the 1990s were somewhat chaotic. The government tended to support the Bulgarian Patriarchate of the BOC and deny the same level of support to the so-called Alternative Synod (or alternative Orthodox Church). This made BOC bolder in trying to persuade Bulgarians to remain faithful to 'the true' tradition.[3] The new Bulgarian Constitution of July 1991 (amended up to December 2015) unequivocally confirmed that 'Eastern Orthodox Christianity shall be considered the traditional religion in the Republic of Bulgaria'.[4] Hostility against some foreign Protestant Christians increased, and these Christians and churches were widely denounced as 'destructive sects' undermining Bulgarian identity and culture.[5]

Such a privileged position gave BOC the opportunity to use central and local authorities to suppress other religious expressions in the country, especially after the former Bulgarian tsar in exile, Simeon Saxe-Coburg-Gotha, returned to Bulgaria and even was prime minister from 2001 to 2005. BOC 'played with monarchy',[6] hoping for the return of the symphonic relations between the church and state.[7] BOC was firm

---

[2] For more on the latter, see Daniela Kalkandjieva, 'The Bulgarian Orthodox Church: Authoring New Visions about the Orthodox Church's Role in Contemporary Bulgarian Society', in *Orthodox Churches and Politics in Southeastern Europe: Nationalism, Conservatism, and Intolerance*, ed. Sabrina P. Ramet (London, UK: Palgrave Macmillan, 2020), 60–65.

[3] Evstatiev et al., 'Christianity, Islam, and Human Rights,' 2015, 3, 9.

[4] National Assembly of the Republic of Bulgaria, *Constitution*, article 13, paragraph 3, at: https://www.parliament.bg/en/const.

[5] Evstatiev et al., 'Christianity, Islam, and Human Rights', 9.

[6] Kalkandjieva, 'Authoring New Visions', 62–64.

[7] See Cyril Hovorun, *Political Orthodoxies. The Unorthodoxies of the Church Coerced* (Minneapolis: Fortress Press, 2018), 14. Authors have suggested that

in its resolution that it could influence local authorities, and even make them appoint Orthodox priests to state positions, to spread Orthodoxy among Bulgarians. This was intended to resist the Protestant churches and communities. Here is one example among many from January 2009: 'A priest joined the team of Mayor Dimitar Nikolov.'[8] His role was to organise Orthodox religious education for all children and young people in Southeast Bulgaria. The aim was to remind them about their own tradition of Orthodoxy and prevent them from adopting other traditions considered foreign and dangerous for Bulgarians.

The Protestant churches opposed the state authorities' attempts at preventing them from free and lawful exercise of their faith and practices.[9] When they found their efforts failing, they had no choice but to turn to the European Court of Human Rights (ECtHR) in Strasburg.[10] At the ECtHR, there have been a number of lawsuits against Bulgaria—most of them concerned human rights and, in most cases, Bulgaria was the loser.[11] Courts of law, however, can do little in situations where politicians in power declare their Orthodoxy, especially in times of parliamentary

---

there has never been a symphony in Orthodoxy. See also Tobias Köllner (Ed.), *Orthodox Religion and Politics in Contemporary Eastern Europe. On Multiple Secularisms and Entanglements* (Milton Park, Abingdon, UK: Routledge, 2019), 5–7.

8   Kristina Valcheva, 'Sveshtenik stana chast ot ekipa na Dimitar Nikolov' (A priest joined the team of mayor Dimitar Nikolov), 13 January 2009, https://www.burgas.bg/bg/posts/view/2660.

9   One of the Pentecostal churches pointed out: 'Burgas municipality to be declared an Orthodox state'. See *Svoboda za vseki, V obshtina Burgas shte bude obiavena pravoslavna darzhava* (Freedom for all, Burgas municipality to be declared an Orthodox state), 11 November 2011, https://svobodazavseki.com/orthodox-member/.

10 See ADF International, 'Religious Freedom Is for Everyone: Europe's Top Human Rights Court Condemns Bulgaria for Discriminating against Christians' 13 December, 2022, https://adfinternational.org/bulgaria-decision/.

11 See Kristen Ghodsee, 'Nationality, Religion, and Symphonic Secularism', in *Islam, Christianity, and Secularism in Bulgaria and Eastern Europe: The Last Half Century*, eds. Dale F. Eickelman and Simeon Evstatiev (Paderborn, Germany: Verlag Ferdinand Schöningh, 2022), 49–73.

or local elections.¹² Courts can do little when churches use local political parties to support their efforts in suppressing other religious expressions, as was the case with BOC 'playing with nationalist parties' in Bulgaria in the years 1992 to 2014.¹³

Relations between the church (BOC) and the state in Bulgaria have often been uneasy. Normally, the state follows its own agenda and the church its own. It is only where their interests intersect that one witnesses what has sometimes been called 'the dialogue' between the church and the state.¹⁴ In my view, however, there have never been dialogues between Bulgarian governments and BOC—it has always been a game of interests and gains/losses. Although researchers would see the current relations between church and state as an attempt to restore former relations of symphony,¹⁵ I am not convinced that this is currently the case in Bulgaria: I maintain that these relations have never been symphonic.

The schism within the Bulgarian Orthodox Church was overcome in 2012. This was followed by an uncertain political situation in the country from March 2013 to May 2017. Bulgaria had five successive governments during this short span. As a result of this uncertainty, since 2012 BOC changed its position on various social issues, including its opposition of the Protestant churches (and other religions) in the country. BOC's rapprochement led it to a more conciliatory outlook. Before I delve into this in more detail, however, it will be helpful to outline the

---

12   The Bulgarian Prime Minister Boyko Borisov 'reasserted the importance of God for him, his party and the Bulgarian people by saying: "Let God save us, walk with us and we walk behind Him"'. See Kristen Ghodsee, 'Nationality, Religion, and Symphonic Secularism,' 81. The Romanian prime minister Viktor Pont (2012–2015) and Lucian Cîrlan, '"Proud to be Orthodox": Religion and politics during the 2014 presidential elections in Romania', in *Orthodox Religion and Politics in Contemporary Eastern Europe. On Multiple Secularisms and Entanglements,* ed. Tobias Köllner (Milton Park, Abingdon, UK: Routledge, 2019), 41–49.

13   Evstatiev et al., 'Christianity, Islam, and Human Rights', 8, 12.

14   See Mariyan Stoyadinov, 'The Church and the Bulgarian Modernities', in *Political Theologies in Orthodox Christianity: Common Challenges and Divergent Positions,* eds. Kristina Stoeckl, Ingeborg Gabriel and Aristotle Papanikolau (London, UK: Bloomsbury T&T Clark, 2017), 308.

15   For instance, Stoyadinov, "The Church and the Bulgarian Modernities", 308.

reasons I see why the Orthodox Church lacked a spirit of cooperation and expressed antipathy.

BOC AND ITS ATTITUDE

The question of why BOC has such an attitude toward other churches and religions in Bulgaria has no easy answers. The best one can do is to note that BOC saw things in simplistic binary categories. BOC is much more ready now to see 'the need for overcoming binary categories, such as tradition/modernisation, us/them, public/private, identity/plurality, religious teaching/secular human rights perspective'.[16] One realises that social processes are far too complex to be confined in binaries. In practice, the Orthodox Church has been slow to embrace its experiments with democratic principles and the rule of law. In addition, Eastern European Orthodox churches faced many challenges that made them take a defensive position, which manifested itself in intolerance and discrimination against others. Nationalism, multiple modernities, desecularization, and cultural disparity are four trends (among others) that defined the undemocratic (compared to Western European standards) attitudes of BOC, which is not atypical of Orthodoxy in the region and the socio-political context it inhabits.

Nationalism

Nationalism seems the most obvious partner of religion both in the past and today. This is especially true for Orthodoxy in Bulgaria and its wider Eastern European context. In Eastern Europe, we have seen that 'nationalism and religion have characteristically similar institutional channels for conveying the narratives, myths, and ideologies, as well as similar, if not always identical, ways of maintaining social segregation'.[17] We need to further reflect on whether it is true for all Eastern European churches that 'religion and nationalism do not merely coexist, they flourish as parallel

---

16   Giuseppe Giordan and Siniša Zrinščak, "Introduction. Global Eastern Orthodoxy: Religion, Politics and Human Rights", in *Global Eastern Orthodoxy. Politics, Religion, and Human Rights,* eds. Giuseppe Giordan and Siniša Zrinščak (Switzerland: Springer Nature Switzerland AG, 2020), 2.

17   Tornike Metreveli, *Orthodox Christianity and the Politics of Transition: Ukraine, Serbia and Georgia* (Milton Park, Abingdon, UK: Routledge, 2021), 8.

institutional structures within (and possibly beyond) the state'.[18] Some ten years ago, Brubaker, while discussing the relations between nationalism and religion, proposed four approaches to how these relations could be interpreted;[19] it is a matter of discussion as to which approach best describes the Orthodox churches in Eastern Europe. What can be affirmed for certain is that state and church would most often partner with each other in their efforts to bring back the nation's supposed previous glory or at least its unique status among other nations.

In this chapter, we focus on nationalism and politics not in the framework of the well-known facts about the ways Eastern Orthodox churches in Eastern Europe have been nationalistic; the focus is mostly on the question of what type of nationalism we observe today and what political circumstances define it. Nationalism seems to be the logical result of recently liberated nations aiming to strengthen national identity and national values in the people who have been under foreign rule for many decades or even centuries. Throughout the world, we observe nationalistic movements in countries that have recently received independence; many churches in these countries act in a similar way by employing nationalist language and theology. Bulgaria is no exception. It gained full independence from Ottoman rule only in 1908, and the Bulgarian Orthodox Church achieved its independent status (the so-called autocephalous status) from the Ecumenical Patriarchate in 1945 when the schism over BOC was annulled. Similar developments took place in all southeastern European countries. This is one of the reasons that there are active (and often influential) nationalist political parties, movements, organisations, and dominant church entities, such as BOC.

Although the nationalist governments or the nationalist political parties and the Orthodox church often partner with each other in order to achieve the same, or similar, goals, their partnership has not always been without problems. When those in power try to undertake certain reforms or to introduce different (i.e., non-traditional) practices in social life, the church often uses its advantage and breaks its partnership. The church is

---

18 Metreveli, *Orthodox Christianity and the Politics of Transition*, 8.
19 Cf. Rogers Brubaker, "Religion and Nationalism: Four Approaches", *Nations and Nationalism* 18 no.1 (2012), 13.

not averse to adopting opposing views and even actions, especially if their differences concern religious or cultural issues. In such circumstances, the Orthodox church takes the position of the defender of 'cultural values' and sees itself as the custodian of national identity.[20] It seems true for the Orthodox churches in Eastern Europe that 'the stronger the elites push for reforms, the stronger the emergence of the churches' resistance'.[21]

Multiple Modernities

Let us note that nationalism is derived from people's understanding of the aspects that define a nation and the values that characterise its life and worth among other nations. From this perspective, nationalism can be understood in terms of postmodernity. Today, we agree that modernity and postmodernity seem to characterise the countries of the world in a different way. Their manifestations across Europe have not been uniform and their manifestations differ from those of Asian and African countries. Many researchers were of the view that religion would die in the face of ever-expanding secularism; they also thought that modernity and Westernisation were identical and that all countries that had undertaken the path of (Western) democratisation and liberalism would eventually experience the same modernisation and postmodern challenges that characterised the West. It took researchers some time to realise that, in fact, there are 'multiple modernities' and that the western type of modernity is not like the eastern one.[22] Considering the Eastern European countries and the enlarging process of Europeanisation, Spohn affirmed that the process 'has been confronted with growing opposition and tensions between the Western European secular-cultural integration mode and the Eastern European revival of nationalism and religion" and that the tensions were "between

---

20 Metreveli, *Orthodox Christianity and the Politics of Transition*, 4.
21 Metreveli, *Orthodox Christianity and the Politics of Transition*, 4.
22 Twenty years ago, Eisenstadt wrote, 'One of the most important implications of the term "multiple modernities" is that modernity and Westernization are not identical' and that Western patterns of modernity are not the only 'authentic' modernities. (Cf. Shmuel Eisenstadt (Ed.), *Comparative Civilizations & Multiple Modernities*, Volume Two (Leiden, the Netherlands: Brill, 2003), 536.

secularized Latin Christian Europe, revived Christian Orthodox Europe and the Islamic civilization'.[23]

Such an understanding of multiple modernities in the world today leads us to the thinking that the values of each 'national' modernity are not the same. While considering religious-secular debates, Rosati and Stoeckl showed that fault-lines of religious-secular conflict oscillate between civilisational borders and ideological secularist-religious conflict lines; they proposed two variants of multiple modernities: comparative-civilisational and post-secular.[24] The authors compared two civilisations: the 'thoroughly secularized western Christian civilization and the Eastern and South-western Orthodox Christian and Muslim civilizations'.[25] It seems, however, that it is the cultural-religious background (or the lack of the religious component, as the case may be) that creates a clash between Eastern and Western Europe. From observing current developments in Europe, we can see that one of the common denominators is the system of values of a nation or people. Religion is enmeshed with culture in Eastern Europe, just as one sees it in Asian and African countries. It is impossible, therefore, in such a context to compartmentalise the church from the state.

In view of this, we can ask ourselves, 'Is the BOC's desire to organise societies according to Christian values and principles out of place or uncharacteristic?' It is not, if one allows the insight from multiple modernities in our analysis of church–state relations. In other words, religion in this part of Europe seems to be one of the most influential players in these societies, and it is likely to remain so for some time.

Desecularisation

Two or three decades after World War Two, many societies in the West took the path to increased secularisation; researchers, and especially sociologists of religion, suggested, 'By the twenty-first century, religious believers are likely to be found only in small sects, huddled together to

---

23 Wilfried Spohn, 'Europeanization, Religion and Collective Identities in an Enlarging Europe: A Multiple Modernities Perspective', *European Journal of Social Theory* 12 no. 3 (2009), 362.

24 Cf. Massimo Rosati and Kristina Stoeckl (Eds.), *Multiple Modernities and Post-secular Societies* (Milton Park, Abingdon, UK: Routledge, 2016), 98.

25 Rosati and Stoeckle, *Multiple Modernities*, 97.

resist a worldwide secular culture'.[26] Three decades later, Berger admitted that, although the argument of sociologists of religion 'was that secularization and modernity go hand in hand' and that 'with more modernization comes more secularization', they made a mistake—'most of the world today is certainly not secular. It's very religious'.[27] What is more, societies are becoming de-secularised, and this process can take multiple forms in different regions or countries of the world, as Karpov has argued.[28]

This was the case with the Bulgarian church. After relentless attempts by the communists to make every Bulgarian an atheist, adherence to religion was one of the first responses to such severe limitations of the free human spirit. The same can be confirmed for all Eastern European countries that were liberated from Soviet and atheistic political regimes. Indeed, in the first several years after the political changes in Eastern Europe, the churches suddenly became so overcrowded that many religious buildings were furnished with amplifiers and loudspeakers because people were standing outside to take part in the church services. Many then left churches because they did not find there what they were hoping for and either remained nominal Christians or practised their faith in a 'cultural way' by celebrating specific Christian feasts that were set in the calendar and reflected the general culture of society—Orthodox Christianity in the case of Bulgaria.

It has been suggested that Bulgarian Christianity be named Secular Orthodox Christianity because it seemed that people found it difficult to distinguish between what is religious and what is national or cultural.[29] In such circumstances, it seems almost impossible for researchers to see any 'symphonic' relations between church and state. The church—here I mean BOC—seems to be the church of Bulgarian people only nominally, with a

---

26 Peter Berger, 'A Bleak Outlook Is Seen for Religion', *New York Times*, 25 February 1968, 3.
27 Peter Berger, 'Epistemological Modesty: An Interview with Peter Berger', *The Christian Century*, 114 (October 29, 1997): 974.
28 Vyacheslav Karpov, 'Desecularization: A Conceptual Framework', *Journal of Church and State* 52, no. 2 (2010): 239–240.
29 See, for example, Daniela Kalkandjieva, '"Secular Orthodox Christianity" versus "Religious Islam" in Postcommunist Bulgaria', *Religion, State and Society* 36 no. 4 (2008): 423–434.

very low percentage of active believers in the Orthodox churches in the country. This fact made authors forge the phrase 'symphonic secularism', applying it to Eastern Orthodoxy and specifically to Bulgaria.[30] More than that: while discussing the issue of human rights in southeastern Europe, Ghodsee developed the idea of secularism without liberalism by maintaining that liberalism is not possible in this region of Europe because the type of secularism that exists here is different from the secularism of the Western European countries.[31]

Cultural Disparity

Historically, Eastern Orthodoxy originated in the Middle East and evolved in Europe. In modern times, most of the so-called Eastern Orthodox countries are situated in these two regions, from where they spread. The Orthodox believers in Europe and the citizens of Eastern Europe did not show obvious cultural differences with the believers of other Christian churches and the peoples of other European countries; however, specific historical developments in Eastern Europe made its peoples feel differently and then act differently. The Ottoman domination in southeastern Europe for almost five centuries, the uncertain political circumstances at the end of the nineteenth century, and then the communist rule for another forty-five years created some disparity among the countries of this region. There was disparity not only in terms of economy, political situations, social life, ideology, and self-perception but also in the understanding of the world and its values. That is, the peoples in Eastern Europe have found themselves to be somewhat different from the peoples in Western Europe. Having been oppressed and deprived of basic human rights and dignity for a very long time in their history, Eastern Europeans longed for liberty, democracy, and freedoms. This experience also made them see things differently.

---

30 Kristen Ghodsee, 'Symphonic Secularism: Eastern Orthodoxy, Ethnic Identity and Religious Freedoms in Contemporary Bulgaria', *Anthropology of East Europe Review* 27 no. 2 (2009): 227–252.

31 Kristen Ghodsee, 'Secularism without Liberalism: Orthodox Churches, Human Rights and American Foreign Policy in Southeastern Europe", in *Eastern Christianity and the Politics in the Twenty-First Century*, ed. Lucian N. Leustean (Milton Park, Abingdon, UK: Routledge, 2014), 754–775.

The people, however, were not prepared to live in democracy: they found it difficult to adapt to the new circumstances of life and realised that they needed a transitional period before they were integrated into the democratic system of the West. It took several decades for this transition, and many think that it has not yet been concluded even after more than thirty-five years. The countries in Central Europe that had been under communism managed to overcome most differences and become more West-like, but those in the east and southeast of Europe still struggle to call themselves Europeans in the way Western Europeans understand European culture and civilisation. These countries realised that it is not so much the economy (becoming wealthier) and politics but the social changes and the understanding of life that baffle them. They still find it possible to live with corruption (though they try to fight it); with laws that function on paper but not in real life; with poverty; and with tradition and culture that are different from those in the West. It is these challenges, but especially the understanding of tradition and culture, that make peoples in the East and Southeast of Europe see themselves as a type of civilisation different from that of Western Europe.

The dominant Orthodox church saw itself as the custodian of the country's traditional memory and this is why BOC vehemently resisted foreign Christian influx into the country. This enabled the BOC to use every possible tool to separate the 'foreign', even if it included seeking governmental support and the backing of the public. Their attempt at protecting tradition was couched in nationalistic and theological language that,[32] in the first two decades after the fall of communism, influenced ordinary citizens and state institutions to such an extent that Orthodox believers would often assume that what is Orthodox is also Bulgarian and national. In some instances, this turned Orthodoxy into political orthodoxy, which served the goals of the politicians and nationalist political parties.[33]

---

32   In fact, in most South-Eastern European Orthodox countries, the language was political-theological, and it was used to justify the suppression of other religious expressions. More on political Orthodoxy can be found in Hovorun, *Political Orthodoxies*, 2, 9, and 13–46.

33   Hovorun calls such Orthodoxy an 'unorthodox Orthodoxy' that seems even heretical, along with other heresies (Hovorun, *Political Orthodoxies*, 2–4). Hovorun points to examples from Russia and his arguments seem well

CHANGING ATTITUDES OF EASTERN ORTHODOXY

Circumstances of life often make people change attitudes, and we can see that today we do not have the same views, understandings, and attitudes as our parents and grandparents had. Christian churches act in the same way—they change attitudes and views (but not theology) in accordance with the new possibilities and new challenges in contemporary societies.

In this section, we deal with the changing attitude of BOC in the last ten years, as it seems to be softening its domineering approach toward other Christian communities and other religions in Bulgaria. Although examples are taken mostly from the life of BOC, in fact the same changed positions characterise most other Eastern Orthodox churches in Eastern Europe. The four trends discussed above remain today but seem to have obtained some specific characteristics that were not so obvious in the past and have now surfaced.

A number of new challenges are prompting such developments in Orthodoxy.[34] It is not possible in a short chapter to consider all of them, so here we focus only on those challenges that made Christians and believers of other religions quell hostilities and fear and seek common responses to the new threats. If we are to use one name for these challenges, it would be the issue of human rights—not human rights in themselves but the interpretation of human rights by politicians and governments and especially by the European Union (EU). For a decade now, the Orthodox churches in Eastern Europe have opposed some of these new interpretations and the introduction of new EU laws and regulations. The new measures taken by the state prompt the Orthodox churches to collaborate with other Christians and believers of other religions. Their goal is to preserve the traditional values of their nation in opposition to the new values and the

---

supported. For Bulgaria, however, this has never been the case, in my view: BOC did not have the opportunity to become political, and Bulgarian Orthodoxy did not turn into political religion in the way this happened in Russia. (For Russia, see Hovorun, *Political Orthodoxies*, 8–9, 77.)

34 See Lucian Leustean. 'The Politics of Orthodox Churches in the European Union', *International Journal for the Study of the Christian Church* 18, no. 2–3 (2018): 146–157.

new understanding of what it means to be human and the foundations of human life, family, children, and society.

The first obvious change is the fact that, since 2013, BOC has been slowly coming to the understanding that it alone, without the support of other Christian believers, would not be able to oppose the government when it tries to introduce new practices that are against traditional Christian teachings. Consequently, there have been no new lawsuits or other major acts by BOC against the Protestant churches or against the believers of any other religion in the country. Those who conduct research on Bulgaria show that there exist no recent acts of hostility or opposition against the non-Orthodox churches and believers.

Another obvious change is that BOC increasingly focusses on social issues and especially on EU regulations that affect life in the member states, especially those that are seen by Eastern Europeans as a threat to their culture and traditional views on life. After BOC recovered from the schismatic divisions in 2012, it realised that too little attention was paid to such social issues as poverty, family and children, education, social care, old people and people with disabilities, human rights, freedoms, and responsibilities. Only in 2012 did BOC adopt one of its first 'legislative' documents on education, catechisation, and culture,[35] and it has only been since that year that BOC in a more meaningful way has discussed the issue of 'traditional values' as compared with some of the values maintained by the EU and some Western governments.[36]

Since 2012, BOC has prepared and distributed documents called 'positions';[37] currently there are more than a dozen such documents, and the Synod is preparing more. The BOC's positions have been supported by addresses (also called appeals) and declarations.[38] What is noticeable, however, is that many of these official documents of BOC discuss such notions as human life, family, children and parenting, medical advances

---

35 Bulgarska Patriarshia, 'Strategia za dukhovna prosveta, katehizatsia i kultura na BPC' (Bulgarian Patriarchate, Strategic principles of spiritual education, catechization and culture in BOC), https://bg-patriarshia.bg/strategies-1.
36 More on this in Kalkandjieva, 'Authoring New Visions,' 2020, 68–72.
37 *Stanovishte* (position, views, opinion). See https://bg-patriarshia.bg/attitude.
38 For appeals, see https://bg-patriarshia.bg/appeal. For declarations, see https://bg-patriarshia.bg/declaration.

and ethical issues, and gender and its expression. A few examples are discussed next.

In December 2011 and June and December 2012, BOC issued three documents about its position on family life, parents, and children. The first document strongly criticises the state in its understanding and efforts to widely introduce in Bulgarian society the practices of assisted reproductive technology, surrogate motherhood, and abortion, taking the position that these practices are incompatible with Christian teaching and the Bulgarian traditional understanding of marriage.[39] The second points to the government's suggestion of giving excessive rights to children over their parents (in the law on children that was just about to be adopted at that time).[40] The third is a statement on the rights of parents and the institutionalisation of children older than the age of four.[41] In this third document, BOC supports the Bulgarian National Network of Parents[42] in its efforts to prevent the adoption of a bill that would give the state excessive rights over parents' rights while introducing compulsory education for children aged four and older.

To save space, let me go to the year 2018 when BOC issued its position on the so-called Istanbul Convention.[43] It highlights in this position the subtle and yet noticeable affirmation of the convention that gender is different from biological sex and that this understanding of gender as well as the different types of sexual expressions should be taught at school as of the earliest age. In June 2021, the chair of the Bulgarian Constitutional court asked BOC about the church's view on gender and sexuality; as expected, BOC unequivocally rejected any understanding other than the biological nature of gender and the natural sexual practice between a man and a woman within the framework of the family.[44] Starting in 2008, when the

---

39   For the first document, see https://bg-patriarshia.bg/attitude-6. More on this also in Kalkandjieva, 'Authoring New Vision', 69.
40   See https://bg-patriarshia.bg/attitude-8.
41   See https://bg-patriarshia.bg/appeal-15.
42   See https://nmr.bg/.
43   See https://bg-patriarshia.bg/news/stanovishte-na-svetia-sinod-po-povod-istanbulskata-konventsi, 22 January 2018. Cf. Kalkandjieva, 'Authoring New Visions', 71–72.
44   See https://bg-patriarshia.bg/news/stanovishte-na-sv-sinod-na-bpts-bp-otnosno-pismo-na-konstitu. The constitutional court of Bulgaria considered

first gay pride was organised in Sofia (in June 2022, the fifteenth anniversary was celebrated), BOC has incessantly opposed any notion of same-sex relations and of any different understanding of man, woman, and child apart from the teaching of the church and of natural law.[45]

What is interesting in BOC's responses to the new challenges is the fact that Protestant churches in Bulgaria were the first to establish Bulgarian non-governmental organisations to fight the new understandings of man and family; only after these NGOs were established did BOC join their activities and publish its own positions and appeals. For example, the above-mentioned statement of BOC on the rights of parents and the institutionalisation of children older than four years followed the Protestant churches' opposition that was supported by 50 organisations of the civil society.[46] In September 2022, another appeal was initiated by thirty-seven Bulgarian organisations,[47] and BOC is now (at time of writing this chapter) preparing its response to it, being resolved to join the efforts of other churches and civil organisations to combat non-traditional values and cultural expressions that have been widely criticised in Bulgarian society.[48]

---

the term 'gender' and the associated documents of the Council of Europe and took its decision four months later; cf. https://constcourt.bg/bg/Acts/GetHtmlContent/5aca41e4-659e-42dc-80a5-c3f31746898b. We need to note here that the court did not follow only BOC's opinion on the issue—it consulted dozens of organisations and scientific committees in Bulgaria before it took the decision. That is, the court took the opinion of different layers of Bulgarian society, including various laws and the constitution of Bulgaria.

45 The last gay pride was in June 2022, when BOC once again expressed its position (its attitude) on "this sinful act of sinful people;" cf. https://bg-patriarshia.bg/news/obrashtenie-na-svetiya-sinod-na-bpts-bp-po-povod-predstoyash.

46 See https://www.sva.bg/105510801089108410721080108710771090108010809410801080/-50.

47 Cf. https://www.sva.bg/1057109810861073109710771085108011031076108610841077107610801080100901077/373351813.

48 March for the Family (Pohod za Semeistvoto, in Bulgarian language) is another Protestant organisation (with several member organisations) whose activities and advocacy were followed by Orthodox Christians; see https://www.family.bg/bg/. The above-mentioned Protestant organisation Svoboda za vseki (Freedom for All) includes members of different Christian churches

The intolerance in language and behaviour in the Bulgarian church has now given way to collaboration. Today we do not read such statements as 'A Bulgarian Orthodox clergyman has said stones should be thrown at parade marchers and that their political allies should be drowned.'[49] Nevertheless, both Christians and people of other faiths are deeply convinced that Bulgaria will never agree to 'the queering of human rights' and the 'twisted' interpretation of fundamental human rights.[50] Pew Research Center admits that Eastern Europe is characterised by 'conservative views' on sexuality and gender and that there is opposition throughout the region.[51] In its technical report of 2020, the EU Agency for Fundamental Rights affirms that there is 'a long way to go for LGBTI equality' in Eastern Europe,[52] including Bulgaria where only 8 percent of Bulgarians believe 'their national government effectively combats prejudice and intolerance against LGBTI people' (compared to 33 percent in the EU).[53]

---

in Bulgaria—Orthodox, Catholic, Pentecostal, etc.—and its activities are closely followed by BOC's representatives and by lecturers of departments of theology at universities; cf. https://svobodazavseki.com/za-nas/.

49 Trudy Ring, 'Bulgarian Priest Urges Violence at Pride Parade', 27 June 2012, https://www.advocate.com/politics/religion/2012/06/27/bulgarian-priest-urges-violence-pride-parade.

50 See one of the petitions, CitizenGo, EU-Parliament to vote on a Roadmap for special LGBT rights, 16 January 2014 at https://www.citizengo.org/en/2882-european-parliament-will-vote-roadmap-special-lgbt-rights-lunacekno, and the Bulgarian appeal to act in supporting it, *Asotsiatsia Obshtestvo i tsennosti, Poiskai ot evrodeputatite da othvurliat pro-homosexualnia doklad "Lunachek"* (Society and Values' Association, Ask the European parliamentaries to reject the Lunacek Report that support homosexuality), 22 January 2014, https://www.sva.bg/105510801089108410721072-1080-10871077109010801094108010801080/7.

51 Cf. Pew Research Center, 'Religious Belief and National Belonging in Central and Eastern Europe', 10 May 2017, 1, https://www.pewresearch.org/religion/2017/05/10/religious-belief-and-national-belonging-in-central-and-eastern-europe/.

52 European Union Agency for Fundamental Rights, 'A Long Way to Go for LGBTI Equality', technical report (Vienna, Austria, 2020), https://fra.europa.eu/sites/default/files/fra_uploads/fra-2020-lgbti-equality-technical-report_en.pdf.

53 European Union Agency for Fundamental Rights, 'EU LGBTI Survey II. A long way to go for LGBTI equality', (Vienna, Austria, 2020), Country

Bulgarian Christians are one with others in Eastern Europe in seeking to safeguard their traditional Orthodox values, but instead of going alone, they seek collaboration with those they previously opposed, namely the other Christian traditions. It seems that the notions of nationalism, the understanding of multiple modernities, the trend of renewed desecularisation, and the increased sensitivity to cultural disparity in comparison to the culture of Western Europe are all still in play but are somewhat differently understood and expressed as compared to the past. Although differences among different traditions of Christianity remain, they are being overcome in the face of common threats.

---

data—Bulgaria, https://fra.europa.eu/sites/default/files/fra_uploads/lgbti-survey-country-data_bulgaria.pdf. This result suggests that it is not so much Orthodox or other Christians or people of other faiths that oppose 'gender ideology', as they call the issue, but also that Bulgarian governments that are not too much in favour of the rights of LGBTI people.

ABOUT THE AUTHORS
(in chapter order)

Dr. David Emmanuel Singh is senior research tutor and PhD stage leader at the Oxford Centre for Mission Studies. He has a BSc (Allahabad), BD and MTh (Islamics; Senate of Serampore), and PhD (Islamics) from the University of Wales, UK. He began as a phenomenologist, focussing on a twelfth-century Islamic theosophist, Ibn 'Arabi, and a sect of Islam called the Mahdawiyya. Over the years, he has branched out into other fields, with new research and supervision in Sufism, Islam, interfaith relations in South Asia, and theology of religions. He is the author of over sixty research papers, eight edited books (including a trilogy on *Jesus and Islam*), and several encyclopaedia entries and book chapters. His two research monographs are *Sainthood and Revelatory Discourse: An Examination of the Basis for the Authority of Bayan in Mahdawi Islam* (Oxford: Regnum and ISPCK, 2003) and *Islamization in Modern South Asia: Deobandi Reform and the Gujjar Response* (Berlin: Walter de Gruyter, 2012).

Dr. Michel Chambon is a French Catholic theologian (Canonical Licence from the Catholic University of Paris) and a cultural anthropologist (PhD from Boston University) focusing on Chinese Christianity. His book *Making Christ Present in China, Actor-Network Theory and the Anthropology of Christianity* (Palgrave Macmillan, 2020) examines the five Christian denominations of Nanping (Fujian) to question the ways in which social science theorises the unity and diversity of Christianity. As a Research Fellow at the Asia Research Institute, National University of Singapore, he coordinates the Initiative for the Study of Asian Catholics, ISAC, www.isac-research.org.

Dr. Farhana A. Nazir was a lecturer and dean of studies at Gujranwala Theological Seminary, Pakistan. She is currently associate editor of *Almushir* (the Counselor, 1966), a journal of the Christian Study Center,

Rawalpindi, Pakistan. She acquired her PhD in World Christianity from the University of Edinburgh, UK, and is the author of a monograph, *The Evolution of Legislation on Religious Offences: A Study of British India and the Implications for Contemporary Pakistan* (Langham). As well as serving the church through preaching, training, and teaching in theological education institutions, her other significant passions are singing, music, and poetry.

Dr. Peter G. Riddell is professor emeritus at the London School of Theology and a professorial research associate in History at SOAS University of London. He took his PhD on Islam in Southeast Asia at the Australian National University and has taught at the ANU, IPB University (Indonesia), SOAS, London School of Theology, and Melbourne School of Theology. He has also held visiting research appointments at the Hebrew University of Jerusalem and L'Ecole Pratique des Hautes Etudes/Sorbonne, Paris. He has published widely on Southeast Asia, Islam, and Christian-Muslim relations. His books include *Transferring a Tradition* (Berkeley, 1990), *Islam and the Malay-Indonesian World* (London, Hawaii, and Singapore, 2001), *Islam in Context* (with Peter Cotterell, Grand Rapids, 2003), *Christians and Muslims* (Leicester, 2004), and *Malay Court Religion, Culture and Language: Interpreting the Qur'an in 17th Century Aceh* (Leiden, 2017).

Dr. Amos Sukamto is the academic dean of INTI Theological Seminary and the director of Unit Penelitian Pelayanan Kontekstual (UPPK, Research Center for Contextual Ministry), Bandung, in Indonesia. His research fields are social theology, the history of Muslim-Christian relations in Indonesia, and the history of Christianity in Indonesia, especially in West Java. His research results have been published in several international journals, such as *Mission Studies*; *Exchange*; *International Bulletin of Mission Research*; *Journal of Law, Religion, and State Transformation*; and *Church History and Religious Culture*.

Rev. Amir S. Bazmjou is an Iranian minister and the CEO of Torch Ministries (*Mashaal* Ministries). He and his wife Rashin Soodmand (the daughter of a martyred pastor, Hossein Soodmand, in Iran) founded Torch Ministries to strengthen, equip, and train leaders from the Church of Iran. Amir has been involved in various types of training, teaching, and preaching ministry among Persian communities over the past twenty-five years. He has also been involved with organising international missions with Operation Mobilisation (OM). For more than fifteen years, he has been involved in pastoral ministry at London's Iranian church (ICF) and with the chaplaincy ministry at the detention centre, Heathrow. He has been part of the translation and editing team of the 'Application Bible Commentary' for Farsi speakers. Amir is a PhD candidate in religious studies and theology at OCMS in Oxford.

Dr. Michael Nazir-Ali is a priest of the Ordinariate of Our Lady of Walsingham and Prelate of Honour to His Holiness Pope Francis. He is president of the Oxford Centre for Training, Research, Advocacy and Dialogue (OXTRAD) and monsignor professor of theology at the Angelicum, Rome. He is an Honourable Fellow of St. Edmund Hall, Oxford, and Fitzwilliam College, Cambridge. He was the 106th Bishop of Rochester for fifteen years, until 1 September 2009. He is originally from Southwest Asia where he was Bishop of Raiwind in Pakistan. In the United Kingdom, he was the first Diocesan Bishop in the Church of England born abroad. He served as the general secretary of CMS from 1989–1994. From 1999, he was a member of the House of Lords, where he was active in a number of areas of national and international concern. He has both a Christian and a Muslim family background.

Dr. Ronald T. Bueno is founder/co-founder and executive director of two organisations in El Salvador: ENLACE, a community development organisation, and CREDATEC, a micro-finance institution. He holds a PhD from the University of Middlesex, London. His doctoral work was ethnographical, focussing on five Pentecostal congregations in El Salvador and evaluating 'Community Engagement as a New and Contested Ritual'. His continuing research and writing focusses on faith and development.

Dr. James G. Huff Jr. is associate director and associate professor of human needs and global resources and anthropology at Wheaton College (Illinois). He received his PhD in Cultural Anthropology from the American University (Washington, DC) in 2004, and worked as associate professor of anthropology at Vanguard University (2002–2014). His scholarship on community development and religion in Latin America considers the role that faith-based NGOs play in generating broader forms of political, economic, and social change. As an applied anthropologist, he has worked with NGOs and community-based organisations across Latin America to evaluate the effectiveness of their programs to alleviate multidimensional poverty and strengthen human well-being.

Dr. Gangri "Philip" Gobu (pen name) is a missionary leader and ordained minister who has served in Tibet and China since 2004. Internationally, he represents his sending agency in Lausanne Congress and Movement, Global BAM Congress, and Chinese Mission Movement. On the ground, he leads his family and teams in running churches, Bible schools, disaster relief centres, girls' schools, kindergartens, safe havens, anti-abortion and pro-life operations, vocational training programs, health-food companies, restaurants, hotels, and medical outreach in the highly restricted and persecuted Tibetan and Uyghur/Tajik areas. He teaches at seminaries and publishes articles and books on Mission Leadership and Maturity Study, Mission Leaders Malfeasance, Mission Strategies, Business as Mission, Tibetan Buddhism, and present-day Chinese politics and culture.

Dr. Marina Ngursangzeli Behera is research tutor, MPhil stage leader, and editor of *Transformation* (SAGE). Marina is from Mizoram, India, and belongs to the Mizoram Synod of the Presbyterian Church of India. She obtained her MTh in missiology from the North India Institute of Post-Graduate Theological Studies (Senate of Serampore College) and her DTh in the history of Christianity from the Federated Faculty for Research in Religion and Culture in Kottayam, Kerala, India (Senate of Serampore College). From 2005 to 2012, she served as an associate professor and chairperson in the department of the history of Christianity at the United Theological College (UTC) in Bangalore, India. From September 2012 to July 2016, supported by the CWM, she held the chair of Ecumenical Missiology at the Ecumenical Institute, Bossey, a program of the World Council of Churches attached to the University of Geneva.

Dr. Gloria Calib is associate vice-rector for academic affairs at Forman Christian College University, one of Pakistan's oldest institutions, founded in 1864. Gloria's key responsibilities include US accreditation work for FCCU, international academic linkages, student academic affairs, and supervision of academic operations. Her key research areas are missiology, women in higher education leadership, and student academic affairs. Gloria holds a PhD in missiology from the London School of Theology (Middlesex University), UK. In this research, she compared the Church of Pakistan (Lahore and Hyderabad dioceses) and the Full Gospel Assemblies of Pakistan. Her findings showed that the Pakistani Church is engaged in inadequate mission, engages in inconsistent theological reflection, and faces overwhelming internal restrictions.

Toby Kan has served as a community development worker in Egypt since 2014. He earned an MPhil in electronic engineering and a master of theology (ThM). He is currently a PhD scholar at the Middlesex University in London. He teaches as an adjunct instructor at the Alliance Bible Seminary in Hong Kong. His major research interests are in interfaith relations, cultural anthropology, and socio-political discourses. He is the author of the paper '"Revolutionary Youth" in Egypt: Interfaith Relations since the 2011 Revolution', *Contemporary Review of the Middle East*, 10 no. 2 (May 29, 2023), https://doi.org/10.1177/23477989231160924.

Dr. Henrik Lindberg Hansen has a degree in theology from Aarhus University and a PhD in sociology of religion from the School of Oriental and African Studies, University of London. After working for six years in Egypt as part of religious dialogues, he completed his research on the need for understanding religious dialogue in Egypt as a socio-political phenomenon. He currently works as an analyst for Udviklingshæmmedes LandsForbund (ULF), the Danish user organisation for and by people with cognitive disabilities. His work involves the development of a research-founded approach to self-advocacy and to projects aimed at improving the lives of the members of the organisation. He is working on a book in association with Aarhus University about Muslims as the political other in Danish society. He is the author of *Christian-Muslim Relations in Egypt: Politics, Society and Interfaith Encounters* (I.B. Tauris, 2015).

Dr. Uchenna D. Anyanwu is a missiologist serving with Calvary Ministries (CAPRO). Uchenna is an ordained minister in the Anglican Church and volunteers part time as a cross-cultural mission specialist with Frontier Fellowship. Uchenna also has an MDiv and MA in intercultural studies from Gordon-Conwell Theological Seminary, where he is currently completing a master's degree in mental health counselling. He obtained his PhD in intercultural studies from Fuller Theological Seminary. His doctoral dissertation was published in the American Society of Missiology Monograph Series as *Pathways to Peacebuilding: Staurocentric Theology in Nigeria's Context of Acute Violence* (Pickwick Publications, 2023).

Dr. Klaus Fiedler is professor emeritus of the Evangelical Theological Faculty, Leuven (Belgium, 1990-2017) and of Mzuzu University (Malawi, 2008-2019). He is a Baptist pastor and was a missionary of the Kanisa la Biblia (Christian Brethren) in Southern Tanzania for seven years. In 1992, he came to Malawi to teach at Chancellor College of the University of Malawi in Zomba, moving to Mzuzu in 2008. He is a church historian and a missiologist, and his special academic interests are the promotion of postgraduate studies, of academic publishing (Kachere Series, 1995-2007, Mzuni Press since 2008, and Luviri Press since 2016), and of Evangelical Feminist Theology. He studied theology at the Baptist/Brethren Seminary in Hamburg but received his most formative education during his two years of study at Makerere University in Kampala (Uganda). He received his PhD in Dar es Salaam (1978), and his Dr theol in Heidelberg (1991). He is the author of *The Story of Faith Missions* (Regnum Books, 1994) and co-author, with Kenneth R. Ross, of *A Malawi Church History 1860-2020* (Mzuni Press, 2020).

Dr. Kenneth R. Ross is professor of theology and dean of postgraduate studies at Zomba Theological University in Malawi. He is also an Honorary Fellow at Edinburgh University School of Divinity; extraordinary professor at the University of Pretoria; senior research associate at Gordon-Conwell Theological Seminary, Boston, USA; affiliate at the University of Glasgow School of Critical Studies; and visiting professor at the University of Livingstonia. He is an advisor to the World Council of Churches Commission on World Mission and Evangelism and series editor of the *Edinburgh Companions to Global Christianity* (Edinburgh University Press). He was general secretary of the Church of Scotland Board of World Mission from 1998 to

2009 and chair of the Scotland Malawi Partnership from 2004 to 2006 and 2010 to 2019. His latest book is *Mission, Race and Colonialism in Malawi: Alexander Hetherwick of Blantyre* (Edinburgh University Press, 2023).

Dr. Pavol Bargár is assistant professor at the Protestant Theological Faculty of Charles University in Prague, Czech Republic. His research interests lie in theology and culture, theological anthropology, mission studies, and interreligious relations. Pavol is a vice-president of the Central and Eastern European Association for Mission Studies (CEEAMS). He also serves on the executive board of the International Council of Christians and Jews (ICCJ). In addition to numerous articles and book chapters, he is the author of *Narrative, Myth, Transformation: Reflecting Theologically on Contemporary Culture* (Mlýn, 2016) and *Embodied Existence: Our Common Life in God* (Cascade Books, 2023). He edited the volume *The Bible, Christianity, and Culture: Essays in Honour of Professor Petr Pokorný* (Karolinum Press, 2023).

Dr. Cristian-Sebastian Sonea is an Orthodox priest and associate professor at the faculty of Orthodox Theology, Babeș-Bolyai University, Cluj-Napoca in Romania. He completed his doctor of theology at the Faculty of Orthodox Theology (2010); studied ecumenical theology at the Ecumenical Institute, Bossey, Switzerland (2014); and studied habilitation in theology at the Institute of Doctoral Studies, Babeș-Bolyai University, Cluj-Napoca in Romania (2020). He also did a specialist program in interreligious studies at the Catholic University of Seattle, USA (2021). He is currently the European representative of IAMS (International Association for Mission Studies) and is interested in the contemporary theology of Orthodox mission, secularisation, and common Christian witness.

Dr. Teofil Stanciu is the editor-in-chief of an interdenominational magazine, *Convergențe*, based in Romania and is the director of a publishing house. He did his PhD at Aurel Vlaicu University, Arad, Romania that focused on a *kenotic* paradigm for Christian public presence. His research fields cover public theology, intra-Christian dialogue, theology, and literature in dialogue. He is currently a member of Osijek Doctoral Colloquium steering committee, a biannual program designed for PhD researchers under CEEAMS (the Central and Eastern European Mission Studies).

Dr. Oliver Kisaka Simiyu is managing director of CORAT Africa, a Christian company headquartered in Nairobi, Kenya, where he empowers Christian leaders through training, consultancy, research, and conferencing. He served as deputy general secretary of the National Council of Churches of Kenya (NCCK) for twelve years and was also a University Chaplain at Africa International University. He serves on numerous boards of Christian organisations. He studied mathematics and physics for his undergrad, and has an MA in biblical studies and a PhD in church and state studies from the Middlesex University through the Oxford Centre for Mission Studies. He is a member of the Friends Church in Kenya, Nairobi, but serves the body of Christ widely as a speaker, teacher, and facilitator. He is the author of *The Grace of Giving: Growing in Faith, Integrity and Community* (Nairobi: Arba Pubications Ltd, 2016).

Dr. Ralph Lee is associate faculty for Orthodox mission at the Oxford Centre for Mission Studies. His research interests include Orthodox theology, non-Chalcedonian Orthodox theology, Oriental Orthodox biblical interpretation, the transmission and textual history of the Bible in Ethiopia, 1Enoch, Ethiopian and Syriac Christian thought, Second Temple Judaism, revival movements in Orthodox churches, Evangelical-Orthodox relations, and Orthodox-Islamic relations. He is chair of Trustees of the Jubilee Centre, a member of the board of trustees of the Lausanne Orthodox Initiative, and a doctoral supervisor in the Cambridge Theological Federation. He is also a representative of the Navigators UK, focussing on disciple making in Orthodox contexts and on ministry to young academics. He has a PhD from SOAS University of London (2011) on Symbolic Interpretations in Ethiopic and Early Syriac Literature; a second PhD is from University of Strathclyde on the Environmental Implications of Industrial Technology in Ethiopia. He was awarded MBE (2014) for service to the British and Commonwealth community in Ethiopia.

Dr. Valentin Kozhuharov is a freelance researcher and lecturer in Christian theology, specifically in Christian Education, Missiology, and Ecumenical Relations. He has taught at different theological institutions of higher education, including at a university's department of Orthodox theology in

Bulgaria, at the Central and Eastern European Institute of Missiology in Budapest, and at a number of theological colleges in Great Britain. He has published nine monographs on topics relating to Christian education, missiology, and ecumenical relations. He has participated in more than one hundred international scholarly conferences/seminars, and he is a member of many professional bodies the world. He has examined and supervised several PhD theses in Christian theology.

SUBJECT INDEX

Anglican, 101, 110–115, 256–260, 317–318, 361
authoritarian, 102, 105, 126, 205, 275

Baptist, 9, 247, 284–288, 294–98, 362
Bharatiya Janata Party (BJP), 4–5, 15–33, 160–168, 173–174
blasphemy, 5, 53–72, 179–183
Boko Haram, 227–239
Brethren, 9, 230–232, 285–287, 298, 362
Buddhism, 2–3, 6, 18, 21, 27, 74, 81, 106, 143, 150, 156, 173
Bulgarian church, 1, 340–344, 347–355
burning, 31, 76–77, 82, 122, 128, 251, 254

Catholic/Catholicism, 8–11, 35–55, 74, 78, 80, 85–94, 110, 117–137, 147, 196, 229, 256, 259, 264, 272–275, 295–297, 304–306, 323–327
Chinese Christianity, 7, 36, 48, 148, 357
Chinese Communist Party, 7, 48–50, 139
Chineseness, 44, 156
Christian experience, 3–4, 13
Christian majority, 3, 5, 7, 10, 73, 308
Christian minority, 3, 52, 62, 101, 196
Christian response, 7, 36, 52, 78, 139, 183, 232
Christian-Muslim relations, 1, 87, 92, 94, 200, 203–204, 222, 358, 361
church and state, 8, 44, 120–121, 245, 314, 342, 347, 364
Citizenship Amendment Act (CAA), 2, 4, 15, 19, 160, 171
clientelism/clientelist, 7, 200–202, 205, 209, 216–217
Confucianism/Confucianists, 43–44, 48, 74

constitutions, 2–6, 16, 22–26, 56–57, 62, 66, 69, 99, 104–107, 112, 120, 144, 159, 166, 169–175, 182, 192, 207, 228, 244, 289–307, 320–321, 333, 340, 352
Copts (Coptic), 200, 202–207, 211–212, 214, 216
COVID-19, 51, 150–157
Cultural Revolution, 37–38, 142
Czech Republic, 4, 8, 263–265, 269, 272–274, 276, 363

dhimmi, 6, 100, 105, 113, 202
dialogue, 7, 11, 50, 78–82, 87–88, 92–94, 164–165, 185, 200, 206–209, 214–217, 233–234, 289, 296, 300–301, 337, 342
dictatorship, 126, 208, 256
discrimination, 7, 51, 65, 71, 84, 108, 112, 160, 177, 191, 200, 203–206, 210, 216, 230, 305, 315, 343
disfavoured, 3, 22, 219, 224, 232, 236

Eastern Orthodoxy, 339–340, 343–344, 348, 350
Ethiopian Orthodox Tewahedo Church (EOTC), 323–331, 333, 336–338
equality, 7, 25, 75, 106, 171, 210–212, 216, 305–306, 329, 354
Evangelical, 9, 10, 85–87, 101, 108–109, 111, 122–124, 128, 216, 235, 283–284, 286–301, 303, 330–331, 333
extrajudicial, 58, 111, 253–254

harmony, 55, 73, 75, 84–88, 92–95
Hindu nationalism, 2, 5, 16, 160–161, 167, 169
Hinduism, 4, 84, 86, 161, 163, 165
Hindutva, 16, 159–175,

SUBJECT INDEX

human rights, 7, 58, 60, 65, 109, 112, 210–212, 216, 243, 253, 276, 307, 341, 343, 348, 350–351, 354

imam, 94, 103–104, 206, 214, 308
intolerance, 60, 87, 171, 223, 257, 340, 343, 354
Islamisation, 5, 84–86, 95, 182, 275–276, 334
Islamism, 203, 207, 211
Islamist acute violence, 228

Jehovah's Witnesses, 8, 243–262

marginalization, 107–108, 304, 306–308, 315
Mizo Christian, 5, 160, 169, 173–175
modernity, 39, 107, 170, 345–347
Maoist (regime), 35, 38, 40, 43, 45, 49, 146
Muslim-Christian relations, 76, 209, 258

National Register of Citizens (NRC), 2, 4, 15–33, 160
nationalism, 5, 8, 16, 48, 160, 182, 210–211, 265, 270, 343–346, 355

one-party state, 247, 261
Orthodoxy, 9, 10, 264, 284, 326, 329, 332, 334–335, 340–355

patriarch/patriarchate, 202, 283, 294, 328, 330, 333, 336–337, 340, 344
Pentecostal, 9–11, 36, 82, 85, 101, 117–137, 284–285, 287–288, 293–295, 298, 324, 329–330
Pentecostalism, 10, 123, 125, 129, 131–132, 331, 334–336, 340
persecution (of), 2, 98, 106, 110, 112, 179, 221, 224, 230, 248, 252–254, 258–259
pluralism/pluralisation, 81, 132, 136–137, 249

politics 4, 8, 27, 88, 163, 170–174, 178–179, 192–198, 203, 205, 209, 247, 261, 265–280, 304, 308, 313, 319, 339–355
populism, 265–266, 268, 272, 279
Protestantism, 9, 35–52, 74–76, 78, 81, 88, 94, 101, 108, 110, 113, 117–118, 122–124, 148, 284, 317, 323, 327–338, 340–342, 351–353

referendum, 275, 289, 295–300
religion and politics, 163, 170, 341–342
religious freedom, 8, 166, 171, 183, 210, 231, 243–262, 288, 300, 324, 332–334
resilience, 48, 51, 233, 263, 277–278, 280, 328
revolution, 5, 7, 37–39, 48, 98–114, 119–217, 324, 329–330, 332–333, 361
Rashtriya Swyamsevak Sangh [RSS], 15–16, 28–29

schism, 10, 125, 337, 340, 342, 344, 351
secularism, 2, 4, 10, 15, 91, 166, 169–171, 175, 345, 348
secularization, 10, 343, 347
secularizing, 8–9, 264
Shari'a, 62, 110, 203, 228, 230
Shi'a theocracy, 6, 102
Sinicization, 144, 148, 150
social relations, 106, 118, 125, 137
solidarity, 5, 80, 134, 174–175, 200, 207, 277–278, 288, 293, 295, 301, 313
staurocentric, 219, 228, 236–239

theocratic, 102, 104, 247
Three-Self church, 35–36, 49, 147, 150, 152–153, 155
Tibetan Christians, 6, 139, 150–157

Vatican II, 47, 127
Velayat-e Faqih, 97, 102–105, 108, 113
victimization, 8, 150, 153, 156, 248, 253

zero-COVID policy, 51, 150–156

COUNTRY/REGION/ PLACE INDEX

Africa, 3-4, 247, 261, 274, 303, 308-309, 311, 316-317, 328, 364

Bulgaria, 4, 8, 269, 339-355, 365

Central and Eastern Europe, 263-281, 363
China, 3, 6-7, 19, 27, 35-52, 97, 100, 140, 144-156, 357, 360
Czech Republic, 4, 8, 263-281, 363

Dzaleka, 252, 258, 260

Egypt, 4, 7, 199-217, 361
El Salvador, 4, 11, 117-137, 359
Ethiopia, 10-11, 317, 323-338, 364

India, 2, 4-5, 8, 15-33, 97, 100, 159-175, 358, 360
Indonesia, 3, 5, 73-83, 89, 94-95, 358
Iran, 4-5, 97-114, 358

Kenya, 4, 9, 303-321, 364

Malawi, 4, 7-8, 243-262, 362
Malaysia, 3, 5, 73, 83-95
Mizoram, 5, 159-174

Nigeria, 4, 10, 219-239, 362

Pakistan, 4-5, 20, 22-29, 54-72, 177-198, 357, 359-361
Philippines, 3, 5, 73, 88, 89-95

Romania, 4, 9, 269, 283-301, 342, 363

South Asia, 24, 62, 72, 160
Southwest Asia, 359

Tibet, 6, 37, 48, 139-156

West Asia, 5
West, the, 8, 19, 72, 101, 110, 148, 161, 170-171, 203, 210, 245, 335, 343, 345-346, 348-349, 355

NAMES INDEX

Ahmed, Abiy, 336–337

Banda, Hastings Kamuzu, 244–246, 248, 250–252, 255–260
Bhatti, Shahbaz 65, 67, 72, 183
Bhutto, Benazir, 56, 60–61, 63
Bibi, Assia, 65–66

Chandrachud, Abhinav, 23, 25
Comșa, Grigore Gheorghe, 285, 287

Desalegn, Hailemariam, 333

Elliot, Charles, 310

Gragn, Ahmed, 323, 326–327

Hardinge, Arthur, 309–310

Jinnah, Muhammad Ali, 54, 57

Kamwana, Elliot Kenan, 247–248
Khomeini, Ayatollah, 6, 102–106, 108–109, 113
Kukah, Matthew Hassan, 229–230, 238–239

Mao Zedong, 37–38, 146–148
Masih, Manzoor, 54–55
Masih, Salamat, 54–55, 58, 61
Modi, Narendra, 19, 27–32, 173
Mubarak, Hosni, 205, 207–208, 211–212
Muhammad Buhari, 229

Nasser, Gamal Abdel, 202, 205, 210–211

Orbán, Viktor, 271–272
Osborn, Robert Durie, 1

Pope Benedict XVI, 51, 56, 65, 207
Pope Francis, 50–51, 207, 275, 297, 359
Pope Tawadros II, 209

Russel, Charles Taze, 246–247

Suharto (President), 75

Taylor, Charles, 4

Xi Jinping, 35, 49, 51, 144–145

Zenawi, Meles, 324, 332–333